Two Thousand Years of Economic Statistics

Volume 2: by Country

2015

Two Thousand Years of Economic Statistics: Population, GDP at PPP, and GDP Per Capita

Years 1 to 2012

Volume 2: by Country

2015

Alexander V. Avakov

Algora Publishing
New York

Library of Congress Cataloging-in-Publication Data

Avakov, Aleksandr V. (Aleksandr Vladimirovich), 1954-

Two thousand years of economic statistics: world population, GDP, and PPP by Country/ Alexander V. Avakov.

p. cm.

Includes bibliographical references.

ISBN 978-1-62894-135-7 (soft cover: alk. paper) — ISBN 978-1-62894-136-4 (case laminate: alk. paper) — ISBN 978-1-62894-137-1 (eBook) 1. Economic history—Statistics. 2. Economic indicators. I. Title. II. Title: 2000 years of economic statistics.

HC21.A97 2010

339.3'1021—dc22

2009037757

Printed in the United States

Table of Contents

Introduction

Two Thousand Years of Economic Statistics presents historical data in two volumes, going far beyond the major powers and the BRICS countries. This is Volume 2, which lists the countries alphabetically, presenting: (1) Population/Growth Rates of Population by country, (2) GDP Per Capita/Growth Rates of GDP Per Capita by country, and (3) GDP/Growth Rates of GDP by country. [In Volume 1 — sold separately — the data is arranged by rank, or size, covering: (1) Population by rank, (2) GDP Per Capita by rank, (3) GDP by rank, (4) Growth Rates of Population by rank, (5) Growth Rates of GDP Per Capita by rank, (6) Growth Rates of GDP by rank.]

This work contains data generally not available elsewhere, presented in ways that help make it possible to draw useful comparisons. First, it provides statistical data for all countries of the world (236 countries, within their 2011 borders) since 1950 (by decade, with 2011 in addition), plus forecasts for 2020 and 2030. Second, it goes back to the year 1000 and provides data for 135 countries (with data for 1000, 1500, 1600, 1700, 1820, 1870, 1880, 1890, 1900, 1913, 1920, 1929, and 1938). Third, it goes back to the first year AD and provides data for 134 countries.

This handbook is based on the groundbreaking works of Angus Maddison, but it differs by giving data up to the most recent year available and calculating GDP (gross and per capita) in the prices of the most recent year. For recent years, I use the World Bank, CIA, and Encyclopedia Britannica as primary sources. But, despite my great debt to them, for the preponderance of the data I rely on original calculations. Among other computational techniques I use a new logarithmic interpolation which resolves cross-country statistical distortions when calculating in the prices of the most recent year. Another point that distinguishes this book is that for every line of data (for every country, each year) I note the technique used in obtaining my estimate (i.e., proxy, exponential interpolation, direct estimate with source citation, etc.).

This book has value with each new edition because every year, the data shown in the prices of the most recent year will be different; plus the logarithmic interpolation used requires recalculation based on the new data. This work is a complement to my annual *Quality of Life, Balance of Power, and Nuclear Weapons*. Where the present work gives the population and current price GDP data in a historical perspective, *Quality of Life* gives a current snapshot of a wide range of world statistics.

Alexander V. Avakov

SOURCES

The sources are shown in the form: XX(Source) or XX(Source A/SourceB), where XX is a year and (Source) (or Source A or Source B) is one of the following:

WB	The World Bank (1)
E	Encyclopedia Britannica
CIA	Central Intelligence Agency
WIKI	Wikipedia or other Internet source
EST	My estimate
REG	Regression is used
POP*GPC	Obtained by multiplication of Population by GDP Per Capita at Purchasing Power Parities
PROXY(X(Source))	Approximation based on data for country or group of countries X from source Source
PROXY(X(Source A/Source B))	Approximation based on data for country or group of countries X from sources Source A and Source B
INTERPOL(X(Source))	Exponential interpolation based on data for country or group of countries X from source Source
INTERPOL(X(Source A/Source B))	Exponential interpolation based on data for country or group of countries X from sources Source A and Source B
YY(Source A)WEIGHT(Country X(Source B))	Data for year YY from Source A weighted to data for Country X from Source B
MIN	When estimated per capita GDP is less than minimum per capita GDP at purchasing power parities in 1990 international dollars (400 dollars) special algorithm described in the Appendix is used.
AVG(Region(Source))	Average for the region Region based on the source Source.

REGIONS

9 European cs	9 small European countries: Andorra, Channel Islands, Faeroe Islands, Gibraltar, Greenland, Isle of Man, Liechtenstein, Monaco, and San Marino, plus Svalbard
7 Caribbean cs	7 small Caribbean countries: Antigua & Barbuda, Bermuda, Guadeloupe, Guiana (Fr.), Martinique, former Netherlends Antilles (now Curacao and Sint Maarten), and Saint. Kitts & Nevis (also now Saint Martin)
8 Caribbean cs	8 small Caribbean countries: Anguilla, Aruba, Cayman Islands, Montserrat, Saint Pierre & Miquelon, Turks & Caicos Islands, Virgin Islands (U.S.), and British Virgin Islands
14 Pacific is	14 Pacific islands: American Samoa, French Polynesia, Guam, Kiribati, Marshall Islands, Micronesia, New Caledonia, Northern Mariana Islands, Palau, Solomon Islands, Tonga, Vanuatu, Wallis & Futuna, and (Western) Samoa
3 Afr. cs	3 small African countries: Mayotte, Saint Helena, and Western Sahara
E. Europe	Eastern Europe
Eur. Russia	European Russia
Eu. Rs./Sb.	European Russia & Siberia
Other W. offshots	Other Western offshots: Canada, Australia, and New Zealand

26 E. Asian cs	26 East Asian countries: Afghanistan, Cambodia, Laos, Mongolia, North Korea, Vietnam, Bhutan, Brunei, Fiji, Macao, Maldives, Papua New Guinea, American Samoa, French Polynesia, Guam, Kiribati, Marshall Islands, Micronesia, New Caledonia, Northern Mariana Islands, Palau, Solomon Islands, Tonga, Vanuatu, Wallis & Futuna, and (Western) Samoa
Other E. Asia	Other East Asia: East Asia other than Japan, China, and India
Pak./wh. India	Pakistan/whole India
Ban./wh. India	Bangladesh/whole India
Ind./wh. India	India/whole India
Other N. Africa	Other North Africa: Algeria, Tunisia, and Libya
Sahel & W. Africa	Sahel & Other West Africa
Sahel	Chad, Mauritania, Mali, and Niger
Other W. Africa	Other West Africa: Senegal, Gambia, Guinea-Bissau, Guinea, Sierra Leone, Liberia, Burkina Faso, Ivory Coast, Ghana, Togo, Benin, Nigeria, Cape Verde, and Western Sahara
Other E. Africa	Other East Africa: Burundi, Djibouti, Kenya, Rwanda, Tanzania, and Uganda
Rest of Africa	Africa other than North Africa, Sahel, and West Africa
Mal., Zam., Zim.	Malawi, Zambia, and Zimbabwe
S. Afr., Sw., Ls.	South Africa, Swaziland, and Lesotho
Ethiopia & Eritr.	Ethiopia & Eritrea
Namibia & Botsw.	Namibia & Botswana
Indian Ocean	Comoros, Mauritius, Mayotte, Reunion, and Seychelles
Gulf Coast	Bahrain, Kuwait, Qatar, and United Arab Emirates
Arabia	Bahrain, Kuwait, Oman, Qatar, Saudi Arabia, United Arab Emirates, and Yemen
W. Asia	West Asia
Other W. Asia	Other West Asia: West Asia other than Arabia, Iran, Iraq, and Turkey
Other L. Am.	Other Latin America: Latin America other than Mexico
8 L. American cs	8 Latin American countries: Argentina, Brazil, Chile, Colombia, Mexico, Peru, Uruguay, and Venezuela
15 L. American cs	15 Latin American countries: Bolivia, Costa Rica, Cuba, Dominican Republic, Ecuador, El Salvador, Guatemala, Haiti, Honduras, Jamaica, Nicaragua, Panama, Paraguay, Puerto Rico, and Trinidad and Tobago
Caribbean cs.	30 Caribbean countries: Cuba, Dominican Republic, Haiti, Jamaica, Puerto Rico, Trinidad and Tobago, Bahamas, Barbados, Belize, Dominica, Grenada, Guyana, former Netherlands Antilles (now Curacao and Sint Maarten), Saint Lucia, Saint Vincent, Suriname, Antigua & Barbuda, Bermuda, Guadeloupe, Guiana (Fr.), Martinique, Saint Kitts & Nevis, Anguilla, Aruba, Cayman Islands, Montserrat, Saint Pierre & Miquelon, Turks & Caicos Islands, Virgin Islands (U.S.), and British Virgin Islands (also now Saint Martin)
Other Sp. Am.	15 Other Spanish America (ex. Caribbean): Argentina, Chile, Colombia, Peru, Uruguay, Venezuela, Bolivia, Costa Rica, Ecuador, El Salvador, Guatemala, Honduras, Nicaragua, Panama, and Paraguay

ABBREVIATIONS

GPC	Gross Domestic Product at Purchasing Power Parities Per Capita
POP	Population
GDP	Gross Domestic Product at Purchasing Power Parities
GPCxxxx	Gross National Income Per Capita at Market Exchange Rates, Year xxxx
GPCxxxx	Gross Domestic Product Per Capita at Purchasing Power Parities, Year xxxx
GRPOP	Population Growth Rates
GRRL	GDP Real Growth Rates
GRPCRL	GDP Per Capita Real Growth Rates

1. Population, by Country

Year	Population, '000s	Growth Rate	Source
		SAS Afghanistan	
0001	582	.	PROXY(Other E. Asia(Maddison))
1000	1,078	0.06	PROXY(Other E. Asia(Maddison))
1500	1,920	0.12	PROXY(Other E. Asia(Maddison))
1600	2,227	0.15	PROXY(Other E. Asia(Maddison))
1700	2,589	0.15	PROXY(Other E. Asia(Maddison))
1820	3,280	0.20	1820(Maddison)
1870	4,207	0.50	1870(Maddison)
1880	4,520	0.72	INTERPOL(Maddison)
1890	4,857	0.72	INTERPOL(Maddison)
1900	5,219	0.72	INTERPOL(Maddison)
1913	5,730	0.72	1913(Maddison)
1920	6,125	0.96	INTERPOL(Maddison)
1929	6,673	0.96	INTERPOL(Maddison)
1938	7,271	0.96	INTERPOL(Maddison)
1950	8,151	0.96	50(E)
1960	9,829	1.89	60(E)
1970	12,431	2.38	70(E)
1980	15,044	1.93	80(E)
1990	13,568	1.03	90(E)
2000	20,016	3.96	00(E)
2010	25,873	2.60	10(E)
2012	26,961	2.08	12(E)
2020	32,420	2.33	12(E)
2030	40,401	2.23	12(E)
		EEU Albania	
0001	200	.	0001(Maddison)
1000	200	0.00	1000(Maddison)

Year	Population, '000s	Growth Rate	Source
1500	200	0.00	1500(Maddison)
1600	200	0.00	1600(Maddison)
1700	300	0.41	1700(Maddison)
1820	437	0.31	1820(Maddison)
1870	603	0.65	1870(Maddison)
1880	662	0.93	INTERPOL(Maddison)
1890	726	0.93	1890(Maddison)
1900	800	0.98	1900(Maddison)
1913	898	0.89	1913(Maddison)
1920	932	0.53	1920(Maddison)
1929	977	0.53	1929(Maddison)
1938	1,040	0.70	1938(Maddison)
1950	1,215	1.30	50(E)
1960	1,611	2.86	60(E)
1970	2,136	2.86	70(E)
1980	2,671	2.26	80(E)
1990	3,289	2.10	90(E)
2000	3,065	0.70	00(E)
2010	2,906	0.53	10(E)
2012	2,817	1.54	12(E)
2020	2,766	0.23	12(E)
2030	2,791	0.09	12(E)
	MEA ALGERIA		
0001	2,000	.	0001(Maddison)
1000	2,000	0.00	1000(Maddison)
1500	1,500	0.06	1500(Maddison)
1600	2,250	0.41	1600(Maddison)
1700	1,750	0.25	1700(Maddison)
1820	2,689	0.36	1820(Maddison)
1870	3,776	0.68	1870(Maddison)
1880	4,183	1.03	1880(Maddison)
1890	4,548	0.84	INTERPOL(Maddison)
1900	4,946	0.84	INTERPOL(Maddison)
1913	5,497	0.82	1913(Maddison)
1920	5,785	0.73	1920(Maddison)
1929	6,431	1.18	INTERPOL(Maddison)
1938	7,326	1.46	INTERPOL(Maddison)
1950	8,753	1.49	50(E)
1960	10,800	2.12	60(E)
1970	13,746	2.44	70(E)
1980	18,811	3.19	80(E)
1990	25,299	3.01	90(E)
2000	30,129	1.76	00(E)
2010	35,978	1.79	10(E)
2012	37,413	1.97	12(E)
2020	41,375	1.27	12(E)
2030	44,768	0.79	12(E)

Year	Population, '000s	Growth Rate	Source
	DME Andorra		
0001	.	.	
1000	.	.	
1500	.	.	
1600	.	.	
1700	.	.	
1820	.	.	
1870	.	.	
1880	.	.	
1890	.	.	
1900	.	.	
1913	.	.	
1920	.	.	
1929	.	.	
1938	.	.	
1950	6	.	50(E)
1960	8	2.92	60(E)
1970	20	9.60	70(E)
1980	34	5.45	80(E)
1990	53	4.54	90(E)
2000	65	2.06	00(E)
2010	85	2.72	10(E)
2012	78	3.96	12(E)
2020	76	0.39	12(E)
2030	74	0.27	12(E)
	AFR Angola		
0001	.	.	
1000	.	.	
1500	.	.	
1600	.	.	
1700	.	.	
1820	.	.	
1870	.	.	
1880	.	.	
1890	.	.	
1900	.	.	
1913	.	.	
1920	.	.	
1929	.	.	
1938	.	.	
1950	4,118	.	50(E)
1960	5,012	1.98	60(E)
1970	6,083	1.96	70(E)
1980	7,854	2.59	80(E)
1990	10,661	3.10	90(E)

Year	Population, '000s	Growth Rate	Source
2000	12,683	1.75	00(E)
2010	17,043	3.00	10(E)
2012	18,043	2.89	12(E)
2020	22,484	2.79	12(E)
2030	29,155	2.63	12(E)
	LAM Anguilla		
0001	.	.	
1000	.	.	
1500	.	.	
1600	.	.	
1700	.	.	
1820	.	.	
1870	.	.	
1880	.	.	
1890	.	.	
1900	.	.	
1913	.	.	
1920	.	.	
1929	.	.	
1938	.	.	
1950	3	.	PROXY(8 Caribbean cs(Maddison))
1960	4	2.29	INTERPOL(8 Caribbean cs(Maddison))
1970	5	2.29	INTERPOL(8 Caribbean cs(Maddison))
1980	6	1.68	INTERPOL(8 Caribbean cs(Maddison))
1990	7	1.41	90(CIA)
2000	12	5.54	00(CIA)
2010	15	2.27	10(CIA)
2012	15	2.21	12(CIA)
2020	18	2.26	12(EST)
2030	23	2.26	12(EST)
	LAM Antigua and Barbuda		
0001	.	.	
1000	.	.	
1500	.	.	
1600	.	.	
1700	.	.	
1820	.	.	
1870	.	.	
1880	.	.	
1890	.	.	
1900	.	.	
1913	.	.	
1920	.	.	
1929	.	.	
1938	.	.	

Year	Population, '000s	Growth Rate	Source
1950	46	.	50(E)
1960	55	1.80	60(E)
1970	66	1.84	70(E)
1980	69	0.45	80(E)
1990	64	0.75	90(E)
2000	76	1.73	00(E)
2010	85	1.13	10(E)
2012	87	1.32	12(E)
2020	94	0.94	12(E)
2030	102	0.82	12(E)
		LAM ARGENTINA	
0001	204	.	PROXY(Other L. Am.(Maddison))
1000	414	0.07	PROXY(Other L. Am.(Maddison))
1500	600	0.07	PROXY(Other Sp. Am.(Maddison))
1600	360	0.51	PROXY(Other Sp. Am.(Maddison))
1700	409	0.13	PROXY(Other Sp. Am.(Maddison))
1820	534	0.22	1820(Maddison)
1870	1,796	2.46	1870(Maddison)
1880	2,462	3.21	INTERPOL(Maddison)
1890	3,376	3.21	1890(Maddison)
1900	4,693	3.35	1900(Maddison)
1913	7,653	3.83	1913(Maddison)
1920	8,861	2.12	1920(Maddison)
1929	11,592	3.03	1929(Maddison)
1938	13,724	1.89	1938(Maddison)
1950	17,150	1.87	50(E)
1960	20,685	1.89	60(E)
1970	24,003	1.50	70(E)
1980	28,154	1.61	80(E)
1990	32,498	1.45	90(E)
2000	36,120	1.06	00(E)
2010	39,968	1.02	10(E)
2012	40,883	1.14	12(E)
2020	43,648	0.82	12(E)
2030	46,539	0.64	12(E)
		USR ARMENIA	
0001	39	.	PROXY(40(E)/Caucasus(Maddison))
1000	66	0.05	PROXY(40(E)/Caucasus(Maddison))
1500	164	0.18	PROXY(40(E)/Caucasus(Maddison))
1600	197	0.18	PROXY(40(E)/Caucasus(Maddison))
1700	230	0.15	PROXY(40(E)/Caucasus(Maddison))
1820	319	0.27	PROXY(40(E)/Caucasus(Maddison))
1870	603	1.28	PROXY(40(E)/USSR(Maddison))
1880	674	1.11	40(E)/INTERPOL(Maddison)
1890	753	1.11	PROXY(40(E)/USSR(Maddison))
1900	847	1.19	PROXY(40(E)/USSR(Maddison))
1913	1,062	1.76	PROXY(40(E)/USSR(Maddison))
1920	1,052	0.15	PROXY(40(E)/USSR(Maddison))
1929	1,170	1.19	PROXY(40(E)/USSR(Maddison))

Year	Population, '000s	Growth Rate	Source
1938	1,282	1.02	PROXY(40(E)/USSR(Maddison))
1950	1,354	0.46	50(E)
1960	1,867	3.26	60(E)
1970	2,518	3.04	70(E)
1980	3,096	2.09	80(E)
1990	3,545	1.36	90(E)
2000	3,076	1.41	00(E)
2010	2,888	0.63	10(E)
2012	2,863	0.44	12(E)
2020	2,876	0.06	12(E)
2030	2,838	0.13	12(E)
		LAM Aruba	
0001	.	.	
1000	.	.	
1500	.	.	
1600	.	.	
1700	.	.	
1820	.	.	
1870	.	.	
1880	.	.	
1890	.	.	
1900	.	.	
1913	.	.	
1920	.	.	
1929	.	.	
1938	.	.	
1950	51	.	50(E)
1960	57	1.12	60(E)
1970	61	0.68	70(E)
1980	60	0.17	80(E)
1990	63	0.49	90(E)
2000	96	4.30	00(E)
2010	101	0.51	10(E)
2012	104	1.30	12(E)
2020	106	0.28	12(E)
2030	107	0.09	12(E)
		DME Australia	
0001	248	.	PROXY(Other W. offshots(Maddison))
1000	321	0.03	PROXY(Other W. offshots(Maddison))
1500	450	0.07	1500(Maddison)
1600	450	0.00	1600(Maddison)
1700	450	0.00	1700(Maddison)
1820	334	0.25	1820(Maddison)
1870	1,775	3.40	1870(Maddison)
1880	2,197	2.16	1880(Maddison)
1890	3,107	3.53	1890(Maddison)
1900	3,741	1.87	1900(Maddison)

Year	Population, '000s	Growth Rate	Source
1913	4,821	1.97	1913(Maddison)
1920	5,358	1.52	1920(Maddison)
1929	6,396	1.99	1929(Maddison)
1938	6,904	0.85	1938(Maddison)
1950	8,219	1.46	50(E)
1960	10,315	2.30	60(E)
1970	12,552	1.98	70(E)
1980	14,471	1.43	80(E)
1990	17,065	1.66	90(E)
2000	18,572	0.85	00(E)
2010	21,130	1.30	10(E)
2012	22,377	2.91	12(E)
2020	25,039	1.41	12(E)
2030	27,549	0.96	12(E)
DME Austria			
0001	500	.	0001(Maddison)
1000	700	0.03	1000(Maddison)
1500	2,000	0.21	1500(Maddison)
1600	2,500	0.22	1600(Maddison)
1700	2,500	0.00	1700(Maddison)
1820	3,369	0.25	1820(Maddison)
1870	4,520	0.59	1870(Maddison)
1880	4,941	0.89	1880(Maddison)
1890	5,394	0.88	1890(Maddison)
1900	5,973	1.02	1900(Maddison)
1913	6,767	0.96	1913(Maddison)
1920	6,455	0.67	1920(Maddison)
1929	6,664	0.35	1929(Maddison)
1938	6,753	0.15	1938(Maddison)
1950	6,935	0.22	50(E)
1960	7,047	0.16	60(E)
1970	7,467	0.58	70(E)
1980	7,549	0.11	80(E)
1990	7,678	0.17	90(E)
2000	8,187	0.64	00(E)
2010	8,379	0.23	10(E)
2012	8,457	0.46	12(E)
2020	8,731	0.40	12(E)
2030	9,004	0.31	12(E)
USR Azerbaijan			
0001	98	.	PROXY(40(E)/Caucasus(Maddison))
1000	163	0.05	PROXY(40(E)/Caucasus(Maddison))
1500	408	0.18	PROXY(40(E)/Caucasus(Maddison))
1600	498	0.20	PROXY(40(E)/Caucasus(Maddison))
1700	571	0.14	PROXY(40(E)/Caucasus(Maddison))
1820	792	0.27	PROXY(40(E)/Caucasus(Maddison))
1870	1,496	1.28	PROXY(40(E)/USSR(Maddison))

Year	Population, '000s	Growth Rate	Source
1880	1,671	1.11	40(E)/INTERPOL(Maddison)
1890	1,867	1.11	PROXY(40(E)/USSR(Maddison))
1900	2,100	1.19	PROXY(40(E)/USSR(Maddison))
1913	2,635	1.76	PROXY(40(E)/USSR(Maddison))
1920	2,608	0.15	PROXY(40(E)/USSR(Maddison))
1929	2,902	1.19	PROXY(40(E)/USSR(Maddison))
1938	3,180	1.02	PROXY(40(E)/USSR(Maddison))
1950	2,885	0.81	50(E)
1960	3,894	3.04	60(E)
1970	5,172	2.88	70(E)
1980	6,161	1.77	80(E)
1990	7,212	1.59	90(E)
2000	8,074	1.14	00(E)
2010	9,054	1.15	10(E)
2012	9,299	1.34	12(E)
2020	10,160	1.11	12(E)
2030	10,732	0.55	12(E)

LAM Bahamas

Year	Population, '000s	Growth Rate	Source
0001	.	.	
1000	.	.	
1500	.	.	
1600	.	.	
1700	.	.	
1820	.	.	
1870	.	.	
1880	.	.	
1890	.	.	
1900	.	.	
1913	.	.	
1920	.	.	
1929	.	.	
1938	.	.	
1950	79	.	50(E)
1960	110	3.37	60(E)
1970	170	4.45	70(E)
1980	210	2.14	80(E)
1990	256	2.00	90(E)
2000	304	1.73	00(E)
2010	352	1.48	10(E)
2012	363	1.49	12(E)
2020	397	1.14	12(E)
2030	430	0.80	12(E)

MEA Bahrain

Year	Population, '000s	Growth Rate	Source
0001	59	.	PROXY(W. Asia(Maddison))
1000	61	0.00	PROXY(W. Asia(Maddison))
1500	54	0.02	PROXY(Arabia(Maddison))
1600	54	0.00	INTERPOL(Maddison)

Year	Population, '000s	Growth Rate	Source
1700	54	0.00	PROXY(Arabia(Maddison))
1820	63	0.12	PROXY(Gulf Coast(Maddison))
1870	63	0.00	PROXY(Gulf Coast(Maddison))
1880	66	0.56	INTERPOL(Maddison)
1890	70	0.56	INTERPOL(Maddison)
1900	74	0.56	INTERPOL(Maddison)
1913	79	0.56	PROXY(Gulf Coast(Maddison))
1920	84	0.89	INTERPOL(Maddison)
1929	91	0.89	INTERPOL(Maddison)
1938	99	0.89	INTERPOL(Maddison)
1950	110	0.89	50(E)
1960	149	3.08	60(E)
1970	210	3.49	70(E)
1980	334	4.75	80(E)
1990	503	4.18	90(E)
2000	638	2.41	00(E)
2010	1,229	6.78	10(E)
2012	1,218	0.46	12(E)
2020	1,373	1.51	12(E)
2030	1,506	0.93	12(E)
	SAS Bangladesh		
0001	7,177	.	PROXY(Undivided India(Maddison))
1000	7,177	0.00	PROXY(Undivided India(Maddison))
1500	10,526	0.08	PROXY(Undivided India(Maddison))
1600	12,919	0.21	PROXY(Undivided India(Maddison))
1700	15,789	0.20	PROXY(Undivided India(Maddison))
1820	20,000	0.20	1820(Maddison)
1870	24,721	0.42	1870(Maddison)
1880	25,536	0.32	INTERPOL(Ban./wh. India(Maddison))
1890	28,210	1.00	INTERPOL(Ban./wh. India(Maddison))
1900	29,164	0.33	INTERPOL(Ban./wh. India(Maddison))
1913	31,786	0.66	1913(Maddison)
1920	32,161	0.17	INTERPOL(Ban./wh. India(Maddison))
1929	34,427	0.76	1929(Maddison)
1938	39,934	1.66	INTERPOL(Ban./wh. India(Maddison))
1950	45,646	1.12	50(E)
1960	54,593	1.81	60(E)
1970	67,331	2.12	70(E)
1980	87,937	2.71	80(E)
1990	111,437	2.40	90(E)
2000	129,592	1.52	00(E)
2010	148,569	1.38	10(E)
2012	152,638	1.36	12(E)
2020	167,603	1.18	12(E)
2030	182,240	0.84	12(E)
	LAM Barbados		
0001	.	.	
1000	.	.	
1500	.	.	

Year	Population, '000s	Growth Rate	Source
1600	.	.	
1700	.	.	
1820	.	.	
1870	.	.	
1880	.	.	
1890	.	.	
1900	.	.	
1913	.	.	
1920	.	.	
1929	.	.	
1938	.	.	
1950	211	.	50(E)
1960	232	0.95	60(E)
1970	239	0.30	70(E)
1980	252	0.53	80(E)
1990	263	0.43	90(E)
2000	269	0.23	00(E)
2010	276	0.26	10(E)
2012	277	0.24	12(E)
2020	282	0.21	12(E)
2030	284	0.07	12(E)

USR Belarus

Year	Population, '000s	Growth Rate	Source
0001	115	.	PROXY(40(E)/Eur. Russia(Maddison))
1000	230	0.07	PROXY(40(E)/Eur. Russia(Maddison))
1500	691	0.22	PROXY(40(E)/Eur. Russia(Maddison))
1600	864	0.22	PROXY(40(E)/Eur. Russia(Maddison))
1700	1,152	0.29	PROXY(40(E)/Eur. Russia(Maddison))
1820	2,545	0.66	PROXY(40(E)/Eur. Russia(Maddison))
1870	4,133	0.97	PROXY(40(E)/USSR(Maddison))
1880	4,617	1.11	40(E)/INTERPOL(Maddison)
1890	5,158	1.11	PROXY(40(E)/USSR(Maddison))
1900	5,803	1.19	PROXY(40(E)/USSR(Maddison))
1913	7,280	1.76	PROXY(40(E)/USSR(Maddison))
1920	7,206	0.15	PROXY(40(E)/USSR(Maddison))
1929	8,018	1.19	PROXY(40(E)/USSR(Maddison))
1938	8,786	1.02	PROXY(40(E)/USSR(Maddison))
1950	7,745	1.05	50(E)
1960	8,190	0.56	60(E)
1970	9,040	0.99	70(E)
1980	9,650	0.66	80(E)
1990	10,186	0.54	90(E)
2000	9,974	0.21	00(E)
2010	9,499	0.49	10(E)
2012	9,460	0.20	12(E)
2020	9,225	0.31	12(E)
2030	8,828	0.44	12(E)

Year	Population, '000s	Growth Rate	Source
		DME Belgium	
0001	300	.	0001(Maddison)
1000	400	0.03	1000(Maddison)
1500	1,400	0.25	1500(Maddison)
1600	1,600	0.13	1600(Maddison)
1700	2,000	0.22	1700(Maddison)
1820	3,434	0.45	1820(Maddison)
1870	5,096	0.79	1870(Maddison)
1880	5,541	0.84	1880(Maddison)
1890	6,096	0.96	1890(Maddison)
1900	6,719	0.98	1900(Maddison)
1913	7,666	1.02	1913(Maddison)
1920	7,552	0.21	1920(Maddison)
1929	8,032	0.69	1929(Maddison)
1938	8,374	0.46	1938(Maddison)
1950	8,639	0.26	50(E)
1960	9,153	0.58	60(E)
1970	9,690	0.57	70(E)
1980	9,859	0.17	80(E)
1990	9,967	0.11	90(E)
2000	10,251	0.28	00(E)
2010	10,919	0.63	10(E)
2012	11,130	0.96	12(E)
2020	11,642	0.56	12(E)
2030	12,256	0.52	12(E)
		LAM Belize	
0001	.	.	
1000	.	.	
1500	.	.	
1600	.	.	
1700	.	.	
1820	.	.	
1870	.	.	
1880	.	.	
1890	.	.	
1900	.	.	
1913	.	.	
1920	.	.	
1929	.	.	
1938	.	.	
1950	68	.	50(E)
1960	90	2.84	60(E)
1970	120	2.92	70(E)
1980	146	1.98	80(E)
1990	189	2.62	90(E)

Year	Population, '000s	Growth Rate	Source
2000	241	2.46	00(E)
2010	314	2.68	10(E)
2012	331	2.69	12(E)
2020	385	1.90	12(E)
2030	448	1.53	12(E)
	AFR Benin		
0001	.	.	
1000	.	.	
1500	.	.	
1600	.	.	
1700	.	.	
1820	.	.	
1870	.	.	
1880	.	.	
1890	.	.	
1900	.	.	
1913	.	.	
1920	.	.	
1929	.	.	
1938	.	.	
1950	1,673	.	50(E)
1960	2,420	3.76	60(E)
1970	2,850	1.65	70(E)
1980	3,611	2.39	80(E)
1990	4,773	2.83	90(E)
2000	6,518	3.16	00(E)
2010	8,850	3.11	10(E)
2012	9,348	2.77	12(E)
2020	11,523	2.65	12(E)
2030	14,630	2.42	12(E)
	DME Bermuda		
0001	.	.	
1000	.	.	
1500	.	.	
1600	.	.	
1700	.	.	
1820	.	.	
1870	.	.	
1880	.	.	
1890	.	.	
1900	.	.	
1913	.	.	
1920	.	.	
1929	.	.	
1938	.	.	

Year	Population, '000s	Growth Rate	Source
1950	39	.	50(E)
1960	44	1.21	60(E)
1970	53	1.88	70(E)
1980	55	0.37	80(E)
1990	58	0.53	90(E)
2000	62	0.67	00(E)
2010	64	0.32	10(E)
2012	65	0.52	12(E)
2020	66	0.26	12(E)
2030	67	0.15	12(E)
SAS Bhutan			
0001	.	.	
1000	.	.	
1500	.	.	
1600	.	.	
1700	.	.	
1820	.	.	
1870	.	.	
1880	.	.	
1890	.	.	
1900	.	.	
1913	.	.	
1920	.	.	
1929	.	.	
1938	.	.	
1950	168	.	50(E)
1960	212	2.35	60(E)
1970	309	3.84	70(E)
1980	446	3.74	80(E)
1990	615	3.27	90(E)
2000	571	0.74	00(E)
2010	726	2.43	10(E)
2012	750	1.63	12(E)
2020	829	1.26	12(E)
2030	899	0.81	12(E)
LAM Bolivia			
0001	420	.	PROXY(Other L. Am.(Maddison))
1000	852	0.07	PROXY(Other L. Am.(Maddison))
1500	1,235	0.07	PROXY(Other Sp. Am.(Maddison))
1600	741	0.51	PROXY(Other Sp. Am.(Maddison))
1700	843	0.13	PROXY(Other Sp. Am.(Maddison))
1820	1,100	0.22	1820(Maddison)
1870	1,495	0.62	1870(Maddison)
1880	1,559	0.42	INTERPOL(Maddison)
1890	1,626	0.42	INTERPOL(Maddison)
1900	1,696	0.42	1900(Maddison)
1913	1,881	0.80	1913(Maddison)

Year	Population, '000s	Growth Rate	Source
1920	2,136	1.83	1920(Maddison)
1929	2,370	1.16	1929(Maddison)
1938	2,629	1.16	1938(Maddison)
1950	2,714	0.27	50(E)
1960	3,355	2.14	60(E)
1970	4,217	2.31	70(E)
1980	5,353	2.41	80(E)
1990	6,658	2.21	90(E)
2000	8,307	2.24	00(E)
2010	9,905	1.77	10(E)
2012	10,308	2.02	12(E)
2020	11,709	1.61	12(E)
2030	13,528	1.45	12(E)
EEU Bosnia			
0001	245	.	PROXY(Yugoslavia(Maddison))
1000	286	0.02	PROXY(Yugoslavia(Maddison))
1500	367	0.05	PROXY(Yugoslavia(Maddison))
1600	449	0.20	PROXY(Yugoslavia(Maddison))
1700	449	0.00	PROXY(YUgoslavia(Maddison))
1820	851	0.53	PROXY(Yugoslavia(Maddison))
1870	1,347	0.92	PROXY(Yugoslavia(Maddison))
1880	1,460	0.81	INTERPOL(Maddison)
1890	1,582	0.81	PROXY(Yugoslavia(Maddison))
1900	1,824	1.44	PROXY(Yugoslavia(Maddison))
1913	2,219	1.52	PROXY(Yugoslavia(Maddison))
1920	2,028	1.28	PROXY(Yugoslavia(Maddison))
1929	2,317	1.49	PROXY(Yugoslavia(Maddison))
1938	2,626	1.40	PROXY(Yugoslavia(Maddison))
1950	2,661	0.11	50(E)
1960	3,180	1.80	60(E)
1970	3,564	1.15	70(E)
1980	3,914	0.94	80(E)
1990	4,308	0.96	90(E)
2000	3,781	1.30	00(E)
2010	3,843	0.16	10(E)
2012	3,843	0.00	12(E)
2020	3,739	0.34	12(E)
2030	3,560	0.49	12(E)
AFR Botswana			
0001	35	.	PROXY(Namibia & Botsw.(Maddison))
1000	46	0.03	PROXY(Namibia & Botsw.(Maddison))
1500	92	0.14	PROXY(Namibia & Botsw.(Maddison))
1600	92	0.00	PROXY(Namibia & Botsw.(Maddison))
1700	92	0.00	PROXY(Namibia & Botsw.(Maddison))
1820	101	0.08	PROXY(Namibia & Botsw.(Maddison))
1870	174	1.09	INTERPOL(Maddison)
1880	194	1.09	INTERPOL(Maddison)
1890	217	1.09	INTERPOL(Maddison)
1900	241	1.09	INTERPOL(Maddison)

Year	Population, '000s	Growth Rate	Source
1913	278	1.09	INTERPOL(Maddison)
1920	300	1.09	INTERPOL(Maddison)
1929	331	1.09	INTERPOL(Maddison)
1938	365	1.09	INTERPOL(Maddison)
1950	430	1.37	50(E)
1960	524	2.00	60(E)
1970	693	2.83	70(E)
1980	996	3.69	80(E)
1990	1,382	3.33	90(E)
2000	1,758	2.44	00(E)
2010	1,982	1.21	10(E)
2012	2,057	1.88	12(E)
2020	2,287	1.33	12(E)
2030	2,595	1.27	12(E)
LAM Brazil			
0001	340	.	PROXY(Other L. Am.(Maddison))
1000	690	0.07	PROXY(Other L. Am.(Maddison))
1500	1,000	0.07	1500(Maddison)
1600	800	0.22	1600(Maddison)
1700	1,250	0.45	1700(Maddison)
1820	4,507	1.07	1820(Maddison)
1870	9,797	1.57	1870(Maddison)
1880	11,794	1.87	1880(Maddison)
1890	14,199	1.87	1890(Maddison)
1900	17,984	2.39	1900(Maddison)
1913	23,660	2.13	1913(Maddison)
1920	27,404	2.12	1920(Maddison)
1929	32,894	2.05	1929(Maddison)
1938	39,480	2.05	1938(Maddison)
1950	53,975	2.64	50(E)
1960	72,742	3.03	60(E)
1970	95,989	2.81	70(E)
1980	118,563	2.13	80(E)
1990	146,593	2.14	90(E)
2000	169,421	1.46	00(E)
2010	190,571	1.18	10(E)
2012	194,158	0.94	12(E)
2020	206,414	0.77	12(E)
2030	218,284	0.56	12(E)
SEA Brunei			
0001	.	.	
1000	.	.	
1500	.	.	
1600	.	.	
1700	.	.	
1820	.	.	
1870	.	.	
1880	.	.	

Year	Population, '000s	Growth Rate	Source
1890	.	.	
1900	.	.	
1913	.	.	
1920	.	.	
1929	.	.	
1938	.	.	
1950	45	.	50(E)
1960	82	6.18	60(E)
1970	130	4.72	70(E)
1980	193	4.03	80(E)
1990	253	2.74	90(E)
2000	325	2.54	00(E)
2010	387	1.76	10(E)
2012	400	1.69	12(E)
2020	452	1.53	12(E)
2030	508	1.17	12(E)
EEU Bulgaria			
0001	500	.	0001(Maddison)
1000	800	0.05	1000(Maddison)
1500	800	0.00	1500(Maddison)
1600	1,250	0.45	1600(Maddison)
1700	1,250	0.00	1700(Maddison)
1820	2,187	0.47	1820(Maddison)
1870	2,586	0.34	1870(Maddison)
1880	2,985	1.44	INTERPOL(Maddison)
1890	3,445	1.44	1890(Maddison)
1900	4,000	1.50	1900(Maddison)
1913	4,720	1.28	1913(Maddison)
1920	5,072	1.03	1920(Maddison)
1929	5,950	1.79	1929(Maddison)
1938	6,564	1.10	1938(Maddison)
1950	7,251	0.83	50(E)
1960	7,867	0.82	60(E)
1970	8,490	0.77	70(E)
1980	8,862	0.43	80(E)
1990	8,718	0.16	90(E)
2000	7,973	0.89	00(E)
2010	7,397	0.75	10(E)
2012	7,311	0.58	12(E)
2020	6,976	0.58	12(E)
2030	6,543	0.64	12(E)
AFR Burkina Faso			
0001	.	.	
1000	.	.	
1500	.	.	
1600	.	.	

Year	Population, '000s	Growth Rate	Source
1700	.	.	
1820	.	.	
1870	.	.	
1880	.	.	
1890	.	.	
1900	.	.	
1913	.	.	
1920	.	.	
1929	.	.	
1938	.	.	
1950	4,376	.	50(E)
1960	4,882	1.10	60(E)
1970	5,807	1.75	70(E)
1980	7,212	2.19	80(E)
1990	9,324	2.60	90(E)
2000	12,294	2.80	00(E)
2010	16,469	2.97	10(E)
2012	17,482	3.03	12(E)
2020	22,150	3.00	12(E)
2030	29,112	2.77	12(E)
		CPA Burma	
0001	622	.	PROXY(Other E. Asia(Maddison))
1000	1,152	0.06	PROXY(Other E. Asia(Maddison))
1500	2,052	0.12	PROXY(Other E. Asia(Maddison))
1600	2,380	0.15	PROXY(Other E. Asia(Maddison))
1700	2,768	0.15	PROXY(Other E. Asia(Maddison))
1820	3,506	0.20	1820(Maddison)
1870	4,245	0.38	1870(Maddison)
1880	5,638	2.88	INTERPOL(Maddison)
1890	7,489	2.88	1890(Maddison)
1900	10,174	3.11	1900(Maddison)
1913	12,326	1.49	1913(Maddison)
1920	13,096	0.87	1920(Maddison)
1929	14,364	1.03	1929(Maddison)
1938	16,145	1.31	1938(Maddison)
1950	19,488	1.58	50(E)
1960	22,839	1.60	60(E)
1970	27,393	1.83	70(E)
1980	33,336	1.98	80(E)
1990	40,464	1.96	90(E)
2000	47,439	1.60	00(E)
2010	53,414	1.19	10(E)
2012	54,576	1.08	12(E)
2020	59,126	1.01	12(E)
2030	64,103	0.81	12(E)
		AFR Burundi	
0001	29	.	PROXY(Other E. Africa(Maddison))

Year	Population, '000s	Growth Rate	Source
1000	293	0.23	PROXY(Other E. Africa(Maddison))
1500	587	0.14	PROXY(Other E. Africa(Maddison))
1600	685	0.15	PROXY(Other E. Africa(Maddison))
1700	782	0.13	PROXY(Other E. Africa(Maddison))
1820	1,016	0.22	PROXY(Other E. Africa(Maddison))
1870	1,406	0.65	INTERPOL(Maddison)
1880	1,500	0.65	INTERPOL(Maddison)
1890	1,601	0.65	INTERPOL(Maddison)
1900	1,708	0.65	INTERPOL(Maddison)
1913	1,858	0.65	INTERPOL(Maddison)
1920	1,945	0.65	INTERPOL(Maddison)
1929	2,062	0.65	INTERPOL(Maddison)
1938	2,186	0.65	INTERPOL(Maddison)
1950	2,363	0.65	50(E)
1960	2,940	2.21	60(E)
1970	3,513	1.80	70(E)
1980	4,130	1.63	80(E)
1990	5,602	3.10	90(E)
2000	6,374	1.30	00(E)
2010	8,383	2.78	10(E)
2012	8,731	2.06	12(E)
2020	10,057	1.78	12(E)
2030	11,441	1.30	12(E)
CPA Cambodia			
0001	371	.	PROXY(Other E. Asia(Maddison))
1000	687	0.06	PROXY(Other E. Asia(Maddison))
1500	1,224	0.12	PROXY(Other E. Asia(Maddison))
1600	1,419	0.15	PROXY(Other E. Asia(Maddison))
1700	1,650	0.15	PROXY(Other E. Asia(Maddison))
1820	2,090	0.20	1820(Maddison)
1870	2,340	0.23	1870(Maddison)
1880	2,493	0.63	INTERPOL(Maddison)
1890	2,655	0.63	INTERPOL(Maddison)
1900	2,828	0.63	INTERPOL(Maddison)
1913	3,070	0.63	1913(Maddison)
1920	3,296	1.02	INTERPOL(Maddison)
1929	3,612	1.02	INTERPOL(Maddison)
1938	3,958	1.02	INTERPOL(Maddison)
1950	4,471	1.02	50(E)
1960	5,761	2.57	60(E)
1970	7,394	2.53	70(E)
1980	6,889	0.70	80(E)
1990	9,368	3.12	90(E)
2000	12,351	2.80	00(E)
2010	14,454	1.58	10(E)
2012	14,951	1.71	12(E)
2020	16,927	1.56	12(E)
2030	19,031	1.18	12(E)

Year	Population, '000s	Growth Rate	Source
		AFR CAMEROON	
0001	.	.	
1000	.	.	
1500	.	.	
1600	.	.	
1700	.	.	
1820	.	.	
1870	.	.	
1880	.	.	
1890	.	.	
1900	.	.	
1913	.	.	
1920	.	.	
1929	.	.	
1938	.	.	
1950	4,888	.	50(E)
1960	5,409	1.02	60(E)
1970	6,842	2.38	70(E)
1980	9,110	2.90	80(E)
1990	12,181	2.95	90(E)
2000	15,678	2.56	00(E)
2010	19,661	2.29	10(E)
2012	20,655	2.50	12(E)
2020	24,383	2.10	12(E)
2030	29,128	1.79	12(E)
		DME CANADA	
0001	80	.	0001(Maddison)
1000	160	0.07	1000(Maddison)
1500	250	0.09	1500(Maddison)
1600	250	0.00	1600(Maddison)
1700	200	0.22	1700(Maddison)
1820	816	1.18	1820(Maddison)
1870	3,781	3.11	1870(Maddison)
1880	4,384	1.49	1880(Maddison)
1890	4,918	1.16	1890(Maddison)
1900	5,457	1.05	1900(Maddison)
1913	7,852	2.84	1913(Maddison)
1920	8,798	1.64	1920(Maddison)
1929	10,305	1.77	1929(Maddison)
1938	11,452	1.18	1938(Maddison)
1950	14,011	1.69	50(E)
1960	17,909	2.48	60(E)
1970	21,717	1.95	70(E)
1980	24,516	1.22	80(E)
1990	27,701	1.23	90(E)
2000	30,667	1.02	00(E)
2010	33,147	0.78	10(E)

Year	Population, '000s	Growth Rate	Source
2012	34,304	1.73	12(E)
2020	36,305	0.71	12(E)
2030	38,929	0.70	12(E)
AFR Cape Verde			
0001	.	.	
1000	.	.	
1500	.	.	
1600	.	.	
1700	.	.	
1820	.	.	
1870	.	.	
1880	.	.	
1890	.	.	
1900	.	.	
1913	.	.	
1920	.	.	
1929	.	.	
1938	.	.	
1950	146	.	50(E)
1960	211	3.75	60(E)
1970	274	2.65	70(E)
1980	300	0.91	80(E)
1990	348	1.50	90(E)
2000	435	2.26	00(E)
2010	492	1.24	10(E)
2012	505	1.27	12(E)
2020	543	0.92	12(E)
2030	587	0.78	12(E)
LAM Cayman Islands			
0001	.	.	
1000	.	.	
1500	.	.	
1600	.	.	
1700	.	.	
1820	.	.	
1870	.	.	
1880	.	.	
1890	.	.	
1900	.	.	
1913	.	.	
1920	.	.	
1929	.	.	
1938	.	.	
1950	6	.	50(E)
1960	8	2.92	60(E)

Year	Population, '000s	Growth Rate	Source
1970	10	2.26	70(E)
1980	17	5.45	80(E)
1990	26	4.34	90(E)
2000	40	4.40	00(E)
2010	56	3.42	10(E)
2012	56	0.00	12(E)
2020	59	0.65	12(E)
2030	62	0.50	12(E)
AFR Central African Republic			
0001	.	.	
1000	.	.	
1500	.	.	
1600	.	.	
1700	.	.	
1820	.	.	
1870	.	.	
1880	.	.	
1890	.	.	
1900	.	.	
1913	.	.	
1920	.	.	
1929	.	.	
1938	.	.	
1950	1,314	.	50(E)
1960	1,467	1.11	60(E)
1970	1,839	2.29	70(E)
1980	2,349	2.48	80(E)
1990	3,085	2.76	90(E)
2000	3,980	2.58	00(E)
2010	4,845	1.99	10(E)
2012	5,057	2.17	12(E)
2020	5,991	2.14	12(E)
2030	7,325	2.03	12(E)
AFR Chad			
0001	.	.	
1000	.	.	
1500	.	.	
1600	.	.	
1700	.	.	
1820	.	.	
1870	.	.	
1880	.	.	
1890	.	.	
1900	.	.	
1913	.	.	
1920	.	.	

Year	Population, '000s	Growth Rate	Source
1929	.	.	
1938	.	.	
1950	2,608	.	50(E)
1960	2,954	1.25	60(E)
1970	3,656	2.15	70(E)
1980	4,554	2.22	80(E)
1990	6,011	2.81	90(E)
2000	8,222	3.18	00(E)
2010	11,707	3.60	10(E)
2012	12,337	2.65	12(E)
2020	15,087	2.55	12(E)
2030	19,225	2.45	12(E)
LAM Chile			
0001	291	.	PROXY(Other L. Am.(Maddison))
1000	591	0.07	PROXY(Other L. Am.(Maddison))
1500	857	0.07	PROXY(Other Sp. Am.(Maddison))
1600	519	0.50	PROXY(Other Sp. Am.(Maddison))
1700	591	0.13	PROXY(Other Sp. Am.(Maddison))
1820	771	0.22	1820(Maddison)
1870	1,945	1.87	1870(Maddison)
1880	2,271	1.56	INTERPOL(Maddison)
1890	2,651	1.56	1890(Maddison)
1900	2,974	1.16	1900(Maddison)
1913	3,431	1.11	1913(Maddison)
1920	3,827	1.57	1920(Maddison)
1929	4,306	1.32	1929(Maddison)
1938	4,915	1.48	1938(Maddison)
1950	6,091	1.80	50(E)
1960	7,652	2.31	60(E)
1970	9,578	2.27	70(E)
1980	11,179	1.56	80(E)
1990	13,188	1.67	90(E)
2000	15,420	1.58	00(E)
2010	16,290	0.55	10(E)
2012	16,608	0.97	12(E)
2020	17,714	0.81	12(E)
2030	18,705	0.55	12(E)
CPA China			
0001	59,600	.	0001(Maddison)
1000	59,000	0.00	1000(Maddison)
1500	103,000	0.11	1500(Maddison)
1600	160,000	0.44	1600(Maddison)
1700	138,000	0.15	1700(Maddison)
1820	381,000	0.85	1820(Maddison)
1870	358,000	0.12	1870(Maddison)
1880	368,000	0.28	1880(Maddison)
1890	380,000	0.32	1890(Maddison)
1900	400,000	0.51	1900(Maddison)
1913	437,140	0.69	1913(Maddison)

Year	Population, '000s	Growth Rate	Source
1920	472,000	1.10	1920(Maddison)
1929	487,273	0.35	1929(Maddison)
1938	513,336	0.58	1938(Maddison)
1950	562,580	0.77	50(E)
1960	658,270	1.58	60(E)
1970	814,623	2.15	70(E)
1980	983,171	1.90	80(E)
1990	1,145,195	1.54	90(E)
2000	1,262,600	0.98	00(E)
2010	1,337,900	0.58	10(E)
2012	1,350,861	0.48	12(E)
2020	1,384,047	0.30	12(E)
2030	1,389,315	0.04	12(E)
LAM Colombia			
0001	460	.	PROXY(Other L. Am.(Maddison))
1000	934	0.07	PROXY(Other L. Am.(Maddison))
1500	1,354	0.07	PROXY(Other Sp. Am.(Maddison))
1600	812	0.51	PROXY(Other Sp. Am.(Maddison))
1700	924	0.13	PROXY(Other Sp. Am.(Maddison))
1820	1,206	0.22	1820(Maddison)
1870	2,392	1.38	1870(Maddison)
1880	2,839	1.73	INTERPOL(Maddison)
1890	3,369	1.73	1890(Maddison)
1900	3,998	1.73	1900(Maddison)
1913	5,195	2.04	1913(Maddison)
1920	6,213	2.59	1920(Maddison)
1929	7,821	2.59	1929(Maddison)
1938	8,702	1.19	1938(Maddison)
1950	12,568	3.11	50(E)
1960	15,953	2.41	60(E)
1970	21,430	3.00	70(E)
1980	26,631	2.20	80(E)
1990	33,147	2.21	90(E)
2000	38,910	1.62	00(E)
2010	44,205	1.28	10(E)
2012	45,226	1.15	12(E)
2020	49,085	1.03	12(E)
2030	52,965	0.76	12(E)
AFR Comoros			
0001	.	.	
1000	.	.	
1500	.	.	
1600	.	.	
1700	.	.	
1820	.	.	
1870	.	.	
1880	.	.	
1890	.	.	

Year	Population, '000s	Growth Rate	Source
1900	.	.	
1913	.	.	
1920	.	.	
1929	.	.	
1938	.	.	
1950	148	.	50(E)
1960	193	2.69	60(E)
1970	238	2.12	70(E)
1980	329	3.29	80(E)
1990	438	2.90	90(E)
2000	545	2.21	00(E)
2010	706	2.62	10(E)
2012	736	2.13	12(E)
2020	846	1.75	12(E)
2030	964	1.31	12(E)

AFR Congo, Democratic Republic of the

Year	Population, '000s	Growth Rate	Source
0001	.	.	
1000	.	.	
1500	.	.	
1600	.	.	
1700	.	.	
1820	.	.	
1870	.	.	
1880	.	.	
1890	.	.	
1900	.	.	
1913	.	.	
1920	.	.	
1929	.	.	
1938	.	.	
1950	13,569	.	50(E)
1960	15,368	1.25	60(E)
1970	20,267	2.81	70(E)
1980	27,019	2.92	80(E)
1990	36,406	3.03	90(E)
2000	49,626	3.15	00(E)
2010	65,966	2.89	10(E)
2012	69,554	2.68	12(E)
2020	85,054	2.55	12(E)
2030	105,956	2.22	12(E)

AFR Congo, Republic of the

Year	Population, '000s	Growth Rate	Source
0001	.	.	
1000	.	.	
1500	.	.	
1600	.	.	
1700	.	.	
1820	.	.	

Year	Population, '000s	Growth Rate	Source
1870	.	.	
1880	.	.	
1890	.	.	
1900	.	.	
1913	.	.	
1920	.	.	
1929	.	.	
1938	.	.	
1950	808	.	50(E)
1960	1,014	2.30	60(E)
1970	1,335	2.79	70(E)
1980	1,798	3.02	80(E)
1990	2,389	2.88	90(E)
2000	3,136	2.76	00(E)
2010	4,043	2.57	10(E)
2012	4,228	2.27	12(E)
2020	5,003	2.13	12(E)
2030	6,169	2.12	12(E)
SEA Cook Islands			
0001	.	.	
1000	.	.	
1500	.	.	
1600	.	.	
1700	.	.	
1820	.	.	
1870	.	.	
1880	.	.	
1890	.	.	
1900	.	.	
1913	.	.	
1920	.	.	
1929	.	.	
1938	.	.	
1950	7	.	PROXY(14 Pacific is(Maddison))
1960	9	2.74	INTERPOL(14 Pacific is(Maddison))
1970	11	2.75	INTERPOL(14 Pacific is(Maddison))
1980	14	2.44	INTERPOL(14 Pacific is(Maddison))
1990	18	2.30	90(CIA)
2000	20	1.16	00(CIA)
2010	11	5.58	10(CIA)
2012	11	3.14	12(CIA)
2020	7	5.18	12(EST)
2030	4	5.18	12(EST)
LAM Costa Rica			
0001	24	.	PROXY(Other L. Am.(Maddison))
1000	49	0.07	PROXY(Other L. Am.(Maddison))
1500	71	0.07	PROXY(Other Sp. Am.(Maddison))
1600	42	0.51	PROXY(Other Sp. Am.(Maddison))

Year	Population, '000s	Growth Rate	Source
1700	48	0.13	PROXY(Other Sp. Am.(Maddison))
1820	63	0.22	1820(Maddison)
1870	137	1.57	1870(Maddison)
1880	177	2.61	INTERPOL(Maddison)
1890	229	2.61	INTERPOL(Maddison)
1900	297	2.61	1900(Maddison)
1913	372	1.75	1913(Maddison)
1920	420	1.75	1920(Maddison)
1929	490	1.73	1929(Maddison)
1938	590	2.08	1938(Maddison)
1950	862	3.21	50(E)
1960	1,277	4.01	60(E)
1970	1,780	3.38	70(E)
1980	2,316	2.67	80(E)
1990	3,057	2.81	90(E)
2000	3,811	2.23	00(E)
2010	4,258	1.12	10(E)
2012	4,353	1.11	12(E)
2020	4,806	1.24	12(E)
2030	5,191	0.77	12(E)
		EEU CROATIA	
0001	353	.	PROXY(Yugoslavia(Maddison))
1000	412	0.02	PROXY(Yugoslavia(Maddison))
1500	530	0.05	PROXY(Yugoslavia(Maddison))
1600	647	0.20	PROXY(Yugoslavia(Maddison))
1700	647	0.00	PROXY(Yugoslavia(Maddison))
1820	1,228	0.53	PROXY(Yugoslavia(Maddison))
1870	1,943	0.92	PROXY(Yugoslavia(Maddison))
1880	2,105	0.81	INTERPOL(Maddison)
1890	2,281	0.81	PROXY(Yugoslavia(Maddison))
1900	2,631	1.44	PROXY(Yugoslavia(Maddison))
1913	3,199	1.52	PROXY(Yugoslavia(Maddison))
1920	2,924	1.28	PROXY(Yugoslavia(Maddison))
1929	3,342	1.49	PROXY(Yugoslavia(Maddison))
1938	3,787	1.40	PROXY(Yugoslavia(Maddison))
1950	3,837	0.11	50(E)
1960	4,036	0.51	60(E)
1970	4,205	0.41	70(E)
1980	4,383	0.42	80(E)
1990	4,508	0.28	90(E)
2000	4,453	0.12	00(E)
2010	4,296	0.36	10(E)
2012	4,266	0.35	12(E)
2020	4,185	0.24	12(E)
2030	4,063	0.30	12(E)
		LAM CUBA	
0001	35	.	PROXY(Other L. Am.(Maddison))
1000	71	0.07	PROXY(Other L. Am.(Maddison))
1500	103	0.07	PROXY(Caribbean cs(Maddison))

Year	Population, '000s	Growth Rate	Source
1600	41	0.91	PROXY(Caribbean cs(Maddison))
1700	103	0.92	PROXY(Caribbean cs(Maddison))
1820	605	1.48	1820(Maddison)
1870	1,331	1.59	1870(Maddison)
1880	1,432	0.73	INTERPOL(Maddison)
1890	1,541	0.73	INTERPOL(Maddison)
1900	1,658	0.73	1900(Maddison)
1913	2,431	2.99	1913(Maddison)
1920	2,997	3.04	1920(Maddison)
1929	3,742	2.50	1929(Maddison)
1938	4,428	1.89	1938(Maddison)
1950	5,920	2.45	50(E)
1960	7,077	1.80	60(E)
1970	8,603	1.97	70(E)
1980	9,694	1.20	80(E)
1990	10,662	0.96	90(E)
2000	11,146	0.44	00(E)
2010	11,167	0.02	10(E)
2012	11,164	0.01	12(E)
2020	11,127	0.04	12(E)
2030	11,017	0.10	12(E)

LAM Curacao

Year	Population, '000s	Growth Rate	Source
0001	.	.	
1000	.	.	
1500	.	.	
1600	.	.	
1700	.	.	
1820	.	.	
1870	.	.	
1880	.	.	
1890	.	.	
1900	.	.	
1913	.	.	
1920	.	.	
1929	.	.	
1938	.	.	
1950	102	.	00(WB)WEIGHT(Neth Antilles(50(E)))
1960	124	1.96	60(E)
1970	145	1.58	70(E)
1980	148	0.20	80(E)
1990	145	0.20	90(E)
2000	134	0.79	00(E)
2010	149	1.07	10(E)
2012	152	0.89	12(E)
2020	158	0.51	12(E)
2030	161	0.19	12(E)

Year	Population, '000s	Growth Rate	Source
		MEA CYPRUS	
0001	200	.	0001(Maddison)
1000	150	0.03	1000(Maddison)
1500	65	0.17	PROXY(Greece(Maddison))
1600	98	0.41	PROXY(Greece(Maddison))
1700	98	0.00	PROXY(Greece(Maddison))
1820	151	0.36	PROXY(Greece(Maddison))
1870	239	0.92	PROXY(Greece(Maddison))
1880	264	1.02	PROXY(Greece(Maddison))
1890	293	1.02	PROXY(Greece(Maddison))
1900	324	1.02	PROXY(Greece(Maddison))
1913	354	0.69	PROXY(Greece(Maddison))
1920	372	0.71	PROXY(Greece(Maddison))
1929	410	1.07	PROXY(Greece(Maddison))
1938	461	1.32	PROXY(Greece(Maddison))
1950	494	0.58	50(E)
1960	579	1.60	60(E)
1970	627	0.80	70(E)
1980	658	0.48	80(E)
1990	751	1.33	90(E)
2000	906	1.89	00(E)
2010	1,108	2.03	10(E)
2012	1,163	2.47	12(E)
2020	1,276	1.16	12(E)
2030	1,387	0.84	12(E)
		EEU CZECH REPUBLIC	
0001	720	.	PROXY(Czechoslovakia(Maddison))
1000	900	0.02	PROXY(Czechoslovakia(Maddison))
1500	2,161	0.18	PROXY(Czechoslovakia(Maddison))
1600	3,242	0.41	PROXY(Czechoslovakia(Maddison))
1700	3,242	0.00	PROXY(Czechoslovakia(Maddison))
1820	5,516	0.44	PROXY(Czechoslovakia(Maddison))
1870	7,316	0.57	PROXY(Czechoslovakia(Maddison))
1880	7,701	0.51	INTERPOL(Maddison)
1890	8,107	0.51	PROXY(Czechoslovakia(Maddison))
1900	8,747	0.76	PROXY(Czechoslovakia(Maddison))
1913	9,542	0.67	PROXY(Czechoslovakia(Maddison))
1920	9,350	0.29	PROXY(Czechoslovakia(Maddison))
1929	10,002	0.75	PROXY(Czechoslovakia(Maddison))
1938	10,520	0.56	PROXY(Czechoslovakia(Maddison))
1950	8,925	1.36	50(E)
1960	9,539	0.67	60(E)
1970	9,805	0.28	70(E)
1980	10,326	0.52	80(E)
1990	10,363	0.04	90(E)
2000	10,208	0.15	00(E)
2010	10,421	0.21	10(E)
2012	10,462	0.20	12(E)

Year	Population, '000s	Growth Rate	Source
2020	10,699	0.28	12(E)
2030	10,722	0.02	12(E)
	DME Denmark		
0001	180	.	0001(Maddison)
1000	360	0.07	1000(Maddison)
1500	600	0.10	1500(Maddison)
1600	650	0.08	1600(Maddison)
1700	700	0.07	1700(Maddison)
1820	1,155	0.42	1820(Maddison)
1870	1,888	0.99	1870(Maddison)
1880	2,081	0.98	1880(Maddison)
1890	2,294	0.98	1890(Maddison)
1900	2,561	1.11	1900(Maddison)
1913	2,983	1.18	1913(Maddison)
1920	3,242	1.20	1920(Maddison)
1929	3,518	0.91	1929(Maddison)
1938	3,777	0.79	1938(Maddison)
1950	4,271	1.03	50(E)
1960	4,585	0.71	60(E)
1970	4,938	0.74	70(E)
1980	5,107	0.34	80(E)
1990	5,135	0.05	90(E)
2000	5,330	0.37	00(E)
2010	5,544	0.39	10(E)
2012	5,606	0.56	12(E)
2020	5,762	0.34	12(E)
2030	5,958	0.34	12(E)
	AFR Djibouti		
0001	.	.	
1000	.	.	
1500	.	.	
1600	.	.	
1700	.	.	
1820	.	.	
1870	.	.	
1880	.	.	
1890	.	.	
1900	.	.	
1913	.	.	
1920	.	.	
1929	.	.	
1938	.	.	
1950	60	.	50(E)
1960	85	3.54	60(E)
1970	162	6.66	70(E)
1980	340	7.70	80(E)
1990	562	5.15	90(E)

Year	Population, '000s	Growth Rate	Source
2000	732	2.68	00(E)
2010	829	1.25	10(E)
2012	850	1.27	12(E)
2020	994	1.97	12(E)
2030	1,178	1.71	12(E)
LAM DOMINICA			
0001	.	.	
1000	.	.	
1500	.	.	
1600	.	.	
1700	.	.	
1820	.	.	
1870	.	.	
1880	.	.	
1890	.	.	
1900	.	.	
1913	.	.	
1920	.	.	
1929	.	.	
1938	.	.	
1950	51	.	50(E)
1960	60	1.64	60(E)
1970	70	1.55	70(E)
1980	74	0.56	80(E)
1990	70	0.55	90(E)
2000	70	0.00	00(E)
2010	71	0.14	10(E)
2012	71	0.33	12(E)
2020	74	0.44	12(E)
2030	77	0.40	12(E)
LAM DOMINICAN REPUBLIC			
0001	5	.	PROXY(Other L. Am.(Maddison))
1000	10	0.07	PROXY(Other L. Am.(Maddison))
1500	15	0.07	PROXY(Caribbean cs(Maddison))
1600	6	0.91	PROXY(Caribbean cs(Maddison))
1700	15	0.92	PROXY(Caribbean cs(Maddison))
1820	89	1.48	1820(Maddison)
1870	242	2.02	1870(Maddison)
1880	311	2.55	INTERPOL(Maddison)
1890	400	2.55	INTERPOL(Maddison)
1900	515	2.55	1900(Maddison)
1913	750	2.93	1913(Maddison)
1920	879	2.29	1920(Maddison)
1929	1,213	3.64	1929(Maddison)
1938	1,596	3.10	1938(Maddison)
1950	2,353	3.29	50(E)
1960	3,294	3.42	60(E)

Year	Population, '000s	Growth Rate	Source
1970	4,502	3.17	70(E)
1980	5,808	2.58	80(E)
1990	7,179	2.14	90(E)
2000	8,328	1.50	00(E)
2010	9,398	1.22	10(E)
2012	9,627	1.21	12(E)
2020	10,543	1.14	12(E)
2030	11,433	0.81	12(E)
SEA East Timor			
0001	.	.	
1000	.	.	
1500	.	.	
1600	.	.	
1700	.	.	
1820	.	.	
1870	.	.	
1880	.	.	
1890	.	.	
1900	.	.	
1913	.	.	
1920	.	.	
1929	.	.	
1938	.	.	
1950	435	.	50(E)
1960	509	1.58	60(E)
1970	598	1.62	70(E)
1980	557	0.71	80(E)
1990	746	2.96	90(E)
2000	767	0.28	00(E)
2010	1,088	3.56	10(E)
2012	1,143	2.51	12(E)
2020	1,384	2.42	12(E)
2030	1,689	2.01	12(E)
LAM Ecuador			
0001	191	.	PROXY(Other L. Am.(Maddison))
1000	387	0.07	PROXY(Other L. Am.(Maddison))
1500	561	0.07	PROXY(Other Sp. Am.(Maddison))
1600	337	0.51	PROXY(Other Sp. Am.(Maddison))
1700	383	0.13	PROXY(Other Sp. Am.(Maddison))
1820	500	0.22	1820(Maddison)
1870	1,013	1.42	1870(Maddison)
1880	1,128	1.08	INTERPOL(Maddison)
1890	1,257	1.08	INTERPOL(Maddison)
1900	1,400	1.08	1900(Maddison)
1913	1,689	1.45	1913(Maddison)
1920	1,790	0.83	1920(Maddison)
1929	1,928	0.83	1929(Maddison)

Year	Population, '000s	Growth Rate	Source
1938	2,355	2.25	1938(Maddison)
1950	3,387	3.07	50(E)
1960	4,439	2.74	60(E)
1970	5,972	3.01	70(E)
1980	7,958	2.91	80(E)
1990	10,261	2.57	90(E)
2000	12,345	1.87	00(E)
2010	14,367	1.53	10(E)
2012	15,157	2.71	12(E)
2020	16,443	1.02	12(E)
2030	17,989	0.90	12(E)
		MEA Egypt	
0001	4,000	.	0001(Maddison)
1000	5,000	0.02	1000(Maddison)
1500	4,000	0.04	1500(Maddison)
1600	5,000	0.22	1600(Maddison)
1700	4,500	0.11	1700(Maddison)
1820	4,394	0.02	1820(Mitchell)
1870	6,394	0.75	1870(MItchell)
1880	7,578	1.71	1880(Mitchell)
1890	8,777	1.48	1890(Mitchell)
1900	10,186	1.50	1900(Mitchell)
1913	12,186	1.39	1913(Mitchell)
1920	13,222	1.17	1920(Mitchell)
1929	14,602	1.11	1929(Mitchell)
1938	16,295	1.23	1938(Mitchell)
1950	20,461	1.92	50(E)
1960	27,903	3.15	60(E)
1970	35,575	2.46	70(E)
1980	44,952	2.37	80(E)
1990	56,843	2.37	90(E)
2000	63,974	1.19	00(E)
2010	78,685	2.09	10(E)
2012	82,852	2.61	12(E)
2020	94,409	1.65	12(E)
2030	106,047	1.17	12(E)
		LAM El Salvador	
0001	95	.	PROXY(Other L. Am.(Maddison))
1000	192	0.07	PROXY(Other L. Am.(Maddison))
1500	278	0.07	PROXY(Other Sp. Am.(Maddison))
1600	167	0.51	PROXY(Other Sp. Am.(Maddison))
1700	190	0.13	PROXY(Other Sp. Am.(Maddison))
1820	248	0.22	1820(Maddison)
1870	492	1.38	1870(Maddison)
1880	570	1.49	INTERPOL(Maddison)
1890	661	1.49	INTERPOL(Maddison)
1900	766	1.49	1900(Maddison)
1913	1,008	2.13	1913(Maddison)
1920	1,170	2.15	1920(Maddison)

Year	Population, '000s	Growth Rate	Source
1929	1,410	2.09	1929(Maddison)
1938	1,590	1.34	1938(Maddison)
1950	1,951	1.72	50(E)
1960	2,582	2.84	60(E)
1970	3,604	3.39	70(E)
1980	4,570	2.40	80(E)
1990	5,110	1.12	90(E)
2000	5,850	1.36	00(E)
2010	6,052	0.34	10(E)
2012	6,090	0.31	12(E)
2020	6,217	0.26	12(E)
2030	6,340	0.20	12(E)
AFR Equatorial Guinea			
0001	.	.	
1000	.	.	
1500	.	.	
1600	.	.	
1700	.	.	
1820	.	.	
1870	.	.	
1880	.	.	
1890	.	.	
1900	.	.	
1913	.	.	
1920	.	.	
1929	.	.	
1938	.	.	
1950	211	.	50(E)
1960	252	1.79	60(E)
1970	291	1.45	70(E)
1980	221	2.71	80(E)
1990	374	5.40	90(E)
2000	520	3.35	00(E)
2010	700	3.02	10(E)
2012	740	2.82	12(E)
2020	905	2.55	12(E)
2030	1,102	1.99	12(E)
AFR Eritrea			
0001	32	.	PROXY(Ethiopia & Eritr.(Maddison))
1000	65	0.07	PROXY(Ethiopia & Eritr.(Maddison))
1500	130	0.14	PROXY(Ethiopia & Eritr.(Maddison))
1600	146	0.12	PROXY(Ethiopia & Eritr.(Maddison))
1700	162	0.11	PROXY(Ethiopia & Eritr.(Maddison))
1820	205	0.19	PROXY(Ethiopia & Eritr.(Maddison))
1870	429	1.49	INTERPOL(Maddison)
1880	498	1.49	INTERPOL(Maddison)
1890	577	1.49	INTERPOL(Maddison)

Year	Population, '000s	Growth Rate	Source
1900	669	1.49	INTERPOL(Maddison)
1913	811	1.49	INTERPOL(Maddison)
1920	900	1.49	INTERPOL(Maddison)
1929	1,028	1.49	INTERPOL(Maddison)
1938	1,174	1.49	INTERPOL(Maddison)
1950	1,402	1.49	50(E)
1960	1,424	0.16	60(E)
1970	1,847	2.64	70(E)
1980	2,469	2.95	80(E)
1990	3,158	2.49	90(E)
2000	3,668	1.51	00(E)
2010	5,254	3.66	10(E)
2012	5,578	3.04	12(E)
2020	6,848	2.60	12(E)
2030	8,394	2.06	12(E)
USR Estonia			
0001	13	.	PROXY(40(E)/Eur. Russia(Maddison))
1000	27	0.07	PROXY(40(E)/Eur. Russia(Maddison))
1500	81	0.22	PROXY(40(E)/Eur. Russia(Maddison))
1600	101	0.22	PROXY(40(E)/Eur. Russia(Maddison))
1700	134	0.29	PROXY(40(E)/Eur. Russia(Maddison))
1820	296	0.66	PROXY(40(E)/Eur. Russia(Maddison))
1870	482	0.97	PROXY(40(E)/USSR(Maddison))
1880	538	1.11	40(E)/INTERPOL(Maddison)
1890	601	1.11	PROXY(40(E)/USSR(Maddison))
1900	676	1.19	PROXY(40(E)/USSR(Maddison))
1913	848	1.76	PROXY(40(E)/USSR(Maddison))
1920	840	0.15	PROXY(40(E)/USSR(Maddison))
1929	934	1.19	PROXY(40(E)/USSR(Maddison))
1938	1,024	1.02	PROXY(40(E)/USSR(Maddison))
1950	1,096	0.57	50(E)
1960	1,216	1.04	60(E)
1970	1,365	1.16	70(E)
1980	1,473	0.76	80(E)
1990	1,568	0.63	90(E)
2000	1,367	1.36	00(E)
2010	1,304	0.47	10(E)
2012	1,291	0.49	12(E)
2020	1,276	0.15	12(E)
2030	1,244	0.25	12(E)
AFR Ethiopia			
0001	468	.	PROXY(Ethiopia & Eritr.(Maddison))
1000	935	0.07	PROXY(Ethiopia & Eritr.(Maddison))
1500	1,870	0.14	PROXY(Ethiopia & Eritr.(Maddison))
1600	2,104	0.12	PROXY(Ethiopia & Eritr.(Maddison))
1700	2,338	0.11	PROXY(Ethiopia & Eritr.(Maddison))
1820	2,949	0.19	PROXY(Ethiopia & Eritr.(Maddison))
1870	6,179	1.49	INTERPOL(Maddison)
1880	7,164	1.49	INTERPOL(Maddison)

Year	Population, '000s	Growth Rate	Source
1890	8,306	1.49	INTERPOL(Maddison)
1900	9,630	1.49	INTERPOL(Maddison)
1913	11,671	1.49	INTERPOL(Maddison)
1920	12,945	1.49	INTERPOL(Maddison)
1929	14,788	1.49	INTERPOL(Maddison)
1938	16,894	1.49	INTERPOL(Maddison)
1950	20,175	1.49	50(E)
1960	22,553	1.12	60(E)
1970	28,959	2.53	70(E)
1980	35,426	2.04	80(E)
1990	48,333	3.16	90(E)
2000	61,856	2.50	00(E)
2010	79,456	2.54	10(E)
2012	84,150	2.91	12(E)
2020	99,038	2.06	12(E)
2030	116,160	1.61	12(E)
DME Falkland Islands			
0001	.	.	
1000	.	.	
1500	.	.	
1600	.	.	
1700	.	.	
1820	.	.	
1870	.	.	
1880	.	.	
1890	.	.	
1900	.	.	
1913	.	.	
1920	.	.	
1929	.	.	
1938	.	.	
1950	2	.	50(E)
1960	2	0.00	60(E)
1970	2	0.00	70(E)
1980	2	0.00	80(E)
1990	2	0.00	90(E)
2000	3	3.52	00(CIA)
2010	3	1.33	10(EST)
2012	3	1.32	12(EST)
2020	4	1.33	12(EST)
2030	4	1.32	12(EST)
DME Faroe Islands			
0001	.	.	
1000	.	.	
1500	.	.	
1600	.	.	
1700	.	.	

Year	Population, '000s	Growth Rate	Source
1820	.	.	
1870	.	.	
1880	.	.	
1890	.	.	
1900	.	.	
1913	.	.	
1920	.	.	
1929	.	.	
1938	.	.	
1950	31	.	50(E)
1960	34	0.93	60(E)
1970	39	1.38	70(E)
1980	43	0.98	80(E)
1990	48	1.11	90(E)
2000	46	0.42	00(E)
2010	49	0.63	10(E)
2012	48	0.55	12(E)
2020	50	0.39	12(E)
2030	52	0.39	12(E)
SEA Fiji			
0001	.	.	
1000	.	.	
1500	.	.	
1600	.	.	
1700	.	.	
1820	.	.	
1870	.	.	
1880	.	.	
1890	.	.	
1900	.	.	
1913	.	.	
1920	.	.	
1929	.	.	
1938	.	.	
1950	289	.	50(E)
1960	393	3.12	60(E)
1970	521	2.86	70(E)
1980	635	2.00	80(E)
1990	728	1.38	90(E)
2000	812	1.10	00(E)
2010	848	0.43	10(E)
2012	856	0.47	12(E)
2020	890	0.49	12(E)
2030	946	0.61	12(E)
DME Finland			
0001	20	.	0001(Maddison)
1000	40	0.07	1000(Maddison)
1500	300	0.40	1500(Maddison)

Year	Population, '000s	Growth Rate	Source
1600	400	0.29	1600(Maddison)
1700	400	0.00	1700(Maddison)
1820	1,169	0.90	1820(Maddison)
1870	1,754	0.81	1870(Maddison)
1880	2,047	1.56	1880(Maddison)
1890	2,364	1.45	1890(Maddison)
1900	2,646	1.13	1900(Maddison)
1913	3,027	1.04	1913(Maddison)
1920	3,133	0.49	1920(Maddison)
1929	3,424	0.99	1929(Maddison)
1938	3,656	0.73	1938(Maddison)
1950	4,009	0.77	50(E)
1960	4,430	1.00	60(E)
1970	4,606	0.39	70(E)
1980	4,799	0.41	80(E)
1990	4,986	0.38	90(E)
2000	5,176	0.37	00(E)
2010	5,362	0.35	10(E)
2012	5,413	0.48	12(E)
2020	5,617	0.46	12(E)
2030	5,833	0.38	12(E)
DME France			
0001	5,000	.	0001(Maddison)
1000	6,500	0.03	1000(Maddison)
1500	15,000	0.17	1500(Maddison)
1600	18,500	0.21	1600(Maddison)
1700	21,471	0.15	1700(Maddison)
1820	31,250	0.31	1820(Maddison)
1870	38,440	0.42	1870(Maddison)
1880	39,045	0.16	1880(Maddison)
1890	40,014	0.25	1890(Maddison)
1900	40,598	0.14	1900(Maddison)
1913	41,463	0.16	1913(Maddison)
1920	39,000	0.87	1920(Maddison)
1929	41,230	0.62	1929(Maddison)
1938	41,960	0.20	1938(Maddison)
1950	41,736	0.04	50(E)
1960	45,689	0.91	60(E)
1970	50,763	1.06	70(E)
1980	53,880	0.60	80(E)
1990	56,708	0.51	90(E)
2000	59,045	0.40	00(E)
2010	62,913	0.64	10(E)
2012	63,538	0.50	12(E)
2020	65,689	0.42	12(E)
2030	67,388	0.26	12(E)

Year	Population, '000s	Growth Rate	Source
	SEA French Polynesia		
0001	.	.	
1000	.	.	
1500	.	.	
1600	.	.	
1700	.	.	
1820	.	.	
1870	.	.	
1880	.	.	
1890	.	.	
1900	.	.	
1913	.	.	
1920	.	.	
1929	.	.	
1938	.	.	
1950	62	.	50(E)
1960	79	2.45	60(E)
1970	111	3.46	70(E)
1980	151	3.13	80(E)
1990	195	2.59	90(E)
2000	238	2.01	00(E)
2010	268	1.19	10(E)
2012	275	1.23	12(E)
2020	296	0.94	12(E)
2030	316	0.66	12(E)
	AFR Gabon		
0001	.	.	
1000	.	.	
1500	.	.	
1600	.	.	
1700	.	.	
1820	.	.	
1870	.	.	
1880	.	.	
1890	.	.	
1900	.	.	
1913	.	.	
1920	.	.	
1929	.	.	
1938	.	.	
1950	416	.	50(E)
1960	486	1.57	60(E)
1970	530	0.87	70(E)
1980	683	2.57	80(E)

Year	Population, '000s	Growth Rate	Source
1990	929	3.12	90(E)
2000	1,235	2.89	00(E)
2010	1,505	2.00	10(E)
2012	1,564	1.93	12(E)
2020	1,818	1.90	12(E)
2030	2,146	1.67	12(E)
	AFR Gambia		
0001	.	.	
1000	.	.	
1500	.	.	
1600	.	.	
1700	.	.	
1820	.	.	
1870	.	.	
1880	.	.	
1890	.	.	
1900	.	.	
1913	.	.	
1920	.	.	
1929	.	.	
1938	.	.	
1950	294	.	50(E)
1960	352	1.82	60(E)
1970	485	3.26	70(E)
1980	652	3.00	80(E)
1990	951	3.85	90(E)
2000	1,357	3.62	00(E)
2010	1,755	2.61	10(E)
2012	1,839	2.37	12(E)
2020	2,174	2.11	12(E)
2030	2,554	1.62	12(E)
	MEA Gaza Strip		
0001	.	.	
1000	.	.	
1500	.	.	
1600	.	.	
1700	.	.	
1820	.	.	
1870	.	.	
1880	.	.	
1890	.	.	
1900	.	.	
1913	.	.	
1920	.	.	
1929	.	.	

Year	Population, '000s	Growth Rate	Source
1938	.	.	
1950	245	.	50(E)
1960	308	2.31	60(E)
1970	343	1.08	70(E)
1980	456	2.89	80(E)
1990	646	3.54	90(E)
2000	1,110	5.56	00(E)
2010	1,535	3.29	10(E)
2012	1,644	3.48	12(E)
2020	2,047	2.78	12(E)
2030	2,475	1.92	12(E)
USR Georgia			
0001	108	.	PROXY(40(E)/Caucasus(Maddison))
1000	180	0.05	PROXY(40(E)/Caucasus(Maddison))
1500	450	0.18	PROXY(40(E)/Caucasus(Maddison))
1600	540	0.18	PROXY(40(E)/Caucasus(Maddison))
1700	630	0.15	PROXY(40(E)/Caucasus(Maddison))
1820	874	0.27	PROXY(40(E)/Caucasus(Maddison))
1870	1,650	1.28	PROXY(40(E)/USSR(Maddison))
1880	1,844	1.11	40(E)/INTERPOL(Maddison)
1890	2,060	1.11	PROXY(40(E)/USSR(Maddison))
1900	2,317	1.19	PROXY(40(E)/USSR(Maddison))
1913	2,907	1.76	PROXY(40(E)/USSR(Maddison))
1920	2,877	0.15	PROXY(40(E)/USSR(Maddison))
1929	3,201	1.19	PROXY(40(E)/USSR(Maddison))
1938	3,508	1.02	PROXY(40(E)/USSR(Maddison))
1950	3,527	0.04	50(E)
1960	4,159	1.66	60(E)
1970	4,707	1.25	70(E)
1980	5,073	0.75	80(E)
1990	5,439	0.70	90(E)
2000	4,418	2.06	00(E)
2010	4,453	0.08	10(E)
2012	4,499	0.51	12(E)
2020	4,322	0.50	12(E)
2030	3,983	0.81	12(E)
DME Germany			
0001	3,000	.	0001(Maddison)
1000	3,500	0.02	1000(Maddison)
1500	12,000	0.25	1500(Maddison)
1600	16,000	0.29	1600(Maddison)
1700	15,000	0.06	1700(Maddison)
1820	24,905	0.42	1820(Maddison)
1870	39,231	0.91	1870(Maddison)
1880	43,500	1.04	1880(Maddison)
1890	47,607	0.91	1890(Maddison)
1900	54,388	1.34	1900(Maddison)
1913	65,058	1.39	1913(Maddison)
1920	60,894	0.94	1920(Maddison)

Year	Population, '000s	Growth Rate	Source
1929	64,739	0.68	1929(Maddison)
1938	68,558	0.64	1938(Maddison)
1950	68,377	0.02	50(E)
1960	73,147	0.68	60(E)
1970	78,069	0.65	70(E)
1980	78,397	0.04	80(E)
1990	79,753	0.17	90(E)
2000	82,197	0.30	00(E)
2010	81,777	0.05	10(E)
2012	81,035	0.45	12(E)
2020	80,287	0.12	12(E)
2030	78,055	0.28	12(E)
AFR GHANA			
0001	198	.	PROXY(Other W. Africa(Maddison))
1000	463	0.08	PROXY(Other W. Africa(Maddison))
1500	727	0.09	PROXY(Other W. Africa(Maddison))
1600	926	0.24	PROXY(Other W. Africa(Maddison))
1700	1,190	0.25	PROXY(Other W. Africa(Maddison))
1820	1,374	0.12	1820(Maddison)
1870	1,500	0.18	1870(Maddison)
1880	1,570	0.45	INTERPOL(Maddison)
1890	1,643	0.45	INTERPOL(Maddison)
1900	1,784	0.83	INTERPOL(Maddison)
1913	2,043	1.05	1913(Maddison)
1920	2,447	2.61	INTERPOL(Maddison)
1929	3,085	2.61	INTERPOL(Maddison)
1938	3,889	2.61	INTERPOL(Maddison)
1950	5,297	2.61	50(E)
1960	6,958	2.77	60(E)
1970	8,789	2.36	70(E)
1980	11,011	2.28	80(E)
1990	15,408	3.42	90(E)
2000	19,043	2.14	00(E)
2010	24,830	2.69	10(E)
2012	26,183	2.69	12(E)
2020	31,305	2.26	12(E)
2030	38,537	2.10	12(E)
DME GIBRALTAR			
0001	.	.	
1000	.	.	
1500	.	.	
1600	.	.	
1700	.	.	
1820	.	.	
1870	.	.	
1880	.	.	
1890	.	.	
1900	.	.	

Year	Population, '000s	Growth Rate	Source
1913	.	.	
1920	.	.	
1929	.	.	
1938	.	.	
1950	23	.	50(E)
1960	24	0.43	60(E)
1970	26	0.80	70(E)
1980	30	1.44	80(E)
1990	31	0.33	90(E)
2000	29	0.50	00(CIA)
2010	29	0.21	10(CIA)
2012	29	0.27	12(CIA)
2020	29	0.13	12(EST)
2030	28	0.13	12(EST)

DME Greece

Year	Population, '000s	Growth Rate	Source
0001	2,000	.	0001(Maddison)
1000	1,100	0.06	1000(Maddison)
1500	1,000	0.02	1500(Maddison)
1600	1,500	0.41	1600(Maddison)
1700	1,500	0.00	1700(Maddison)
1820	2,312	0.36	1820(Maddison)
1870	3,657	0.92	1870(Maddison)
1880	4,049	1.02	1880(Maddison)
1890	4,482	1.02	1890(Maddison)
1900	4,962	1.02	1900(Maddison)
1913	5,425	0.69	1913(Maddison)
1920	5,700	0.71	1920(Maddison)
1929	6,275	1.07	1929(Maddison)
1938	7,061	1.32	1938(Maddison)
1950	7,566	0.58	50(E)
1960	8,333	0.97	60(E)
1970	8,793	0.54	70(E)
1980	9,643	0.93	80(E)
1990	10,161	0.52	90(E)
2000	10,987	0.78	00(E)
2010	10,782	0.19	10(E)
2012	10,856	0.34	12(E)
2020	11,042	0.21	12(E)
2030	11,091	0.04	12(E)

DME Greenland

Year	Population, '000s	Growth Rate	Source
0001	.	.	
1000	.	.	
1500	.	.	
1600	.	.	
1700	.	.	
1820	.	.	
1870	.	.	
1880	.	.	

Year	Population, '000s	Growth Rate	Source
1890	.	.	
1900	.	.	
1913	.	.	
1920	.	.	
1929	.	.	
1938	.	.	
1950	23	.	50(E)
1960	33	3.68	60(E)
1970	46	3.38	70(E)
1980	50	0.84	80(E)
1990	56	1.14	90(E)
2000	56	0.00	00(E)
2010	56	0.00	10(E)
2012	56	0.12	12(E)
2020	56	0.03	12(E)
2030	56	0.00	12(E)
		LAM Grenada	
0001	.	.	
1000	.	.	
1500	.	.	
1600	.	.	
1700	.	.	
1820	.	.	
1870	.	.	
1880	.	.	
1890	.	.	
1900	.	.	
1913	.	.	
1920	.	.	
1929	.	.	
1938	.	.	
1950	76	.	50(E)
1960	90	1.71	60(E)
1970	95	0.54	70(E)
1980	90	0.54	80(E)
1990	94	0.44	90(E)
2000	103	0.92	00(E)
2010	103	0.00	10(E)
2012	103	0.00	12(E)
2020	107	0.48	12(E)
2030	107	0.00	12(E)
		LAM Guadeloupe	
0001	.	.	
1000	.	.	
1500	.	.	

Year	Population, '000s	Growth Rate	Source
1600	.	.	
1700	.	.	
1820	.	.	
1870	.	.	
1880	.	.	
1890	.	.	
1900	.	.	
1913	.	.	
1920	.	.	
1929	.	.	
1938	.	.	
1950	208	.	50(Maddison)
1960	266	2.49	60(E)
1970	310	1.54	70(E)
1980	318	0.26	80(E)
1990	355	1.11	90(E)
2000	388	0.89	00(E)
2010	403	0.38	10(E)
2012	404	0.17	12(E)
2020	415	0.33	12(E)
2030	425	0.24	12(E)
		SEA Guam	
0001	.	.	
1000	.	.	
1500	.	.	
1600	.	.	
1700	.	.	
1820	.	.	
1870	.	.	
1880	.	.	
1890	.	.	
1900	.	.	
1913	.	.	
1920	.	.	
1929	.	.	
1938	.	.	
1950	60	.	50(E)
1960	67	1.11	60(E)
1970	85	2.41	70(E)
1980	107	2.33	80(E)
1990	134	2.28	90(E)
2000	155	1.47	00(E)
2010	159	0.26	10(E)
2012	160	0.42	12(E)
2020	169	0.66	12(E)
2030	185	0.91	12(E)

Year	Population, '000s	Growth Rate	Source
		LAM GUATEMALA	
0001	227	.	PROXY(Other L. Am.(Maddison))
1000	461	0.07	PROXY(Other L. Am.(Maddison))
1500	668	0.07	PROXY(Other Sp. Am.(Maddison))
1600	401	0.51	PROXY(Other Sp. Am.(Maddison))
1700	456	0.13	PROXY(Other Sp. Am.(Maddison))
1820	595	0.22	1820(Maddison)
1870	1,080	1.20	1870(Maddison)
1880	1,149	0.62	INTERPOL(Maddison)
1890	1,222	0.62	INTERPOL(Maddison)
1900	1,300	0.62	1900(Maddison)
1913	1,486	1.03	1913(Maddison)
1920	1,597	1.03	1920(Maddison)
1929	1,753	1.04	1929(Maddison)
1938	2,110	2.08	1938(Maddison)
1950	2,969	2.89	50(E)
1960	4,159	3.43	60(E)
1970	5,448	2.74	70(E)
1980	7,036	2.59	80(E)
1990	8,923	2.40	90(E)
2000	11,237	2.33	00(E)
2010	14,389	2.50	10(E)
2012	15,139	2.57	12(E)
2020	18,382	2.46	12(E)
2030	22,726	2.14	12(E)
		DME GUERNSEY	
0001	.	.	
1000	.	.	
1500	.	.	
1600	.	.	
1700	.	.	
1820	.	.	
1870	.	.	
1880	.	.	
1890	.	.	
1900	.	.	
1913	.	.	
1920	.	.	
1929	.	.	
1938	.	.	
1950	44	.	50(E)
1960	45	0.22	60(E)
1970	51	1.26	70(E)
1980	53	0.39	80(E)
1990	61	1.42	90(E)
2000	62	0.16	00(E)
2010	65	0.47	10(E)

Year	Population, '000s	Growth Rate	Source
2012	66	0.51	12(E)
2020	69	0.62	12(E)
2030	72	0.43	12(E)
	LAM GUIANA, FRENCH		
0001	.	.	
1000	.	.	
1500	.	.	
1600	.	.	
1700	.	.	
1820	.	.	
1870	.	.	
1880	.	.	
1890	.	.	
1900	.	.	
1913	.	.	
1920	.	.	
1929	.	.	
1938	.	.	
1950	27	.	50(E)
1960	32	1.71	60(E)
1970	49	4.35	70(E)
1980	68	3.33	80(E)
1990	117	5.58	90(E)
2000	165	3.50	00(E)
2010	233	3.51	10(E)
2012	238	1.13	12(E)
2020	298	2.83	12(E)
2030	369	2.16	12(E)
	AFR GUINEA		
0001	135	.	PROXY(Other W. Africa(Maddison))
1000	315	0.08	PROXY(Other W. Africa(Maddison))
1500	495	0.09	PROXY(Other W. Africa(Maddison))
1600	630	0.24	PROXY(Other W. Africa(Maddison))
1700	810	0.25	PROXY(Other W. Africa(Maddison))
1820	935	0.12	PROXY(Other W. Africa(Maddison))
1870	1,389	0.80	INTERPOL(Maddison)
1880	1,504	0.80	INTERPOL(Maddison)
1890	1,628	0.80	INTERPOL(Maddison)
1900	1,762	0.80	INTERPOL(Maddison)
1913	1,953	0.80	INTERPOL(Maddison)
1920	2,065	0.80	INTERPOL(Maddison)
1929	2,217	0.80	INTERPOL(Maddison)
1938	2,381	0.80	INTERPOL(Maddison)
1950	2,619	0.80	50(E)
1960	3,541	3.06	60(E)
1970	4,154	1.61	70(E)
1980	4,407	0.59	80(E)

Year	Population, '000s	Growth Rate	Source
1990	5,759	2.71	90(E)
2000	8,344	3.78	00(E)
2010	9,982	1.81	10(E)
2012	10,490	2.51	12(E)
2020	12,765	2.48	12(E)
2030	15,946	2.25	12(E)
AFR GuineaBissau			
0001	30	.	PROXY(Other W. Africa(Maddison))
1000	69	0.08	PROXY(Other W. Africa(Maddison))
1500	108	0.09	PROXY(Other W. Africa(Maddison))
1600	138	0.24	PROXY(Other W. Africa(Maddison))
1700	177	0.25	PROXY(Other W. Africa(Maddison))
1820	205	0.12	PROXY(Other W. Africa(Maddison))
1870	304	0.80	INTERPOL(Maddison)
1880	329	0.80	INTERPOL(Maddison)
1890	356	0.80	INTERPOL(Maddison)
1900	386	0.80	INTERPOL(Maddison)
1913	427	0.80	INTERPOL(Maddison)
1920	452	0.80	INTERPOL(Maddison)
1929	485	0.80	INTERPOL(Maddison)
1938	521	0.80	INTERPOL(Maddison)
1950	573	0.80	50(E)
1960	593	0.34	60(E)
1970	603	0.17	70(E)
1980	835	3.31	80(E)
1990	1,017	1.99	90(E)
2000	1,241	2.01	00(E)
2010	1,569	2.37	10(E)
2012	1,645	2.39	12(E)
2020	1,935	2.05	12(E)
2030	2,350	1.96	12(E)
LAM Guyana			
0001	.	.	
1000	.	.	
1500	.	.	
1600	.	.	
1700	.	.	
1820	.	.	
1870	.	.	
1880	.	.	
1890	.	.	
1900	.	.	
1913	.	.	
1920	.	.	
1929	.	.	
1938	.	.	
1950	423	.	50(E)

Year	Population, '000s	Growth Rate	Source
1960	560	2.85	60(E)
1970	721	2.56	70(E)
1980	777	0.75	80(E)
1990	725	0.69	90(E)
2000	733	0.11	00(E)
2010	754	0.28	10(E)
2012	757	0.22	12(E)
2020	773	0.26	12(E)
2030	795	0.28	12(E)
LAM Haiti			
0001	42	.	PROXY(Other L. Am.(Maddison))
1000	85	0.07	PROXY(Other L. Am.(Maddison))
1500	124	0.07	PROXY(Caribbean cs(Maddison))
1600	49	0.91	PROXY(Caribbean cs(Maddison))
1700	124	0.92	PROXY(Caribbean cs(Maddison))
1820	723	1.48	1820(Maddison)
1870	1,150	0.93	1870(Maddison)
1880	1,273	1.02	INTERPOL(Maddison)
1890	1,409	1.02	INTERPOL(Maddison)
1900	1,560	1.02	1900(Maddison)
1913	1,891	1.49	1913(Maddison)
1920	2,124	1.67	1920(Maddison)
1929	2,390	1.32	1929(Maddison)
1938	2,682	1.29	1938(Maddison)
1950	3,221	1.54	50(E)
1960	3,697	1.39	60(E)
1970	4,541	2.08	70(E)
1980	5,508	1.95	80(E)
1990	6,798	2.13	90(E)
2000	8,413	2.15	00(E)
2010	9,649	1.38	10(E)
2012	9,812	0.84	12(E)
2020	10,693	1.08	12(E)
2030	11,784	0.98	12(E)
LAM Honduras			
0001	52	.	PROXY(Other L. Am.(Maddison))
1000	105	0.07	PROXY(Other L. Am.(Maddison))
1500	152	0.07	PROXY(Other Sp. Am.(Maddison))
1600	91	0.51	PROXY(Other Sp. Am.(Maddison))
1700	103	0.13	PROXY(Other Sp. Am.(Maddison))
1820	135	0.22	1820(Maddison)
1870	404	2.22	1870(Maddison)
1880	434	0.71	INTERPOL(Maddison)
1890	466	0.71	INTERPOL(Maddison)
1900	500	0.71	1900(Maddison)
1913	660	2.16	1913(Maddison)
1920	720	1.25	1920(Maddison)

Year	Population, '000s	Growth Rate	Source
1929	930	2.88	1929(Maddison)
1938	1,100	1.88	1938(Maddison)
1950	1,431	2.22	50(E)
1960	2,000	3.40	60(E)
1970	2,688	3.00	70(E)
1980	3,628	3.04	80(E)
1990	4,889	3.03	90(E)
2000	6,218	2.43	00(E)
2010	7,601	2.03	10(E)
2012	7,912	2.02	12(E)
2020	9,179	1.87	12(E)
2030	10,657	1.50	12(E)
SEA Hong Kong			
0001	3	.	PROXY(China(Maddison))
1000	3	0.00	PROXY(China(Maddison))
1500	5	0.11	PROXY(China(Maddison))
1600	8	0.44	PROXY(China(Maddison))
1700	7	0.15	PROXY(China(Maddison))
1820	20	0.85	1820(Maddison)
1870	123	3.70	1870(Maddison)
1880	162	2.81	INTERPOL(Maddison)
1890	214	2.81	1890(Maddison)
1900	306	3.64	1900(Maddison)
1913	487	3.64	1913(Maddison)
1920	648	4.16	1920(Maddison)
1929	785	2.15	1929(Maddison)
1938	1,479	7.29	1938(Maddison)
1950	2,237	3.51	50(E)
1960	3,076	3.24	60(E)
1970	3,958	2.55	70(E)
1980	5,054	2.47	80(E)
1990	5,794	1.38	90(E)
2000	6,665	1.41	00(E)
2010	7,030	0.53	10(E)
2012	7,114	0.60	12(E)
2020	7,648	0.91	12(E)
2030	8,309	0.83	12(E)
EEU Hungary			
0001	300	.	0001(Maddison)
1000	500	0.05	1000(Maddison)
1500	1,250	0.18	1500(Maddison)
1600	1,250	0.00	1600(Maddison)
1700	1,500	0.18	1700(Maddison)
1820	4,146	0.85	1820(Maddison)
1870	5,917	0.71	1870(Maddison)
1880	6,260	0.56	INTERPOL(Maddison)
1890	6,622	0.56	1890(Maddison)
1900	7,127	0.74	1900(Maddison)
1913	7,840	0.74	1913(Maddison)

Year	Population, '000s	Growth Rate	Source
1920	7,950	0.20	1920(Maddison)
1929	8,583	0.85	1929(Maddison)
1938	9,167	0.73	1938(Maddison)
1950	9,338	0.15	50(E)
1960	9,961	0.65	60(E)
1970	10,301	0.34	70(E)
1980	10,709	0.39	80(E)
1990	10,374	0.32	90(E)
2000	10,211	0.16	00(E)
2010	10,005	0.20	10(E)
2012	9,877	0.64	12(E)
2020	9,648	0.29	12(E)
2030	9,306	0.36	12(E)
DME ICELAND			
0001	.	.	
1000	26	.	PROXY(Denmark)
1500	43	0.10	PROXY(Denmark)
1600	47	0.08	PROXY(Denmark)
1700	50	0.07	1700(WIKI)
1820	48	0.04	1820(WIKI)
1870	70	0.75	1870(WIKI)
1880	72	0.36	1880(WIKI)
1890	71	0.24	1890(WIKI)
1900	78	1.00	1900(WIKI)
1913	87	0.84	1913(WIKI)
1920	94	1.11	1920(WIKI)
1929	106	1.34	1929(WIKI)
1938	118	1.20	1938(WIKI)
1950	143	1.61	50(E)
1960	176	2.10	60(E)
1970	204	1.49	70(E)
1980	228	1.12	80(E)
1990	255	1.13	90(E)
2000	281	0.98	00(E)
2010	318	1.24	10(E)
2012	321	0.52	12(E)
2020	346	0.93	12(E)
2030	376	0.83	12(E)
SAS INDIA			
0001	62,924	.	PROXY(Undivided India(Maddison))
1000	62,924	0.00	PROXY(Undivided India(Maddison))
1500	92,289	0.08	PROXY(Undivided India(Maddison))
1600	113,264	0.21	PROXY(Undivided India(Maddison))
1700	138,433	0.20	PROXY(Undivided India(Maddison))
1820	175,349	0.20	1820(Maddison)
1870	212,189	0.38	1870(Maddison)
1880	215,157	0.14	INTERPOL(Ind./wh. India(Maddison))
1890	233,315	0.81	INTERPOL(Ind./wh. India(Maddison))
1900	236,772	0.15	INTERPOL(Ind./wh. India(Maddison))

Year	Population, '000s	Growth Rate	Source
1913	251,906	0.48	1913(Maddison)
1920	253,309	0.08	INTERPOL(Ind./wh. India(Maddison))
1929	275,861	0.95	1929(Maddison)
1938	309,434	1.28	INTERPOL(Ind./wh. India(Maddison))
1950	369,880	1.50	50(E)
1960	447,844	1.93	60(E)
1970	553,874	2.15	70(E)
1980	700,059	2.37	80(E)
1990	873,785	2.24	90(E)
2000	1,053,898	1.89	00(E)
2010	1,195,520	1.27	10(E)
2012	1,235,002	1.64	12(E)
2020	1,364,293	1.25	12(E)
2030	1,498,634	0.94	12(E)
		SEA Indonesia	
0001	3,244	.	PROXY(Other E. Asia)
1000	6,005	0.06	PROXY(Other E. Asia)
1500	10,700	0.12	1500(Maddison)
1600	11,839	0.10	INTERPOL(Maddison)
1700	13,100	0.10	1700(Maddison)
1820	17,927	0.26	1820(Maddison)
1870	28,922	0.96	1870(Maddison)
1880	32,876	1.29	1880(Maddison)
1890	37,579	1.35	1890(Maddison)
1900	42,746	1.30	1900(Maddison)
1913	49,934	1.20	1913(Maddison)
1920	53,723	1.05	1920(Maddison)
1929	59,863	1.21	1929(Maddison)
1938	68,131	1.45	1938(Maddison)
1950	79,538	1.30	50(E)
1960	91,947	1.46	60(E)
1970	118,362	2.56	70(E)
1980	150,820	2.45	80(E)
1990	184,346	2.03	90(E)
2000	206,265	1.13	00(E)
2010	237,920	1.44	10(E)
2012	244,814	1.44	12(E)
2020	264,023	0.95	12(E)
2030	281,941	0.66	12(E)
		MEA Iran	
0001	4,360	.	PROXY(W. Asia(Maddison))
1000	4,494	0.00	PROXY(W. Asia(Maddison))
1500	4,000	0.02	1500(Maddison)
1600	4,472	0.11	INTERPOL(Maddison)
1700	5,000	0.11	1700(Maddison)
1820	6,560	0.23	1820(Maddison)
1870	8,415	0.50	1870(Maddison)
1880	8,955	0.62	INTERPOL(Maddison)
1890	9,529	0.62	INTERPOL(Maddison)

Year	Population, '000s	Growth Rate	Source
1900	10,140	0.62	INTERPOL(Maddison)
1913	10,994	0.62	1913(Maddison)
1920	11,927	1.17	INTERPOL(Maddison)
1929	13,245	1.17	INTERPOL(Maddison)
1938	14,708	1.17	INTERPOL(Maddison)
1950	16,913	1.17	50(E)
1960	21,999	2.66	60(E)
1970	28,662	2.68	70(E)
1980	38,577	3.02	80(E)
1990	54,871	3.59	90(E)
2000	65,458	1.78	00(E)
2010	73,893	1.22	10(E)
2012	75,805	1.29	12(E)
2020	81,440	0.90	12(E)
2030	84,850	0.41	12(E)
		MEA Iraq	
0001	1,090	.	PROXY(W. Asia(Maddison))
1000	1,124	0.00	PROXY(W. Asia(Maddison))
1500	1,000	0.02	1500(Maddison)
1600	1,000	0.00	INTERPOL(Maddison)
1700	1,000	0.00	1700(Maddison)
1820	1,093	0.07	1820(Maddison)
1870	1,580	0.74	1870(Maddison)
1880	1,776	1.18	INTERPOL(Maddison)
1890	1,997	1.18	INTERPOL(Maddison)
1900	2,244	1.18	INTERPOL(Maddison)
1913	2,613	1.18	1913(Maddison)
1920	2,991	1.95	INTERPOL(Maddison)
1929	3,559	1.95	INTERPOL(Maddison)
1938	4,235	1.95	INTERPOL(Maddison)
1950	5,340	1.95	50(E)
1960	7,380	3.29	60(E)
1970	10,022	3.11	70(E)
1980	13,744	3.21	80(E)
1990	17,374	2.37	90(E)
2000	23,857	3.22	00(E)
2010	31,672	2.87	10(E)
2012	33,709	3.17	12(E)
2020	42,684	2.99	12(E)
2030	55,257	2.62	12(E)
		DME Ireland	
0001	116	.	PROXY(UK(Maddison))
1000	289	0.09	PROXY(UK(Maddison))
1500	569	0.14	PROXY(whole Ireland(Maddison))
1600	712	0.22	PROXY(whole Ireland(Maddison))
1700	1,370	0.66	PROXY(whole Ireland(Maddison))
1820	5,053	1.09	PROXY(whole Ireland(Maddison))
1870	3,856	0.54	PROXY(whole Ireland(Maddison))
1880	3,702	0.41	PROXY(whole Ireland(Maddison))

Year	Population, '000s	Growth Rate	Source
1890	3,357	0.97	PROXY(whole Ireland(Maddison))
1900	3,180	0.54	PROXY(whole Ireland(Maddison))
1913	3,092	0.21	PROXY(whole Ireland(Maddison))
1920	3,103	0.05	1920(Maddison)
1929	2,937	0.61	1929(Maddison)
1938	2,937	0.00	1938(Maddison)
1950	2,969	0.09	50(E)
1960	2,832	0.47	60(E)
1970	2,950	0.41	70(E)
1980	3,401	1.43	80(E)
1990	3,506	0.30	90(E)
2000	3,801	0.81	00(E)
2010	4,537	1.79	10(E)
2012	4,575	0.42	12(E)
2020	4,963	1.02	12(E)
2030	5,347	0.75	12(E)
		DME Isle of Man	
0001	.	.	
1000	.	.	
1500	.	.	
1600	.	.	
1700	.	.	
1820	.	.	
1870	.	.	
1880	.	.	
1890	.	.	
1900	.	.	
1913	.	.	
1920	.	.	
1929	.	.	
1938	.	.	
1950	55	.	50(E)
1960	48	1.35	60(E)
1970	53	1.00	70(E)
1980	64	1.90	80(E)
1990	69	0.76	90(E)
2000	76	0.97	00(E)
2010	84	1.01	10(E)
2012	86	1.02	12(E)
2020	91	0.75	12(E)
2030	94	0.32	12(E)
		DME Israel	
0001	180	.	PROXY(W. Asia(Maddison))
1000	186	0.00	PROXY(W. Asia(Maddison))
1500	166	0.02	PROXY(Other W. Asia(Maddison))
1600	161	0.03	INTERPOL(Maddison)
1700	157	0.03	PROXY(Other W. Asia(Maddison))

Year	Population, '000s	Growth Rate	Source
1820	184	0.13	PROXY(Palestine(Maddison))
1870	238	0.52	PROXY(Palestine(Maddison))
1880	266	1.12	INTERPOL(Maddison)
1890	298	1.15	INTERPOL(Maddison)
1900	334	1.15	INTERPOL(Maddison)
1913	387	1.15	PROXY(Palestine(Maddison))
1920	486	3.30	INTERPOL(Maddison)
1929	650	3.30	INTERPOL(Maddison)
1938	871	3.30	INTERPOL(Maddison)
1950	1,258	3.11	50(E)
1960	2,090	5.21	60(E)
1970	2,850	3.15	70(E)
1980	3,746	2.77	80(E)
1990	4,500	1.85	90(E)
2000	6,098	3.09	00(E)
2010	7,306	1.82	10(E)
2012	7,557	1.70	12(E)
2020	8,519	1.51	12(E)
2030	9,650	1.25	12(E)
DME Italy			
0001	8,000	.	0001(Maddison)
1000	5,000	0.05	1000(Maddison)
1500	10,500	0.15	1500(Maddison)
1600	13,100	0.22	1600(Maddison)
1700	13,300	0.02	1700(Maddison)
1820	20,176	0.35	1820(Maddison)
1870	27,888	0.65	1870(Maddison)
1880	29,534	0.58	1880(Maddison)
1890	31,702	0.71	1890(Maddison)
1900	33,672	0.60	1900(Maddison)
1913	37,248	0.78	1913(Maddison)
1920	37,398	0.06	1920(Maddison)
1929	40,469	0.88	1929(Maddison)
1938	43,419	0.78	1938(Maddison)
1950	47,104	0.68	50(E)
1960	49,519	0.50	60(E)
1970	53,325	0.74	70(E)
1980	56,221	0.53	80(E)
1990	56,832	0.11	90(E)
2000	57,646	0.14	00(E)
2010	59,116	0.25	10(E)
2012	59,615	0.42	12(E)
2020	60,951	0.28	12(E)
2030	62,039	0.18	12(E)
AFR Ivory Coast			
0001	.	.	
1000	.	.	
1500	.	.	
1600	.	.	

Year	Population, '000s	Growth Rate	Source
1700	.	.	
1820	.	.	
1870	.	.	
1880	.	.	
1890	.	.	
1900	.	.	
1913	.	.	
1920	.	.	
1929	.	.	
1938	.	.	
1950	2,505	.	50(E)
1960	3,576	3.62	60(E)
1970	5,579	4.55	70(E)
1980	8,593	4.41	80(E)
1990	12,491	3.81	90(E)
2000	16,885	3.06	00(E)
2010	21,059	2.23	10(E)
2012	21,944	2.08	12(E)
2020	25,504	1.90	12(E)
2030	29,724	1.54	12(E)
LAM JAMAICA			
0001	23	.	PROXY(Other L. Am.(Maddison))
1000	47	0.07	PROXY(Other L. Am.(Maddison))
1500	69	0.07	PROXY(Caribbean cs(Maddison))
1600	27	0.91	PROXY(Caribbean cs(Maddison))
1700	69	0.92	PROXY(Caribbean cs(Maddison))
1820	401	1.48	1820(Maddison)
1870	499	0.44	1870(Maddison)
1880	564	1.23	INTERPOL(Maddison)
1890	637	1.23	INTERPOL(Maddison)
1900	720	1.23	1900(Maddison)
1913	837	1.16	1913(Maddison)
1920	855	0.30	1920(Maddison)
1929	985	1.59	1929(Maddison)
1938	1,163	1.86	1938(Maddison)
1950	1,403	1.58	50(E)
1960	1,629	1.50	60(E)
1970	1,869	1.38	70(E)
1980	2,132	1.33	80(E)
1990	2,365	1.04	90(E)
2000	2,582	0.88	00(E)
2010	2,691	0.41	10(E)
2012	2,710	0.36	12(E)
2020	2,775	0.30	12(E)
2030	2,789	0.05	12(E)
DME JAPAN			
0001	3,000	.	0001(Maddison)
1000	7,500	0.09	1000(Maddison)

Year	Population, '000s	Growth Rate	Source
1500	15,400	0.14	1500(Maddison)
1600	18,500	0.18	1600(Maddison)
1700	27,000	0.38	1700(Maddison)
1820	31,000	0.12	1820(Maddison)
1870	34,437	0.21	1870(Maddison)
1880	36,807	0.67	1880(Maddison)
1890	40,077	0.85	1890(Maddison)
1900	44,103	0.96	1900(Maddison)
1913	51,672	1.23	1913(Maddison)
1920	55,818	1.11	1920(Maddison)
1929	63,244	1.40	1929(Maddison)
1938	71,879	1.43	1938(Maddison)
1950	83,625	1.27	50(E)
1960	92,501	1.01	60(E)
1970	103,710	1.15	70(E)
1980	115,915	1.12	80(E)
1990	122,251	0.53	90(E)
2000	126,861	0.37	00(E)
2010	128,070	0.09	10(E)
2012	127,529	0.21	12(E)
2020	125,707	0.18	12(E)
2030	121,088	0.37	12(E)
DME JERSEY			
0001	.	.	
1000	.	.	
1500	.	.	
1600	.	.	
1700	.	.	
1820	.	.	
1870	.	.	
1880	.	.	
1890	.	.	
1900	.	.	
1913	.	.	
1920	.	.	
1929	.	.	
1938	.	.	
1950	57	.	50(E)
1960	63	1.01	60(E)
1970	69	0.91	70(E)
1980	76	0.97	80(E)
1990	84	1.01	90(E)
2000	87	0.35	00(E)
2010	97	1.09	10(E)
2012	99	0.82	12(E)
2020	105	0.79	12(E)
2030	110	0.47	12(E)

Year	Population, '000s	Growth Rate	Source
			MEA Jordan
0001	213	.	PROXY(W. Asia(Maddison))
1000	220	0.00	PROXY(W. Asia(Maddison))
1500	196	0.02	PROXY(Other W. Asia(Maddison))
1600	191	0.03	INTERPOL(Maddison)
1700	186	0.03	PROXY(Other W. Asia(Maddison))
1820	217	0.13	1820(Maddison)
1870	266	0.41	1870(Maddison)
1880	283	0.63	INTERPOL(Maddison)
1890	301	0.63	INTERPOL(Maddison)
1900	321	0.63	INTERPOL(Maddison)
1913	348	0.63	1913(Maddison)
1920	369	0.83	INTERPOL(Maddison)
1929	397	0.83	INTERPOL(Maddison)
1938	428	0.83	INTERPOL(Maddison)
1950	472	0.83	50(E)
1960	895	6.61	60(E)
1970	1,667	6.42	70(E)
1980	2,299	3.27	80(E)
1990	3,416	4.04	90(E)
2000	4,798	3.46	00(E)
2010	6,047	2.34	10(E)
2012	6,318	2.22	12(E)
2020	7,297	1.82	12(E)
2030	8,336	1.34	12(E)
			USR Kazakhstan
0001	464	.	PROXY(40(E)/Turkestan(Maddison))
1000	773	0.05	PROXY(40(E)/Turkestan(Maddison))
1500	1,082	0.07	PROXY(40(E)/Turkestan(Maddison))
1600	1,236	0.13	PROXY(40(E)/Turkestan(Maddison))
1700	1,391	0.12	PROXY(40(E)/Turkestan(Maddison))
1820	2,081	0.34	PROXY(40(E)/Turkestan(Maddison))
1870	2,809	0.60	PROXY(40(E)/USSR(Maddison))
1880	3,138	1.11	40(E)/INTERPOL(Maddison)
1890	3,506	1.11	PROXY(40(E)/USSR(Maddison))
1900	3,944	1.19	PROXY(40(E)/USSR(Maddison))
1913	4,948	1.76	PROXY(40(E)/USSR(Maddison))
1920	4,898	0.15	PROXY(40(E)/USSR(Maddison))
1929	5,449	1.19	PROXY(40(E)/USSR(Maddison))
1938	5,971	1.02	PROXY(40(E)/USSR(Maddison))
1950	6,693	0.96	50(E)
1960	9,982	4.08	60(E)
1970	13,106	2.76	70(E)
1980	15,000	1.36	80(E)
1990	16,775	1.12	90(E)
2000	14,884	1.19	00(E)
2010	16,311	0.92	10(E)
2012	16,809	1.52	12(E)
2020	18,395	1.13	12(E)

Year	Population, '000s	Growth Rate	Source
2030	19,634	0.65	12(E)
		AFR KENYA	
0001	.	.	
1000	.	.	
1500	.	.	
1600	.	.	
1700	.	.	
1820	.	.	
1870	.	.	
1880	.	.	
1890	.	.	
1900	.	.	
1913	.	.	
1920	.	.	
1929	.	.	
1938	.	.	
1950	6,121	.	50(E)
1960	8,157	2.91	60(E)
1970	11,247	3.26	70(E)
1980	16,331	3.80	80(E)
1990	23,361	3.64	90(E)
2000	30,606	2.74	00(E)
2010	40,843	2.93	10(E)
2012	42,946	2.54	12(E)
2020	49,858	1.88	12(E)
2030	56,552	1.27	12(E)
		SEA KIRIBATI	
0001	.	.	
1000	.	.	
1500	.	.	
1600	.	.	
1700	.	.	
1820	.	.	
1870	.	.	
1880	.	.	
1890	.	.	
1900	.	.	
1913	.	.	
1920	.	.	
1929	.	.	
1938	.	.	
1950	33	.	50(E)
1960	41	2.19	60(E)
1970	49	1.80	70(E)
1980	58	1.70	80(E)

Year	Population, '000s	Growth Rate	Source
1990	71	2.04	90(E)
2000	85	1.82	00(E)
2010	102	1.84	10(E)
2012	107	2.24	12(E)
2020	121	1.59	12(E)
2030	138	1.32	12(E)
	CPA KOREA, NORTH		
0001	767	.	PROXY(Other E. Asia(Maddison))
1000	1,420	0.06	PROXY(Other E. Asia(Maddison))
1500	2,530	0.12	1500(Maddison)
1600	3,124	0.21	INTERPOL(Maddison)
1700	3,858	0.21	1700(Maddison)
1820	4,345	0.10	1820(Maddison)
1870	4,511	0.08	1870(Maddison)
1880	4,598	0.19	INTERPOL(Maddison)
1890	4,697	0.21	INTERPOL(Maddison)
1900	4,777	0.17	INTERPOL(Maddison)
1913	4,897	0.19	1913(Maddison)
1920	5,577	1.87	INTERPOL(Maddison)
1929	6,592	1.87	INTERPOL(Maddison)
1938	7,791	1.87	INTERPOL(Maddison)
1950	9,737	1.87	50(E)
1960	10,946	1.18	60(E)
1970	14,247	2.67	70(E)
1980	17,239	1.92	80(E)
1990	20,143	1.57	90(E)
2000	22,785	1.24	00(E)
2010	24,326	0.66	10(E)
2012	24,588	0.54	12(E)
2020	25,643	0.53	12(E)
2030	26,688	0.40	12(E)
	SEA KOREA, SOUTH		
0001	1,658	.	PROXY(Other E. Asia(Maddison))
1000	3,070	0.06	PROXY(Other E. Asia(Maddison))
1500	5,470	0.12	1500(Maddison)
1600	6,755	0.21	INTERPOL(Maddison)
1700	8,342	0.21	1700(Maddison)
1820	9,395	0.10	1820(Maddison)
1870	9,753	0.07	1870(Maddison)
1880	9,800	0.05	INTERPOL(Maddison)
1890	9,848	0.05	1890(Maddison)
1900	9,896	0.05	1900(Maddison)
1913	10,589	0.52	1913(Maddison)
1920	11,804	1.56	1920(Maddison)
1929	13,716	1.68	1929(Maddison)
1938	15,381	1.28	1938(Maddison)
1950	20,846	2.57	50(E)
1960	25,074	1.86	60(E)
1970	31,443	2.29	70(E)

Year	Population, '000s	Growth Rate	Source
1980	37,460	1.77	80(E)
1990	42,980	1.38	90(E)
2000	46,059	0.69	00(E)
2010	49,410	0.70	10(E)
2012	49,905	0.50	12(E)
2020	51,435	0.38	12(E)
2030	52,160	0.14	12(E)
EEU Kosovo			
0001	77	.	PROXY(Yugoslavia(Maddison))
1000	82	0.01	PROXY(Yugoslavia(Maddison))
1500	105	0.05	PROXY(Yugoslavia(Maddison))
1600	129	0.20	PROXY(Yugoslavia(Maddison))
1700	129	0.00	PROXY(Yugoslavia(Maddison))
1820	244	0.53	PROXY(Yugoslavia(Maddison))
1870	387	0.92	PROXY(Yugoslavia(Maddison))
1880	419	0.81	INTERPOL(Maddison)
1890	454	0.81	PROXY(Yugoslavia(Maddison))
1900	524	1.44	PROXY(Yugoslavia(Maddison))
1913	637	1.52	PROXY(Yugoslavia(Maddison))
1920	582	1.28	PROXY(Yugoslavia(Maddison))
1929	665	1.49	PROXY(Yugoslavia(Maddison))
1938	754	1.40	PROXY(Yugoslavia(Maddison))
1950	764	0.11	50(E)
1960	947	2.17	60(E)
1970	1,219	2.56	70(E)
1980	1,521	2.24	80(E)
1990	1,862	2.04	90(E)
2000	1,700	0.91	00(E)
2010	1,815	0.66	10(E)
2012	1,837	0.60	12(E)
2020	1,933	0.64	12(E)
2030	2,066	0.67	12(E)
MEA Kuwait			
0001	78	.	PROXY(W. Asia(Maddison))
1000	80	0.00	PROXY(W. Asia(Maddison))
1500	71	0.02	PROXY(Arabia(Maddison))
1600	71	0.00	INTERPOL(Maddison)
1700	71	0.00	PROXY(Arabia(Maddison))
1820	82	0.12	PROXY(Gulf Coast(Maddison))
1870	82	0.00	PROXY(Gulf Coast(Maddison))
1880	87	0.56	INTERPOL(Maddison)
1890	92	0.56	INTERPOL(Maddison)
1900	97	0.56	INTERPOL(Maddison)
1913	105	0.56	PROXY(Gulf Coast(Maddison))
1920	111	0.89	INTERPOL(Maddison)
1929	120	0.89	INTERPOL(Maddison)
1938	130	0.89	INTERPOL(Maddison)
1950	145	0.89	50(E)
1960	292	7.25	60(E)

Year	Population, '000s	Growth Rate	Source
1970	748	9.86	70(E)
1980	1,370	6.24	80(E)
1990	2,131	4.52	90(E)
2000	2,236	0.48	00(E)
2010	3,566	4.78	10(E)
2012	3,807	3.32	12(E)
2020	4,511	2.14	12(E)
2030	5,332	1.69	12(E)
USR Kyrgyzstan			
0001	115	.	PROXY(40(E)/Turkestan(Maddison))
1000	192	0.05	PROXY(40(E)/Turkestan(Maddison))
1500	269	0.07	PROXY(40(E)/Turkestan(Maddison))
1600	307	0.13	PROXY(40(E)/Turkestan(Maddison))
1700	346	0.12	PROXY(40(E)/Turkestan(Maddison))
1820	517	0.34	PROXY(40(E)/Turkestan(Maddison))
1870	698	0.60	PROXY(40(E)/USSR(Maddison))
1880	780	1.11	40(E)/INTERPOL(Maddison)
1890	871	1.11	PROXY(40(E)/USSR(Maddison))
1900	980	1.19	PROXY(40(E)/USSR(Maddison))
1913	1,230	1.76	PROXY(40(E)/USSR(Maddison))
1920	1,217	0.15	PROXY(40(E)/USSR(Maddison))
1929	1,354	1.19	PROXY(40(E)/USSR(Maddison))
1938	1,484	1.02	PROXY(40(E)/USSR(Maddison))
1950	1,740	1.33	50(E)
1960	2,173	2.25	60(E)
1970	2,964	3.15	70(E)
1980	3,627	2.04	80(E)
1990	4,395	1.94	90(E)
2000	4,883	1.06	00(E)
2010	5,448	1.10	10(E)
2012	5,567	1.09	12(E)
2020	6,126	1.20	12(E)
2030	6,793	1.04	12(E)
CPA Laos			
0001	83	.	PROXY(Other E. Asia(Maddison))
1000	154	0.06	PROXY(Other E. Asia(Maddison))
1500	275	0.12	PROXY(Other E. Asia(Maddison))
1600	319	0.15	PROXY(Other E. Asia(Maddison))
1700	371	0.15	PROXY(Other E. Asia(Maddison))
1820	470	0.20	1820(Maddison)
1870	755	0.95	1870(Maddison)
1880	870	1.42	INTERPOL(Maddison)
1890	1,002	1.42	INTERPOL(Maddison)
1900	1,154	1.42	INTERPOL(Maddison)
1913	1,387	1.42	1913(Maddison)
1920	1,412	0.25	INTERPOL(Maddison)
1929	1,445	0.25	INTERPOL(Maddison)
1938	1,478	0.25	INTERPOL(Maddison)
1950	1,524	0.25	50(E)

Year	Population, '000s	Growth Rate	Source
1960	2,130	3.40	60(E)
1970	2,691	2.37	70(E)
1980	3,235	1.86	80(E)
1990	4,192	2.63	90(E)
2000	5,245	2.27	00(E)
2010	6,256	1.78	10(E)
2012	6,517	2.06	12(E)
2020	7,272	1.38	12(E)
2030	8,004	0.96	12(E)
		USR LATVIA	
0001	24	.	PROXY(40(E)/Eur. Russia(Maddison))
1000	48	0.07	PROXY(40(E)/Eur. Russia(Maddison))
1500	144	0.22	PROXY(40(E)/Eur. Russia(Maddison))
1600	180	0.22	PROXY(40(E)/Eur. Russia(Maddison))
1700	240	0.29	PROXY(40(E)/Eur. Russia(Maddison))
1820	531	0.66	PROXY(40(E)/Eur. Russia(Maddison))
1870	862	0.97	PROXY(40(E)/USSR(Maddison))
1880	963	1.11	40(E)/INTERPOL(Maddison)
1890	1,075	1.11	PROXY(40(E)/USSR(Maddison))
1900	1,210	1.19	PROXY(40(E)/USSR(Maddison))
1913	1,518	1.76	PROXY(40(E)/USSR(Maddison))
1920	1,502	0.15	PROXY(40(E)/USSR(Maddison))
1929	1,672	1.19	PROXY(40(E)/USSR(Maddison))
1938	1,832	1.02	PROXY(40(E)/USSR(Maddison))
1950	1,949	0.52	50(E)
1960	2,132	0.90	60(E)
1970	2,366	1.05	70(E)
1980	2,513	0.60	80(E)
1990	2,664	0.59	90(E)
2000	2,370	1.16	00(E)
2010	2,098	1.21	10(E)
2012	2,046	1.24	12(E)
2020	1,970	0.47	12(E)
2030	1,883	0.45	12(E)
		MEA LEBANON	
0001	326	.	PROXY(W. Asia(Maddison))
1000	336	0.00	PROXY(W. Asia(Maddison))
1500	299	0.02	PROXY(Other W. Asia(Maddison))
1600	292	0.03	INTERPOL(Maddison)
1700	284	0.03	PROXY(Other W. Asia(Maddison))
1820	332	0.13	1820(Maddison)
1870	476	0.72	1870(Maddison)
1880	512	0.72	INTERPOL(Maddison)
1890	550	0.72	INTERPOL(Maddison)
1900	591	0.72	INTERPOL(Maddison)
1913	649	0.72	1913(Maddison)
1920	755	2.18	INTERPOL(Maddison)
1929	917	2.18	INTERPOL(Maddison)
1938	1,114	2.18	INTERPOL(Maddison)

Year	Population, '000s	Growth Rate	Source
1950	1,443	2.18	50(E)
1960	1,786	2.16	60(E)
1970	2,383	2.93	70(E)
1980	2,899	1.98	80(E)
1990	3,440	1.73	90(E)
2000	3,791	0.98	00(E)
2010	4,125	0.85	10(E)
2012	4,130	0.06	12(E)
2020	4,243	0.34	12(E)
2030	4,335	0.21	12(E)
		AFR Lesotho	
0001	5	.	PROXY(S. Afr., Sw., Ls.(Maddison))
1000	15	0.11	PROXY(S. Afr., Sw., Ls.(Maddison))
1500	30	0.14	PROXY(S. Afr., Sw., Ls.(Maddison))
1600	35	0.15	PROXY(S. Afr., Sw., Ls.(Maddison))
1700	50	0.36	PROXY(S. Afr., Sw., Ls.(Maddison))
1820	77	0.37	PROXY(S. Afr., Sw., Ls.(Maddison))
1870	184	1.74	INTERPOL(Maddison)
1880	219	1.74	INTERPOL(Maddison)
1890	260	1.74	INTERPOL(Maddison)
1900	309	1.74	INTERPOL(Maddison)
1913	387	1.74	INTERPOL(Maddison)
1920	437	1.74	INTERPOL(Maddison)
1929	510	1.74	INTERPOL(Maddison)
1938	596	1.74	INTERPOL(Maddison)
1950	734	1.74	50(E)
1960	859	1.59	60(E)
1970	1,067	2.19	70(E)
1980	1,359	2.45	80(E)
1990	1,703	2.28	90(E)
2000	1,916	1.19	00(E)
2010	1,920	0.02	10(E)
2012	1,931	0.28	12(E)
2020	1,969	0.25	12(E)
2030	1,952	0.09	12(E)
		AFR Liberia	
0001	.	.	
1000	.	.	
1500	.	.	
1600	.	.	
1700	.	.	
1820	.	.	
1870	.	.	
1880	.	.	
1890	.	.	
1900	.	.	
1913	.	.	
1920	.	.	

Year	Population, '000s	Growth Rate	Source
1929	.	.	
1938	.	.	
1950	824	.	50(E)
1960	1,116	3.08	60(E)
1970	1,440	2.58	70(E)
1980	1,923	2.93	80(E)
1990	2,127	1.01	90(E)
2000	2,847	2.96	00(E)
2010	3,823	2.99	10(E)
2012	4,039	2.79	12(E)
2020	4,945	2.56	12(E)
2030	6,254	2.38	12(E)
MEA Libya			
0001	400	.	0001(Maddison)
1000	500	0.02	1000(Maddison)
1500	500	0.00	1500(Maddison)
1600	500	0.00	1600(Maddison)
1700	500	0.00	1700(Maddison)
1820	538	0.06	1820(Maddison)
1870	660	0.41	INTERPOL(Maddison/Mitchell)
1880	688	0.41	INTERPOL(Maddison/Mitchell)
1890	717	0.41	INTERPOL(Maddison/Mitchell)
1900	747	0.41	INTERPOL(Maddison/Mitchell)
1913	788	0.41	INTERPOL(Maddison/Mitchell)
1920	811	0.41	INTERPOL(Maddison/Mitchell)
1929	841	0.41	INTERPOL(Maddison/Mitchell)
1938	873	0.41	INTERPOL(Mitchell/E)
1950	1,029	1.38	50(E)
1960	1,349	2.74	60(E)
1970	1,994	3.99	70(E)
1980	3,063	4.39	80(E)
1990	4,334	3.53	90(E)
2000	5,025	1.49	00(E)
2010	6,110	1.97	10(E)
2012	6,038	0.59	12(E)
2020	6,943	1.76	12(E)
2030	7,773	1.14	12(E)
DME Liechtenstein			
0001	.	.	
1000	.	.	
1500	.	.	
1600	.	.	
1700	.	.	
1820	.	.	
1870	.	.	
1880	.	.	

Year	Population, '000s	Growth Rate	Source
1890	.	.	
1900	.	.	
1913	.	.	
1920	.	.	
1929	.	.	
1938	.	.	
1950	14	.	50(E)
1960	16	1.34	60(E)
1970	21	2.76	70(E)
1980	25	1.76	80(E)
1990	29	1.50	90(E)
2000	33	1.30	00(E)
2010	36	0.87	10(E)
2012	37	0.92	12(E)
2020	39	0.78	12(E)
2030	42	0.74	12(E)
		USR LITHUANIA	
0001	37	.	PROXY(40(E)/Eur. Russia(Maddison))
1000	75	0.07	PROXY(40(E)/Eur. Russia(Maddison))
1500	224	0.22	PROXY(40(E)/Eur. Russia(Maddison))
1600	279	0.22	PROXY(40(E)/Eur. Russia(Maddison))
1700	373	0.29	PROXY(40(E)/Eur. Russia(Maddison))
1820	823	0.66	PROXY(40(E)/Eur. Russia(Maddison))
1870	1,336	0.97	PROXY(40(E)/USSR(Maddison))
1880	1,493	1.11	40(E)/INTERPOL(Maddison)
1890	1,668	1.11	PROXY(40(E)/USSR(Maddison))
1900	1,876	1.19	PROXY(40(E)/USSR(Maddison))
1913	2,354	1.76	PROXY(40(E)/USSR(Maddison))
1920	2,330	0.15	PROXY(40(E)/USSR(Maddison))
1929	2,593	1.19	PROXY(40(E)/USSR(Maddison))
1938	2,841	1.02	PROXY(40(E)/USSR(Maddison))
1950	2,553	0.89	50(E)
1960	2,765	0.80	60(E)
1970	3,138	1.27	70(E)
1980	3,436	0.91	80(E)
1990	3,698	0.74	90(E)
2000	3,500	0.55	00(E)
2010	3,100	1.21	10(E)
2012	3,009	1.48	12(E)
2020	2,879	0.55	12(E)
2030	2,769	0.39	12(E)
		DME LUXEMBOURG	
0001	.	.	
1000	.	.	
1500	.	.	
1600	.	.	
1700	.	.	

Year	Population, '000s	Growth Rate	Source
1820	.	.	
1870	.	.	
1880	.	.	
1890	.	.	
1900	.	.	
1913	.	.	
1920	.	.	
1929	.	.	
1938	.	.	
1950	296	.	50(E)
1960	314	0.59	60(E)
1970	339	0.77	70(E)
1980	364	0.71	80(E)
1990	381	0.46	90(E)
2000	435	1.33	00(E)
2010	507	1.54	10(E)
2012	533	2.50	12(E)
2020	594	1.37	12(E)
2030	657	1.01	12(E)
		SEA Macao	
0001	.	.	
1000	.	.	
1500	.	.	
1600	.	.	
1700	.	.	
1820	.	.	
1870	.	.	
1880	.	.	
1890	.	.	
1900	.	.	
1913	.	.	
1920	.	.	
1929	.	.	
1938	.	.	
1950	205	.	50(E)
1960	173	1.68	60(E)
1970	254	3.92	70(E)
1980	252	0.08	80(E)
1990	372	3.97	90(E)
2000	431	1.48	00(E)
2010	541	2.30	10(E)
2012	575	3.11	12(E)
2020	680	2.12	12(E)
2030	745	0.92	12(E)
		EEU Macedonia	
0001	113	.	PROXY(Yugoslavia(Maddison))

Year	Population, '000s	Growth Rate	Source
1000	132	0.02	PROXY(Yugoslavia(Maddison))
1500	170	0.05	PROXY(Yugoslavia(Maddison))
1600	208	0.20	PROXY(Yugoslavia(Maddison))
1700	208	0.00	PROXY(Yugoslavia(Maddison))
1820	394	0.53	PROXY(Yugoslavia(Maddison))
1870	623	0.92	PROXY(Yugoslavia(Maddison))
1880	675	0.81	INTERPOL(Maddison)
1890	731	0.81	PROXY(Yugoslavia(Maddison))
1900	843	1.44	PROXY(Yugoslavia(Maddison))
1913	1,026	1.52	PROXY(Yugoslavia(Maddison))
1920	937	1.28	PROXY(Yugoslavia(Maddison))
1929	1,071	1.49	PROXY(Yugoslavia(Maddison))
1938	1,214	1.40	PROXY(Yugoslavia(Maddison))
1950	1,230	0.11	50(E)
1960	1,392	1.24	60(E)
1970	1,568	1.20	70(E)
1980	1,795	1.36	80(E)
1990	1,909	0.62	90(E)
2000	2,009	0.51	00(E)
2010	2,055	0.23	10(E)
2012	2,061	0.15	12(E)
2020	2,068	0.04	12(E)
2030	2,038	0.15	12(E)
AFR Madagascar			
0001	1	.	0001(EST)
1000	200	0.53	1000(Maddison)
1500	700	0.25	1500(Maddison)
1600	800	0.13	1600(Maddison)
1700	1,000	0.22	1700(Maddison)
1820	1,683	0.43	1820(Maddison)
1870	2,400	0.71	INTERPOL(Maddison)
1880	2,576	0.71	INTERPOL(Maddison)
1890	2,766	0.71	INTERPOL(Maddison)
1900	2,969	0.71	INTERPOL(Maddison)
1913	3,256	0.71	INTERPOL(Maddison)
1920	3,422	0.71	INTERPOL(Maddison)
1929	3,648	0.71	INTERPOL(Maddison)
1938	3,888	0.71	INTERPOL(Maddison)
1950	4,234	0.71	50(E)
1960	5,104	1.89	60(E)
1970	6,549	2.52	70(E)
1980	8,609	2.77	80(E)
1990	11,281	2.74	90(E)
2000	15,712	3.37	00(E)
2010	20,847	2.87	10(E)
2012	21,999	2.73	12(E)
2020	26,956	2.57	12(E)
2030	33,417	2.17	12(E)
AFR Malawi			

Year	Population, '000s	Growth Rate	Source
0001	26	.	PROXY(Mal., Zam., Zim.(Maddison))
1000	171	0.19	PROXY(Mal., Zam., Zim.(Maddison))
1500	343	0.14	PROXY(Mal., Zam., Zim.(Maddison))
1600	377	0.10	PROXY(Mal., Zam., Zim.(Maddison))
1700	411	0.09	PROXY(Mal., Zam., Zim.(Maddison))
1820	461	0.10	PROXY(Mal., Zam., Zim.(Maddison))
1870	924	1.40	INTERPOL(Maddison)
1880	1,063	1.40	INTERPOL(Maddison)
1890	1,221	1.40	INTERPOL(Maddison)
1900	1,404	1.40	INTERPOL(Maddison)
1913	1,683	1.40	INTERPOL(Maddison)
1920	1,855	1.40	INTERPOL(Maddison)
1929	2,103	1.40	INTERPOL(Maddison)
1938	2,383	1.40	INTERPOL(Maddison)
1950	2,817	1.40	50(E)
1960	3,525	2.27	60(E)
1970	4,531	2.54	70(E)
1980	6,240	3.25	80(E)
1990	9,381	4.16	90(E)
2000	11,229	1.81	00(E)
2010	14,901	2.87	10(E)
2012	15,889	3.26	12(E)
2020	20,677	3.35	12(E)
2030	28,174	3.14	12(E)
		SEA Malaysia	
0001	51	.	PROXY(Other E. Asia(Maddison))
1000	94	0.06	PROXY(Other E. Asia(Maddison))
1500	168	0.12	PROXY(Other E. Asia(Maddison))
1600	195	0.15	PROXY(Other E. Asia(Maddison))
1700	227	0.15	PROXY(Other E. Asia(Maddison))
1820	287	0.20	1820(Maddison)
1870	800	2.07	1870(Maddison)
1880	1,126	3.48	INTERPOL(Maddison)
1890	1,585	3.48	1890(Maddison)
1900	2,232	3.48	1900(Maddison)
1913	3,084	2.52	1913(Maddison)
1920	3,545	2.01	1920(Maddison)
1929	4,316	2.21	1929(Maddison)
1938	5,207	2.11	1938(Maddison)
1950	6,110	1.34	50(E)
1960	8,428	3.27	60(E)
1970	10,910	2.61	70(E)
1980	13,460	2.12	80(E)
1990	17,882	2.88	90(E)
2000	22,198	2.19	00(E)
2010	28,325	2.47	10(E)
2012	29,740	2.47	12(E)
2020	32,897	1.27	12(E)
2030	37,166	1.23	12(E)

Year	Population, '000s	Growth Rate	Source
	SAS Maldives		
0001	.	.	
1000	.	.	
1500	.	.	
1600	.	.	
1700	.	.	
1820	.	.	
1870	.	.	
1880	.	.	
1890	.	.	
1900	.	.	
1913	.	.	
1920	.	.	
1929	.	.	
1938	.	.	
1950	79	.	50(E)
1960	99	2.28	60(E)
1970	121	2.03	70(E)
1980	158	2.70	80(E)
1990	216	3.18	90(E)
2000	272	2.33	00(E)
2010	320	1.64	10(E)
2012	331	1.64	12(E)
2020	364	1.21	12(E)
2030	391	0.72	12(E)
	AFR Mali		
0001	.	.	
1000	.	.	
1500	.	.	
1600	.	.	
1700	.	.	
1820	.	.	
1870	.	.	
1880	.	.	
1890	.	.	
1900	.	.	
1913	.	.	
1920	.	.	
1929	.	.	
1938	.	.	
1950	3,688	.	50(E)
1960	4,495	2.00	60(E)
1970	5,546	2.12	70(E)
1980	6,822	2.09	80(E)
1990	8,327	2.01	90(E)

Year	Population, '000s	Growth Rate	Source
2000	10,788	2.62	00(E)
2010	14,583	3.06	10(E)
2012	15,493	3.07	12(E)
2020	19,623	3.00	12(E)
2030	25,619	2.70	12(E)
		DME Malta	
0001	.	.	
1000	.	.	
1500	.	.	
1600	.	.	
1700	.	.	
1820	.	.	
1870	.	.	
1880	.	.	
1890	.	.	
1900	.	.	
1913	.	.	
1920	.	.	
1929	.	.	
1938	.	.	
1950	312	.	50(E)
1960	313	0.03	60(E)
1970	304	0.29	70(E)
1980	327	0.73	80(E)
1990	368	1.19	90(E)
2000	390	0.58	00(E)
2010	413	0.57	10(E)
2012	415	0.24	12(E)
2020	426	0.33	12(E)
2030	429	0.07	12(E)
		SEA Marshall Islands	
0001	.	.	
1000	.	.	
1500	.	.	
1600	.	.	
1700	.	.	
1820	.	.	
1870	.	.	
1880	.	.	
1890	.	.	
1900	.	.	
1913	.	.	
1920	.	.	
1929	.	.	
1938	.	.	

Year	Population, '000s	Growth Rate	Source
1950	11	.	50(E)
1960	15	3.15	60(E)
1970	22	3.90	70(E)
1980	31	3.49	80(E)
1990	44	3.56	90(E)
2000	51	1.49	00(E)
2010	53	0.39	10(E)
2012	53	0.38	12(E)
2020	59	1.25	12(E)
2030	64	0.82	12(E)
LAM Martinique			
0001	.	.	
1000	.	.	
1500	.	.	
1600	.	.	
1700	.	.	
1820	.	.	
1870	.	.	
1880	.	.	
1890	.	.	
1900	.	.	
1913	.	.	
1920	.	.	
1929	.	.	
1938	.	.	
1950	222	.	50(E)
1960	282	2.42	60(E)
1970	325	1.43	70(E)
1980	326	0.03	80(E)
1990	360	1.00	90(E)
2000	383	0.62	00(E)
2010	393	0.26	10(E)
2012	389	0.51	12(E)
2020	392	0.10	12(E)
2030	392	0.00	12(E)
AFR Mauritania			
0001	.	.	
1000	.	.	
1500	.	.	
1600	.	.	
1700	.	.	
1820	.	.	
1870	.	.	
1880	.	.	
1890	.	.	
1900	.	.	

Year	Population, '000s	Growth Rate	Source
1913	.	.	
1920	.	.	
1929	.	.	
1938	.	.	
1950	692	.	50(E)
1960	1,117	4.90	60(E)
1970	1,289	1.44	70(E)
1980	1,545	1.83	80(E)
1990	1,925	2.22	90(E)
2000	2,501	2.65	00(E)
2010	3,205	2.51	10(E)
2012	3,359	2.37	12(E)
2020	4,005	2.22	12(E)
2030	4,851	1.93	12(E)

AFR Mauritius

Year	Population, '000s	Growth Rate	Source
0001	.	.	
1000	.	.	
1500	.	.	
1600	.	.	
1700	.	.	
1820	.	.	
1870	.	.	
1880	.	.	
1890	.	.	
1900	.	.	
1913	.	.	
1920	.	.	
1929	.	.	
1938	.	.	
1950	479	.	50(E)
1960	662	3.29	60(E)
1970	829	2.28	70(E)
1980	966	1.54	80(E)
1990	1,059	0.92	90(E)
2000	1,179	1.08	00(E)
2010	1,232	0.44	10(E)
2012	1,243	0.43	12(E)
2020	1,290	0.47	12(E)
2030	1,321	0.24	12(E)

AFR Mayotte

Year	Population, '000s	Growth Rate	Source
0001	.	.	
1000	.	.	
1500	.	.	
1600	.	.	
1700	.	.	
1820	.	.	

Year	Population, '000s	Growth Rate	Source
1870	.	.	
1880	.	.	
1890	.	.	
1900	.	.	
1913	.	.	
1920	.	.	
1929	.	.	
1938	.	.	
1950	17	.	50(E)
1960	25	3.93	60(E)
1970	35	3.42	70(E)
1980	52	4.04	80(E)
1990	89	5.52	90(E)
2000	147	5.15	00(E)
2010	204	3.33	10(E)
2012	216	3.01	12(E)
2020	265	2.56	12(E)
2030	324	2.03	12(E)
		LAM Mexico	
0001	2,200	.	0001(Maddison)
1000	4,500	0.07	1000(Maddison)
1500	7,500	0.10	1500(Maddison)
1600	2,500	1.09	1600(Maddison)
1700	4,500	0.59	1700(Maddison)
1820	6,587	0.32	1820(Maddison)
1870	9,219	0.67	1870(Maddison)
1880	10,399	1.21	1880(Maddison)
1890	11,729	1.21	1890(Maddison)
1900	13,607	1.50	1900(Maddison)
1913	14,970	0.74	1913(Maddison)
1920	14,900	0.07	1920(Maddison)
1929	16,875	1.39	1929(Maddison)
1938	19,705	1.74	1938(Maddison)
1950	27,741	2.89	50(E)
1960	38,419	3.31	60(E)
1970	51,868	3.05	70(E)
1980	68,776	2.86	80(E)
1990	84,307	2.06	90(E)
2000	98,439	1.56	00(E)
2010	112,437	1.34	10(E)
2012	116,585	1.83	12(E)
2020	125,792	0.95	12(E)
2030	135,251	0.73	12(E)
		SEA Micronesia	
0001	.	.	
1000	.	.	
1500	.	.	
1600	.	.	

Year	Population, '000s	Growth Rate	Source
1700	.	.	
1820	.	.	
1870	.	.	
1880	.	.	
1890	.	.	
1900	.	.	
1913	.	.	
1920	.	.	
1929	.	.	
1938	.	.	
1950	32	.	50(E)
1960	45	3.47	60(E)
1970	61	3.09	70(E)
1980	73	1.81	80(E)
1990	96	2.78	90(E)
2000	107	1.09	00(E)
2010	103	0.38	10(E)
2012	102	0.33	12(E)
2020	100	0.29	12(E)
2030	103	0.30	12(E)
USR MOLDOVA			
0001	31	.	PROXY(40(E)/Eur. Russia(Maddison))
1000	63	0.07	PROXY(40(E)/Eur. Russia(Maddison))
1500	189	0.22	PROXY(40(E)/Eur. Russia(Maddison))
1600	236	0.22	PROXY(40(E)/Eur. Russia(Maddison))
1700	314	0.29	PROXY(40(E)/Eur. Russia(Maddison))
1820	694	0.66	PROXY(40(E)/Eur. Russia(Maddison))
1870	1,128	0.97	PROXY(40(E)/USSR(Maddison))
1880	1,260	1.11	40(E)/INTERPOL(Maddison)
1890	1,407	1.11	PROXY(40(E)/USSR(Maddison))
1900	1,583	1.19	PROXY(40(E)/USSR(Maddison))
1913	1,986	1.76	PROXY(40(E)/USSR(Maddison))
1920	1,966	0.15	PROXY(40(E)/USSR(Maddison))
1929	2,187	1.19	PROXY(40(E)/USSR(Maddison))
1938	2,397	1.02	PROXY(40(E)/USSR(Maddison))
1950	2,341	0.20	50(E)
1960	3,004	2.53	60(E)
1970	3,595	1.81	70(E)
1980	4,010	1.10	80(E)
1990	4,364	0.85	90(E)
2000	4,223	0.33	00(E)
2010	3,935	0.70	10(E)
2012	3,918	0.21	12(E)
2020	3,713	0.67	12(E)
2030	3,480	0.65	12(E)
DME MONACO			
0001	.	.	
1000	.	.	

Year	Population, '000s	Growth Rate	Source
1500	.	.	
1600	.	.	
1700	.	.	
1820	.	.	
1870	.	.	
1880	.	.	
1890	.	.	
1900	.	.	
1913	.	.	
1920	.	.	
1929	.	.	
1938	.	.	
1950	18	.	50(E)
1960	21	1.55	60(E)
1970	24	1.34	70(E)
1980	27	1.18	80(E)
1990	30	1.06	90(E)
2000	35	1.55	00(E)
2010	36	0.28	10(E)
2012	37	1.01	12(E)
2020	38	0.43	12(E)
2030	39	0.26	12(E)
CPA Mongolia			
0001	110	.	PROXY(Other E. Asia(Maddison))
1000	203	0.06	PROXY(Other E. Asia(Maddison))
1500	362	0.12	PROXY(Other E. Asia(Maddison))
1600	420	0.15	PROXY(Other E. Asia(Maddison))
1700	489	0.15	PROXY(Other E. Asia(Maddison))
1820	619	0.20	1820(Maddison)
1870	668	0.15	1870(Maddison)
1880	681	0.19	INTERPOL(Maddison)
1890	694	0.19	INTERPOL(Maddison)
1900	707	0.19	INTERPOL(Maddison)
1913	725	0.19	1913(Maddison)
1920	729	0.08	INTERPOL(Maddison)
1929	734	0.08	INTERPOL(Maddison)
1938	740	0.08	INTERPOL(Maddison)
1950	747	0.08	50(E)
1960	931	2.23	60(E)
1970	1,248	2.97	70(E)
1980	1,663	2.91	80(E)
1990	2,086	2.29	90(E)
2000	2,385	1.35	00(E)
2010	2,637	1.01	10(E)
2012	2,691	1.03	12(E)
2020	3,022	1.46	12(E)
2030	3,343	1.01	12(E)

Year	Population, '000s	Growth Rate	Source
EEU Montenegro			
0001	37	.	PROXY(Yugoslavia(Maddison))
1000	43	0.02	PROXY(Yugoslavia(Maddison))
1500	55	0.05	PROXY(Yugoslavia(Maddison))
1600	67	0.20	PROXY(Yugoslavia(Maddison))
1700	67	0.00	PROXY(Yugoslavia(Maddison))
1820	127	0.53	PROXY(Yugoslavia(Maddison))
1870	201	0.92	PROXY(Yugoslavia(Maddison))
1880	218	0.81	INTERPOL(Maddison)
1890	236	0.81	PROXY(Yugoslavia(Maddison))
1900	272	1.44	PROXY(Yugoslavia(Maddison))
1913	331	1.52	PROXY(Yugoslavia(Maddison))
1920	303	1.28	PROXY(Yugoslavia(Maddison))
1929	346	1.49	PROXY(Yugoslavia(Maddison))
1938	392	1.40	PROXY(Yugoslavia(Maddison))
1950	397	0.11	50(E)
1960	467	1.64	60(E)
1970	519	1.06	70(E)
1980	576	1.05	80(E)
1990	609	0.56	90(E)
2000	633	0.39	00(E)
2010	620	0.21	10(E)
2012	620	0.00	12(E)
2020	624	0.08	12(E)
2030	622	0.03	12(E)
LAM Montserrat			
0001	.	.	
1000	.	.	
1500	.	.	
1600	.	.	
1700	.	.	
1820	.	.	
1870	.	.	
1880	.	.	
1890	.	.	
1900	.	.	
1913	.	.	
1920	.	.	
1929	.	.	
1938	.	.	
1950	6	.	PROXY(8 Caribbean cs(Maddison))
1960	7	2.29	INTERPOL(8 Caribbean cs(Maddison))
1970	9	2.29	INTERPOL(8 Caribbean cs(Maddison))
1980	11	1.67	INTERPOL(8 Caribbean cs(Maddison))
1990	12	1.41	90(CIA)
2000	6	6.44	00(CIA)
2010	5	2.22	10(CIA)

Year	Population, '000s	Growth Rate	Source
2012	5	0.45	12(CIA)
2020	4	1.79	12(EST)
2030	4	1.78	12(EST)
MEA Morocco			
0001	1,000	.	0001(Maddison)
1000	2,000	0.07	1000(Maddison)
1500	1,500	0.06	1500(Maddison)
1600	2,250	0.41	1600(Maddison)
1700	1,750	0.25	1700(Maddison)
1820	2,689	0.36	1820(Maddison)
1870	3,776	0.68	1870(Maddison)
1880	4,051	0.71	INTERPOL(Maddison)
1890	4,347	0.71	INTERPOL(Maddison)
1900	4,664	0.71	INTERPOL(Maddison)
1913	5,111	0.71	1913(Maddison)
1920	5,683	1.53	INTERPOL(Maddison)
1929	6,513	1.53	INTERPOL(Maddison)
1938	7,465	1.53	INTERPOL(Maddison)
1950	8,953	1.53	50(E)
1960	12,423	3.33	60(E)
1970	15,909	2.50	70(E)
1980	19,487	2.05	80(E)
1990	24,000	2.10	90(E)
2000	28,113	1.59	00(E)
2010	31,627	1.18	10(E)
2012	32,305	1.07	12(E)
2020	34,956	0.99	12(E)
2030	37,887	0.81	12(E)
AFR Mozambique			
0001	50	.	0001(Maddison)
1000	300	0.18	1000(Maddison)
1500	1,000	0.24	1500(Maddison)
1600	1,250	0.22	1600(Maddison)
1700	1,500	0.18	1700(Maddison)
1820	2,096	0.28	1820(Maddison)
1870	3,191	0.84	INTERPOL(Maddison)
1880	3,470	0.84	INTERPOL(Maddison)
1890	3,775	0.84	INTERPOL(Maddison)
1900	4,106	0.84	INTERPOL(Maddison)
1913	4,580	0.84	INTERPOL(Maddison)
1920	4,857	0.84	INTERPOL(Maddison)
1929	5,239	0.84	INTERPOL(Maddison)
1938	5,650	0.84	INTERPOL(Maddison)
1950	6,250	0.84	50(E)
1960	7,472	1.80	60(E)
1970	9,304	2.22	70(E)
1980	12,103	2.66	80(E)
1990	12,989	0.71	90(E)
2000	17,997	3.31	00(E)

Year	Population, '000s	Growth Rate	Source
2010	22,417	2.22	10(E)
2012	23,523	2.44	12(E)
2020	28,603	2.47	12(E)
2030	36,622	2.50	12(E)
		AFR Namibia	
0001	40	.	PROXY(Namibia & Botsw.(Maddison))
1000	54	0.03	PROXY(Namibia & Botsw.(Maddison))
1500	108	0.14	PROXY(Namibia & Botsw.(Maddison))
1600	108	0.00	PROXY(Namibia & Botsw.(Maddison))
1700	108	0.00	PROXY(Namibia & Botsw.(Maddison))
1820	118	0.08	PROXY(Namibia & Botsw.(Maddison))
1870	203	1.09	INTERPOL(Maddison)
1880	226	1.09	INTERPOL(Maddison)
1890	252	1.09	INTERPOL(Maddison)
1900	282	1.09	INTERPOL(Maddison)
1913	324	1.09	INTERPOL(Maddison)
1920	350	1.09	INTERPOL(Maddison)
1929	386	1.09	INTERPOL(Maddison)
1938	426	1.09	INTERPOL(Maddison)
1950	464	0.72	50(E)
1960	603	2.65	60(E)
1970	780	2.61	70(E)
1980	1,013	2.65	80(E)
1990	1,415	3.40	90(E)
2000	1,896	2.97	00(E)
2010	2,071	0.89	10(E)
2012	2,130	1.41	12(E)
2020	2,415	1.58	12(E)
2030	2,750	1.31	12(E)
		SEA Nauru	
0001	.	.	
1000	.	.	
1500	.	.	
1600	.	.	
1700	.	.	
1820	.	.	
1870	.	.	
1880	.	.	
1890	.	.	
1900	.	.	
1913	.	.	
1920	.	.	
1929	.	.	
1938	.	.	
1950	3	.	50(E)
1960	4	2.92	60(E)
1970	7	5.76	70(E)

Year	Population, '000s	Growth Rate	Source
1980	8	1.34	80(E)
1990	9	1.18	90(E)
2000	10	1.06	00(E)
2010	10	0.00	10(E)
2012	10	0.34	12(E)
2020	10	0.08	12(E)
2030	11	0.96	12(E)
		SAS Nepal	
0001	689	.	PROXY(Other E. Asia(Maddison))
1000	1,275	0.06	PROXY(Other E. Asia(Maddison))
1500	2,272	0.12	PROXY(Other E. Asia(Maddison))
1600	2,635	0.15	PROXY(Other E. Asia(Maddison))
1700	3,064	0.15	PROXY(Other E. Asia(Maddison))
1820	3,881	0.20	1820(Maddison)
1870	4,698	0.38	1870(Maddison)
1880	4,939	0.50	INTERPOL(Maddison)
1890	5,192	0.50	1890(Maddison)
1900	5,283	0.17	1900(Maddison)
1913	5,639	0.50	1913(Maddison)
1920	6,113	1.16	INTERPOL(Maddison)
1929	6,783	1.16	INTERPOL(Maddison)
1938	7,525	1.16	INTERPOL(Maddison)
1950	8,643	1.16	50(E)
1960	10,035	1.50	60(E)
1970	11,919	1.74	70(E)
1980	14,665	2.09	80(E)
1990	18,918	2.58	90(E)
2000	24,818	2.75	00(E)
2010	26,147	0.52	10(E)
2012	26,862	1.36	12(E)
2020	30,359	1.54	12(E)
2030	34,485	1.28	12(E)
		DME Netherlands	
0001	200	.	0001(Maddison)
1000	300	0.04	1000(Maddison)
1500	950	0.23	1500(Maddison)
1600	1,500	0.46	1600(Maddison)
1700	1,900	0.24	1700(Maddison)
1820	2,333	0.17	1820(Maddison)
1870	3,610	0.88	1870(Maddison)
1880	4,043	1.14	1880(Maddison)
1890	4,535	1.16	1890(Maddison)
1900	5,142	1.26	1900(Maddison)
1913	6,164	1.40	1913(Maddison)
1920	6,848	1.51	1920(Maddison)
1929	7,782	1.43	1929(Maddison)
1938	8,685	1.23	1938(Maddison)
1950	10,090	1.26	50(E)
1960	11,494	1.31	60(E)

Year	Population, '000s	Growth Rate	Source
1970	13,020	1.25	70(E)
1980	14,150	0.84	80(E)
1990	14,952	0.55	90(E)
2000	15,926	0.63	00(E)
2010	16,606	0.42	10(E)
2012	16,736	0.39	12(E)
2020	17,166	0.32	12(E)
2030	17,620	0.26	12(E)
	SEA New Caledonia		
0001	.	.	
1000	.	.	
1500	.	.	
1600	.	.	
1700	.	.	
1820	.	.	
1870	.	.	
1880	.	.	
1890	.	.	
1900	.	.	
1913	.	.	
1920	.	.	
1929	.	.	
1938	.	.	
1950	65	.	50(E)
1960	79	1.97	60(E)
1970	112	3.55	70(E)
1980	139	2.18	80(E)
1990	169	1.97	90(E)
2000	211	2.24	00(E)
2010	249	1.67	10(E)
2012	256	1.45	12(E)
2020	282	1.20	12(E)
2030	311	0.98	12(E)
	DME New Zealand		
0001	55	.	PROXY(Other W. offshots(Maddison))
1000	71	0.03	PROXY(Other W. offshots(Maddison))
1500	100	0.07	1500(Maddison)
1600	100	0.00	1600(Maddison)
1700	100	0.00	1700(Maddison)
1820	100	0.00	1820(Maddison)
1870	291	2.16	1870(Maddison)
1880	520	5.98	1880(Maddison)
1890	665	2.49	1890(Maddison)
1900	807	1.95	1900(Maddison)
1913	1,122	2.57	1913(Maddison)
1920	1,241	1.45	1920(Maddison)
1929	1,471	1.91	1929(Maddison)

Year	Population, '000s	Growth Rate	Source
1938	1,604	0.97	1938(Maddison)
1950	1,909	1.46	50(E)
1960	2,377	2.22	60(E)
1970	2,820	1.72	70(E)
1980	3,144	1.09	80(E)
1990	3,452	0.94	90(E)
2000	3,860	1.12	00(E)
2010	4,368	1.24	10(E)
2012	4,430	0.70	12(E)
2020	4,744	0.86	12(E)
2030	5,145	0.81	12(E)
LAM NICARAGUA			
0001	71	.	PROXY(Other L. Am.(Maddison))
1000	144	0.07	PROXY(Other L. Am.(Maddison))
1500	209	0.07	PROXY(Other Sp. Am.(Maddison))
1600	125	0.51	PROXY(Other Sp. Am.(Maddison))
1700	142	0.13	PROXY(Other Sp. Am.(Maddison))
1820	186	0.22	1820(Maddison)
1870	337	1.20	1870(Maddison)
1880	379	1.17	INTERPOL(Maddison)
1890	425	1.17	INTERPOL(Maddison)
1900	478	1.17	1900(Maddison)
1913	578	1.47	1913(Maddison)
1920	640	1.47	1920(Maddison)
1929	680	0.68	1929(Maddison)
1938	780	1.54	1938(Maddison)
1950	1,295	4.32	50(E)
1960	1,773	3.19	60(E)
1970	2,398	3.07	70(E)
1980	3,242	3.06	80(E)
1990	4,121	2.43	90(E)
2000	5,074	2.10	00(E)
2010	5,788	1.33	10(E)
2012	5,956	1.44	12(E)
2020	6,603	1.30	12(E)
2030	7,240	0.93	12(E)
AFR NIGER			
0001	.	.	
1000	.	.	
1500	.	.	
1600	.	.	
1700	.	.	
1820	.	.	
1870	.	.	
1880	.	.	
1890	.	.	
1900	.	.	
1913	.	.	

Year	Population, '000s	Growth Rate	Source
1920	.	.	
1929	.	.	
1938	.	.	
1950	2,208	.	50(E)
1960	3,250	3.94	60(E)
1970	4,373	3.01	70(E)
1980	5,871	2.99	80(E)
1990	7,788	2.87	90(E)
2000	10,922	3.44	00(E)
2010	15,512	3.57	10(E)
2012	16,644	3.58	12(E)
2020	22,071	3.59	12(E)
2030	30,841	3.40	12(E)
AFR Nigeria			
0001	.	.	
1000	.	.	
1500	.	.	
1600	.	.	
1700	.	.	
1820	.	.	
1870	.	.	
1880	.	.	
1890	.	.	
1900	.	.	
1913	.	.	
1920	.	.	
1929	.	.	
1938	.	.	
1950	31,797	.	50(E)
1960	45,926	3.75	60(E)
1970	57,357	2.25	70(E)
1980	75,543	2.79	80(E)
1990	97,552	2.59	90(E)
2000	124,208	2.45	00(E)
2010	161,605	2.67	10(E)
2012	170,096	2.59	12(E)
2020	207,699	2.53	12(E)
2030	263,626	2.41	12(E)
SEA Niue			
0001	.	.	
1000	.	.	
1500	.	.	
1600	.	.	
1700	.	.	
1820	.	.	
1870	.	.	

Year	Population, '000s	Growth Rate	Source
1880	.	.	
1890	.	.	
1900	.	.	
1913	.	.	
1920	.	.	
1929	.	.	
1938	.	.	
1950	1	.	PROXY(14 Pacific is(Maddison))
1960	1	2.75	INTERPOL(14 Pacific is(Maddison))
1970	1	2.75	INTERPOL(14 Pacific is(Maddison))
1980	2	2.44	INTERPOL(14 Pacific is(Maddison))
1990	2	2.30	90(CIA)
2000	2	0.46	00(CIA)
2010	1	4.35	10(CIA)
2012	1	3.19	12(CIA)
2020	1	4.16	12(EST)
2030	1	4.15	12(EST)
SEA Northern Mariana Islands			
0001	.	.	
1000	.	.	
1500	.	.	
1600	.	.	
1700	.	.	
1820	.	.	
1870	.	.	
1880	.	.	
1890	.	.	
1900	.	.	
1913	.	.	
1920	.	.	
1929	.	.	
1938	.	.	
1950	6	.	50(E)
1960	9	4.14	60(E)
1970	12	2.92	70(E)
1980	17	3.54	80(E)
1990	44	9.98	90(E)
2000	69	4.60	00(E)
2010	54	2.42	10(E)
2012	51	2.73	12(E)
2020	56	1.15	12(E)
2030	64	1.34	12(E)
DME Norway			
0001	100	.	0001(Maddison)
1000	200	0.07	1000(Maddison)
1500	300	0.08	1500(Maddison)

Year	Population, '000s	Growth Rate	Source
1600	400	0.29	1600(Maddison)
1700	500	0.22	1700(Maddison)
1820	970	0.55	1820(Maddison)
1870	1,735	1.17	1870(Maddison)
1880	1,919	1.01	1880(Maddison)
1890	1,997	0.40	1890(Maddison)
1900	2,230	1.11	1900(Maddison)
1913	2,447	0.72	1913(Maddison)
1920	2,625	1.01	1920(Maddison)
1929	2,795	0.70	1929(Maddison)
1938	2,936	0.55	1938(Maddison)
1950	3,265	0.89	50(E)
1960	3,583	0.93	60(E)
1970	3,877	0.79	70(E)
1980	4,086	0.53	80(E)
1990	4,241	0.37	90(E)
2000	4,491	0.57	00(E)
2010	4,914	0.90	10(E)
2012	5,027	1.14	12(E)
2020	5,546	1.24	12(E)
2030	6,075	0.92	12(E)
MEA Oman			
0001	300	.	PROXY(W. Asia(Maddison))
1000	309	0.00	PROXY(W. Asia(Maddison))
1500	275	0.02	PROXY(Arabia(Maddison))
1600	275	0.00	INTERPOL(Maddison)
1700	275	0.00	PROXY(Arabia(Maddison))
1820	318	0.12	1820(Maddison)
1870	367	0.29	1870(Maddison)
1880	384	0.44	INTERPOL(Maddison)
1890	401	0.44	INTERPOL(Maddison)
1900	419	0.44	INTERPOL(Maddison)
1913	444	0.44	1913(Maddison)
1920	446	0.07	INTERPOL(Maddison)
1929	449	0.07	INTERPOL(Maddison)
1938	452	0.07	INTERPOL(Maddison)
1950	456	0.07	50(E)
1960	601	2.80	60(E)
1970	783	2.68	70(E)
1980	1,185	4.23	80(E)
1990	1,794	4.23	90(E)
2000	2,264	2.35	00(E)
2010	2,743	1.94	10(E)
2012	2,879	2.45	12(E)
2020	3,262	1.57	12(E)
2030	3,572	0.91	12(E)
SAS Pakistan			
0001	4,899	.	PROXY(Undivided India(Maddison))
1000	4,899	0.00	PROXY(Undivided India(Maddison))

Year	Population, '000s	Growth Rate	Source
1500	7,185	0.08	PROXY(Undivided India(Maddison))
1600	8,818	0.21	PROXY(Undivided India(Maddison))
1700	10,777	0.20	PROXY(Undivided India(Maddison))
1820	13,651	0.20	1820(Maddison)
1870	16,090	0.33	1870(Maddison)
1880	16,492	0.25	INTERPOL(Pak./wh. India(Maddison))
1890	18,078	0.92	INTERPOL(Pak./wh. India(Maddison))
1900	18,544	0.26	INTERPOL(Pak./wh. India(Maddison))
1913	20,008	0.59	1913(Maddison)
1920	20,477	0.33	INTERPOL(Pak./wh. India(Maddison))
1929	22,812	1.21	1929(Maddison)
1938	26,719	1.77	INTERPOL(Pak./wh. India(Maddison))
1950	39,448	3.30	50(E)
1960	51,719	2.75	60(E)
1970	67,491	2.70	70(E)
1980	85,219	2.36	80(E)
1990	118,816	3.38	90(E)
2000	152,429	2.52	00(E)
2010	184,405	1.92	10(E)
2012	190,248	1.57	12(E)
2020	213,719	1.46	12(E)
2030	242,862	1.29	12(E)

SEA Palau

Year	Population, '000s	Growth Rate	Source
0001	.	.	
1000	.	.	
1500	.	.	
1600	.	.	
1700	.	.	
1820	.	.	
1870	.	.	
1880	.	.	
1890	.	.	
1900	.	.	
1913	.	.	
1920	.	.	
1929	.	.	
1938	.	.	
1950	7	.	50(E)
1960	9	2.54	60(E)
1970	12	2.92	70(E)
1980	13	0.80	80(E)
1990	15	1.44	90(E)
2000	19	2.39	00(E)
2010	21	0.76	10(E)
2012	21	0.65	12(E)
2020	22	0.72	12(E)
2030	23	0.45	12(E)

Year	Population, '000s	Growth Rate	Source
		LAM PANAMA	
0001	36	.	PROXY(Other L. Am.(Maddison))
1000	73	0.07	PROXY(Other L. Am.(Maddison))
1500	106	0.07	PROXY(Other Sp. Am.(Maddison))
1600	64	0.51	PROXY(Other Sp. Am.(Maddison))
1700	72	0.13	PROXY(Other Sp. Am.(Maddison))
1820	94	0.22	PROXY(15 L. American cs(Maddison))
1870	176	1.26	1870(Maddison)
1880	201	1.35	INTERPOL(Maddison)
1890	230	1.35	INTERPOL(Maddison)
1900	263	1.35	1900(Maddison)
1913	348	2.18	1913(Maddison)
1920	487	4.92	1920(Maddison)
1929	506	0.43	1929(Maddison)
1938	640	2.64	1938(Maddison)
1950	893	2.81	50(E)
1960	1,136	2.44	60(E)
1970	1,524	2.98	70(E)
1980	1,982	2.66	80(E)
1990	2,474	2.24	90(E)
2000	3,041	2.08	00(E)
2010	3,662	1.88	10(E)
2012	3,787	1.69	12(E)
2020	4,279	1.54	12(E)
2030	4,835	1.23	12(E)
		SEA PAPUA NEW GUINEA	
0001	.	.	
1000	.	.	
1500	.	.	
1600	.	.	
1700	.	.	
1820	.	.	
1870	.	.	
1880	.	.	
1890	.	.	
1900	.	.	
1913	.	.	
1920	.	.	
1929	.	.	
1938	.	.	
1950	1,485	.	50(EST)
1960	1,718	1.47	60(E)
1970	2,214	2.57	70(E)
1980	2,846	2.54	80(E)
1990	3,683	2.61	90(E)
2000	5,191	3.49	00(E)
2010	6,860	2.83	10(E)

Year	Population, '000s	Growth Rate	Source
2012	7,134	1.98	12(E)
2020	8,584	2.34	12(E)
2030	10,329	1.87	12(E)
		LAM Paraguay	
0001	55	.	PROXY(Other L. Am.(Maddison))
1000	111	0.07	PROXY(Other L. Am.(Maddison))
1500	161	0.07	PROXY(Other Sp. Am.(Maddison))
1600	96	0.51	PROXY(Other Sp. Am.(Maddison))
1700	110	0.13	PROXY(Other Sp. Am.(Maddison))
1820	143	0.22	1820(Maddison)
1870	384	2.00	1870(Maddison)
1880	402	0.45	INTERPOL(Maddison)
1890	420	0.45	INTERPOL(Maddison)
1900	440	0.45	1900(Maddison)
1913	594	2.34	1913(Maddison)
1920	699	2.35	1920(Maddison)
1929	860	2.33	1929(Maddison)
1938	1,061	2.36	1938(Maddison)
1950	1,473	2.77	50(E)
1960	1,910	2.63	60(E)
1970	2,477	2.63	70(E)
1980	3,172	2.50	80(E)
1990	4,200	2.85	90(E)
2000	5,418	2.58	00(E)
2010	6,376	1.64	10(E)
2012	6,540	1.27	12(E)
2020	7,192	1.20	12(E)
2030	7,974	1.04	12(E)
		LAM Peru	
0001	503	.	PROXY(Other L. Am.(Maddison))
1000	1,020	0.07	PROXY(Other L. Am.(Maddison))
1500	1,479	0.07	PROXY(Other Sp. Am.(Maddison))
1600	887	0.51	PROXY(Other Sp. Am.(Maddison))
1700	1,009	0.13	PROXY(Other Sp. Am.(Maddison))
1820	1,317	0.22	1820(Maddison)
1870	2,606	1.37	1870(Maddison)
1880	2,953	1.26	INTERPOL(Maddison)
1890	3,346	1.26	1890(Maddison)
1900	3,791	1.26	1900(Maddison)
1913	4,339	1.04	1913(Maddison)
1920	4,667	1.05	1920(Maddison)
1929	5,294	1.41	1929(Maddison)
1938	6,093	1.57	1938(Maddison)
1950	7,632	1.89	50(E)
1960	9,931	2.67	60(E)
1970	13,193	2.88	70(E)
1980	17,295	2.74	80(E)
1990	21,565	2.23	90(E)
2000	25,797	1.81	00(E)

Year	Population, '000s	Growth Rate	Source
2010	28,948	1.16	10(E)
2012	29,546	1.03	12(E)
2020	31,915	0.97	12(E)
2030	34,444	0.77	12(E)
		SEA Philippines	
0001	152	.	PROXY(Other E. Asia(Maddison))
1000	281	0.06	PROXY(Other E. Asia(Maddison))
1500	500	0.12	1500(Maddison)
1600	791	0.46	INTERPOL(Maddison)
1700	1,250	0.46	1700(Maddison)
1820	2,176	0.46	1820(Maddison)
1870	5,063	1.70	1870(Maddison)
1880	5,726	1.24	INTERPOL(Maddison)
1890	6,476	1.24	1890(Maddison)
1900	7,324	1.24	1900(Maddison)
1913	9,384	1.92	1913(Maddison)
1920	10,725	1.93	1920(Maddison)
1929	12,890	2.06	1929(Maddison)
1938	15,934	2.38	1938(Maddison)
1950	19,996	1.91	50(E)
1960	27,057	3.07	60(E)
1970	36,567	3.06	70(E)
1980	48,112	2.78	80(E)
1990	60,939	2.39	90(E)
2000	76,748	2.33	00(E)
2010	92,628	1.90	10(E)
2012	94,191	0.84	12(E)
2020	106,173	1.51	12(E)
2030	122,212	1.42	12(E)
		EEU Poland	
0001	450	.	0001(Maddison)
1000	1,200	0.10	1000(Maddison)
1500	4,000	0.24	1500(Maddison)
1600	5,000	0.22	1600(Maddison)
1700	6,000	0.18	1700(Maddison)
1820	10,426	0.46	1820(Maddison)
1870	16,865	0.97	1870(Maddison)
1880	19,632	1.53	INTERPOL(Maddison)
1890	22,854	1.53	1890(Maddison)
1900	24,750	0.80	1900(Maddison)
1913	26,710	0.59	1913(Maddison)
1920	23,968	1.54	1920(Maddison)
1929	27,856	1.68	1929(Maddison)
1938	31,062	1.22	1938(Maddison)
1950	24,824	1.85	50(E)
1960	29,561	1.76	60(E)
1970	32,526	0.96	70(E)
1980	35,578	0.90	80(E)
1990	38,031	0.67	90(E)

Year	Population, '000s	Growth Rate	Source
2000	38,230	0.05	00(E)
2010	38,456	0.06	10(E)
2012	38,513	0.07	12(E)
2020	38,703	0.06	12(E)
2030	37,866	0.22	12(E)
DME Portugal			
0001	400	.	0001(Maddison)
1000	600	0.04	1000(Maddison)
1500	1,000	0.10	1500(Maddison)
1600	1,100	0.10	1600(Maddison)
1700	2,000	0.60	1700(Maddison)
1820	3,297	0.42	1820(Maddison)
1870	4,327	0.55	1870(Maddison)
1880	4,610	0.64	1880(Maddison)
1890	5,028	0.87	1890(Maddison)
1900	5,404	0.72	1900(Maddison)
1913	5,972	0.77	1913(Maddison)
1920	6,029	0.14	1920(Maddison)
1929	6,701	1.18	1929(Maddison)
1938	7,488	1.24	1938(Maddison)
1950	8,443	1.01	50(E)
1960	9,037	0.68	60(E)
1970	9,044	0.01	70(E)
1980	9,778	0.78	80(E)
1990	9,923	0.15	90(E)
2000	10,235	0.31	00(E)
2010	10,547	0.30	10(E)
2012	10,589	0.20	12(E)
2020	10,672	0.10	12(E)
2030	10,724	0.05	12(E)
LAM Puerto Rico			
0001	14	.	PROXY(Other L. Am.(Maddison))
1000	29	0.07	PROXY(Other L. Am.(Maddison))
1500	42	0.07	PROXY(Caribbean cs(Maddison))
1600	17	0.91	PROXY(Caribbean cs(Maddison))
1700	42	0.92	PROXY(Caribbean cs(Maddison))
1820	248	1.48	1820(Maddison)
1870	645	1.93	1870(Maddison)
1880	736	1.33	INTERPOL(Maddison)
1890	840	1.33	INTERPOL(Maddison)
1900	959	1.33	1900(Maddison)
1913	1,181	1.61	1913(Maddison)
1920	1,312	1.51	1920(Maddison)
1929	1,526	1.69	1929(Maddison)
1938	1,810	1.91	1938(Maddison)
1950	2,218	1.71	50(E)
1960	2,358	0.61	60(E)
1970	2,722	1.45	70(E)
1980	3,210	1.66	80(E)

Year	Population, '000s	Growth Rate	Source
1990	3,537	0.97	90(E)
2000	3,811	0.75	00(E)
2010	3,722	0.24	10(E)
2012	3,690	0.43	12(E)
2020	3,528	0.56	12(E)
2030	3,220	0.91	12(E)
		MEA QATAR	
0001	13	.	PROXY(W. Asia(Maddison))
1000	14	0.00	PROXY(W. Asia(Maddison))
1500	12	0.02	PROXY(Arabia(Maddison))
1600	12	0.00	INTERPOL(Maddison)
1700	12	0.00	PROXY(Arabia(Maddison))
1820	14	0.12	PROXY(Gulf Coast(Maddison))
1870	14	0.00	PROXY(Gulf Coast(Maddison))
1880	15	0.56	INTERPOL(Maddison)
1890	16	0.56	INTERPOL(Maddison)
1900	17	0.56	INTERPOL(Maddison)
1913	18	0.56	PROXY(Gulf Coast(Maddison))
1920	19	0.89	INTERPOL(Maddison)
1929	21	0.89	INTERPOL(Maddison)
1938	22	0.89	INTERPOL(Maddison)
1950	25	0.89	50(E)
1960	45	6.05	60(E)
1970	111	9.45	70(E)
1980	229	7.51	80(E)
1990	467	7.39	90(E)
2000	591	2.38	00(E)
2010	1,674	10.97	10(E)
2012	1,879	5.95	12(E)
2020	2,215	2.08	12(E)
2030	2,388	0.75	12(E)
		AFR REUNION	
0001	.	.	
1000	.	.	
1500	.	.	
1600	.	.	
1700	.	.	
1820	.	.	
1870	.	.	
1880	.	.	
1890	.	.	
1900	.	.	
1913	.	.	
1920	.	.	
1929	.	.	
1938	.	.	
1950	244	.	50(E)

Year	Population, '000s	Growth Rate	Source
1960	338	3.31	60(E)
1970	447	2.83	70(E)
1980	507	1.27	80(E)
1990	601	1.72	90(E)
2000	723	1.87	00(E)
2010	825	1.33	10(E)
2012	842	1.04	12(E)
2020	910	0.97	12(E)
2030	978	0.72	12(E)
EEU Romania			
0001	800	.	0001(Maddison)
1000	800	0.00	1000(Maddison)
1500	2,000	0.18	1500(Maddison)
1600	2,000	0.00	1600(Maddison)
1700	2,500	0.22	1700(Maddison)
1820	6,389	0.78	1820(Maddison)
1870	9,179	0.73	1870(Maddison)
1880	9,758	0.61	INTERPOL(Maddison)
1890	10,373	0.61	1890(Maddison)
1900	11,000	0.59	1900(Maddison)
1913	12,527	1.00	1913(Maddison)
1920	12,340	0.21	1920(Maddison)
1929	13,952	1.37	1929(Maddison)
1938	15,601	1.25	1938(Maddison)
1950	16,311	0.37	50(E)
1960	18,407	1.22	60(E)
1970	20,253	0.96	70(E)
1980	22,201	0.92	80(E)
1990	23,207	0.44	90(E)
2000	22,435	0.34	00(E)
2010	20,327	0.98	10(E)
2012	19,910	1.03	12(E)
2020	19,502	0.26	12(E)
2030	18,588	0.48	12(E)
USR Russia			
0001	1,409	.	PROXY(40(E)/Eu. Rs./Sb.(Maddison))
1000	2,750	0.07	PROXY(40(E)/Eu. Rs./Sb.(Maddison))
1500	8,183	0.22	PROXY(40(E)/Eu. Rs./Sb.(Maddison))
1600	10,195	0.22	PROXY(40(E)/Eu. Rs./Sb.(Maddison))
1700	13,616	0.29	PROXY(40(E)/Eu. Rs./Sb.(Maddison))
1820	30,588	0.68	PROXY(40(E)/Eu. Rs./Sb.(Maddison))
1870	50,303	1.00	PROXY(40(E)/USSR(Maddison))
1880	56,196	1.11	40(E)/INTERPOL(Maddison)
1890	62,779	1.11	PROXY(40(E)/USSR(Maddison))
1900	70,628	1.19	PROXY(40(E)/USSR(Maddison))
1913	88,606	1.76	PROXY(40(E)/USSR(Maddison))
1920	87,707	0.15	PROXY(40(E)/USSR(Maddison))
1929	97,584	1.19	PROXY(40(E)/USSR(Maddison))
1938	106,933	1.02	PROXY(40(E)/USSR(Maddison))

Year	Population, '000s	Growth Rate	Source
1950	101,937	0.40	50(E)
1960	119,906	1.64	60(E)
1970	130,392	0.84	70(E)
1980	138,655	0.62	80(E)
1990	148,244	0.67	90(E)
2000	146,670	0.11	00(E)
2010	142,939	0.26	10(E)
2012	143,182	0.09	12(E)
2020	141,760	0.12	12(E)
2030	137,142	0.33	12(E)
AFR Rwanda			
0001	.	.	
1000	.	.	
1500	.	.	
1600	.	.	
1700	.	.	
1820	.	.	
1870	.	.	
1880	.	.	
1890	.	.	
1900	.	.	
1913	.	.	
1920	.	.	
1929	.	.	
1938	.	.	
1950	2,162	.	50(E)
1960	2,771	2.51	60(E)
1970	3,749	3.07	70(E)
1980	5,179	3.28	80(E)
1990	7,110	3.22	90(E)
2000	8,098	1.31	00(E)
2010	9,971	2.10	10(E)
2012	10,501	2.62	12(E)
2020	13,037	2.74	12(E)
2030	16,321	2.27	12(E)
AFR Saint Helena			
0001	.	.	
1000	.	.	
1500	.	.	
1600	.	.	
1700	.	.	
1820	.	.	
1870	.	.	
1880	.	.	
1890	.	.	
1900	.	.	

Year	Population, '000s	Growth Rate	Source
1913	.	.	
1920	.	.	
1929	.	.	
1938	.	.	
1950	7	.	PROXY(Falkland Islands(E))
1960	7	0.00	PROXY(Falkland Islands(E))
1970	7	0.00	PROXY(Falkland Islands(E))
1980	7	0.00	PROXY(Falkland Islands(E))
1990	7	0.00	90(CIA)
2000	7	0.80	00(CIA)
2010	8	0.62	10(CIA)
2012	8	0.38	12(CIA)
2020	8	0.58	12(EST)
2030	9	0.58	12(EST)
LAM Saint Kitts and Nevis			
0001	.	.	
1000	.	.	
1500	.	.	
1600	.	.	
1700	.	.	
1820	.	.	
1870	.	.	
1880	.	.	
1890	.	.	
1900	.	.	
1913	.	.	
1920	.	.	
1929	.	.	
1938	.	.	
1950	49	.	50(E)
1960	51	0.40	60(E)
1970	46	1.03	70(E)
1980	44	0.44	80(E)
1990	42	0.46	90(E)
2000	46	0.91	00(E)
2010	50	0.84	10(E)
2012	51	0.73	12(E)
2020	54	0.78	12(E)
2030	57	0.54	12(E)
LAM Saint Lucia			
0001	.	.	
1000	.	.	
1500	.	.	
1600	.	.	
1700	.	.	
1820	.	.	

Year	Population, '000s	Growth Rate	Source
1870	.	.	
1880	.	.	
1890	.	.	
1900	.	.	
1913	.	.	
1920	.	.	
1929	.	.	
1938	.	.	
1950	83	.	50(E)
1960	90	0.81	60(E)
1970	104	1.46	70(E)
1980	118	1.27	80(E)
1990	138	1.58	90(E)
2000	157	1.30	00(E)
2010	166	0.56	10(E)
2012	169	0.99	12(E)
2020	186	1.18	12(E)
2030	196	0.53	12(E)
LAM Saint Martin			
0001	.	.	
1000	.	.	
1500	.	.	
1600	.	.	
1700	.	.	
1820	.	.	
1870	.	.	
1880	.	.	
1890	.	.	
1900	.	.	
1913	.	.	
1920	.	.	
1929	.	.	
1938	.	.	
1950	4	.	60(WB)WEIGHT(Neth Antilles(50(E)))
1960	4	1.96	60(WB)
1970	5	2.45	70(WB)
1980	8	3.35	80(WB)
1990	30	14.76	90(WB)
2000	28	0.56	00(WB)
2010	30	0.63	10(WB)
2012	31	1.19	12(WB)
2020	33	0.73	12(EST)
2030	35	0.73	12(EST)
DME Saint Pierre and Miquelon			
0001	.	.	
1000	.	.	

Year	Population, '000s	Growth Rate	Source
1500	.	.	
1600	.	.	
1700	.	.	
1820	.	.	
1870	.	.	
1880	.	.	
1890	.	.	
1900	.	.	
1913	.	.	
1920	.	.	
1929	.	.	
1938	.	.	
1950	3	.	PROXY(8 Caribbean cs(Maddison))
1960	4	2.29	INTERPOL(8 Caribbean cs(Maddison))
1970	5	2.29	INTERPOL(8 Caribbean cs(Maddison))
1980	6	1.67	INTERPOL(8 Caribbean cs(Maddison))
1990	6	1.41	90(CIA)
2000	7	0.86	00(CIA)
2010	6	1.37	10(CIA)
2012	6	1.50	12(CIA)
2020	5	1.39	12(EST)
2030	5	1.39	12(EST)
LAM Saint Vincent and the Grenadines			
0001	.	.	
1000	.	.	
1500	.	.	
1600	.	.	
1700	.	.	
1820	.	.	
1870	.	.	
1880	.	.	
1890	.	.	
1900	.	.	
1913	.	.	
1920	.	.	
1929	.	.	
1938	.	.	
1950	67	.	50(E)
1960	81	1.92	60(E)
1970	88	0.83	70(E)
1980	98	1.08	80(E)
1990	107	0.88	90(E)
2000	110	0.28	00(E)
2010	101	0.85	10(E)
2012	103	0.98	12(E)
2020	105	0.24	12(E)

Year	Population, '000s	Growth Rate	Source
2030	106	0.09	12(E)
	SEA Samoa		
0001	.	.	
1000	.	.	
1500	.	.	
1600	.	.	
1700	.	.	
1820	.	.	
1870	.	.	
1880	.	.	
1890	.	.	
1900	.	.	
1913	.	.	
1920	.	.	
1929	.	.	
1938	.	.	
1950	82	.	50(E)
1960	110	2.98	60(E)
1970	142	2.59	70(E)
1980	155	0.88	80(E)
1990	161	0.38	90(E)
2000	175	0.84	00(E)
2010	186	0.61	10(E)
2012	189	0.71	12(E)
2020	194	0.35	12(E)
2030	204	0.50	12(E)
	SEA Samoa, American		
0001	.	.	
1000	.	.	
1500	.	.	
1600	.	.	
1700	.	.	
1820	.	.	
1870	.	.	
1880	.	.	
1890	.	.	
1900	.	.	
1913	.	.	
1920	.	.	
1929	.	.	
1938	.	.	
1950	19	.	50(E)
1960	20	0.51	60(E)
1970	27	3.05	70(E)
1980	32	1.71	80(E)

Year	Population, '000s	Growth Rate	Source
1990	47	3.92	90(E)
2000	57	1.95	00(E)
2010	55	0.36	10(E)
2012	55	0.18	12(E)
2020	54	0.18	12(E)
2030	52	0.38	12(E)
DME San Marino			
0001	.	.	
1000	.	.	
1500	.	.	
1600	.	.	
1700	.	.	
1820	.	.	
1870	.	.	
1880	.	.	
1890	.	.	
1900	.	.	
1913	.	.	
1920	.	.	
1929	.	.	
1938	.	.	
1950	13	.	50(E)
1960	15	1.44	60(E)
1970	19	2.39	70(E)
1980	21	1.01	80(E)
1990	24	1.34	90(E)
2000	27	1.18	00(E)
2010	32	1.71	10(E)
2012	32	0.62	12(E)
2020	33	0.23	12(E)
2030	34	0.30	12(E)
AFR Sao Tome and Principe			
0001	.	.	
1000	.	.	
1500	.	.	
1600	.	.	
1700	.	.	
1820	.	.	
1870	.	.	
1880	.	.	
1890	.	.	
1900	.	.	
1913	.	.	
1920	.	.	
1929	.	.	

Year	Population, '000s	Growth Rate	Source
1938	.	.	
1950	60	.	50(E)
1960	64	0.65	60(E)
1970	74	1.46	70(E)
1980	95	2.53	80(E)
1990	116	2.02	90(E)
2000	141	1.97	00(E)
2010	178	2.36	10(E)
2012	189	2.91	12(E)
2020	221	2.01	12(E)
2030	260	1.64	12(E)
	MEA Saudi Arabia		
0001	1,971	.	PROXY(W. Asia(Maddison))
1000	2,032	0.00	PROXY(W. Asia(Maddison))
1500	1,809	0.02	PROXY(Arabia(Maddison))
1600	1,809	0.00	INTERPOL(Maddison)
1700	1,809	0.00	PROXY(Arabia(Maddison))
1820	2,091	0.12	1820(Maddison)
1870	2,338	0.22	1870(Maddison)
1880	2,413	0.31	INTERPOL(Maddison)
1890	2,490	0.31	INTERPOL(Maddison)
1900	2,569	0.31	INTERPOL(Maddison)
1913	2,676	0.31	1913(Maddison)
1920	2,768	0.49	INTERPOL(Maddison)
1929	2,892	0.49	INTERPOL(Maddison)
1938	3,020	0.49	INTERPOL(Maddison)
1950	3,201	0.49	50(E)
1960	4,718	3.96	60(E)
1970	6,109	2.62	70(E)
1980	10,022	5.07	80(E)
1990	16,061	4.83	90(E)
2000	21,312	2.87	00(E)
2010	27,287	2.50	10(E)
2012	29,088	3.25	12(E)
2020	32,689	1.47	12(E)
2030	37,081	1.27	12(E)
	AFR Senegal		
0001	.	.	
1000	.	.	
1500	.	.	
1600	.	.	
1700	.	.	
1820	.	.	
1870	.	.	
1880	.	.	
1890	.	.	
1900	.	.	
1913	.	.	

Year	Population, '000s	Growth Rate	Source
1920	.	.	
1929	.	.	
1938	.	.	
1950	2,543	.	50(E)
1960	3,270	2.55	60(E)
1970	4,318	2.82	70(E)
1980	5,611	2.65	80(E)
1990	7,348	2.73	90(E)
2000	9,469	2.57	00(E)
2010	12,323	2.67	10(E)
2012	12,966	2.58	12(E)
2020	15,736	2.45	12(E)
2030	19,485	2.16	12(E)
		EEU Serbia	
0001	540	.	PROXY(Yugoslavia(Maddison))
1000	630	0.02	PROXY(Yugoslavia(Maddison))
1500	810	0.05	PROXY(Yugoslavia(Maddison))
1600	990	0.20	PROXY(Yugoslavia(Maddison))
1700	990	0.00	PROXY(Yugoslavia(Maddison))
1820	1,878	0.53	PROXY(Yugoslavia(Maddison))
1870	2,972	0.92	PROXY(Yugoslavia(Maddison))
1880	3,220	0.81	INTERPOL(Maddison)
1890	3,489	0.81	PROXY(Yugoslavia(Maddison))
1900	4,024	1.44	PROXY(Yugoslavia(Maddison))
1913	4,894	1.52	PROXY(Yugoslavia(Maddison))
1920	4,473	1.28	PROXY(Yugoslavia(Maddison))
1929	5,111	1.49	PROXY(Yugoslavia(Maddison))
1938	5,792	1.40	PROXY(Yugoslavia(Maddison))
1950	5,869	0.11	50(E)
1960	6,659	1.27	60(E)
1970	7,248	0.85	70(E)
1980	7,588	0.46	80(E)
1990	7,786	0.26	90(E)
2000	7,516	0.35	00(E)
2010	7,227	0.39	10(E)
2012	7,163	0.44	12(E)
2020	6,904	0.46	12(E)
2030	6,569	0.50	12(E)
		AFR Seychelles	
0001	.	.	
1000	.	.	
1500	.	.	
1600	.	.	
1700	.	.	
1820	.	.	
1870	.	.	
1880	.	.	
1890	.	.	

Year	Population, '000s	Growth Rate	Source
1900	.	.	
1913	.	.	
1920	.	.	
1929	.	.	
1938	.	.	
1950	34	.	50(E)
1960	41	1.89	60(E)
1970	52	2.41	70(E)
1980	63	1.94	80(E)
1990	71	1.20	90(E)
2000	80	1.20	00(E)
2010	91	1.30	10(E)
2012	88	1.52	12(E)
2020	96	1.06	12(E)
2030	98	0.21	12(E)
	AFR Sierra Leone		
0001	100	.	PROXY(Other W. Africa(Maddison))
1000	234	0.08	PROXY(Other W. Africa(Maddison))
1500	367	0.09	PROXY(Other W. Africa(Maddison))
1600	468	0.24	PROXY(Other W. Africa(Maddison))
1700	601	0.25	PROXY(Other W. Africa(Maddison))
1820	694	0.12	PROXY(Other W. Africa(Maddison))
1870	1,031	0.80	INTERPOL(Maddison)
1880	1,116	0.80	INTERPOL(Maddison)
1890	1,208	0.80	INTERPOL(Maddison)
1900	1,308	0.80	INTERPOL(Maddison)
1913	1,450	0.80	INTERPOL(Maddison)
1920	1,533	0.80	INTERPOL(Maddison)
1929	1,646	0.80	INTERPOL(Maddison)
1938	1,768	0.80	INTERPOL(Maddison)
1950	1,944	0.80	50(E)
1960	2,187	1.18	60(E)
1970	2,593	1.72	70(E)
1980	3,162	2.00	80(E)
1990	3,982	2.33	90(E)
2000	4,143	0.40	00(E)
2010	5,868	3.54	10(E)
2012	6,123	2.15	12(E)
2020	7,178	2.01	12(E)
2030	8,532	1.74	12(E)
	SEA Singapore		
0001	1	.	PROXY(Other E. Asia(Maddison))
1000	2	0.06	PROXY(Other E. Asia(Maddison))
1500	3	0.12	PROXY(Other E. Asia(Maddison))
1600	3	0.15	PROXY(Other E. Asia(Maddison))
1700	4	0.15	PROXY(Other E. Asia(Maddison))
1820	5	0.20	1820(Maddison)
1870	84	5.80	1870(Maddison)
1880	115	3.18	INTERPOL(Maddison)

Year	Population, '000s	Growth Rate	Source
1890	157	3.18	1890(Maddison)
1900	215	3.19	1900(Maddison)
1913	323	3.18	1913(Maddison)
1920	391	2.77	1920(Maddison)
1929	575	4.38	1929(Maddison)
1938	710	2.37	1938(Maddison)
1950	1,022	3.08	50(E)
1960	1,634	4.80	60(E)
1970	2,074	2.41	70(E)
1980	2,415	1.53	80(E)
1990	3,017	2.25	90(E)
2000	4,028	2.93	00(E)
2010	5,077	2.34	10(E)
2012	5,319	2.35	12(E)
2020	6,191	1.92	12(E)
2030	7,201	1.52	12(E)
	LAM SINT MAARTEN		
0001	.	.	
1000	.	.	
1500	.	.	
1600	.	.	
1700	.	.	
1820	.	.	
1870	.	.	
1880	.	.	
1890	.	.	
1900	.	.	
1913	.	.	
1920	.	.	
1929	.	.	
1938	.	.	
1950	2	.	60(E)WEIGHT(Neth Antilles(50(E)))
1960	3	1.96	60(E)
1970	6	9.13	70(E)
1980	12	6.72	80(E)
1990	29	8.96	90(E)
2000	31	0.41	00(E)
2010	38	2.21	10(E)
2012	39	0.70	12(E)
2020	41	0.71	12(E)
2030	43	0.43	12(E)
	EEU SLOVAKIA		
0001	280	.	PROXY(Czechoslovakia(Maddison))
1000	349	0.02	PROXY(Czechoslovakia(Maddison))
1500	839	0.18	PROXY(Czechoslovakia(Maddison))
1600	1,258	0.41	PROXY(Czechoslovakia(Maddison))
1700	1,258	0.00	PROXY(Czechoslovakia(Maddison))

Year	Population, '000s	Growth Rate	Source
1820	2,140	0.44	PROXY(Czechoslovakia(Maddison))
1870	2,839	0.57	PROXY(Czechoslovakia(Maddison))
1880	2,988	0.51	INTERPOL(Maddison)
1890	3,145	0.51	PROXY(Czechoslovakia(Maddison))
1900	3,394	0.76	PROXY(Czechoslovakia(Maddison))
1913	3,702	0.67	PROXY(Czechoslovakia(Maddison))
1920	3,628	0.29	PROXY(Czechoslovakia(Maddison))
1929	3,881	0.75	PROXY(Czechoslovakia(Maddison))
1938	4,082	0.56	PROXY(Czechoslovakia(Maddison))
1950	3,463	1.36	50(E)
1960	4,145	1.81	60(E)
1970	4,528	0.89	70(E)
1980	4,976	0.95	80(E)
1990	5,256	0.55	90(E)
2000	5,401	0.27	00(E)
2010	5,379	0.04	10(E)
2012	5,408	0.27	12(E)
2020	5,513	0.24	12(E)
2030	5,516	0.01	12(E)

EEU Slovenia

Year	Population, '000s	Growth Rate	Source
0001	135	.	PROXY(Yugoslavia(Maddison))
1000	158	0.02	PROXY(Yugoslavia(Maddison))
1500	203	0.05	PROXY(Yugoslavia(Maddison))
1600	248	0.20	PROXY(Yugoslavia(Maddison))
1700	248	0.00	PROXY(Yugoslavia(Maddison))
1820	469	0.53	PROXY(Yugoslavia(Maddison))
1870	743	0.92	PROXY(Yugoslavia(Maddison))
1880	805	0.81	INTERPOL(Maddison)
1890	872	0.81	PROXY(Yugoslavia(Maddison))
1900	1,006	1.44	PROXY(Yugoslavia(Maddison))
1913	1,223	1.52	PROXY(Yugoslavia(Maddison))
1920	1,118	1.28	PROXY(Yugoslavia(Maddison))
1929	1,278	1.49	PROXY(Yugoslavia(Maddison))
1938	1,448	1.40	PROXY(Yugoslavia(Maddison))
1950	1,467	0.11	50(E)
1960	1,580	0.74	60(E)
1970	1,670	0.56	70(E)
1980	1,832	0.93	80(E)
1990	1,927	0.51	90(E)
2000	1,985	0.30	00(E)
2010	2,049	0.32	10(E)
2012	2,056	0.18	12(E)
2020	2,110	0.32	12(E)
2030	2,122	0.06	12(E)

SEA Solomon Islands

Year	Population, '000s	Growth Rate	Source
0001	.	.	
1000	.	.	
1500	.	.	
1600	.	.	

Year	Population, '000s	Growth Rate	Source
1700	.	.	
1820	.	.	
1870	.	.	
1880	.	.	
1890	.	.	
1900	.	.	
1913	.	.	
1920	.	.	
1929	.	.	
1938	.	.	
1950	90	.	50(E)
1960	118	2.75	60(E)
1970	160	3.09	70(E)
1980	229	3.65	80(E)
1990	310	3.07	90(E)
2000	415	2.96	00(E)
2010	530	2.48	10(E)
2012	578	4.45	12(E)
2020	685	2.14	12(E)
2030	846	2.13	12(E)
		AFR Somalia	
0001	200	.	0001(Maddison)
1000	400	0.07	1000(Maddison)
1500	800	0.14	1500(Maddison)
1600	800	0.00	1600(Maddison)
1700	950	0.17	1700(Maddison)
1820	1,000	0.04	1820(Maddison)
1870	1,369	0.63	INTERPOL(Maddison)
1880	1,458	0.63	INTERPOL(Maddison)
1890	1,553	0.63	INTERPOL(Maddison)
1900	1,653	0.63	INTERPOL(Maddison)
1913	1,794	0.63	INTERPOL(Maddison)
1920	1,875	0.63	INTERPOL(Maddison)
1929	1,984	0.63	INTERPOL(Maddison)
1938	2,100	0.63	INTERPOL(Maddison)
1950	2,264	0.63	50(E)
1960	2,956	2.70	60(E)
1970	3,667	2.18	70(E)
1980	5,794	4.68	80(E)
1990	6,692	1.45	90(E)
2000	7,501	1.15	00(E)
2010	9,768	2.68	10(E)
2012	10,088	1.63	12(E)
2020	11,757	1.93	12(E)
2030	15,041	2.49	12(E)
		AFR South Africa	
0001	93	.	PROXY(S. Afr., Sw., Ls.(Maddison))
1000	279	0.11	PROXY(S. Afr., Sw., Ls.(Maddison))

Year	Population, '000s	Growth Rate	Source
1500	559	0.14	PROXY(S. Afr., Sw., Ls.(Maddison))
1600	652	0.15	PROXY(S. Afr., Sw., Ls.(Maddison))
1700	931	0.36	PROXY(S. Afr., Sw., Ls.(Maddison))
1820	1,444	0.37	PROXY(S. Afr., Sw., Ls.(Maddison))
1870	2,547	1.14	1870(Maddison)
1880	3,127	2.07	INTERPOL(Maddison)
1890	3,839	2.07	INTERPOL(Maddison)
1900	4,713	2.07	INTERPOL(Maddison)
1913	6,153	2.07	1913(Maddison)
1920	7,157	2.18	INTERPOL(Maddison)
1929	8,693	2.18	INTERPOL(Maddison)
1938	10,559	2.18	INTERPOL(Maddison)
1950	13,596	2.13	50(E)
1960	17,396	2.50	60(E)
1970	22,502	2.61	70(E)
1980	29,075	2.60	80(E)
1990	36,745	2.37	90(E)
2000	44,872	2.02	00(E)
2010	50,824	1.25	10(E)
2012	52,311	1.45	12(E)
2020	54,728	0.57	12(E)
2030	56,953	0.40	12(E)
		AFR South Sudan	
0001	346	.	PROXY(0001(Maddison))
1000	519	0.04	PROXY(1000(Maddison))
1500	692	0.06	PROXY(1500(Maddison))
1600	726	0.05	PROXY(1600(Maddison))
1700	761	0.05	PROXY(1700(Maddison))
1820	891	0.13	PROXY(1820(Maddison))
1870	1,058	0.34	INTERPOL(Maddison)
1880	1,095	0.34	INTERPOL(Maddison)
1890	1,133	0.34	INTERPOL(Maddison)
1900	1,173	0.34	INTERPOL(Maddison)
1913	1,226	0.34	INTERPOL(Maddison)
1920	1,256	0.34	INTERPOL(Maddison)
1929	1,295	0.34	INTERPOL(Maddison)
1938	1,336	0.34	INTERPOL(Maddison)
1950	1,589	1.46	PROXY(Sudan+S.Sudan)
1960	1,831	1.43	PROXY(Sudan+S.Sudan)
1970	2,384	2.67	PROXY(Sudan+S.Sudan)
1980	3,368	3.52	PROXY(Sudan+S.Sudan)
1990	4,476	2.88	PROXY(Sudan+S.Sudan)
2000	6,296	3.47	00(E)
2010	9,584	4.29	10(E)
2012	10,563	4.99	12(E)
2020	14,558	4.09	12(E)
2030	18,682	2.53	12(E)
		DME Spain	
0001	3,750	.	0001(Maddison)

Year	Population, '000s	Growth Rate	Source
1000	4,000	0.01	1000(Maddison)
1500	6,800	0.11	1500(Maddison)
1600	8,240	0.19	1600(Maddison)
1700	8,770	0.06	1700(Maddison)
1820	12,203	0.28	1820(Maddison)
1870	16,201	0.57	1870(Maddison)
1880	16,859	0.40	1880(Maddison)
1890	17,757	0.52	1890(Maddison)
1900	18,566	0.45	1900(Maddison)
1913	20,263	0.68	1913(Maddison)
1920	21,232	0.67	1920(Maddison)
1929	23,210	0.99	1929(Maddison)
1938	25,279	0.95	1938(Maddison)
1950	27,868	0.82	50(E)
1960	30,641	0.95	60(E)
1970	33,876	1.01	70(E)
1980	37,488	1.02	80(E)
1990	39,351	0.49	90(E)
2000	40,589	0.31	00(E)
2010	45,968	1.25	10(E)
2012	47,239	1.37	12(E)
2020	49,378	0.56	12(E)
2030	51,437	0.41	12(E)
		SAS Sri Lanka	
0001	303	.	PROXY(Other E. Asia(Maddison))
1000	561	0.06	PROXY(Other E. Asia(Maddison))
1500	1,000	0.12	1500(Maddison)
1600	1,095	0.09	INTERPOL(Maddison)
1700	1,200	0.09	1700(Maddison)
1820	1,213	0.01	1820(Maddison)
1870	2,786	1.68	1870(Maddison)
1880	3,021	0.81	1880(Maddison)
1890	3,343	1.02	1890(Maddison)
1900	3,912	1.58	1900(Maddison)
1913	4,811	1.60	1913(Maddison)
1920	5,250	1.26	1920(Maddison)
1929	5,669	0.86	1929(Maddison)
1938	6,045	0.72	1938(Maddison)
1950	7,339	1.63	50(E)
1960	10,020	3.16	60(E)
1970	12,555	2.28	70(E)
1980	15,083	1.85	80(E)
1990	17,337	1.40	90(E)
2000	18,745	0.78	00(E)
2010	20,032	0.67	10(E)
2012	20,318	0.71	12(E)
2020	21,699	0.83	12(E)
2030	22,865	0.52	12(E)

Year	Population, '000s	Growth Rate	Source
		AFR Sudan	
0001	1,654	.	PROXY(0001(Maddison))
1000	2,481	0.04	PROXY(1000(Maddison))
1500	3,308	0.06	PROXY(1500(Maddison))
1600	3,474	0.05	PROXY(1600(Maddison))
1700	3,639	0.05	PROXY(1700(Maddison))
1820	4,265	0.13	PROXY(1820(Maddison))
1870	5,062	0.34	INTERPOL(Maddison)
1880	5,238	0.34	INTERPOL(Maddison)
1890	5,421	0.34	INTERPOL(Maddison)
1900	5,610	0.34	INTERPOL(Maddison)
1913	5,866	0.34	INTERPOL(Maddison)
1920	6,008	0.34	INTERPOL(Maddison)
1929	6,197	0.34	INTERPOL(Maddison)
1938	6,391	0.34	INTERPOL(Maddison)
1950	7,601	1.46	PROXY(Sudan+S.Sudan)
1960	8,758	1.43	PROXY(Sudan+S.Sudan)
1970	11,404	2.67	PROXY(Sudan+S.Sudan)
1980	16,114	3.52	PROXY(Sudan+S.Sudan)
1990	21,412	2.88	PROXY(Sudan+S.Sudan)
2000	27,067	2.37	00(E)
2010	32,997	2.00	10(E)
2012	34,220	1.84	12(E)
2020	39,161	1.70	12(E)
2030	46,338	1.70	12(E)
		LAM Suriname	
0001	.	.	
1000	.	.	
1500	.	.	
1600	.	.	
1700	.	.	
1820	.	.	
1870	.	.	
1880	.	.	
1890	.	.	
1900	.	.	
1913	.	.	
1920	.	.	
1929	.	.	
1938	.	.	
1950	215	.	50(E)
1960	290	3.04	60(E)
1970	372	2.52	70(E)
1980	366	0.16	80(E)
1990	407	1.07	90(E)
2000	467	1.38	00(E)
2010	531	1.29	10(E)

Year	Population, '000s	Growth Rate	Source
2012	547	1.48	12(E)
2020	584	0.82	12(E)
2030	618	0.57	12(E)
		DME Svalbard	
0001	.	.	
1000	.	.	
1500	.	.	
1600	.	.	
1700	.	.	
1820	.	.	
1870	.	.	
1880	.	.	
1890	.	.	
1900	.	.	
1913	.	.	
1920	.	.	
1929	.	.	
1938	.	.	
1950	3	.	PROXY(Norway(E))
1960	3	0.93	PROXY(Norway(E))
1970	4	0.79	PROXY(Norway(E))
1980	4	0.53	PROXY(Norway(E))
1990	4	0.37	90(CIA)
2000	2	4.78	00(CIA)
2010	2	1.55	10(CIA)
2012	2	2.37	12(CIA)
2020	2	1.30	PROXY(Norway(E))
2030	2	0.92	PROXY(Norway(E))
		AFR Swaziland	
0001	2	.	PROXY(S. Afr., Sw., Ls.(Maddison))
1000	6	0.11	PROXY(S. Afr., Sw., Ls.(Maddison))
1500	11	0.14	PROXY(S. Afr., Sw., Ls.(Maddison))
1600	13	0.15	PROXY(S. Afr., Sw., Ls.(Maddison))
1700	19	0.36	PROXY(S. Afr., Sw., Ls.(Maddison))
1820	29	0.37	PROXY(S. Afr., Sw., Ls.(Maddison))
1870	68	1.74	INTERPOL(Maddison)
1880	81	1.75	INTERPOL(Maddison)
1890	97	1.75	INTERPOL(Maddison)
1900	115	1.74	INTERPOL(Maddison)
1913	144	1.75	INTERPOL(Maddison)
1920	162	1.74	INTERPOL(Maddison)
1929	190	1.75	INTERPOL(Maddison)
1938	222	1.74	INTERPOL(Maddison)
1950	273	1.74	50(E)
1960	349	2.49	60(E)
1970	446	2.48	70(E)
1980	603	3.06	80(E)

Year	Population, '000s	Growth Rate	Source
1990	863	3.65	90(E)
2000	1,064	2.12	00(E)
2010	1,186	1.09	10(E)
2012	1,220	1.41	12(E)
2020	1,341	1.19	12(E)
2030	1,462	0.87	12(E)
DME Sweden			
0001	200	.	0001(Maddison)
1000	400	0.07	1000(Maddison)
1500	550	0.06	1500(Maddison)
1600	760	0.32	1600(Maddison)
1700	1,260	0.51	1700(Maddison)
1820	2,585	0.60	1820(Maddison)
1870	4,169	0.96	1870(Maddison)
1880	4,572	0.93	1880(Maddison)
1890	4,780	0.45	1890(Maddison)
1900	5,117	0.68	1900(Maddison)
1913	5,621	0.73	1913(Maddison)
1920	5,876	0.64	1920(Maddison)
1929	6,113	0.44	1929(Maddison)
1938	6,298	0.33	1938(Maddison)
1950	7,014	0.90	50(E)
1960	7,498	0.67	60(E)
1970	8,042	0.70	70(E)
1980	8,310	0.33	80(E)
1990	8,559	0.30	90(E)
2000	8,872	0.36	00(E)
2010	9,378	0.56	10(E)
2012	9,520	0.75	12(E)
2020	10,137	0.79	12(E)
2030	10,594	0.44	12(E)
DME Switzerland			
0001	300	.	0001(Maddison)
1000	300	0.00	1000(Maddison)
1500	650	0.15	1500(Maddison)
1600	1,000	0.43	1600(Maddison)
1700	1,200	0.18	1700(Maddison)
1820	1,986	0.42	1820(Maddison)
1870	2,655	0.58	1870(Maddison)
1880	2,839	0.67	1880(Maddison)
1890	2,951	0.39	1890(Maddison)
1900	3,300	1.12	1900(Maddison)
1913	3,864	1.22	1913(Maddison)
1920	3,877	0.05	1920(Maddison)
1929	4,022	0.41	1929(Maddison)
1938	4,192	0.46	1938(Maddison)
1950	4,694	0.95	50(E)
1960	5,328	1.27	60(E)
1970	6,181	1.50	70(E)

Year	Population, '000s	Growth Rate	Source
1980	6,319	0.22	80(E)
1990	6,712	0.61	90(E)
2000	7,184	0.68	00(E)
2010	7,828	0.86	10(E)
2012	7,997	1.07	12(E)
2020	8,472	0.72	12(E)
2030	8,811	0.39	12(E)
MEA Syria			
0001	1,314	.	PROXY(W. Asia(Maddison))
1000	1,355	0.00	PROXY(W. Asia(Maddison))
1500	1,206	0.02	PROXY(Other W. Asia(Maddison))
1600	1,175	0.03	INTERPOL(Maddison)
1700	1,145	0.03	PROXY(Other W. Asia(Maddison))
1820	1,337	0.13	1820(Maddison)
1870	1,582	0.34	1870(Maddison)
1880	1,669	0.54	INTERPOL(Maddison)
1890	1,762	0.54	INTERPOL(Maddison)
1900	1,859	0.54	INTERPOL(Maddison)
1913	1,994	0.54	1913(Maddison)
1920	2,217	1.53	INTERPOL(Maddison)
1929	2,542	1.53	INTERPOL(Maddison)
1938	2,913	1.53	INTERPOL(Maddison)
1950	3,495	1.53	50(E)
1960	4,567	2.71	60(E)
1970	6,368	3.38	70(E)
1980	8,907	3.41	80(E)
1990	12,324	3.30	90(E)
2000	15,989	2.64	00(E)
2010	20,411	2.47	10(E)
2012	21,110	1.70	12(E)
2020	24,079	1.66	12(E)
2030	27,859	1.47	12(E)
SEA Taiwan			
0001	61	.	PROXY(Other E. Asia(Maddison))
1000	112	0.06	PROXY(Other E. Asia(Maddison))
1500	200	0.12	1500(Maddison)
1600	447	0.81	INTERPOL(Maddison)
1700	1,000	0.81	1700(Maddison)
1820	2,000	0.58	1820(Maddison)
1870	2,345	0.32	1870(Maddison)
1880	2,421	0.32	INTERPOL(Maddison)
1890	2,500	0.32	1890(Maddison)
1900	2,864	1.37	1900(Maddison)
1913	3,469	1.49	1913(Maddison)
1920	3,736	1.06	1920(Maddison)
1929	4,493	2.07	1929(Maddison)
1938	5,678	2.63	1938(Maddison)
1950	7,619	2.48	50(E)
1960	10,668	3.42	60(E)

Year	Population, '000s	Growth Rate	Source
1970	14,583	3.18	70(E)
1980	17,642	1.92	80(E)
1990	20,279	1.40	90(E)
2000	22,185	0.90	00(E)
2010	23,138	0.42	10(E)
2012	23,286	0.32	12(E)
2020	23,594	0.16	12(E)
2030	23,532	0.03	12(E)
USR TAJIKISTAN			
0001	115	.	PROXY(40(E)/Turkestan(Maddison))
1000	192	0.05	PROXY(40(E)/Turkestan(Maddison))
1500	268	0.07	PROXY(40(E)/Turkestan(Maddison))
1600	307	0.13	PROXY(40(E)/Turkestan(Maddison))
1700	345	0.12	PROXY(40(E)/Turkestan(Maddison))
1820	516	0.34	PROXY(40(E)/Turkestan(Maddison))
1870	697	0.60	PROXY(40(E)/USSR(Maddison))
1880	778	1.11	40(E)/INTERPOL(Maddison)
1890	870	1.11	PROXY(40(E)/USSR(Maddison))
1900	978	1.19	PROXY(40(E)/USSR(Maddison))
1913	1,227	1.76	PROXY(40(E)/USSR(Maddison))
1920	1,215	0.15	PROXY(40(E)/USSR(Maddison))
1929	1,352	1.19	PROXY(40(E)/USSR(Maddison))
1938	1,481	1.02	PROXY(40(E)/USSR(Maddison))
1950	1,532	0.28	50(E)
1960	2,082	3.12	60(E)
1970	2,942	3.52	70(E)
1980	3,953	3.00	80(E)
1990	5,303	2.98	90(E)
2000	6,181	1.54	00(E)
2010	7,531	2.00	10(E)
2012	7,835	2.00	12(E)
2020	8,761	1.41	12(E)
2030	9,922	1.25	12(E)
AFR TANZANIA			
0001	.	.	
1000	.	.	
1500	.	.	
1600	.	.	
1700	.	.	
1820	.	.	
1870	.	.	
1880	.	.	
1890	.	.	
1900	.	.	
1913	.	.	
1920	.	.	
1929	.	.	

Year	Population, '000s	Growth Rate	Source
1938	.	.	
1950	7,935	.	50(E)
1960	10,074	2.42	60(E)
1970	13,605	3.05	70(E)
1980	18,686	3.22	80(E)
1990	25,479	3.15	90(E)
2000	34,038	2.94	00(E)
2010	42,446	2.23	10(E)
2012	44,745	2.67	12(E)
2020	55,737	2.78	12(E)
2030	72,411	2.65	12(E)
		SEA THAILAND	
0001	606	.	PROXY(Other E. Asia(Maddison))
1000	1,122	0.06	PROXY(Other E. Asia(Maddison))
1500	2,000	0.12	1500(Maddison)
1600	2,236	0.11	INTERPOL(Maddison)
1700	2,500	0.11	1700(Maddison)
1820	4,665	0.52	1820(Maddison)
1870	5,775	0.43	1870(Maddison)
1880	6,206	0.72	INTERPOL(Maddison)
1890	6,670	0.72	1890(Maddison)
1900	7,320	0.93	1900(Maddison)
1913	8,689	1.33	1913(Maddison)
1920	9,802	1.74	1920(Maddison)
1929	12,058	2.33	1929(Maddison)
1938	14,980	2.44	1938(Maddison)
1950	20,607	2.69	50(E)
1960	27,513	2.93	60(E)
1970	37,091	3.03	70(E)
1980	47,026	2.40	80(E)
1990	55,197	1.61	90(E)
2000	61,022	1.01	00(E)
2010	65,403	0.70	10(E)
2012	66,316	0.70	12(E)
2020	68,753	0.45	12(E)
2030	70,465	0.25	12(E)
		AFR TOGO	
0001	.	.	
1000	.	.	
1500	.	.	
1600	.	.	
1700	.	.	
1820	.	.	
1870	.	.	
1880	.	.	
1890	.	.	
1900	.	.	
1913	.	.	

Year	Population, '000s	Growth Rate	Source
1920	.	.	
1929	.	.	
1938	.	.	
1950	1,329	.	50(E)
1960	1,578	1.73	60(E)
1970	2,097	2.88	70(E)
1980	2,667	2.43	80(E)
1990	3,666	3.23	90(E)
2000	4,629	2.36	00(E)
2010	6,127	2.84	10(E)
2012	6,481	2.85	12(E)
2020	7,589	1.99	12(E)
2030	8,975	1.69	12(E)
SEA Tokelau			
0001	.	.	
1000	.	.	
1500	.	.	
1600	.	.	
1700	.	.	
1820	.	.	
1870	.	.	
1880	.	.	
1890	.	.	
1900	.	.	
1913	.	.	
1920	.	.	
1929	.	.	
1938	.	.	
1950	1	.	PROXY(14 Pacific is(Maddison))
1960	1	2.75	INTERPOL(14 Pacific is(Maddison))
1970	1	2.74	INTERPOL(14 Pacific is(Maddison))
1980	1	2.44	INTERPOL(14 Pacific is(Maddison))
1990	2	2.30	90(CIA)
2000	1	1.52	00(CIA)
2010	1	0.41	10(CIA)
2012	1	1.15	12(CIA)
2020	1	0.53	12(EST)
2030	1	0.53	12(EST)
SEA Tonga			
0001	.	.	
1000	.	.	
1500	.	.	
1600	.	.	
1700	.	.	
1820	.	.	
1870	.	.	

Year	Population, '000s	Growth Rate	Source
1880	.	.	
1890	.	.	
1900	.	.	
1913	.	.	
1920	.	.	
1929	.	.	
1938	.	.	
1950	50	.	50(E)
1960	65	2.66	60(E)
1970	80	2.10	70(E)
1980	92	1.41	80(E)
1990	96	0.43	90(E)
2000	99	0.31	00(E)
2010	103	0.40	10(E)
2012	103	0.00	12(E)
2020	106	0.36	12(E)
2030	111	0.46	12(E)
LAM Trinidad and Tobago			
0001	3	.	PROXY(Other L. Am.(Maddison))
1000	7	0.07	PROXY(Other L. Am.(Maddison))
1500	10	0.07	PROXY(Caribbean cs(Maddison))
1600	4	0.91	PROXY(Caribbean cs(Maddison))
1700	10	0.92	PROXY(Caribbean cs(Maddison))
1820	60	1.48	1820(Maddison)
1870	124	1.46	1870(Maddison)
1880	160	2.60	INTERPOL(Maddison)
1890	207	2.60	INTERPOL(Maddison)
1900	268	2.60	1900(Maddison)
1913	352	2.12	1913(Maddison)
1920	389	1.44	1920(Maddison)
1929	398	0.25	1929(Maddison)
1938	458	1.57	1938(Maddison)
1950	668	3.20	50(E)
1960	828	2.17	60(E)
1970	941	1.29	70(E)
1980	1,082	1.41	80(E)
1990	1,235	1.33	90(E)
2000	1,263	0.22	00(E)
2010	1,318	0.43	10(E)
2012	1,335	0.65	12(E)
2020	1,362	0.25	12(E)
2030	1,343	0.14	12(E)
MEA Tunisia			
0001	800	.	0001(Maddison)
1000	1,000	0.02	1000(Maddison)
1500	800	0.04	1500(Maddison)
1600	1,000	0.22	1600(Maddison)
1700	800	0.22	1700(Maddison)

Year	Population, '000s	Growth Rate	Source
1820	875	0.07	1820(Maddison)
1870	1,176	0.59	1870(Maddison)
1880	1,310	1.08	INTERPOL(Maddison)
1890	1,459	1.08	INTERPOL(Maddison)
1900	1,625	1.08	INTERPOL(Maddison)
1913	1,870	1.08	1913(Maddison)
1920	2,107	1.72	INTERPOL(Maddison)
1929	2,457	1.72	INTERPOL(Maddison)
1938	2,865	1.72	INTERPOL(Maddison)
1950	3,517	1.72	50(E)
1960	4,221	1.84	60(E)
1970	5,127	1.96	70(E)
1980	6,457	2.33	80(E)
1990	8,215	2.44	90(E)
2000	9,553	1.52	00(E)
2010	10,547	0.99	10(E)
2012	10,769	1.05	12(E)
2020	11,543	0.87	12(E)
2030	12,138	0.50	12(E)
MEA TURKEY			
0001	6,866	.	PROXY(W. Asia(Maddison))
1000	7,079	0.00	PROXY(W. Asia(Maddison))
1500	6,300	0.02	1500(Maddison)
1600	7,275	0.14	INTERPOL(Maddison)
1700	8,400	0.14	1700(Maddison)
1820	10,074	0.15	1820(Maddison)
1870	11,793	0.32	1870(Maddison)
1880	12,472	0.56	INTERPOL(Maddison)
1890	13,189	0.56	INTERPOL(Maddison)
1900	13,948	0.56	INTERPOL(Maddison)
1913	15,000	0.56	1913(Maddison)
1920	13,877	1.11	1923(Maddison)
1929	14,705	0.65	1929(Maddison)
1938	17,016	1.64	1938(Maddison)
1950	21,484	1.96	50(E)
1960	27,506	2.50	60(E)
1970	35,231	2.51	70(E)
1980	44,439	2.35	80(E)
1990	55,120	2.18	90(E)
2000	64,252	1.54	00(E)
2010	73,135	1.30	10(E)
2012	75,189	1.39	12(E)
2020	81,705	1.04	12(E)
2030	87,687	0.71	12(E)
USR TURKMENISTAN			
0001	98	.	PROXY(40(E)/Turkestan(Maddison))
1000	164	0.05	PROXY(40(E)/Turkestan(Maddison))
1500	229	0.07	PROXY(40(E)/Turkestan(Maddison))
1600	262	0.13	PROXY(40(E)/Turkestan(Maddison))

Year	Population, '000s	Growth Rate	Source
1700	295	0.12	PROXY(40(E)/Turkestan(Maddison))
1820	441	0.34	PROXY(40(E)/Turkestan(Maddison))
1870	595	0.60	PROXY(40(E)/USSR(Maddison))
1880	665	1.11	40(E)/INTERPOL(Maddison)
1890	742	1.11	PROXY(40(E)/USSR(Maddison))
1900	835	1.19	PROXY(40(E)/USSR(Maddison))
1913	1,048	1.76	PROXY(40(E)/USSR(Maddison))
1920	1,037	0.15	PROXY(40(E)/USSR(Maddison))
1929	1,154	1.19	PROXY(40(E)/USSR(Maddison))
1938	1,265	1.02	PROXY(40(E)/USSR(Maddison))
1950	1,204	0.41	50(E)
1960	1,585	2.79	60(E)
1970	2,181	3.24	70(E)
1980	2,875	2.80	80(E)
1990	3,658	2.44	90(E)
2000	4,385	1.83	00(E)
2010	4,941	1.20	10(E)
2012	5,055	1.15	12(E)
2020	5,529	1.13	12(E)
2030	6,027	0.87	12(E)
LAM Turks and Caicos Islands			
0001	.	.	
1000	.	.	
1500	.	.	
1600	.	.	
1700	.	.	
1820	.	.	
1870	.	.	
1880	.	.	
1890	.	.	
1900	.	.	
1913	.	.	
1920	.	.	
1929	.	.	
1938	.	.	
1950	5	.	PROXY(8 Caribbean cs(Maddison))
1960	6	2.29	60(WB)
1970	6	0.16	70(WB)
1980	8	2.94	80(WB)
1990	12	4.38	90(WB)
2000	19	5.03	00(WB)
2010	31	5.08	10(WB)
2012	32	2.29	12(WB)
2020	47	4.61	12(EST)
2030	73	4.61	12(EST)
SEA Tuvalu			
0001	.	.	

Year	Population, '000s	Growth Rate	Source
1000	.	.	
1500	.	.	
1600	.	.	
1700	.	.	
1820	.	.	
1870	.	.	
1880	.	.	
1890	.	.	
1900	.	.	
1913	.	.	
1920	.	.	
1929	.	.	
1938	.	.	
1950	5	.	50(E)
1960	5	0.00	60(E)
1970	6	1.84	70(E)
1980	8	2.92	80(E)
1990	9	1.18	90(E)
2000	9	0.00	00(E)
2010	11	2.03	10(E)
2012	11	0.90	12(E)
2020	12	0.87	12(E)
2030	12	0.00	12(E)
	AFR Uganda		
0001	.	.	
1000	.	.	
1500	.	.	
1600	.	.	
1700	.	.	
1820	.	.	
1870	.	.	
1880	.	.	
1890	.	.	
1900	.	.	
1913	.	.	
1920	.	.	
1929	.	.	
1938	.	.	
1950	5,158	.	50(E)
1960	7,262	3.48	60(E)
1970	9,715	2.95	70(E)
1980	12,020	2.15	80(E)
1990	16,549	3.25	90(E)
2000	22,916	3.31	00(E)
2010	31,507	3.23	10(E)
2012	33,639	3.33	12(E)

Year	Population, '000s	Growth Rate	Source
2020	43,518	3.27	12(E)
2030	58,488	3.00	12(E)
USR Ukraine			
0001	527	.	PROXY(40(E)/Eur. Russia(Maddison))
1000	1,053	0.07	PROXY(40(E)/Eur. Russia(Maddison))
1500	3,160	0.22	PROXY(40(E)/Eur. Russia(Maddison))
1600	3,950	0.22	PROXY(40(E)/Eur. Russia(Maddison))
1700	5,267	0.29	PROXY(40(E)/Eur. Russia(Maddison))
1820	11,629	0.66	PROXY(40(E)/Eur. Russia(Maddison))
1870	18,888	0.97	PROXY(40(E)/USSR(Maddison))
1880	21,101	1.11	40(E)/INTERPOL(Maddison)
1890	23,572	1.11	PROXY(40(E)/USSR(Maddison))
1900	26,520	1.19	PROXY(40(E)/USSR(Maddison))
1913	33,270	1.76	PROXY(40(E)/USSR(Maddison))
1920	32,933	0.15	PROXY(40(E)/USSR(Maddison))
1929	36,641	1.19	PROXY(40(E)/USSR(Maddison))
1938	40,152	1.02	PROXY(40(E)/USSR(Maddison))
1950	36,906	0.70	50(E)
1960	42,783	1.49	60(E)
1970	47,317	1.01	70(E)
1980	50,034	0.56	80(E)
1990	51,892	0.37	90(E)
2000	49,177	0.54	00(E)
2010	45,860	0.70	10(E)
2012	45,635	0.25	12(E)
2020	43,843	0.50	12(E)
2030	41,264	0.60	12(E)
MEA United Arab Emirates			
0001	39	.	PROXY(W. Asia(Maddison))
1000	40	0.00	PROXY(W. Asia(Maddison))
1500	35	0.02	PROXY(Arabia(Maddison))
1600	35	0.00	INTERPOL(Maddison)
1700	35	0.00	PROXY(Arabia(Maddison))
1820	41	0.12	PROXY(Gulf Coast(Maddison))
1870	41	0.00	PROXY(Gulf Coast(Maddison))
1880	43	0.56	INTERPOL(Maddison)
1890	46	0.56	INTERPOL(Maddison)
1900	48	0.56	INTERPOL(Maddison)
1913	52	0.56	PROXY(Gulf Coast(Maddison))
1920	55	0.89	INTERPOL(Maddison)
1929	60	0.89	INTERPOL(Maddison)
1938	65	0.89	INTERPOL(Maddison)
1950	72	0.89	50(E)
1960	90	2.26	60(E)
1970	232	9.93	70(E)
1980	1,016	15.92	80(E)
1990	1,809	5.94	90(E)
2000	3,033	5.30	00(E)
2010	7,512	9.49	10(E)

Year	Population, '000s	Growth Rate	Source
2012	7,969	3.00	12(E)
2020	9,174	1.78	12(E)
2030	10,489	1.35	12(E)
DME United Kingdom			
0001	747	.	PROXY(UK & Irealnd(Maddison))
1000	1,867	0.09	PROXY(UK & Ireland(Maddison))
1500	3,681	0.14	PROXY(UK & Ireland(Maddison))
1600	5,761	0.45	PROXY(UK & Ireland(Maddison))
1700	7,997	0.33	PROXY(UK & Ireland(Maddison))
1820	19,831	0.76	PROXY(UK & Ireland(Maddison))
1870	29,319	0.79	PROXY(UK & Ireland(Maddison))
1880	32,328	0.98	PROXY(UK & Ireland(Maddison))
1890	35,001	0.80	PROXY(UK & Ireland(Maddison))
1900	38,428	0.94	PROXY(UK & Ireland(Maddison))
1913	42,624	0.80	PROXY(UK & Ireland(Maddison))
1920	43,718	0.36	1920(Maddison)
1929	45,672	0.49	1929(Maddison)
1938	47,494	0.44	1938(Maddison)
1950	50,290	0.48	50(E)
1960	52,372	0.41	60(E)
1970	55,632	0.61	70(E)
1980	56,330	0.12	80(E)
1990	57,237	0.16	90(E)
2000	58,887	0.28	00(E)
2010	62,843	0.65	10(E)
2012	63,764	0.73	12(E)
2020	69,281	1.04	12(E)
2030	73,611	0.61	12(E)
DME United States			
0001	680	.	0001(Maddison)
1000	1,300	0.06	1000(Maddison)
1500	2,000	0.09	1500(Maddison)
1600	1,500	0.29	1600(Maddison)
1700	1,000	0.40	1700(Maddison)
1820	9,981	1.94	1820(Maddison)
1870	40,241	2.83	1870(Maddison)
1880	50,458	2.29	1880(Maddison)
1890	63,302	2.29	1890(Maddison)
1900	76,391	1.90	1900(Maddison)
1913	97,606	1.90	1913(Maddison)
1920	106,881	1.31	1920(Maddison)
1929	122,245	1.50	1929(Maddison)
1938	130,476	0.73	1938(Maddison)
1950	152,271	1.30	50(E)
1960	180,671	1.72	60(E)
1970	204,879	1.27	70(E)
1980	227,726	1.06	80(E)
1990	249,806	0.93	90(E)
2000	282,385	1.23	00(E)

Year	Population, '000s	Growth Rate	Source
2010	309,746	0.93	10(E)
2012	314,231	0.72	12(E)
2020	337,268	0.89	12(E)
2030	366,152	0.83	12(E)
		LAM Uruguay	
0001	21	.	PROXY(Other L. Am.(Maddison))
1000	43	0.07	PROXY(Other L. Am.(Maddison))
1500	62	0.07	PROXY(Other Sp. Am.(Maddison))
1600	37	0.51	PROXY(Other Sp. Am.(Maddison))
1700	42	0.13	PROXY(Other Sp. Am.(Maddison))
1820	55	0.22	1820(Maddison)
1870	343	3.73	1870(Maddison)
1880	464	3.07	1880(Maddison)
1890	686	3.99	1890(Maddison)
1900	915	2.92	1900(Maddison)
1913	1,177	1.96	1913(Maddison)
1920	1,371	2.20	1920(Maddison)
1929	1,685	2.32	1929(Maddison)
1938	1,952	1.65	1938(Maddison)
1950	2,239	1.15	50(E)
1960	2,538	1.26	60(E)
1970	2,809	1.02	70(E)
1980	2,915	0.37	80(E)
1990	3,109	0.65	90(E)
2000	3,220	0.35	00(E)
2010	3,279	0.18	10(E)
2012	3,292	0.19	12(E)
2020	3,362	0.26	12(E)
2030	3,441	0.23	12(E)
		USR Uzbekistan	
0001	494	.	PROXY(40(E)/Turkestan(Maddison))
1000	823	0.05	PROXY(40(E)/Turkestan(Maddison))
1500	1,153	0.07	PROXY(40(E)/Turkestan(Maddison))
1600	1,318	0.13	PROXY(40(E)/Turkestan(Maddison))
1700	1,482	0.12	PROXY(40(E)/Turkestan(Maddison))
1820	2,217	0.34	PROXY(40(E)/Turkestan(Maddison))
1870	2,993	0.60	PROXY(40(E)/USSR(Maddison))
1880	3,344	1.11	40(E)/INTERPOL(Maddison)
1890	3,735	1.11	PROXY(40(E)/USSR(Maddison))
1900	4,202	1.19	PROXY(40(E)/USSR(Maddison))
1913	5,272	1.76	PROXY(40(E)/USSR(Maddison))
1920	5,219	0.15	PROXY(40(E)/USSR(Maddison))
1929	5,806	1.19	PROXY(40(E)/USSR(Maddison))
1938	6,363	1.02	PROXY(40(E)/USSR(Maddison))
1950	6,293	0.09	50(E)
1960	8,531	3.09	60(E)
1970	11,940	3.42	70(E)
1980	15,994	2.97	80(E)
1990	20,530	2.53	90(E)

Year	Population, '000s	Growth Rate	Source
2000	24,488	1.78	00(E)
2010	28,001	1.35	10(E)
2012	29,314	2.32	12(E)
2020	32,505	1.30	12(E)
2030	35,250	0.81	12(E)
	SEA Vanuatu		
0001	.	.	
1000	.	.	
1500	.	.	
1600	.	.	
1700	.	.	
1820	.	.	
1870	.	.	
1880	.	.	
1890	.	.	
1900	.	.	
1913	.	.	
1920	.	.	
1929	.	.	
1938	.	.	
1950	48	.	50(E)
1960	64	2.92	60(E)
1970	86	3.00	70(E)
1980	117	3.13	80(E)
1990	149	2.45	90(E)
2000	189	2.41	00(E)
2010	241	2.46	10(E)
2012	257	3.22	12(E)
2020	309	2.34	12(E)
2030	370	1.82	12(E)
	LAM Venezuela		
0001	274	.	PROXY(Other L. Am.(Maddison))
1000	556	0.07	PROXY(Other L. Am.(Maddison))
1500	806	0.07	PROXY(Other Sp. Am.(Maddison))
1600	484	0.51	PROXY(Other Sp. Am.(Maddison))
1700	550	0.13	PROXY(Other Sp. Am.(Maddison))
1820	718	0.22	1820(Maddison)
1870	1,653	1.68	1870(Maddison)
1880	1,952	1.68	1880(Maddison)
1890	2,224	1.31	1890(Maddison)
1900	2,542	1.35	1900(Maddison)
1913	2,874	0.95	1913(Maddison)
1920	2,992	0.58	1920(Maddison)
1929	3,259	0.95	1929(Maddison)
1938	3,623	1.18	1938(Maddison)
1950	5,094	2.88	50(E)
1960	7,562	4.03	60(E)

Year	Population, '000s	Growth Rate	Source
1970	10,681	3.51	70(E)
1980	15,036	3.48	80(E)
1990	19,685	2.73	90(E)
2000	24,311	2.13	00(E)
2010	28,369	1.56	10(E)
2012	29,534	2.03	12(E)
2020	32,612	1.25	12(E)
2030	36,232	1.06	12(E)
		CPA Vietnam	
0001	1,163	.	PROXY(Other E. Asia(Maddison))
1000	2,152	0.06	PROXY(Other E. Asia(Maddison))
1500	3,835	0.12	PROXY(Other E. Asia(Maddison))
1600	4,447	0.15	PROXY(Other E. Asia(Maddison))
1700	5,171	0.15	PROXY(Other E. Asia(Maddison))
1820	6,551	0.20	1820(Maddison)
1870	10,528	0.95	1870(Maddison)
1880	12,127	1.42	INTERPOL(Maddison)
1890	13,969	1.42	INTERPOL(Maddison)
1900	16,091	1.42	INTERPOL(Maddison)
1913	19,339	1.42	1913(Maddison)
1920	20,652	0.94	INTERPOL(Maddison)
1929	22,472	0.94	INTERPOL(Maddison)
1938	24,452	0.94	INTERPOL(Maddison)
1950	27,367	0.94	50(E)
1960	31,656	1.47	60(E)
1970	42,577	3.01	70(E)
1980	53,715	2.35	80(E)
1990	67,258	2.27	90(E)
2000	77,631	1.44	00(E)
2010	86,933	1.14	10(E)
2012	88,788	1.06	12(E)
2020	96,309	1.02	12(E)
2030	103,257	0.70	12(E)
		LAM Virgin Islands, British	
0001	.	.	
1000	.	.	
1500	.	.	
1600	.	.	
1700	.	.	
1820	.	.	
1870	.	.	
1880	.	.	
1890	.	.	
1900	.	.	
1913	.	.	
1920	.	.	
1929	.	.	

Year	Population, '000s	Growth Rate	Source
1938	.	.	
1950	6	.	PROXY(8 Caribbean cs(Maddison))
1960	7	2.29	INTERPOL(8 Caribbean cs(Maddison))
1970	9	2.29	INTERPOL(8 Caribbean cs(Maddison))
1980	11	1.67	INTERPOL(8 Caribbean cs(Maddison))
1990	12	1.41	90(CIA)
2000	20	4.81	00(CIA)
2010	25	2.43	10(CIA)
2012	31	11.76	12(CIA)
2020	42	3.93	12(EST)
2030	62	3.93	12(EST)

LAM Virgin Islands, U.S.

Year	Population, '000s	Growth Rate	Source
0001	.	.	
1000	.	.	
1500	.	.	
1600	.	.	
1700	.	.	
1820	.	.	
1870	.	.	
1880	.	.	
1890	.	.	
1900	.	.	
1913	.	.	
1920	.	.	
1929	.	.	
1938	.	.	
1950	27	.	50(E)
1960	33	2.03	60(E)
1970	63	6.68	70(E)
1980	97	4.41	80(E)
1990	102	0.50	90(E)
2000	109	0.67	00(E)
2010	106	0.28	10(E)
2012	105	0.32	12(E)
2020	100	0.65	12(E)
2030	91	0.94	12(E)

SEA Wallis and Futuna

Year	Population, '000s	Growth Rate	Source
0001	.	.	
1000	.	.	
1500	.	.	
1600	.	.	
1700	.	.	
1820	.	.	
1870	.	.	
1880	.	.	
1890	.	.	

Year	Population, '000s	Growth Rate	Source
1900	.	.	
1913	.	.	
1920	.	.	
1929	.	.	
1938	.	.	
1950	5	.	PROXY(14 Pacific is(Maddison))
1960	7	2.75	INTERPOL(14 Pacific is(Maddison))
1970	9	2.75	INTERPOL(14 Pacific is(Maddison))
1980	12	2.44	INTERPOL(14 Pacific is(Maddison))
1990	15	2.30	90(CIA)
2000	15	0.25	00(CIA)
2010	15	0.04	10(CIA)
2012	15	0.36	12(CIA)
2020	16	0.09	12(EST)
2030	16	0.09	12(EST)
MEA West Bank			
0001	.	.	
1000	.	.	
1500	.	.	
1600	.	.	
1700	.	.	
1820	.	.	
1870	.	.	
1880	.	.	
1890	.	.	
1900	.	.	
1913	.	.	
1920	.	.	
1929	.	.	
1938	.	.	
1950	772	.	50(W Bank/Gaza(Maddison)Gaza(E))
1960	805	0.42	60(W Bank/Gaza(Maddison)Gaza(E))
1970	608	2.77	70(E)
1980	733	1.89	80(E)
1990	1,011	3.27	90(E)
2000	2,175	7.96	00(E)
2010	2,830	2.67	10(E)
2012	2,994	2.85	12(E)
2020	3,518	2.04	12(E)
2030	4,127	1.61	12(E)
AFR Western Sahara			
0001	.	.	
1000	.	.	
1500	.	.	
1600	.	.	
1700	.	.	

Year	Population, '000s	Growth Rate	Source
1820	.	.	
1870	.	.	
1880	.	.	
1890	.	.	
1900	.	.	
1913	.	.	
1920	.	.	
1929	.	.	
1938	.	.	
1950	14	.	50(E)
1960	28	7.18	60(E)
1970	89	12.26	70(E)
1980	124	3.37	80(E)
1990	217	5.76	90(E)
2000	336	4.47	00(E)
2010	492	3.89	10(E)
2012	523	3.09	12(E)
2020	652	2.80	12(E)
2030	821	2.33	12(E)
MEA Yemen			
0001	2,445	.	PROXY(W. Asia(Maddison))
1000	2,520	0.00	PROXY(W. Asia(Maddison))
1500	2,243	0.02	PROXY(Arabia(Maddison))
1600	2,243	0.00	INTERPOL(Maddison)
1700	2,243	0.00	PROXY(Arabia(Maddison))
1820	2,593	0.12	1820(Maddison)
1870	2,840	0.18	1870(Maddison)
1880	2,938	0.34	INTERPOL(Maddison)
1890	3,039	0.34	INTERPOL(Maddison)
1900	3,143	0.34	INTERPOL(Maddison)
1913	3,284	0.34	1913(Maddison)
1920	3,525	1.02	INTERPOL(Maddison)
1929	3,862	1.02	INTERPOL(Maddison)
1938	4,230	1.02	INTERPOL(Maddison)
1950	4,777	1.02	50(E)
1960	5,872	2.09	60(E)
1970	7,098	1.91	70(E)
1980	9,133	2.55	80(E)
1990	12,416	3.12	90(E)
2000	17,723	3.62	00(E)
2010	23,939	3.05	10(E)
2012	25,526	3.26	12(E)
2020	32,232	2.96	12(E)
2030	41,342	2.52	12(E)
AFR Zambia			
0001	23	.	PROXY(Mal., Zam., Zim.(Maddison))
1000	155	0.19	PROXY(Mal., Zam., Zim.(Maddison))
1500	310	0.14	PROXY(Mal., Zam., Zim.(Maddison))

Year	Population, '000s	Growth Rate	Source
1600	342	0.10	PROXY(Mal., Zam., Zim.(Maddison))
1700	373	0.09	PROXY(Mal., Zam., Zim.(Maddison))
1820	418	0.10	PROXY(Mal., Zam., Zim.(Maddison))
1870	838	1.40	INTERPOL(Maddison)
1880	963	1.40	INTERPOL(Maddison)
1890	1,107	1.40	INTERPOL(Maddison)
1900	1,272	1.40	INTERPOL(Maddison)
1913	1,525	1.40	INTERPOL(Maddison)
1920	1,681	1.40	INTERPOL(Maddison)
1929	1,906	1.40	INTERPOL(Maddison)
1938	2,160	1.40	INTERPOL(Maddison)
1950	2,553	1.40	50(E)
1960	3,254	2.46	60(E)
1970	4,248	2.70	70(E)
1980	5,643	2.88	80(E)
1990	7,858	3.37	90(E)
2000	9,984	2.42	00(E)
2010	12,984	2.66	10(E)
2012	13,995	3.82	12(E)
2020	17,804	3.05	12(E)
2030	23,637	2.87	12(E)
	AFR ZIMBABWE		
0001	26	.	PROXY(Mal., Zam., Zim.(Maddison))
1000	173	0.19	PROXY(Mal., Zam., Zim.(Maddison))
1500	347	0.14	PROXY(Mal., Zam., Zim.(Maddison))
1600	382	0.10	PROXY(Mal., Zam., Zim.(Maddison))
1700	416	0.09	PROXY(Mal., Zam., Zim.(Maddison))
1820	467	0.10	PROXY(Mal., Zam., Zim.(Maddison))
1870	936	1.40	INTERPOL(Maddison)
1880	1,076	1.40	INTERPOL(Maddison)
1890	1,237	1.40	INTERPOL(Maddison)
1900	1,422	1.40	INTERPOL(Maddison)
1913	1,704	1.40	INTERPOL(Maddison)
1920	1,879	1.40	INTERPOL(Maddison)
1929	2,130	1.40	INTERPOL(Maddison)
1938	2,414	1.40	INTERPOL(Maddison)
1950	2,853	1.40	50(E)
1960	4,011	3.47	60(E)
1970	5,515	3.24	70(E)
1980	7,170	2.66	80(E)
1990	10,156	3.54	90(E)
2000	11,820	1.53	00(E)
2010	12,675	0.70	10(E)
2012	12,955	1.10	12(E)
2020	15,274	2.08	12(E)
2030	17,322	1.27	12(E)

2. GDP at PPP Per Capita, by Country

Year	GDP at PPP Per Capita, 2012 doll.	Growth Rate	Source
SAS Afghanistan			
0001	403	.	0001(MIN)
1000	595	0.04	1000(MIN)
1500	780	0.05	PROXY(Other E. Asia(Maddison))
1600	794	0.02	PROXY(Other E. Asia(Maddison))
1700	790	0.01	PROXY(Other E. Asia(Maddison))
1820	799	0.01	PROXY(26 E. Asian cs(Maddison))
1870	769	0.08	PROXY(26 E. Asian cs(Maddison))
1880	833	0.79	INTERPOL(Maddison)
1890	901	0.79	INTERPOL(Maddison)
1900	975	0.80	INTERPOL(Maddison)
1913	1,081	0.79	PROXY(26 E. Asian cs(Maddison))
1920	1,067	0.19	INTERPOL(Maddison)
1929	1,050	0.19	INTERPOL(Maddison)
1938	1,032	0.19	INTERPOL(Maddison)
1950	1,009	0.19	50(Maddison)
1960	1,299	2.56	60(Maddison)
1970	1,203	0.77	70(Maddison)
1980	1,162	0.34	80(Maddison)
1990	883	2.72	90(Maddison)
2000	1,033	1.58	00(CIA)WEIGHT(US(WB))
2010	1,206	1.56	10(WB)
2012	1,561	13.76	12(WB)
2020	1,995	3.12	FORECAST
2030	2,511	2.33	FORECAST

Year	GDP at PPP Per Capita, 2012 doll.	Growth Rate	Source
EEU ALBANIA			
0001	338	.	0001(MIN)
1000	463	0.03	1000(MIN)
1500	568	0.04	1500(MIN)
1600	595	0.05	1600(MIN)
1700	624	0.05	1700(MIN)
1820	664	0.05	PROXY(E. Europe(Maddison))
1870	698	0.10	1870(Maddison)
1880	808	1.48	INTERPOL(Maddison)
1890	936	1.48	1890(Maddison)
1900	1,072	1.37	1900(Maddison)
1913	1,269	1.31	1913(Maddison)
1920	1,345	0.83	INTERPOL(Maddison)
1929	1,449	0.83	1920(Maddison)
1938	1,498	0.37	INTERPOL(Maddison)
1950	1,566	0.37	50(Maddison)
1960	2,378	4.26	60(Maddison)
1970	3,430	3.73	70(Maddison)
1980	4,150	1.92	80(WB)
1990	3,712	1.11	90(WB)
2000	4,967	2.96	00(WB)
2010	8,996	6.12	10(WB)
2012	9,403	2.24	12(WB)
2020	13,058	4.19	FORECAST
2030	16,825	2.57	FORECAST
MEA ALGERIA			
0001	673	.	PROXY(Other N. Africa(Maddison))
1000	673	0.00	PROXY(Other N. Africa(Maddison))
1500	673	0.00	PROXY(Other N. Africa(Maddison))
1600	673	0.00	PROXY(Other N. Africa(Maddison))
1700	673	0.00	PROXY(Other N. Africa(Maddison))
1820	673	0.00	1820(Maddison)
1870	1,119	1.02	1870(Maddison)
1880	1,239	1.03	1880(Maddison)
1890	1,392	1.17	INTERPOL(Maddison)
1900	1,564	1.17	INTERPOL(Maddison)
1913	1,820	1.17	1913(Maddison)
1920	1,976	1.19	1920(Maddison)
1929	2,136	0.87	INTERPOL(Maddison)
1938	2,147	0.06	INTERPOL(Maddison)
1950	2,136	0.04	50(Maddison)
1960	3,626	5.43	60(Maddison)
1970	4,306	1.73	70(Maddison)
1980	6,666	4.47	80(WB)
1990	6,498	0.26	90(WB)
2000	6,510	0.02	00(WB)
2010	8,272	2.42	10(WB)
2012	8,447	1.05	12(WB)

Year	GDP at PPP Per Capita, 2012 doll.	Growth Rate	Source
2020	9,660	1.69	FORECAST
2030	11,476	1.74	FORECAST
		DME ANDORRA	
0001	.	.	
1000	.	.	
1500	.	.	
1600	.	.	
1700	.	.	
1820	.	.	
1870	.	.	
1880	.	.	
1890	.	.	
1900	.	.	
1913	.	.	
1920	.	.	
1929	.	.	
1938	.	.	
1950	6,502	.	PROXY(9 European cs(Maddison))
1960	9,495	3.86	INTERPOL(9 European cs(Maddison))
1970	13,865	3.86	INTERPOL(9 European cs(Maddison))
1980	17,777	2.52	INTERPOL(9 European cs(Maddison))
1990	21,556	1.95	92(CIA)WEIGHT(US(Maddison))
2000	24,511	1.29	00(CIA)WEIGHT(US(WB))
2010	39,084	4.78	10(CIA)WEIGHT(US(WB))
2012	37,176	2.47	12(CIA)
2020	47,482	3.11	FORECAST
2030	59,753	2.33	FORECAST
		AFR ANGOLA	
0001	.	.	
1000	.	.	
1500	.	.	
1600	.	.	
1700	.	.	
1820	.	.	
1870	.	.	
1880	.	.	
1890	.	.	
1900	.	.	
1913	.	.	
1920	.	.	
1929	.	.	
1938	.	.	
1950	1,646	.	50(Maddison)
1960	2,457	4.09	60(Maddison)

Year	GDP at PPP Per Capita, 2012 doll.	Growth Rate	Source
1970	4,347	5.87	70(Maddison)
1980	2,961	3.77	80(Maddison)
1990	3,451	1.54	90(WB)
2000	2,766	2.19	00(WB)
2010	5,762	7.61	10(WB)
2012	6,006	2.10	12(WB)
2020	8,415	4.31	FORECAST
2030	10,862	2.58	FORECAST
LAM Anguilla			
0001	.	.	
1000	.	.	
1500	.	.	
1600	.	.	
1700	.	.	
1820	.	.	
1870	.	.	
1880	.	.	
1890	.	.	
1900	.	.	
1913	.	.	
1920	.	.	
1929	.	.	
1938	.	.	
1950	4,783	.	PROXY(8 Caribbean cs(Maddison))
1960	6,224	2.67	INTERPOL(8 Caribbean cs(Maddison))
1970	8,098	2.67	INTERPOL(8 Caribbean cs(Maddison))
1980	9,522	1.63	INTERPOL(8 Caribbean cs(Maddison))
1990	10,720	1.19	93(CIA)WEIGHT(US(Maddison))
2000	11,094	0.34	99(CIA)WEIGHT(US(WB))
2010	12,975	1.58	09(CIA)WEIGHT(US(WB))
2012	13,378	1.54	09(CIA)WEIGHT(US(WB))
2020	14,953	1.40	FORECAST
2030	17,468	1.57	FORECAST
LAM Antigua and Barbuda			
0001	.	.	
1000	.	.	
1500	.	.	
1600	.	.	
1700	.	.	
1820	.	.	
1870	.	.	
1880	.	.	
1890	.	.	
1900	.	.	
1913	.	.	

Year	GDP at PPP Per Capita, 2012 doll.	Growth Rate	Source
1920	.	.	
1929	.	.	
1938	.	.	
1950	2,790	.	50(Maddison)
1960	3,845	3.26	INTERPOL
1970	5,300	3.26	INTERPOL
1980	7,306	3.26	80(WB)
1990	15,424	7.76	90(WB)
2000	18,923	2.07	00(WB)
2010	20,120	0.62	10(WB)
2012	19,640	1.20	12(WB)
2020	23,063	2.03	FORECAST
2030	27,869	1.91	FORECAST
LAM Argentina			
0001	364	.	0001(MIN)
1000	513	0.03	1000(MIN)
1500	645	0.05	AVG(Other Sp. Am.(Maddison))
1600	919	0.35	INTERPOL(Maddison)
1700	1,309	0.35	INTERPOL(Maddison)
1820	2,003	0.35	PROXY(Other L. Am.(Maddison))
1870	2,052	0.05	1870(Maddison)
1880	2,628	2.51	INTERPOL(Maddison)
1890	3,368	2.51	1890(Maddison)
1900	4,313	2.50	1900(Maddison)
1913	5,942	2.50	1913(Maddison)
1920	5,435	1.27	1920(Maddison)
1929	6,834	2.58	1929(Maddison)
1938	6,372	0.77	1938(Maddison)
1950	7,804	1.70	50(Maddison)
1960	8,340	0.67	60(Maddison)
1970	10,523	2.35	70(Maddison)
1980	11,339	0.75	80(WB)
1990	8,367	2.99	90(WB)
2000	11,689	3.40	00(WB)
2010	16,792	3.69	10(CIA)WEIGHT(US(WB))
2012	18,200	4.11	12(CIA)
2020	23,511	3.25	FORECAST
2030	29,708	2.37	FORECAST
USR Armenia			
0001	406	.	0001(MIN)
1000	601	0.04	1000(MIN)
1500	790	0.05	PROXY(USSR(Maddison))
1600	874	0.10	PROXY(USSR(Maddison))
1700	966	0.10	PROXY(USSR(Maddison))
1820	1,090	0.10	PROXY(USSR(Maddison))
1870	1,493	0.63	PROXY(USSR(Maddison))
1880	1,635	0.91	INTERPOL(Maddison)
1890	1,790	0.91	INTERPOL(Maddison)

Year	GDP at PPP Per Capita, 2012 doll.	Growth Rate	Source
1900	1,959	0.91	PROXY(USSR(Maddison))
1913	2,356	1.43	PROXY(USSR(Maddison))
1920	913	12.67	PROXY(USSR(Davies))
1929	2,254	10.56	PROXY(USSR(Maddison))
1938	3,496	5.00	PROXY(USSR(Maddison))
1950	4,499	2.12	PROXY(USSR(Maddison))
1960	5,161	1.38	PROXY(USSR(Maddison))
1970	5,963	1.46	PROXY(USSR(Maddison))
1980	6,163	0.33	INTERPOL(Armenia(Maddison))
1990	6,155	0.01	90(WB)
2000	4,464	3.16	00(WB)
2010	6,241	3.41	10(WB)
2012	6,544	2.40	12(WB)
2020	7,688	2.03	FORECAST
2030	9,292	1.91	FORECAST

LAM Aruba

Year	GDP at PPP Per Capita, 2012 doll.	Growth Rate	Source
0001	.	.	
1000	.	.	
1500	.	.	
1600	.	.	
1700	.	.	
1820	.	.	
1870	.	.	
1880	.	.	
1890	.	.	
1900	.	.	
1913	.	.	
1920	.	.	
1929	.	.	
1938	.	.	
1950	11,617	.	PROXY(8 Caribbean cs(Maddison))
1960	15,560	2.97	INTERPOL(8 Caribbean cs(Maddison))
1970	20,840	2.97	INTERPOL(8 Caribbean cs(Maddison))
1980	24,945	1.81	INTERPOL(8 Caribbean cs(Maddison))
1990	28,453	1.32	93(CIA)WEIGHT(US(Maddison))
2000	34,640	1.99	00(CIA)WEIGHT(US(WB))
2010	22,993	4.02	09(CIA)WEIGHT(US(WB))
2012	24,582	3.40	11(CIA)WEIGHT(US(WB))
2020	27,363	1.35	FORECAST
2030	31,864	1.53	FORECAST

DME Australia

Year	GDP at PPP Per Capita, 2012 doll.	Growth Rate	Source
0001	372	.	0001(MIN)
1000	529	0.04	1000(MIN)
1500	671	0.05	1500(MIN)
1600	710	0.06	1600(MIN)
1700	752	0.06	1700(MIN)

Year	GDP at PPP Per Capita, 2012 doll.	Growth Rate	Source
1820	811	0.06	1820(Maddison)
1870	5,122	3.76	1870(Maddison)
1880	6,705	2.73	1880(Maddison)
1890	6,976	0.40	1890(Maddison)
1900	6,280	1.05	1900(Maddison)
1913	8,070	1.95	1913(Maddison)
1920	7,458	1.12	1920(Maddison)
1929	8,236	1.11	1929(Maddison)
1938	9,211	1.25	1938(Maddison)
1950	11,599	1.94	50(Maddison)
1960	13,952	1.86	60(Maddison)
1970	19,507	3.41	70(Maddison)
1980	23,728	1.98	80(WB)
1990	28,914	2.00	90(WB)
2000	35,937	2.20	00(WB)
2010	42,606	1.72	10(WB)
2012	43,818	1.41	12(WB)
2020	51,380	2.01	FORECAST
2030	62,032	1.90	FORECAST
DME Austria			
0001	665	.	0001(Maddison)
1000	665	0.00	1000(Maddison)
1500	1,106	0.10	1500(Maddison)
1600	1,310	0.17	1600(Maddison)
1700	1,554	0.17	1700(Maddison)
1820	1,906	0.17	1820(Maddison)
1870	2,915	0.85	1870(Maddison)
1880	3,253	1.10	1880(Maddison)
1890	3,823	1.63	1890(Maddison)
1900	4,510	1.67	1900(Maddison)
1913	5,422	1.43	1913(Maddison)
1920	3,774	5.04	1920(Maddison)
1929	5,788	4.87	1929(Maddison)
1938	5,569	0.43	1938(Maddison)
1950	5,799	0.34	50(Maddison)
1960	10,737	6.35	60(Maddison)
1970	16,814	4.59	70(Maddison)
1980	24,819	3.97	80(WB)
1990	30,665	2.14	90(WB)
2000	38,427	2.28	00(WB)
2010	42,699	1.06	10(WB)
2012	44,122	1.65	12(WB)
2020	51,652	1.99	FORECAST
2030	62,298	1.89	FORECAST
USR Azerbaijan			
0001	350	.	0001(MIN)
1000	485	0.03	1000(MIN)
1500	602	0.04	1500(MIN)

Year	GDP at PPP Per Capita, 2012 doll.	Growth Rate	Source
1600	632	0.05	PROXY(USSR(Maddison))
1700	699	0.10	PROXY(USSR(Maddison))
1820	788	0.10	PROXY(USSR(Maddison))
1870	1,080	0.63	PROXY(USSR(Maddison))
1880	1,182	0.91	INTERPOL(Maddison)
1890	1,294	0.91	INTERPOL(Maddison)
1900	1,417	0.91	PROXY(USSR(Maddison))
1913	1,704	1.43	PROXY(USSR(Maddison))
1920	660	12.67	PROXY(USSR(Davies))
1929	1,630	10.56	PROXY(USSR(Maddison))
1938	2,528	5.00	PROXY(USSR(Maddison))
1950	3,253	2.12	PROXY(USSR(Maddison))
1960	4,198	2.58	PROXY(USSR(Maddison))
1970	5,514	2.76	PROXY(USSR(Maddison))
1980	5,672	0.28	INTERPOL(Azerbaijan(Maddison))
1990	5,410	0.47	90(WB)
2000	2,836	6.25	00(WB)
2010	10,167	13.62	10(WB)
2012	10,127	0.19	12(WB)
2020	16,834	6.56	FORECAST
2030	21,956	2.69	FORECAST

LAM Bahamas

Year	GDP at PPP Per Capita, 2012 doll.	Growth Rate	Source
0001	.	.	
1000	.	.	
1500	.	.	
1600	.	.	
1700	.	.	
1820	.	.	
1870	.	.	
1880	.	.	
1890	.	.	
1900	.	.	
1913	.	.	
1920	.	.	
1929	.	.	
1938	.	.	
1950	14,975	.	50(Maddison)
1960	20,531	3.21	INTERPOL(Maddison)
1970	28,149	3.21	INTERPOL(Maddison)
1980	31,132	1.01	80(WB)
1990	34,391	1.00	90(WB)
2000	34,929	0.16	00(WB)
2010	31,019	1.18	10(WB)
2012	31,116	0.16	12(WB)
2020	32,070	0.38	FORECAST
2030	34,751	0.81	FORECAST

Year	GDP at PPP Per Capita, 2012 doll.	Growth Rate	Source
		MEA Bahrain	
0001	761	.	PROXY(W. Asia(Maddison))
1000	906	0.02	PROXY(W. Asia(Maddison))
1500	861	0.01	AVG(Arabia(Maddison))
1600	861	0.00	INTERPOL(Maddison)
1700	861	0.00	AVG(Arabia(Maddison))
1820	861	0.00	AVG(Arabia(Maddison))
1870	900	0.09	AVG(Arabia(Maddison))
1880	909	0.10	INTERPOL(Maddison)
1890	918	0.10	INTERPOL(Maddison)
1900	927	0.10	INTERPOL(Maddison)
1913	939	0.10	AVG(Arabia(Maddison))
1920	1,190	3.45	INTERPOL(Maddison)
1929	1,615	3.45	INTERPOL(Maddison)
1938	2,192	3.45	INTERPOL(Maddison)
1950	3,292	3.45	50(Maddison)
1960	6,869	7.63	60(Maddison)
1970	14,103	7.46	70(Maddison)
1980	24,663	5.75	80(WB)
1990	20,378	1.89	90(Maddison)
2000	32,202	4.68	00(WB)
2010	28,839	1.10	10(WB)
2012	28,924	0.15	12(WB)
2020	33,352	1.80	FORECAST
2030	39,841	1.79	FORECAST
		SAS Bangladesh	
0001	704	.	0001(Undivided India(Maddison))
1000	704	0.00	1000(Undivided India(Maddison))
1500	861	0.04	1500(Undivided India(Maddison))
1600	861	0.00	1600(Undivided India(Maddison))
1700	861	0.00	1700(Undivided India(Maddison))
1820	831	0.03	1820(Maddison)
1870	879	0.11	INTERPOL(Maddison)
1880	889	0.11	INTERPOL(Maddison)
1890	899	0.11	INTERPOL(Maddison)
1900	909	0.11	1900(Maddison)
1913	966	0.46	1913(Maddison)
1920	967	0.02	INTERPOL(Maddison)
1929	969	0.02	1929(Maddison)
1938	895	0.87	1938(Maddison)
1950	845	0.48	50(Maddison)
1960	813	0.39	60(Maddison)
1970	898	1.00	70(Maddison)
1980	746	1.84	80(WB)
1990	827	1.03	90(WB)
2000	1,080	2.70	00(WB)
2010	1,670	4.46	10(WB)
2012	1,851	5.27	12(WB)

Year	GDP at PPP Per Capita, 2012 doll.	Growth Rate	Source
2020	2,465	3.65	FORECAST
2030	3,145	2.46	FORECAST
		LAM BARBADOS	
0001	.	.	
1000	.	.	
1500	.	.	
1600	.	.	
1700	.	.	
1820	.	.	
1870	.	.	
1880	.	.	
1890	.	.	
1900	.	.	
1913	.	.	
1920	.	.	
1929	.	.	
1938	.	.	
1950	3,323	.	50(Maddison)
1960	6,487	6.92	INTERPOL(Maddison)
1970	12,664	6.92	INTERPOL(Maddison)
1980	18,735	3.99	80(WB)
1990	20,271	0.79	90(WB)
2000	25,428	2.29	00(WB)
2010	26,554	0.43	10(WB)
2012	26,488	0.12	12(WB)
2020	29,557	1.38	FORECAST
2030	34,486	1.55	FORECAST
		USR BELARUS	
0001	373	.	0001(MIN)
1000	531	0.04	1000(MIN)
1500	674	0.05	PROXY(USSR(Maddison))
1600	746	0.10	PROXY(USSR(Maddison))
1700	824	0.10	PROXY(USSR(Maddison))
1820	930	0.10	PROXY(USSR(Maddison))
1870	1,274	0.63	PROXY(USSR(Maddison))
1880	1,395	0.91	INTERPOL(Maddison)
1890	1,527	0.91	INTERPOL(Maddison)
1900	1,672	0.91	PROXY(USSR(Maddison))
1913	2,011	1.43	PROXY(USSR(Maddison))
1920	779	12.67	PROXY(USSR(Davies))
1929	1,923	10.56	PROXY(USSR(Maddison))
1938	2,984	5.00	PROXY(USSR(Maddison))
1950	3,840	2.12	PROXY(USSR(Maddison))
1960	4,790	2.24	PROXY(USSR(Maddison))
1970	6,082	2.42	PROXY(USSR(Maddison))
1980	6,766	1.07	INTERPOL(Belarus(Maddison))

Year	GDP at PPP Per Capita, 2012 doll.	Growth Rate	Source
1990	7,323	0.79	90(WB)
2000	6,624	1.00	00(WB)
2010	14,272	7.98	10(WB)
2012	15,327	3.63	12(WB)
2020	21,867	4.54	FORECAST
2030	28,309	2.62	FORECAST
DME Belgium			
0001	704	.	0001(Maddison)
1000	665	0.01	1000(Maddison)
1500	1,369	0.14	1500(Maddison)
1600	1,527	0.11	1600(Maddison)
1700	1,790	0.16	1700(Maddison)
1820	2,064	0.12	1820(Maddison)
1870	4,213	1.44	1870(Maddison)
1880	4,796	1.31	1880(Maddison)
1890	5,364	1.13	1890(Maddison)
1900	5,838	0.85	1900(Maddison)
1913	6,604	0.95	1913(Maddison)
1920	6,200	0.90	1920(Maddison)
1929	7,909	2.74	1929(Maddison)
1938	7,561	0.50	1938(Maddison)
1950	8,547	1.03	50(Maddison)
1960	11,260	2.80	60(Maddison)
1970	17,956	4.78	70(Maddison)
1980	25,430	3.54	80(WB)
1990	30,990	2.00	90(WB)
2000	37,594	1.95	00(WB)
2010	40,777	0.82	10(WB)
2012	40,566	0.26	12(WB)
2020	45,593	1.47	FORECAST
2030	53,488	1.61	FORECAST
LAM Belize			
0001	.	.	
1000	.	.	
1500	.	.	
1600	.	.	
1700	.	.	
1820	.	.	
1870	.	.	
1880	.	.	
1890	.	.	
1900	.	.	
1913	.	.	
1920	.	.	
1929	.	.	
1938	.	.	

Year	GDP at PPP Per Capita, 2012 doll.	Growth Rate	Source
1950	2,531	.	50(Maddison)
1960	2,932	1.48	INTERPOL(Maddison)
1970	3,395	1.48	INTERPOL(Maddison)
1980	4,021	1.71	80(WB)
1990	4,981	2.16	90(WB)
2000	6,734	3.06	00(WB)
2010	7,739	1.40	10(WB)
2012	7,937	1.27	12(WB)
2020	9,288	1.99	FORECAST
2030	11,201	1.89	FORECAST
AFR Benin			
0001	.	.	
1000	.	.	
1500	.	.	
1600	.	.	
1700	.	.	
1820	.	.	
1870	.	.	
1880	.	.	
1890	.	.	
1900	.	.	
1913	.	.	
1920	.	.	
1929	.	.	
1938	.	.	
1950	1,696	.	50(Maddison)
1960	1,856	0.90	60(Maddison)
1970	1,778	0.43	70(Maddison)
1980	1,632	0.86	80(WB)
1990	1,601	0.19	90(WB)
2000	1,702	0.61	00(WB)
2010	1,601	0.61	10(WB)
2012	1,557	1.39	12(WB)
2020	1,577	0.16	FORECAST
2030	1,675	0.60	FORECAST
DME Bermuda			
0001	.	.	
1000	.	.	
1500	.	.	
1600	.	.	
1700	.	.	
1820	.	.	
1870	.	.	
1880	.	.	
1890	.	.	

Year	GDP at PPP Per Capita, 2012 doll.	Growth Rate	Source
1900	.	.	
1913	.	.	
1920	.	.	
1929	.	.	
1938	.	.	
1950	2,608	.	50(Maddison)
1960	4,502	5.61	INTERPOL(Maddison)
1970	7,773	5.61	INTERPOL(Maddison)
1980	9,938	2.49	INTERPOL(Maddison)
1990	11,172	1.18	90(Maddison)
2000	34,666	11.99	00(CIA)WEIGHT(US(WB))
2010	85,831	9.49	11(CIA)WEIGHT(US(WB))
2012	89,269	1.98	11(CIA)WEIGHT(US(WB))
2020	166,705	8.12	FORECAST
2030	215,348	2.59	FORECAST
SAS Bhutan			
0001	.	.	
1000	.	.	
1500	.	.	
1600	.	.	
1700	.	.	
1820	.	.	
1870	.	.	
1880	.	.	
1890	.	.	
1900	.	.	
1913	.	.	
1920	.	.	
1929	.	.	
1938	.	.	
1950	787	.	50(Maddison)
1960	838	0.63	INTERPOL(Maddison)
1970	892	0.63	INTERPOL(Maddison)
1980	1,036	1.51	80(WB)
1990	2,051	7.06	90(WB)
2000	3,169	4.45	00(WB)
2010	5,742	6.12	10(WB)
2012	6,591	7.14	12(WB)
2020	10,431	5.91	FORECAST
2030	13,614	2.70	FORECAST
LAM Bolivia			
0001	367	.	0001(MIN)
1000	518	0.03	1000(MIN)
1500	653	0.05	1500(MIN)
1600	689	0.05	1600(MIN)
1700	729	0.06	1700(MIN)

Year	GDP at PPP Per Capita, 2012 doll.	Growth Rate	Source
1820	784	0.06	PROXY(Other L. Am.(Maddison))
1870	803	0.05	PROXY(Other L. Am.(Maddison))
1880	957	1.77	INTERPOL(Maddison)
1890	1,140	1.77	INTERPOL(Maddison)
1900	1,359	1.77	INTERPOL(Maddison)
1913	1,706	1.77	PROXY(Other L. Am.(Maddison))
1920	1,899	1.54	INTERPOL(Maddison)
1929	2,179	1.54	INTERPOL(Maddison)
1938	2,500	1.54	INTERPOL(Maddison)
1950	3,003	1.54	50(Maddison)
1960	2,481	1.89	60(Maddison)
1970	3,427	3.28	70(Maddison)
1980	4,093	1.79	80(WB)
1990	3,224	2.36	90(WB)
2000	3,911	1.95	00(WB)
2010	4,832	2.14	10(WB)
2012	5,196	3.70	12(WB)
2020	6,183	2.20	FORECAST
2030	7,529	1.99	FORECAST
EEU Bosnia			
0001	346	.	0001(MIN)
1000	478	0.03	1000(MIN)
1500	590	0.04	1500(MIN)
1600	619	0.05	1600(MIN)
1700	652	0.05	1700(MIN)
1820	695	0.05	1820(MIN)
1870	715	0.06	1870(MIN)
1880	719	0.06	PROXY(Yugoslavia(Maddison))
1890	853	1.72	PROXY(Yugoslavia(Maddison))
1900	913	0.68	PROXY(Yugoslavia(Maddison))
1913	1,070	1.23	PROXY(Yugoslavia(Maddison))
1920	1,043	0.36	PROXY(Yugoslavia(Maddison))
1929	1,380	3.16	PROXY(Yugoslavia(Maddison))
1938	1,372	0.07	PROXY(Yugoslavia(Maddison))
1950	1,569	1.13	PROXY(Yugoslavia(Maddison))
1960	2,642	5.35	PROXY(Yugoslavia(Maddison))
1970	4,348	5.11	PROXY(Yugoslavia(Maddison))
1980	7,552	5.68	PROXY(Yugoslavia(Maddison))
1990	7,146	0.55	90(Maddison)
2000	5,893	1.91	00(WB)
2010	9,295	4.66	10(WB)
2012	9,392	0.52	12(WB)
2020	11,749	2.84	FORECAST
2030	14,663	2.24	FORECAST
AFR Botswana			
0001	295	.	0001(MIN)
1000	386	0.03	1000(MIN)
1500	457	0.03	1500(MIN)

Year	GDP at PPP Per Capita, 2012 doll.	Growth Rate	Source
1600	474	0.04	1600(MIN)
1700	492	0.04	1700(MIN)
1820	517	0.04	1820(MIN)
1870	528	0.04	1870(MIN)
1880	530	0.04	1880(MIN)
1890	532	0.04	1890(MIN)
1900	534	0.04	1900(MIN)
1913	537	0.04	1913(MIN)
1920	539	0.04	1920(MIN)
1929	541	0.04	1929(MIN)
1938	543	0.04	1938(MIN)
1950	546	0.04	50(Maddison)
1960	732	2.97	60(Maddison)
1970	1,367	6.45	70(Maddison)
1980	4,288	12.11	80(WB)
1990	8,727	7.37	90(WB)
2000	11,381	2.69	00(WB)
2010	14,816	2.67	10(WB)
2012	16,105	4.26	12(WB)
2020	22,589	4.32	FORECAST
2030	29,161	2.59	FORECAST
		LAM BRAZIL	
0001	361	.	0001(MIN)
1000	507	0.03	1000(MIN)
1500	636	0.05	1500(MIN)
1600	670	0.05	1600(Maddison)
1700	718	0.07	1700(Maddison)
1820	1,011	0.29	1820(Maddison)
1870	1,116	0.20	1870(Maddison)
1880	1,177	0.53	1880(Maddison)
1890	1,242	0.54	1890(Maddison)
1900	1,061	1.57	1900(Maddison)
1913	1,269	1.39	1913(Maddison)
1920	1,507	2.48	1920(Maddison)
1929	1,779	1.86	1929(Maddison)
1938	1,997	1.29	1938(Maddison)
1950	2,616	2.28	50(Maddison)
1960	3,714	3.56	60(Maddison)
1970	4,940	2.89	70(Maddison)
1980	8,548	5.64	80(WB)
1990	8,105	0.53	90(WB)
2000	9,011	1.06	00(WB)
2010	11,504	2.47	10(WB)
2012	11,716	0.92	12(WB)
2020	13,747	2.02	FORECAST
2030	16,603	1.91	FORECAST

Year	GDP at PPP Per Capita, 2012 doll.	Growth Rate	Source
SEA Brunei			
0001	.	.	
1000	.	.	
1500	.	.	
1600	.	.	
1700	.	.	
1820	.	.	
1870	.	.	
1880	.	.	
1890	.	.	
1900	.	.	
1913	.	.	
1920	.	.	
1929	.	.	
1938	.	.	
1950	7,789	.	50(Maddison)
1960	14,084	6.10	INTERPOL(Maddison)
1970	25,465	6.10	INTERPOL(Maddison)
1980	53,816	7.77	80(WB)
1990	28,208	6.26	90(WB)
2000	55,340	6.97	00(WB)
2010	51,448	0.73	10(WB)
2012	52,482	1.00	12(WB)
2020	64,018	2.51	FORECAST
2030	78,981	2.12	FORECAST
EEU Bulgaria			
0001	665	.	AVG(Danubian provinces(Maddison))
1000	626	0.01	1000(Maddison)
1500	908	0.07	PROXY(E. Europe(Maddison))
1600	1,003	0.10	PROXY(E. Europe(Maddison))
1700	1,109	0.10	PROXY(E. Europe(Maddison))
1820	1,250	0.10	PROXY(E. Europe(Maddison))
1870	1,314	0.10	1870(Maddison)
1880	1,525	1.50	INTERPOL(Maddison)
1890	1,770	1.50	1890(Maddison)
1900	1,914	0.79	1900(Maddison)
1913	2,400	1.76	1913(Maddison)
1920	1,422	7.20	1924(Maddison)
1929	1,847	2.94	1929(Maddison)
1938	2,496	3.41	1938(Maddison)
1950	2,584	0.29	50(Maddison)
1960	4,490	5.68	60(Maddison)
1970	7,257	4.92	70(Maddison)
1980	9,085	2.27	80(WB)
1990	11,700	2.56	90(WB)
2000	9,422	2.14	00(WB)

Year	GDP at PPP Per Capita, 2012 doll.	Growth Rate	Source
2010	15,449	5.07	10(WB)
2012	16,041	1.90	12(WB)
2020	20,842	3.33	FORECAST
2030	26,388	2.39	FORECAST
AFR Burkina Faso			
0001	.	.	
1000	.	.	
1500	.	.	
1600	.	.	
1700	.	.	
1820	.	.	
1870	.	.	
1880	.	.	
1890	.	.	
1900	.	.	
1913	.	.	
1920	.	.	
1929	.	.	
1938	.	.	
1950	742	.	50(Maddison)
1960	864	1.53	60(Maddison)
1970	907	0.49	70(Maddison)
1980	790	1.37	80(WB)
1990	860	0.86	90(WB)
2000	1,049	2.00	00(WB)
2010	1,380	2.77	10(WB)
2012	1,482	3.63	12(WB)
2020	1,797	2.44	FORECAST
2030	2,210	2.09	FORECAST
CPA Burma			
0001	400	.	0001(MIN)
1000	588	0.04	1000(MIN)
1500	769	0.05	PROXY(Other E. Asia(Maddison))
1600	783	0.02	PROXY(Other E. Asia(Maddison))
1700	779	0.01	PROXY(Other E. Asia(Maddison))
1820	789	0.01	1820(Maddison)
1870	789	0.00	1870(Maddison)
1880	847	0.72	INTERPOL(Maddison)
1890	910	0.72	INTERPOL(Maddison)
1900	977	0.72	INTERPOL(Maddison)
1913	1,072	0.72	1913(Maddison)
1920	1,146	0.95	INTERPOL(Maddison)
1929	1,355	1.88	INTERPOL(Maddison)
1938	1,158	1.73	1938(Maddison)
1950	620	5.08	50(Maddison)
1960	852	3.24	60(Maddison)

Year	GDP at PPP Per Capita, 2012 doll.	Growth Rate	Source
1970	958	1.17	70(Maddison)
1980	1,199	2.26	80(Maddison)
1990	1,168	0.26	90(Maddison)
2000	1,709	3.88	00(CIA)WEIGHT(US(WB))
2010	1,529	1.11	10(CIA)WEIGHT(US(WB))
2012	1,600	2.29	12(CIA)
2020	1,797	1.46	FORECAST
2030	2,106	1.60	FORECAST
		AFR Burundi	
0001	300	.	0001(MIN)
1000	395	0.03	1000(MIN)
1500	468	0.03	1500(MIN)
1600	487	0.04	1600(MIN)
1700	506	0.04	1700(MIN)
1820	532	0.04	1820(MIN)
1870	544	0.04	1870(MIN)
1880	546	0.04	1880(MIN)
1890	549	0.04	1890(MIN)
1900	551	0.04	1900(MIN)
1913	554	0.04	1913(MIN)
1920	556	0.04	1920(MIN)
1929	558	0.04	1929(MIN)
1938	560	0.04	1938(MIN)
1950	563	0.04	50(Maddison)
1960	548	0.28	60(Maddison)
1970	533	0.27	70(Maddison)
1980	522	0.20	80(WB)
1990	514	0.17	90(WB)
2000	553	0.73	00(WB)
2010	552	0.00	10(WB)
2012	551	0.10	12(WB)
2020	559	0.17	FORECAST
2030	595	0.62	FORECAST
		CPA Cambodia	
0001	358	.	0001(MIN)
1000	501	0.03	1000(MIN)
1500	626	0.04	PROXY(Other E. Asia(Maddison))
1600	637	0.02	PROXY(Other E. Asia(Maddison))
1700	634	0.01	PROXY(Other E. Asia(Maddison))
1820	642	0.01	PROXY(26 E. Asian cs(Maddison))
1870	626	0.05	MIN(PROXY(26 E. Asian cs(Maddison)
1880	669	0.66	INTERPOL(Maddison)
1890	724	0.79	INTERPOL(Maddison)
1900	783	0.79	INTERPOL(Maddison)
1913	868	0.80	PROXY(26 E. Asian cs(Maddison))
1920	857	0.19	INTERPOL(Maddison)
1929	843	0.19	INTERPOL(Maddison)
1938	829	0.19	INTERPOL(Maddison)

Year	GDP at PPP Per Capita, 2012 doll.	Growth Rate	Source
1950	811	0.19	50(Maddison)
1960	1,063	2.75	60(Maddison)
1970	1,019	0.42	70(Maddison)
1980	1,252	2.08	80(Maddison)
1990	1,330	0.61	90(Maddison)
2000	1,365	0.26	00(WB)
2010	2,252	5.13	10(WB)
2012	2,454	4.38	12(WB)
2020	3,193	3.34	FORECAST
2030	4,044	2.39	FORECAST
AFR Cameroon			
0001	.	.	
1000	.	.	
1500	.	.	
1600	.	.	
1700	.	.	
1820	.	.	
1870	.	.	
1880	.	.	
1890	.	.	
1900	.	.	
1913	.	.	
1920	.	.	
1929	.	.	
1938	.	.	
1950	1,050	.	50(Maddison)
1960	1,389	2.84	60(Maddison)
1970	1,745	2.31	70(Maddison)
1980	2,262	2.63	80(WB)
1990	2,325	0.27	90(WB)
2000	2,073	1.14	00(WB)
2010	2,231	0.74	10(WB)
2012	2,312	1.79	12(WB)
2020	2,484	0.90	FORECAST
2030	2,806	1.23	FORECAST
DME Canada			
0001	352	.	0001(MIN)
1000	489	0.03	1000(MIN)
1500	608	0.04	1500(MIN)
1600	639	0.05	1600(MIN)
1700	673	0.05	1700(Maddison)
1820	1,415	0.62	1820(Maddison)
1870	2,652	1.27	1870(Maddison)
1880	2,842	0.69	1880(Maddison)
1890	3,721	2.73	1890(Maddison)
1900	4,555	2.04	1900(Maddison)

Year	GDP at PPP Per Capita, 2012 doll.	Growth Rate	Source
1913	6,959	3.31	1913(Maddison)
1920	6,042	2.00	1920(Maddison)
1929	7,926	3.06	1929(Maddison)
1938	7,114	1.19	1938(Maddison)
1950	11,409	4.02	50(Maddison)
1960	13,840	1.95	60(Maddison)
1970	19,271	3.37	70(Maddison)
1980	26,160	3.10	80(WB)
1990	30,585	1.57	90(WB)
2000	37,123	1.96	00(WB)
2010	40,469	0.87	10(WB)
2012	41,298	1.02	12(WB)
2020	46,567	1.51	FORECAST
2030	54,763	1.63	FORECAST

AFR Cape Verde

Year	GDP at PPP Per Capita, 2012 doll.	Growth Rate	Source
0001	.	.	
1000	.	.	
1500	.	.	
1600	.	.	
1700	.	.	
1820	.	.	
1870	.	.	
1880	.	.	
1890	.	.	
1900	.	.	
1913	.	.	
1920	.	.	
1929	.	.	
1938	.	.	
1950	704	.	50(Maddison)
1960	700	0.06	60(Maddison)
1970	750	0.69	70(Maddison)
1980	893	1.76	80(WB)
1990	1,264	3.54	90(WB)
2000	2,763	8.13	00(WB)
2010	4,594	5.22	10(WB)
2012	4,846	2.71	12(WB)
2020	7,328	5.31	FORECAST
2030	9,548	2.68	FORECAST

LAM Cayman Islands

Year	GDP at PPP Per Capita, 2012 doll.	Growth Rate	Source
0001	.	.	
1000	.	.	
1500	.	.	
1600	.	.	
1700	.	.	

Year	GDP at PPP Per Capita, 2012 doll.	Growth Rate	Source
1820	.	.	
1870	.	.	
1880	.	.	
1890	.	.	
1900	.	.	
1913	.	.	
1920	.	.	
1929	.	.	
1938	.	.	
1950	15,717	.	PROXY(8 Caribbean cs(Maddison))
1960	20,718	2.80	INTERPOL(8 Caribbean cs(Maddison))
1970	27,309	2.80	INTERPOL(8 Caribbean cs(Maddison))
1980	32,368	1.71	INTERPOL(8 Caribbean cs(Maddison))
1990	36,656	1.25	93(CIA)WEIGHT(US(Maddison))
2000	40,176	0.92	99(CIA)WEIGHT(US(WB))
2010	48,666	1.94	08(CIA)WEIGHT(US(WB))
2012	50,255	1.62	08(CIA)WEIGHT(US(WB))
2020	57,665	1.73	FORECAST
2030	68,658	1.76	FORECAST

AFR Central African Republic

Year	GDP at PPP Per Capita, 2012 doll.	Growth Rate	Source
0001	.	.	
1000	.	.	
1500	.	.	
1600	.	.	
1700	.	.	
1820	.	.	
1870	.	.	
1880	.	.	
1890	.	.	
1900	.	.	
1913	.	.	
1920	.	.	
1929	.	.	
1938	.	.	
1950	1,208	.	50(Maddison)
1960	1,359	1.19	60(Maddison)
1970	1,234	0.96	70(Maddison)
1980	995	2.13	80(WB)
1990	860	1.45	90(WB)
2000	772	1.08	00(WB)
2010	994	2.56	10(WB)
2012	1,077	4.06	12(WB)
2020	1,242	1.81	FORECAST
2030	1,485	1.80	FORECAST

Year	GDP at PPP Per Capita, 2012 doll.	Growth Rate	Source
AFR Chad			
0001	.	.	
1000	.	.	
1500	.	.	
1600	.	.	
1700	.	.	
1820	.	.	
1870	.	.	
1880	.	.	
1890	.	.	
1900	.	.	
1913	.	.	
1920	.	.	
1929	.	.	
1938	.	.	
1950	745	.	50(Maddison)
1960	1,053	3.52	60(Maddison)
1970	1,101	0.45	70(Maddison)
1980	827	2.83	80(WB)
1990	1,059	2.51	90(WB)
2000	1,014	0.43	00(WB)
2010	2,077	7.43	10(WB)
2012	2,135	1.38	12(WB)
2020	2,936	4.06	FORECAST
2030	3,775	2.55	FORECAST
LAM Chile			
0001	364	.	0001(MIN)
1000	513	0.03	1000(MIN)
1500	645	0.05	AVG(Other Sp. Am.(Maddison))
1600	759	0.16	INTERPOL(Maddison)
1700	893	0.16	INTERPOL(Maddison)
1820	1,086	0.16	1820(Maddison)
1870	2,019	1.25	1870(Maddison)
1880	2,410	1.79	INTERPOL(Maddison)
1890	2,877	1.79	INTERPOL(Maddison)
1900	3,435	1.79	1900(Maddison)
1913	4,676	2.40	1913(Maddison)
1920	4,283	1.25	1920(Maddison)
1929	5,985	3.79	1929(Maddison)
1938	5,532	0.87	1938(Maddison)
1950	5,979	0.65	50(Maddison)
1960	6,173	0.32	60(Maddison)
1970	6,980	1.23	70(Maddison)

Year	GDP at PPP Per Capita, 2012 doll.	Growth Rate	Source
1980	6,872	0.16	80(WB)
1990	8,650	2.33	90(WB)
2000	14,199	5.08	00(WB)
2010	19,332	3.13	10(WB)
2012	21,468	5.38	12(WB)
2020	28,844	3.76	FORECAST
2030	36,885	2.49	FORECAST
CPA China			
0001	704	.	0001(Maddison)
1000	704	0.00	1000(Maddison)
1500	939	0.06	1500(Maddison)
1600	939	0.00	1600(Maddison)
1700	939	0.00	1700(Maddison)
1820	939	0.00	1820(Maddison)
1870	829	0.25	1870(Maddison)
1880	837	0.09	INTERPOL(Maddison)
1890	845	0.09	1890(Maddison)
1900	853	0.09	1900(Maddison)
1913	864	0.10	1913(Maddison)
1920	871	0.11	INTERPOL(Maddison)
1929	879	0.11	1929(Maddison)
1938	879	0.00	1938(Maddison)
1950	687	2.04	50(Maddison)
1960	840	2.03	60(Maddison)
1970	795	0.55	70(Maddison)
1980	871	0.92	80(WB)
1990	1,737	7.14	90(WB)
2000	3,290	6.60	00(WB)
2010	7,870	9.11	10(WB)
2012	9,083	7.43	12(WB)
2020	16,617	7.84	FORECAST
2030	21,516	2.62	FORECAST
LAM Colombia			
0001	346	.	0001(MIN)
1000	477	0.03	1000(MIN)
1500	590	0.04	1500(MIN)
1600	619	0.05	1600(MIN)
1700	651	0.05	PROXY(Other Sp. Am.(Maddison))
1820	889	0.26	PROXY(Other L. Am.(Maddison))
1870	911	0.05	PROXY(Other L. Am.(Maddison))
1880	1,081	1.73	INTERPOL(Maddison)
1890	1,283	1.73	INTERPOL(Maddison)
1900	1,523	1.73	1900(Maddison)
1913	1,934	1.86	1913(Maddison)
1920	1,964	0.22	1920(Maddison)
1929	2,355	2.04	1929(Maddison)
1938	2,884	2.28	1938(Maddison)

Year	GDP at PPP Per Capita, 2012 doll.	Growth Rate	Source
1950	3,369	1.30	50(Maddison)
1960	3,812	1.24	60(Maddison)
1970	4,604	1.91	70(Maddison)
1980	6,177	2.98	80(WB)
1990	7,090	1.39	90(WB)
2000	7,564	0.65	00(WB)
2010	9,656	2.47	10(WB)
2012	10,436	3.96	12(WB)
2020	12,517	2.30	FORECAST
2030	15,309	2.03	FORECAST
AFR Comoros			
0001	.	.	
1000	.	.	
1500	.	.	
1600	.	.	
1700	.	.	
1820	.	.	
1870	.	.	
1880	.	.	
1890	.	.	
1900	.	.	
1913	.	.	
1920	.	.	
1929	.	.	
1938	.	.	
1950	876	.	50(Maddison)
1960	1,304	4.05	60(Maddison)
1970	2,222	5.48	70(Maddison)
1980	1,391	4.58	80(WB)
1990	1,414	0.17	90(WB)
2000	1,293	0.90	00(WB)
2010	1,207	0.69	10(WB)
2012	1,210	0.13	12(WB)
2020	1,235	0.26	FORECAST
2030	1,324	0.70	FORECAST
AFR Congo, Democratic Republic of the			
0001	.	.	
1000	.	.	
1500	.	.	
1600	.	.	
1700	.	.	
1820	.	.	
1870	.	.	
1880	.	.	
1890	.	.	

Year	GDP at PPP Per Capita, 2012 doll.	Growth Rate	Source
1900	.	.	
1913	.	.	
1920	.	.	
1929	.	.	
1938	.	.	
1950	892	.	50(Maddison)
1960	1,152	2.59	60(Maddison)
1970	1,165	0.12	70(Maddison)
1980	900	2.55	80(WB)
1990	743	1.90	90(WB)
2000	315	8.23	00(WB)
2010	383	2.00	10(WB)
2012	415	4.08	12(WB)
2020	470	1.57	FORECAST
2030	555	1.67	FORECAST
AFR Congo, Republic of the			
0001	.	.	
1000	.	.	
1500	.	.	
1600	.	.	
1700	.	.	
1820	.	.	
1870	.	.	
1880	.	.	
1890	.	.	
1900	.	.	
1913	.	.	
1920	.	.	
1929	.	.	
1938	.	.	
1950	2,017	.	50(Maddison)
1960	2,386	1.69	60(Maddison)
1970	2,859	1.82	70(Maddison)
1980	3,710	2.64	80(WB)
1990	4,399	1.72	90(WB)
2000	3,640	1.87	00(WB)
2010	4,285	1.64	10(WB)
2012	4,354	0.80	12(WB)
2020	4,839	1.33	FORECAST
2030	5,627	1.52	FORECAST
SEA Cook Islands			
0001	.	.	
1000	.	.	
1500	.	.	
1600	.	.	

Year	GDP at PPP Per Capita, 2012 doll.	Growth Rate	Source
1700	.	.	
1820	.	.	
1870	.	.	
1880	.	.	
1890	.	.	
1900	.	.	
1913	.	.	
1920	.	.	
1929	.	.	
1938	.	.	
1950	2,946	.	PROXY(14 Pacific is(Maddison))
1960	3,483	1.69	INTERPOL(14 Pacific is(Maddison))
1970	4,119	1.69	INTERPOL(14 Pacific is(Maddison))
1980	4,399	0.66	INTERPOL(14 Pacific is(Maddison))
1990	4,497	0.22	93(CIA)WEIGHT(US(Maddison))
2000	6,369	3.54	99(CIA)WEIGHT(US(WB))
2010	10,262	4.88	05(CIA)WEIGHT(US(WB))
2012	10,627	1.76	05(CIA)WEIGHT(US(WB))
2020	14,027	3.53	FORECAST
2030	17,848	2.44	FORECAST
LAM Costa Rica			
0001	370	.	0001(MIN)
1000	526	0.04	1000(MIN)
1500	666	0.05	1500(MIN)
1600	703	0.05	1600(MIN)
1700	745	0.06	1700(MIN)
1820	802	0.06	PROXY(Other L. Am.(Maddison))
1870	822	0.05	PROXY(Other L. Am.(Maddison))
1880	979	1.77	INTERPOL(Maddison)
1890	1,166	1.77	INTERPOL(Maddison)
1900	1,390	1.77	INTERPOL(Maddison)
1913	1,745	1.77	PROXY(Other L. Am.(Maddison))
1920	2,541	5.51	1920(Maddison)
1929	2,476	0.29	1929(Maddison)
1938	2,936	1.91	1938(Maddison)
1950	3,072	0.38	50(Maddison)
1960	4,188	3.15	60(Maddison)
1970	5,708	3.15	70(Maddison)
1980	7,364	2.58	80(WB)
1990	7,201	0.22	90(WB)
2000	9,284	2.57	00(WB)
2010	11,940	2.55	10(WB)
2012	12,733	3.27	12(WB)
2020	15,596	2.57	FORECAST
2030	19,279	2.14	FORECAST
EEU Croatia			
0001	415	.	0001(MIN)

Year	GDP at PPP Per Capita, 2012 doll.	Growth Rate	Source
1000	620	0.04	1000(MIN)
1500	824	0.06	PROXY(E. Europe(Maddison))
1600	910	0.10	PROXY(E. Europe(Maddison))
1700	1,006	0.10	PROXY(E. Europe(Maddison))
1820	1,134	0.10	PROXY(E. Europe(Maddison))
1870	1,192	0.10	PROXY(Yugoslavia(Maddison))
1880	1,414	1.72	INTERPOL(Maddison)
1890	1,678	1.72	PROXY(Yugoslavia(Maddison))
1900	1,795	0.68	PROXY(Yugoslavia(Maddison))
1913	2,104	1.23	PROXY(Yugoslavia(Maddison))
1920	2,052	0.36	PROXY(Yugoslavia(Maddison))
1929	2,715	3.16	PROXY(Yugoslavia(Maddison))
1938	2,699	0.07	PROXY(Yugoslavia(Maddison))
1950	3,087	1.13	PROXY(Yugoslavia(Maddison))
1960	5,261	5.47	PROXY(Yugoslavia(Maddison))
1970	8,760	5.23	PROXY(Yugoslavia(Maddison))
1980	15,416	5.81	PROXY(Yugoslavia(Maddison))
1990	14,568	0.56	90(Maddison)
2000	15,472	0.60	00(WB)
2010	20,829	3.02	10(WB)
2012	20,961	0.32	12(WB)
2020	24,924	2.19	FORECAST
2030	30,339	1.99	FORECAST
		LAM Cuba	
0001	396	.	0001(MIN)
1000	579	0.04	1000(MIN)
1500	753	0.05	1500(MIN)
1600	801	0.06	1600(MIN)
1700	856	0.07	PROXY(Caribean cs(Maddison))
1820	836	0.02	PROXY(Other L. Am.(Maddison))
1870	856	0.05	PROXY(Other L. Am.(Maddison))
1880	1,020	1.77	INTERPOL(Maddison)
1890	1,216	1.77	INTERPOL(Maddison)
1900	1,449	1.77	INTERPOL(Maddison)
1913	1,819	1.77	PROXY(Other L. Am.(Maddison))
1920	2,024	1.54	INTERPOL(Maddison)
1929	2,565	2.66	1929(Maddison)
1938	2,125	2.07	1938(Maddison)
1950	3,202	3.47	50(Maddison)
1960	3,209	0.02	60(Maddison)
1970	3,036	0.55	70(Maddison)
1980	3,948	2.66	80(Maddison)
1990	4,315	0.89	90(Maddison)
2000	2,928	3.80	00(CIA)WEIGHT(US(WB))
2010	10,601	13.73	10(CIA)WEIGHT(US(WB))
2012	10,925	1.52	12(CIA)

Year	GDP at PPP Per Capita, 2012 doll.	Growth Rate	Source
2020	18,710	6.96	FORECAST
2030	24,366	2.68	FORECAST
LAM CURACAO			
0001	.	.	
1000	.	.	
1500	.	.	
1600	.	.	
1700	.	.	
1820	.	.	
1870	.	.	
1880	.	.	
1890	.	.	
1900	.	.	
1913	.	.	
1920	.	.	
1929	.	.	
1938	.	.	
1950	5,148	.	50(Maddison)WEIGHT(Neth Antilles)
1960	7,201	3.41	INTERPOL(Maddison)
1970	10,073	3.41	INTERPOL(Maddison)
1980	9,870	0.20	INTERPOL(Maddison)
1990	8,303	1.71	90(Maddison)WEIGHT(Neth Antilles)
2000	12,606	4.26	00(CIA)WEIGHT(US(WB))/(Neth Antill
2010	20,159	4.81	08(CIA)WEIGHT(US(WB))
2012	20,928	1.89	08(CIA)WEIGHT(US(WB))
2020	27,973	3.69	FORECAST
2030	35,720	2.48	FORECAST
MEA CYPRUS			
0001	861	.	0001(Maddison)
1000	939	0.01	1000(Maddison)
1500	666	0.07	PROXY(Greece(Maddison))
1600	743	0.11	PROXY(Greece(Maddison))
1700	815	0.09	PROXY(Greece(Maddison))
1820	986	0.16	PROXY(Greece(Maddison))
1870	1,354	0.64	PROXY(Greece(Maddison))
1880	1,566	1.47	PROXY(Greece(Maddison))
1890	1,812	1.47	PROXY(Greece(Maddison))
1900	2,078	1.38	PROXY(Greece(Maddison))
1913	2,449	1.27	PROXY(Greece(Maddison))
1920	2,883	2.36	PROXY(Greece(Maddison))
1929	3,603	2.51	PROXY(Greece(Maddison))
1938	4,118	1.50	PROXY(Greece(Maddison))
1950	2,946	2.75	50(Maddison)
1960	5,037	5.51	INTERPOL(Maddison)
1970	8,614	5.51	INTERPOL(Maddison)

Year	GDP at PPP Per Capita, 2012 doll.	Growth Rate	Source
1980	14,729	5.51	80(WB)
1990	24,220	5.10	90(WB)
2000	29,779	2.09	00(WB)
2010	33,174	1.09	10(WB)
2012	30,768	3.69	12(WB)
2020	36,545	2.17	FORECAST
2030	44,456	1.98	FORECAST
		EEU CZECH REPUBLIC	
0001	457	.	0001(MIN)
1000	719	0.05	1000(MIN)
1500	1,008	0.07	PROXY(E. Europe(Maddison))
1600	1,114	0.10	PROXY(E. Europe(Maddison))
1700	1,232	0.10	PROXY(E. Europe(Maddison))
1820	1,388	0.10	PROXY(Czechoslovakia(Maddison))
1870	1,903	0.63	PROXY(Czechoslovakia(Maddison))
1880	2,164	1.29	INTERPOL(Maddison)
1890	2,461	1.29	PROXY(Czechoslovakia(Maddison))
1900	2,827	1.40	PROXY(Czechoslovakia(Maddison))
1913	3,427	1.49	PROXY(Czechoslovakia(Maddison))
1920	3,161	1.15	PROXY(Czechoslovakia(Maddison))
1929	4,974	5.17	PROXY(Czechoslovakia(Maddison))
1938	4,712	0.60	PROXY(37Czechoslovakia(Maddison))
1950	5,724	1.63	PROXY(Czechoslovakia(Maddison))
1960	9,034	4.67	PROXY(Czechoslovakia(Maddison))
1970	12,422	3.24	PROXY(Czechoslovakia(Maddison))
1980	16,626	2.96	PROXY(Czechoslovakia(Maddison))
1990	19,234	1.47	90(WB)
2000	20,085	0.43	00(WB)
2010	27,405	3.16	10(WB)
2012	27,523	0.21	12(WB)
2020	32,586	2.13	FORECAST
2030	39,568	1.96	FORECAST
		DME DENMARK	
0001	485	.	0001(MIN)
1000	790	0.05	1000(MIN)
1500	1,155	0.08	1500(Maddison)
1600	1,369	0.17	1600(Maddison)
1700	1,626	0.17	1700(Maddison)
1820	1,994	0.17	1820(Maddison)
1870	3,134	0.91	1870(Maddison)
1880	3,413	0.86	1880(Maddison)
1890	3,948	1.47	1890(Maddison)
1900	4,721	1.80	1900(Maddison)
1913	6,122	2.02	1913(Maddison)
1920	6,247	0.29	1920(Maddison)
1929	7,942	2.70	1929(Maddison)
1938	9,017	1.42	1938(Maddison)
1950	10,865	1.57	50(Maddison)

Year	GDP at PPP Per Capita, 2012 doll.	Growth Rate	Source
1960	14,190	2.71	60(Maddison)
1970	21,341	4.17	70(Maddison)
1980	26,183	2.07	80(WB)
1990	32,827	2.29	90(WB)
2000	41,828	2.45	00(WB)
2010	42,814	0.23	10(WB)
2012	42,775	0.05	12(WB)
2020	47,217	1.24	FORECAST
2030	54,618	1.47	FORECAST
AFR DJIBOUTI			
0001	.	.	
1000	.	.	
1500	.	.	
1600	.	.	
1700	.	.	
1820	.	.	
1870	.	.	
1880	.	.	
1890	.	.	
1900	.	.	
1913	.	.	
1920	.	.	
1929	.	.	
1938	.	.	
1950	2,347	.	50(Maddison)
1960	2,974	2.39	60(Maddison)
1970	3,727	2.28	70(Maddison)
1980	3,193	1.53	80(Maddison)
1990	2,975	0.71	90(WB)
2000	2,020	3.79	00(WB)
2010	2,680	2.87	10(CIA)WEIGHT(US(WB))
2012	2,700	0.37	12(CIA)
2020	3,043	1.51	FORECAST
2030	3,578	1.63	FORECAST
LAM DOMINICA			
0001	.	.	
1000	.	.	
1500	.	.	
1600	.	.	
1700	.	.	
1820	.	.	
1870	.	.	
1880	.	.	
1890	.	.	
1900	.	.	

Year	GDP at PPP Per Capita, 2012 doll.	Growth Rate	Source
1913	.	.	
1920	.	.	
1929	.	.	
1938	.	.	
1950	2,516	.	50(Maddison)
1960	3,301	2.75	INTERPOL(Maddison)
1970	4,331	2.75	INTERPOL(Maddison)
1980	4,538	0.47	80(WB)
1990	8,156	6.04	90(WB)
2000	9,534	1.57	00(WB)
2010	12,778	2.97	10(WB)
2012	12,426	1.39	12(WB)
2020	15,299	2.63	FORECAST
2030	18,958	2.17	FORECAST

LAM Dominican Republic

Year	GDP at PPP Per Capita, 2012 doll.	Growth Rate	Source
0001	347	.	0001(MIN)
1000	479	0.03	1000(MIN)
1500	593	0.04	1500(MIN)
1600	622	0.05	1600(MIN)
1700	655	0.05	1700(MIN)
1820	699	0.05	1820(MIN)
1870	719	0.06	1870(MIN)
1880	723	0.06	1880(MIN)
1890	727	0.06	INTERPOL(Maddison)
1900	903	2.19	INTERPOL(Maddison)
1913	913	0.09	PROXY(Other L. Am.(Maddison))
1920	1,016	1.54	INTERPOL(Maddison)
1929	1,166	1.54	INTERPOL(Maddison)
1938	1,338	1.54	INTERPOL(Maddison)
1950	1,607	1.54	50(Maddison)
1960	2,104	2.73	60(Maddison)
1970	2,603	2.15	70(Maddison)
1980	4,096	4.64	80(WB)
1990	4,164	0.17	90(WB)
2000	6,504	4.56	00(WB)
2010	9,479	3.84	10(WB)
2012	10,038	2.91	12(WB)
2020	13,422	3.70	FORECAST
2030	17,141	2.48	FORECAST

SEA East Timor

Year	GDP at PPP Per Capita, 2012 doll.	Growth Rate	Source
0001	.	.	
1000	.	.	
1500	.	.	
1600	.	.	
1700	.	.	
1820	.	.	
1870	.	.	

Year	GDP at PPP Per Capita, 2012 doll.	Growth Rate	Source
1880	.	.	
1890	.	.	
1900	.	.	
1913	.	.	
1920	.	.	
1929	.	.	
1938	.	.	
1950	655	.	PROXY(14 Pacific is(Maddison))
1960	765	1.55	INTERPOL(14 Pacific is(Maddison))
1970	892	1.55	INTERPOL(14 Pacific is(Maddison))
1980	948	0.61	INTERPOL(14 Pacific is(Maddison))
1990	968	0.20	00(WB)WEIGHT(US(Maddison))
2000	1,188	2.07	00(WB)
2010	1,557	2.74	10(WB)
2012	1,660	3.27	12(WB)
2020	2,004	2.38	FORECAST
2030	2,459	2.07	FORECAST
LAM Ecuador			
0001	361	.	0001(MIN)
1000	508	0.03	1000(MIN)
1500	637	0.05	1500(MIN)
1600	672	0.05	1600(MIN)
1700	710	0.06	1700(MIN)
1820	761	0.06	PROXY(Other L. Am.(Maddison))
1870	780	0.05	PROXY(Other L. Am.(Maddison))
1880	929	1.77	INTERPOL(Maddison)
1890	1,107	1.77	INTERPOL(Maddison)
1900	1,319	1.77	INTERPOL(Maddison)
1913	1,656	1.77	PROXY(Other L. Am.(Maddison))
1920	1,843	1.54	INTERPOL(Maddison)
1929	2,115	1.54	INTERPOL(Maddison)
1938	2,427	1.54	INTERPOL(Maddison)
1950	2,915	1.54	50(Maddison)
1960	3,713	2.45	60(Maddison)
1970	4,784	2.57	70(Maddison)
1980	7,187	4.15	80(WB)
1990	7,258	0.10	90(WB)
2000	7,080	0.25	00(WB)
2010	8,788	2.18	10(WB)
2012	9,637	4.72	12(WB)
2020	11,356	2.07	FORECAST
2030	13,752	1.93	FORECAST
MEA Egypt			
0001	782	.	0001(Maddison)
1000	782	0.00	1000(Maddison)
1500	743	0.01	1500(Maddison)
1600	743	0.00	1600(Maddison)

Year	GDP at PPP Per Capita, 2012 doll.	Growth Rate	Source
1700	743	0.00	1700(Maddison)
1820	743	0.00	1820(Maddison)
1870	1,016	0.63	1870(Maddison)
1880	1,079	0.60	INTERPOL(Maddison)
1890	1,155	0.69	INTERPOL(Maddison)
1900	1,260	0.88	INTERPOL(Maddison)
1913	1,411	0.88	1913(Maddison)
1920	1,391	0.20	INTERPOL(Maddison)
1929	1,366	0.20	1929(Maddison)
1938	1,393	0.22	INTERPOL(Maddison)
1950	1,424	0.18	50(Maddison)
1960	1,523	0.68	60(Maddison)
1970	1,883	2.14	70(Maddison)
1980	3,005	4.78	80(WB)
1990	4,035	2.99	90(WB)
2000	4,892	1.94	00(WB)
2010	6,576	3.00	10(WB)
2012	6,614	0.29	12(WB)
2020	8,137	2.62	FORECAST
2030	10,080	2.16	FORECAST
LAM El Salvador			
0001	351	.	0001(MIN)
1000	488	0.03	1000(MIN)
1500	606	0.04	1500(MIN)
1600	637	0.05	1600(MIN)
1700	671	0.05	1700(MIN)
1820	717	0.06	1820(MIN)
1870	738	0.06	1870(MIN)
1880	743	0.06	INTERPOL(Maddison)
1890	885	1.77	INTERPOL(Maddison)
1900	1,054	1.77	INTERPOL(Maddison)
1913	1,324	1.77	PROXY(Other L. Am.(Maddison))
1920	1,458	1.39	1920(Maddison)
1929	1,629	1.24	1929(Maddison)
1938	1,529	0.70	1938(Maddison)
1950	2,330	3.57	50(Maddison)
1960	2,965	2.44	60(Maddison)
1970	3,960	2.94	70(Maddison)
1980	4,550	1.40	80(WB)
1990	3,775	1.85	90(WB)
2000	5,820	4.42	00(WB)
2010	6,783	1.54	10(WB)
2012	6,991	1.52	12(WB)
2020	8,316	2.19	FORECAST
2030	10,125	1.99	FORECAST
AFR Equatorial Guinea			
0001	.	.	
1000	.	.	

Year	GDP at PPP Per Capita, 2012 doll.	Growth Rate	Source
1500	.	.	
1600	.	.	
1700	.	.	
1820	.	.	
1870	.	.	
1880	.	.	
1890	.	.	
1900	.	.	
1913	.	.	
1920	.	.	
1929	.	.	
1938	.	.	
1950	845	.	50(Maddison)
1960	1,146	3.10	60(Maddison)
1970	1,975	5.59	70(Maddison)
1980	2,188	1.03	80(Maddison)
1990	2,275	0.39	90(WB)
2000	9,856	15.79	00(WB)
2010	29,243	11.49	10(WB)
2012	29,742	0.85	12(WB)
2020	61,840	9.58	FORECAST
2030	78,661	2.44	FORECAST

AFR Eritrea

Year	GDP at PPP Per Capita, 2012 doll.	Growth Rate	Source
0001	257	.	0001(MIN)l & W. Africa(Maddison))
1000	324	0.02	1000(MIN)
1500	372	0.03	1500(MIN)
1600	383	0.03	1600(MIN)
1700	395	0.03	1700(MIN)
1820	411	0.03	1820(MIN)
1870	417	0.03	1870(MIN)
1880	419	0.03	1880(MIN)
1890	420	0.03	1890(MIN)
1900	422	0.03	1900(MIN)
1913	424	0.03	1913(MIN)
1920	425	0.03	1920(MIN)
1929	426	0.03	1929(MIN)
1938	427	0.03	1938(MIN)
1950	429	0.03	PROXY(Ethiopia & Eritr.(Maddison))
1960	482	1.18	PROXY(Ethiopia & Eritr.(Maddison))
1970	647	2.99	PROXY(Ethiopia & Eritr.(Maddison))
1980	703	0.82	PROXY(Ethiopia & Eritr.(Maddison))
1990	637	0.98	90(WB)
2000	682	0.69	00(WB)
2010	512	2.82	10(WB)

Year	GDP at PPP Per Capita, 2012 doll.	Growth Rate	Source
2012	557	4.32	12(WB)
2020	600	0.93	FORECAST
2030	680	1.25	FORECAST
		USR Estonia	
0001	474	.	0001(MIN)
1000	764	0.05	1000(MIN)
1500	1,099	0.07	INTERPOL(Maddison)
1600	1,229	0.11	INTERPOL(Maddison)
1700	1,376	0.11	INTERPOL(Maddison)
1820	1,575	0.11	PROXY(USSR(Maddison))
1870	2,158	0.63	PROXY(USSR(Maddison))
1880	2,363	0.91	INTERPOL(Maddison)
1890	2,587	0.91	INTERPOL(Maddison)
1900	2,831	0.91	PROXY(USSR(Maddison))
1913	3,406	1.43	PROXY(USSR(Maddison))
1920	2,978	1.90	PROXY(Finland(Maddison))
1929	4,384	4.39	PROXY(Finland(Maddison))
1938	5,791	3.14	PROXY(Finland(Maddison))
1950	6,503	0.97	PROXY(USSR(Maddison))
1960	8,991	3.29	PROXY(USSR(Maddison))
1970	12,649	3.47	PROXY(USSR(Maddison))
1980	15,020	1.73	INTERPOL(Estonia(Maddison))
1990	16,682	1.05	90(Maddison)
2000	14,753	1.22	00(WB)
2010	21,387	3.78	10(WB)
2012	24,450	6.92	12(WB)
2020	31,337	3.15	FORECAST
2030	39,487	2.34	FORECAST
		AFR Ethiopia	
0001	253	.	0001(MIN)
1000	317	0.02	1000(MIN)
1500	363	0.03	1500(MIN)
1600	373	0.03	1600(MIN)
1700	385	0.03	1700(MIN)
1820	400	0.03	1820(MIN)
1870	406	0.03	1870(MIN)
1880	408	0.03	1880(MIN)
1890	409	0.03	1890(MIN)
1900	410	0.03	1900(MIN)
1913	412	0.03	1913(MIN)
1920	413	0.03	1920(MIN)
1929	414	0.03	1929(MIN)
1938	415	0.03	1938(MIN)
1950	417	0.03	PROXY(Ethiopia & Eritr.(Maddison))
1960	469	1.18	PROXY(Ethiopia & Eritr.(Maddison))
1970	631	3.01	PROXY(Ethiopia & Eritr.(Maddison))
1980	684	0.82	PROXY(Ethiopia & Eritr.(Maddison))
1990	618	1.01	90(WB)

Year	GDP at PPP Per Capita, 2012 doll.	Growth Rate	Source
2000	591	0.44	00(WB)
2010	1,003	5.43	10(WB)
2012	1,109	5.13	12(WB)
2020	1,454	3.45	FORECAST
2030	1,847	2.42	FORECAST
	DME FALKLAND ISLANDS		
0001	.	.	
1000	.	.	
1500	.	.	
1600	.	.	
1700	.	.	
1820	.	.	
1870	.	.	
1880	.	.	
1890	.	.	
1900	.	.	
1913	.	.	
1920	.	.	
1929	.	.	
1938	.	.	
1950	12,450	.	PROXY(8 Caribbean cs(Maddison))
1960	16,302	2.73	INTERPOL(8 Caribbean cs(Maddison))
1970	21,347	2.73	INTERPOL(8 Caribbean cs(Maddison))
1980	25,199	1.67	INTERPOL(8 Caribbean cs(Maddison))
1990	28,452	1.22	95(CIA)WEIGHT(US(Maddison))
2000	30,393	0.66	02(CIA)WEIGHT(US(WB))
2010	55,272	6.16	07(CIA)WEIGHT(US(WB))
2012	57,033	1.58	07(CIA)WEIGHT(US(WB))
2020	75,989	3.65	FORECAST
2030	96,951	2.47	FORECAST
	DME FAROE ISLANDS		
0001	.	.	
1000	.	.	
1500	.	.	
1600	.	.	
1700	.	.	
1820	.	.	
1870	.	.	
1880	.	.	
1890	.	.	
1900	.	.	
1913	.	.	
1920	.	.	
1929	.	.	

Year	GDP at PPP Per Capita, 2012 doll.	Growth Rate	Source
1938	.	.	
1950	6,533	.	PROXY(9 European cs(Maddison))
1960	9,588	3.91	INTERPOL(9 European cs(Maddison))
1970	14,072	3.91	INTERPOL(9 European cs(Maddison))
1980	18,101	2.55	INTERPOL(9 European cs(Maddison))
1990	22,005	1.97	89(CIA)WEIGHT(US(Maddison))
2000	25,653	1.55	00(CIA)WEIGHT(US(WB))
2010	31,146	1.96	10(CIA)WEIGHT(US(WB))
2012	32,088	1.50	10(CIA)WEIGHT(US(WB))
2020	37,771	2.06	FORECAST
2030	45,706	1.93	FORECAST
SEA Fiji			
0001	.	.	
1000	.	.	
1500	.	.	
1600	.	.	
1700	.	.	
1820	.	.	
1870	.	.	
1880	.	.	
1890	.	.	
1900	.	.	
1913	.	.	
1920	.	.	
1929	.	.	
1938	.	.	
1950	4,608	.	50(Maddison)
1960	4,597	0.02	INTERPOL(14 Pacific is(Maddison))
1970	4,586	0.02	INTERPOL(14 Pacific is(Maddison))
1980	4,420	0.37	80(WB)
1990	4,419	0.00	90(WB)
2000	4,623	0.45	00(WB)
2010	4,809	0.39	10(WB)
2012	4,877	0.71	12(WB)
2020	5,033	0.39	FORECAST
2030	5,461	0.82	FORECAST
DME Finland			
0001	383	.	0001(MIN)
1000	552	0.04	1000(MIN)
1500	709	0.05	1500(Maddison)
1600	842	0.17	1600(Maddison)
1700	998	0.17	1700(Maddison)
1820	1,222	0.17	1820(Maddison)
1870	1,784	0.76	1870(Maddison)
1880	1,807	0.13	1880(Maddison)
1890	2,161	1.80	1890(Maddison)

Year	GDP at PPP Per Capita, 2012 doll.	Growth Rate	Source
1900	2,610	1.91	1900(Maddison)
1913	3,303	1.83	1913(Maddison)
1920	2,889	1.90	1920(Maddison)
1929	4,252	4.39	1929(Maddison)
1938	5,616	3.14	1938(Maddison)
1950	6,655	1.42	50(Maddison)
1960	10,012	4.17	60(Maddison)
1970	15,837	4.69	70(Maddison)
1980	21,919	3.30	80(WB)
1990	28,708	2.74	90(WB)
2000	33,691	1.61	00(WB)
2010	38,825	1.43	10(WB)
2012	39,199	0.48	12(WB)
2020	45,354	1.84	FORECAST
2030	54,298	1.82	FORECAST
DME France			
0001	740	.	0001(Maddison)
1000	665	0.01	1000(Maddison)
1500	1,138	0.11	1500(Maddison)
1600	1,316	0.15	1600(Maddison)
1700	1,424	0.08	1700(Maddison)
1820	1,776	0.18	1820(Maddison)
1870	2,936	1.01	1870(Maddison)
1880	3,317	1.23	1880(Maddison)
1890	3,718	1.15	1890(Maddison)
1900	4,500	1.93	1900(Maddison)
1913	5,453	1.49	1913(Maddison)
1920	5,050	1.09	1920(Maddison)
1929	7,370	4.29	1929(Maddison)
1938	6,989	0.59	1938(Maddison)
1950	8,248	1.39	50(Maddison)
1960	11,902	3.74	60(Maddison)
1970	18,631	4.58	70(Maddison)
1980	24,172	2.64	80(WB)
1990	29,229	1.92	90(WB)
2000	34,682	1.73	00(WB)
2010	36,396	0.48	10(WB)
2012	36,785	0.53	12(WB)
2020	40,734	1.28	FORECAST
2030	47,240	1.49	FORECAST
SEA French Polynesia			
0001	.	.	
1000	.	.	
1500	.	.	
1600	.	.	
1700	.	.	
1820	.	.	

Year	GDP at PPP Per Capita, 2012 doll.	Growth Rate	Source
1870	.	.	
1880	.	.	
1890	.	.	
1900	.	.	
1913	.	.	
1920	.	.	
1929	.	.	
1938	.	.	
1950	6,874	.	PROXY(14 Pacific is(Maddison))
1960	8,139	1.70	INTERPOL(14 Pacific is(Maddison))
1970	9,636	1.70	INTERPOL(14 Pacific is(Maddison))
1980	10,297	0.67	INTERPOL(14 Pacific is(Maddison))
1990	10,529	0.22	93(CIA)WEIGHT(US(Maddison))
2000	15,087	3.66	97(CIA)WEIGHT(US(WB))
2010	23,664	4.60	06(CIA)WEIGHT(US(WB))
2012	24,513	1.78	06(CIA)WEIGHT(US(WB))
2020	32,105	3.43	FORECAST
2030	40,752	2.41	FORECAST
		AFR GABON	
0001	.	.	
1000	.	.	
1500	.	.	
1600	.	.	
1700	.	.	
1820	.	.	
1870	.	.	
1880	.	.	
1890	.	.	
1900	.	.	
1913	.	.	
1920	.	.	
1929	.	.	
1938	.	.	
1950	4,864	.	50(Maddison)
1960	7,901	4.97	60(Maddison)
1970	13,361	5.39	70(Maddison)
1980	18,691	3.41	80(WB)
1990	17,187	0.84	90(WB)
2000	15,258	1.18	00(WB)
2010	14,649	0.41	10(WB)
2012	15,765	3.74	12(WB)
2020	17,028	0.97	FORECAST
2030	19,334	1.28	FORECAST
		AFR GAMBIA	
0001	.	.	

Year	GDP at PPP Per Capita, 2012 doll.	Growth Rate	Source
1000	.	.	
1500	.	.	
1600	.	.	
1700	.	.	
1820	.	.	
1870	.	.	
1880	.	.	
1890	.	.	
1900	.	.	
1913	.	.	
1920	.	.	
1929	.	.	
1938	.	.	
1950	950	.	50(Maddison)
1960	1,208	2.43	60(Maddison)
1970	1,572	2.67	70(Maddison)
1980	1,987	2.37	80(WB)
1990	1,872	0.59	90(WB)
2000	1,889	0.09	00(WB)
2010	2,010	0.62	10(WB)
2012	1,903	2.69	12(WB)
2020	1,991	0.57	FORECAST
2030	2,193	0.97	FORECAST
MEA Gaza Strip			
0001	.	.	
1000	.	.	
1500	.	.	
1600	.	.	
1700	.	.	
1820	.	.	
1870	.	.	
1880	.	.	
1890	.	.	
1900	.	.	
1913	.	.	
1920	.	.	
1929	.	.	
1938	.	.	
1950	1,120	.	PROXY(West Bank & Gaza(Maddison))
1960	1,233	0.96	PROXY(West Bank & Gaza(Maddison))
1970	1,354	0.94	PROXY(West Bank & Gaza(Maddison))
1980	1,472	0.84	PROXY(West Bank & Gaza(Maddison))
1990	1,601	0.84	PROXY(West Bank & Gaza(Maddison))
2000	1,543	0.37	00(WB)
2010	1,325	1.51	10(CIA)WEIGHT(US(WB))

Year	GDP at PPP Per Capita, 2012 doll.	Growth Rate	Source
2012	1,306	0.75	11(CIA)WEIGHT(US(WB))
2020	1,326	0.19	FORECAST
2030	1,412	0.64	FORECAST
USR GEORGIA			
0001	400	.	0001(MIN)
1000	588	0.04	1000(MIN)
1500	769	0.05	PROXY(USSR(Maddison))
1600	850	0.10	PROXY(USSR(Maddison))
1700	940	0.10	PROXY(USSR(Maddison))
1820	1,060	0.10	PROXY(USSR(Maddison))
1870	1,453	0.63	PROXY(USSR(Maddison))
1880	1,590	0.91	INTERPOL(Maddison)
1890	1,741	0.91	INTERPOL(Maddison)
1900	1,906	0.91	PROXY(USSR(Maddison))
1913	2,293	1.43	PROXY(USSR(Maddison))
1920	1,359	7.20	PROXY(Bulgaria(Maddison))
1929	2,193	5.46	PROXY(USSR(Maddison))
1938	3,401	5.00	PROXY(USSR(Maddison))
1950	4,377	2.12	PROXY(USSR(Maddison))
1960	5,609	2.51	PROXY(USSR(Maddison))
1970	7,349	2.74	PROXY(USSR(Maddison))
1980	7,844	0.65	80(WB)
1990	6,816	1.39	90(WB)
2000	2,363	10.05	00(WB)
2010	5,030	7.85	10(WB)
2012	5,833	7.69	12(WB)
2020	8,589	4.96	FORECAST
2030	11,165	2.66	FORECAST
DME GERMANY			
0001	638	.	0001(Maddison)
1000	642	0.00	1000(Maddison)
1500	1,077	0.10	1500(Maddison)
1600	1,238	0.14	1600(Maddison)
1700	1,424	0.14	1700(Maddison)
1820	1,685	0.14	1820(Maddison)
1870	2,878	1.08	1870(Maddison)
1880	3,116	0.80	1880(Maddison)
1890	3,799	2.00	1890(Maddison)
1900	4,671	2.09	1900(Maddison)
1913	5,709	1.55	1913(Maddison)
1920	4,375	3.73	1920(Maddison)
1929	6,339	4.21	1929(Maddison)
1938	7,815	2.35	1938(Maddison)
1950	6,073	2.08	50(Maddison)
1960	12,687	7.64	60(Maddison)
1970	18,662	3.94	70(Maddison)
1980	25,376	3.12	80(WB)
1990	31,606	2.22	90(WB)

Year	GDP at PPP Per Capita, 2012 doll.	Growth Rate	Source
2000	36,388	1.42	00(WB)
2010	40,321	1.03	10(WB)
2012	42,700	2.91	12(WB)
2020	49,683	1.91	FORECAST
2030	59,695	1.85	FORECAST
AFR GHANA			
0001	334	.	0001(MIN)
1000	456	0.03	1000(MIN)
1500	557	0.04	1500(MIN)
1600	583	0.05	1600(MIN)
1700	611	0.05	1700(MIN)
1820	649	0.05	1820(Maddison)
1870	723	0.21	1870(Maddison)
1880	739	0.22	INTERPOL(Maddison)
1890	756	0.22	INTERPOL(Maddison)
1900	826	0.89	INTERPOL(Maddison)
1913	1,222	3.06	1913(Maddison)
1920	1,309	0.98	INTERPOL(Maddison)
1929	1,429	0.98	INTERPOL(Maddison)
1938	1,561	0.98	INTERPOL(Maddison)
1950	1,756	0.98	50(Maddison)
1960	1,871	0.64	60(Maddison)
1970	1,762	0.60	70(Maddison)
1980	1,396	2.30	80(WB)
1990	1,308	0.65	90(WB)
2000	1,421	0.83	00(WB)
2010	1,780	2.28	10(WB)
2012	2,014	6.36	12(WB)
2020	2,395	2.19	FORECAST
2030	2,915	1.99	FORECAST
DME GIBRALTAR			
0001	.	.	
1000	.	.	
1500	.	.	
1600	.	.	
1700	.	.	
1820	.	.	
1870	.	.	
1880	.	.	
1890	.	.	
1900	.	.	
1913	.	.	
1920	.	.	
1929	.	.	
1938	.	.	
1950	3,025	.	PROXY(9 European cs(Maddison))

Year	GDP at PPP Per Capita, 2012 doll.	Growth Rate	Source
1960	4,883	4.90	INTERPOL(9 European cs(Maddison))
1970	7,882	4.90	INTERPOL(9 European cs(Maddison))
1980	10,793	3.19	INTERPOL(9 European cs(Maddison))
1990	13,772	2.47	93(CIA)WEIGHT(US(Maddison))
2000	33,161	9.19	00(CIA)WEIGHT(US(WB))
2010	46,831	3.51	08(CIA)WEIGHT(US(WB))
2012	48,676	1.95	08(CIA)WEIGHT(US(WB))
2020	70,812	4.80	FORECAST
2030	91,921	2.64	FORECAST
		DME Greece	
0001	861	.	0001(Maddison)
1000	626	0.03	1000(Maddison)
1500	678	0.02	1500(Maddison)
1600	756	0.11	1600(Maddison)
1700	829	0.09	1700(Maddison)
1820	1,003	0.16	1820(Maddison)
1870	1,377	0.64	1870(Maddison)
1880	1,593	1.47	INTERPOL(Maddison)
1890	1,843	1.47	1890(Maddison)
1900	2,114	1.38	1900(Maddison)
1913	2,491	1.27	1913(Maddison)
1920	2,932	2.36	INTERPOL(Maddison)
1929	3,665	2.51	1929(Maddison)
1938	4,189	1.50	1938(Maddison)
1950	2,997	2.75	50(Maddison)
1960	5,436	6.14	60(Maddison)
1970	12,006	8.25	70(Maddison)
1980	18,974	4.68	80(WB)
1990	19,310	0.18	90(WB)
2000	24,786	2.53	00(WB)
2010	29,625	1.80	10(WB)
2012	26,041	6.24	12(WB)
2020	30,691	2.08	FORECAST
2030	37,167	1.93	FORECAST
		DME Greenland	
0001	.	.	
1000	.	.	
1500	.	.	
1600	.	.	
1700	.	.	
1820	.	.	
1870	.	.	
1880	.	.	
1890	.	.	
1900	.	.	
1913	.	.	
1920	.	.	

Year	GDP at PPP Per Capita, 2012 doll.	Growth Rate	Source
1929	.	.	
1938	.	.	
1950	6,812	.	PROXY(9 European cs(Maddison))
1960	9,953	3.86	INTERPOL(9 European cs(Maddison))
1970	14,540	3.86	INTERPOL(9 European cs(Maddison))
1980	18,648	2.52	INTERPOL(9 European cs(Maddison))
1990	22,617	1.95	95(CIA)WEIGHT(US(Maddison))
2000	25,782	1.32	00(CIA)WEIGHT(US(WB))
2010	37,704	3.87	10(CIA)WEIGHT(US(WB))
2012	38,392	0.91	11(CIA)WEIGHT(US(WB))
2020	47,947	2.82	FORECAST
2030	59,798	2.23	FORECAST

LAM Grenada

Year	GDP at PPP Per Capita, 2012 doll.	Growth Rate	Source
0001	.	.	
1000	.	.	
1500	.	.	
1600	.	.	
1700	.	.	
1820	.	.	
1870	.	.	
1880	.	.	
1890	.	.	
1900	.	.	
1913	.	.	
1920	.	.	
1929	.	.	
1938	.	.	
1950	1,462	.	50(Maddison)
1960	2,170	4.03	INTERPOL(Maddison)
1970	3,221	4.03	INTERPOL(Maddison)
1980	4,118	2.49	80(WB)
1990	6,620	4.86	90(WB)
2000	9,252	3.40	00(WB)
2010	10,837	1.59	10(WB)
2012	10,928	0.42	12(WB)
2020	13,328	2.51	FORECAST
2030	16,441	2.12	FORECAST

LAM Guadeloupe

Year	GDP at PPP Per Capita, 2012 doll.	Growth Rate	Source
0001	.	.	
1000	.	.	
1500	.	.	
1600	.	.	
1700	.	.	
1820	.	.	
1870	.	.	

Year	GDP at PPP Per Capita, 2012 doll.	Growth Rate	Source
1880	.	.	
1890	.	.	
1900	.	.	
1913	.	.	
1920	.	.	
1929	.	.	
1938	.	.	
1950	2,701	.	50(Maddison)
1960	4,357	4.90	INTERPOL(Maddison)
1970	7,029	4.90	INTERPOL(Maddison)
1980	8,507	1.93	INTERPOL(Maddison)
1990	8,681	0.20	90(Maddison)
2000	12,459	3.68	97(CIA)WEIGHT(US(WB))
2010	31,214	9.62	10(REG)WEIGHT(US(WB))
2012	30,074	1.84	12(REG)
2020	47,065	5.76	FORECAST
2030	61,413	2.70	FORECAST
SEA Guam			
0001	.	.	
1000	.	.	
1500	.	.	
1600	.	.	
1700	.	.	
1820	.	.	
1870	.	.	
1880	.	.	
1890	.	.	
1900	.	.	
1913	.	.	
1920	.	.	
1929	.	.	
1938	.	.	
1950	14,860	.	PROXY(14 Pacific is(Maddison))
1960	17,343	1.56	INTERPOL(14 Pacific is(Maddison))
1970	20,242	1.56	INTERPOL(14 Pacific is(Maddison))
1980	21,507	0.61	INTERPOL(14 Pacific is(Maddison))
1990	21,951	0.20	91(CIA)WEIGHT(US(Maddison))
2000	26,785	2.01	00(CIA)WEIGHT(US(WB))
2010	29,738	1.05	10(CIA)WEIGHT(US(WB))
2012	30,712	1.62	10(CIA)WEIGHT(US(WB))
2020	34,139	1.33	FORECAST
2030	39,712	1.52	FORECAST
LAM Guatemala			
0001	381	.	0001(MIN)
1000	547	0.04	1000(MIN)

Year	GDP at PPP Per Capita, 2012 doll.	Growth Rate	Source
1500	700	0.05	1500(MIN)
1600	741	0.06	1600(MIN)
1700	788	0.06	1700(MIN)
1820	852	0.07	PROXY(Other L. Am.(Maddison))
1870	873	0.05	PROXY(Other L. Am.(Maddison))
1880	1,040	1.77	INTERPOL(Maddison)
1890	1,239	1.77	INTERPOL(Maddison)
1900	1,476	1.77	INTERPOL(Maddison)
1913	1,854	1.77	PROXY(Other L. Am.(Maddison))
1920	1,990	1.02	1920(Maddison)
1929	2,692	3.41	1929(Maddison)
1938	3,480	2.90	1938(Maddison)
1950	3,263	0.54	50(Maddison)
1960	3,346	0.25	60(Maddison)
1970	3,991	1.78	70(Maddison)
1980	4,704	1.66	80(WB)
1990	4,105	1.35	90(WB)
2000	4,581	1.10	00(WB)
2010	4,929	0.73	10(WB)
2012	5,019	0.91	12(WB)
2020	5,389	0.89	FORECAST
2030	6,084	1.22	FORECAST

DME Guernsey

Year	GDP at PPP Per Capita, 2012 doll.	Growth Rate	Source
0001	.	.	
1000	.	.	
1500	.	.	
1600	.	.	
1700	.	.	
1820	.	.	
1870	.	.	
1880	.	.	
1890	.	.	
1900	.	.	
1913	.	.	
1920	.	.	
1929	.	.	
1938	.	.	
1950	7,544	.	PROXY(9 European cs(Maddison))
1960	10,974	3.82	INTERPOL(9 European cs(Maddison))
1970	15,963	3.82	INTERPOL(9 European cs(Maddison))
1980	20,414	2.49	INTERPOL(9 European cs(Maddison))
1990	24,706	1.93	97(CIA)WEIGHT(US(Maddison))
2000	27,436	1.05	99(CIA)WEIGHT(US(WB))
2010	50,532	6.30	05(CIA)WEIGHT(US(WB))
2012	52,083	1.52	05(CIA)WEIGHT(US(WB))

Year	GDP at PPP Per Capita, 2012 doll.	Growth Rate	Source
2020	71,166	3.98	FORECAST
2030	91,380	2.53	FORECAST
LAM Guiana, French			
0001	.	.	
1000	.	.	
1500	.	.	
1600	.	.	
1700	.	.	
1820	.	.	
1870	.	.	
1880	.	.	
1890	.	.	
1900	.	.	
1913	.	.	
1920	.	.	
1929	.	.	
1938	.	.	
1950	7,998	.	50(Maddison)
1960	7,549	0.58	INTERPOL(Maddison)
1970	7,126	0.58	INTERPOL(Maddison)
1980	6,976	0.21	INTERPOL(Maddison)
1990	6,937	0.06	90(Maddison)
2000	8,302	1.81	98(CIA)WEIGHT(US(WB))
2010	25,706	11.97	10(REG)WEIGHT(US(WB))
2012	23,356	4.68	12(REG)
2020	37,426	6.07	FORECAST
2030	48,849	2.70	FORECAST
AFR Guinea			
0001	273	.	0001(MIN)
1000	349	0.02	1000(MIN)
1500	405	0.03	1500(MIN)
1600	419	0.03	1600(MIN)
1700	433	0.03	1700(MIN)
1820	452	0.04	1820(MIN)
1870	460	0.04	1870(MIN)
1880	462	0.04	1880(MIN)
1890	464	0.04	1890(MIN)
1900	465	0.04	1900(MIN)
1913	468	0.04	1913(MIN)
1920	469	0.04	1920(MIN)
1929	470	0.04	1929(MIN)
1938	472	0.04	1938(MIN)
1950	474	0.04	50(Maddison)
1960	640	3.04	60(Maddison)
1970	788	2.11	70(Maddison)
1980	978	2.18	80(Maddison)

Year	GDP at PPP Per Capita, 2012 doll.	Growth Rate	Source
1990	973	0.05	90(WB)
2000	985	0.12	00(WB)
2010	1,025	0.40	10(WB)
2012	1,051	1.29	12(WB)
2020	1,106	0.64	FORECAST
2030	1,225	1.02	FORECAST
AFR GuineaBissau			
0001	265	.	0001(MIN)
1000	337	0.02	1000(MIN)
1500	389	0.03	1500(MIN)
1600	401	0.03	1600(MIN)
1700	415	0.03	1700(MIN)
1820	432	0.03	1820(MIN)
1870	440	0.03	1870(MIN)
1880	441	0.04	1880(MIN)
1890	443	0.04	1890(MIN)
1900	444	0.04	1900(MIN)
1913	446	0.04	1913(MIN)
1920	447	0.04	1920(MIN)
1929	449	0.04	1929(MIN)
1938	450	0.04	1938(MIN)
1950	452	0.04	50(Maddison)
1960	761	5.34	60(Maddison)
1970	1,285	5.38	70(Maddison)
1980	1,151	1.09	80(WB)
1990	1,467	2.46	90(WB)
2000	1,147	2.43	00(WB)
2010	1,174	0.23	10(WB)
2012	1,101	3.13	12(WB)
2020	1,159	0.64	FORECAST
2030	1,283	1.02	FORECAST
LAM Guyana			
0001	.	.	
1000	.	.	
1500	.	.	
1600	.	.	
1700	.	.	
1820	.	.	
1870	.	.	
1880	.	.	
1890	.	.	
1900	.	.	
1913	.	.	
1920	.	.	
1929	.	.	
1938	.	.	

Year	GDP at PPP Per Capita, 2012 doll.	Growth Rate	Source
1950	1,709	.	50(Maddison)
1960	1,906	1.09	INTERPOL(Maddison)
1970	2,125	1.09	INTERPOL(Maddison)
1980	2,536	1.78	80(WB)
1990	1,966	2.51	90(WB)
2000	2,839	3.74	00(WB)
2010	3,082	0.82	10(WB)
2012	3,344	4.17	12(WB)
2020	3,925	2.02	FORECAST
2030	4,741	1.91	FORECAST
LAM Haiti			
0001	350	.	0001(MIN)
1000	485	0.03	1000(MIN)
1500	601	0.04	1500(MIN)
1600	631	0.05	1600(MIN)
1700	665	0.05	1700(MIN)
1820	710	0.05	1820(MIN)
1870	731	0.06	1870(MIN)
1880	735	0.06	1880(MIN)
1890	740	0.06	1890(MIN)
1900	744	0.06	INTERPOL(Maddison)
1913	934	1.77	PROXY(Other L. Am.(Maddison))
1920	1,040	1.54	INTERPOL(Maddison)
1929	1,193	1.54	INTERPOL(Maddison)
1938	1,369	1.54	INTERPOL(Maddison)
1950	1,645	1.54	50(Maddison)
1960	1,651	0.04	60(Maddison)
1970	1,428	1.44	70(Maddison)
1980	2,019	3.53	80(Maddison)
1990	1,630	2.12	90(Maddison)
2000	1,303	2.21	00(WB)
2010	1,147	1.27	10(WB)
2012	1,208	2.63	12(WB)
2020	1,266	0.58	FORECAST
2030	1,396	0.98	FORECAST
LAM Honduras			
0001	330	.	0001(MIN)
1000	448	0.03	1000(MIN)
1500	546	0.04	1500(MIN)
1600	571	0.04	1600(MIN)
1700	598	0.05	1700(MIN)
1820	635	0.05	1820(MIN)
1870	651	0.05	1870(MIN)
1880	655	0.05	INTERPOL(Maddison)
1890	780	1.77	INTERPOL(Maddison)
1900	930	1.77	INTERPOL(Maddison)
1913	1,167	1.77	PROXY(Other L. Am.(Maddison))
1920	1,994	7.95	1920(Maddison)

Year	GDP at PPP Per Capita, 2012 doll.	Growth Rate	Source
1929	2,346	1.82	1929(Maddison)
1938	1,729	3.33	1938(Maddison)
1950	2,055	1.45	50(Maddison)
1960	2,208	0.72	60(Maddison)
1970	2,557	1.48	70(Maddison)
1980	3,123	2.02	80(WB)
1990	2,937	0.61	90(WB)
2000	3,265	1.06	00(WB)
2010	4,026	2.12	10(WB)
2012	4,174	1.82	12(WB)
2020	4,771	1.68	FORECAST
2030	5,665	1.73	FORECAST
SEA Hong Kong			
0001	704	.	PROXY(China(Maddison))
1000	704	0.00	PROXY(China(Maddison))
1500	939	0.06	PROXY(China(Maddison))
1600	939	0.00	PROXY(China(Maddison))
1700	939	0.00	PROXY(China(Maddison))
1820	939	0.00	1820(Maddison)
1870	1,069	0.26	1870(Maddison)
1880	1,237	1.47	INTERPOL(Maddison)
1890	1,431	1.47	INTERPOL(Maddison)
1900	1,656	1.47	INTERPOL(Maddison)
1913	2,001	1.47	1913(Maddison)
1920	2,221	1.50	INTERPOL(Maddison)
1929	2,539	1.50	INTERPOL(Maddison)
1938	2,903	1.50	INTERPOL(Maddison)
1950	3,471	1.50	50(Maddison)
1960	4,893	3.49	60(Maddison)
1970	8,865	6.12	70(Maddison)
1980	16,299	6.28	80(WB)
1990	27,687	5.44	90(WB)
2000	34,615	2.26	00(WB)
2010	48,915	3.52	10(WB)
2012	51,103	2.21	12(WB)
2020	68,614	3.75	FORECAST
2030	87,724	2.49	FORECAST
EEU Hungary			
0001	665	.	AVG(Danubian provinces(Maddison))
1000	626	0.01	1000(Maddison)
1500	1,115	0.12	INTERPOL(Maddison)
1600	1,251	0.12	INTERPOL(Maddison)
1700	1,404	0.12	INTERPOL(Maddison)
1820	1,613	0.12	INTERPOL(Maddison)
1870	1,709	0.12	1870(Maddison)
1880	1,985	1.51	INTERPOL(Maddison)
1890	2,305	1.51	1890(Maddison)
1900	2,632	1.34	1900(Maddison)

Year	GDP at PPP Per Capita, 2012 doll.	Growth Rate	Source
1913	3,283	1.71	1913(Maddison)
1920	2,674	2.89	1920(Maddison)
1929	3,875	4.21	1929(Maddison)
1938	4,155	0.78	1938(Maddison)
1950	3,881	0.57	50(Maddison)
1960	6,496	5.29	60(Maddison)
1970	10,115	4.53	70(Maddison)
1980	14,199	3.45	80(WB)
1990	16,664	1.61	90(WB)
2000	17,720	0.62	00(WB)
2010	22,468	2.40	10(WB)
2012	22,635	0.37	12(WB)
2020	26,389	1.94	FORECAST
2030	31,746	1.87	FORECAST
DME Iceland			
0001	.	.	
1000	655	.	1000(MIN)
1500	886	0.06	PROXY(Denmark)
1600	1,051	0.17	PROXY(Denmark)
1700	1,248	0.17	PROXY(Denmark)
1820	1,530	0.17	PROXY(Denmark)
1870	2,406	0.91	PROXY(Denmark)
1880	2,619	0.85	PROXY(Denmark)
1890	3,030	1.47	PROXY(Denmark)
1900	3,623	1.80	PROXY(Denmark)
1913	4,698	2.02	PROXY(Denmark)
1920	4,794	0.29	PROXY(Denmark)
1929	6,095	2.70	PROXY(Denmark)
1938	6,920	1.42	PROXY(Denmark)
1950	8,339	1.57	50(Maddison)
1960	12,962	4.51	INTERPOL(Maddison)
1970	20,150	4.51	INTERPOL(Maddison)
1980	26,614	2.82	80(WB)
1990	31,122	1.58	90(WB)
2000	34,615	1.07	00(WB)
2010	37,891	0.91	10(WB)
2012	39,097	1.58	12(WB)
2020	43,896	1.46	FORECAST
2030	51,458	1.60	FORECAST
SAS India			
0001	704	.	0001(Undivided India(Maddison))
1000	704	0.00	1000(Undivided India(Maddison))
1500	861	0.04	1500(Undivided India(Maddison))
1600	861	0.00	1600(Undivided India(Maddison))
1700	861	0.00	1700(Undivided India(Maddison))
1820	831	0.03	1820(Maddison)
1870	873	0.10	1870(Maddison)
1880	911	0.43	INTERPOL(Maddison)

Year	GDP at PPP Per Capita, 2012 doll.	Growth Rate	Source
1890	951	0.43	1890(Maddison)
1900	978	0.28	1900(Maddison)
1913	1,037	0.46	1913(Maddison)
1920	984	0.75	1920(Maddison)
1929	1,041	0.62	1929(Maddison)
1938	969	0.79	1938(Maddison)
1950	969	0.00	50(Maddison)
1960	1,065	0.95	60(Maddison)
1970	1,112	0.43	70(Maddison)
1980	1,090	0.20	80(WB)
1990	1,491	3.18	90(WB)
2000	2,031	3.14	00(WB)
2010	3,563	5.78	10(WB)
2012	3,870	4.22	12(WB)
2020	5,491	4.47	FORECAST
2030	7,103	2.61	FORECAST
SEA Indonesia			
0001	678	.	PROXY(Other E. Asia(Maddison))
1000	678	0.00	PROXY(Other E. Asia(Maddison))
1500	884	0.05	1500(Maddison)
1600	896	0.01	INTERPOL(Maddison)
1700	908	0.01	1700(Maddison)
1820	958	0.04	1820(Maddison)
1870	1,023	0.13	1870(Maddison)
1880	1,036	0.12	1880(Maddison)
1890	1,033	0.03	1890(Maddison)
1900	1,163	1.19	1900(Maddison)
1913	1,415	1.52	1913(Maddison)
1920	1,479	0.64	1920(Maddison)
1929	1,831	2.40	1929(Maddison)
1938	1,839	0.05	1938(Maddison)
1950	1,314	2.76	50(Maddison)
1960	1,395	0.60	60(Maddison)
1970	1,434	0.28	70(Maddison)
1980	1,923	2.98	80(WB)
1990	2,807	3.86	90(WB)
2000	3,180	1.26	00(WB)
2010	4,458	3.43	10(WB)
2012	4,876	4.59	12(WB)
2020	6,282	3.22	FORECAST
2030	7,930	2.36	FORECAST
MEA Iran			
0001	831	.	PROXY(W. Asia(Maddison))
1000	988	0.02	PROXY(W. Asia(Maddison))
1500	939	0.01	1500(Maddison)
1600	939	0.00	INTERPOL(Maddison)
1700	939	0.00	1700(Maddison)
1820	920	0.02	1820(Maddison)

Year	GDP at PPP Per Capita, 2012 doll.	Growth Rate	Source
1870	1,125	0.40	1870(Maddison)
1880	1,215	0.77	INTERPOL(Maddison)
1890	1,312	0.77	INTERPOL(Maddison)
1900	1,416	0.77	INTERPOL(Maddison)
1913	1,565	0.77	1913(Maddison)
1920	1,734	1.48	INTERPOL(Maddison)
1929	1,978	1.48	INTERPOL(Maddison)
1938	2,257	1.48	INTERPOL(Maddison)
1950	2,692	1.48	50(Maddison)
1960	3,607	2.97	60(Maddison)
1970	7,594	7.73	70(Maddison)
1980	7,637	0.06	80(WB)
1990	6,430	1.70	90(WB)
2000	8,387	2.69	00(WB)
2010	12,475	4.05	10(WB)
2012	12,275	0.80	12(WB)
2020	15,333	2.82	FORECAST
2030	19,125	2.23	FORECAST
MEA IRAQ			
0001	791	.	PROXY(W. Asia(Maddison))
1000	941	0.02	PROXY(W. Asia(Maddison))
1500	894	0.01	PROXY(W. Asia(Maddison))
1600	896	0.00	PROXY(W. Asia(Maddison))
1700	896	0.00	PROXY(W. Asia(Maddison))
1820	920	0.02	1820(Maddison)
1870	1,125	0.40	1870(Maddison)
1880	1,215	0.77	INTERPOL(Maddison)
1890	1,312	0.77	INTERPOL(Maddison)
1900	1,416	0.77	INTERPOL(Maddison)
1913	1,565	0.77	1913(Maddison)
1920	1,660	0.84	INTERPOL(Maddison)
1929	1,790	0.84	INTERPOL(Maddison)
1938	1,930	0.84	INTERPOL(Maddison)
1950	2,134	0.84	50(Maddison)
1960	4,568	7.91	60(Maddison)
1970	5,933	2.65	70(Maddison)
1980	11,532	6.87	80(Maddison)
1990	6,622	5.40	90(Maddison)WEIGHT(00(WB))
2000	6,047	0.90	00(WB)
2010	6,455	0.66	10(WB)
2012	7,435	7.32	12(WB)
2020	8,681	1.96	FORECAST
2030	10,453	1.87	FORECAST
DME IRELAND			
0001	415	.	0001(MIN)
1000	619	0.04	1000(MIN)

Year	GDP at PPP Per Capita, 2012 doll.	Growth Rate	Source
1500	823	0.06	1500(Maddison)
1600	962	0.16	1600(Maddison)
1700	1,119	0.15	1700(Maddison)
1820	1,372	0.17	1820(Maddison)
1870	2,778	1.42	1870(Maddison)
1880	3,072	1.01	INTERPOL(Maddison)
1890	3,397	1.01	INTERPOL(Maddison)
1900	3,756	1.01	INTERPOL(Maddison)
1913	4,281	1.01	1913(Maddison)
1920	4,002	0.96	INTERPOL(Maddison)
1929	4,419	1.11	1929(Maddison)
1938	4,776	0.87	1938(Maddison)
1950	5,403	1.03	50(Maddison)
1960	6,931	2.52	60(Maddison)
1970	10,431	4.17	70(Maddison)
1980	14,916	3.64	80(WB)
1990	20,893	3.43	90(WB)
2000	40,445	6.83	00(WB)
2010	43,064	0.63	10(WB)
2012	43,834	0.89	12(WB)
2020	54,727	2.81	FORECAST
2030	68,245	2.23	FORECAST

DME Isle of Man

Year	GDP at PPP Per Capita, 2012 doll.	Growth Rate	Source
0001	.	.	
1000	.	.	
1500	.	.	
1600	.	.	
1700	.	.	
1820	.	.	
1870	.	.	
1880	.	.	
1890	.	.	
1900	.	.	
1913	.	.	
1920	.	.	
1929	.	.	
1938	.	.	
1950	4,816	.	PROXY(9 European cs(Maddison))
1960	7,266	4.20	INTERPOL(9 European cs(Maddison))
1970	10,962	4.20	INTERPOL(9 European cs(Maddison))
1980	14,358	2.74	INTERPOL(9 European cs(Maddison))
1990	17,701	2.12	94(CIA)WEIGHT(US(Maddison))
2000	24,915	3.48	01(CIA)WEIGHT(US(WB))
2010	56,027	8.44	07(CIA)WEIGHT(US(WB))
2012	57,917	1.67	07(CIA)WEIGHT(US(WB))
2020	89,808	5.64	FORECAST
2030	117,153	2.69	FORECAST

Year	GDP at PPP Per Capita, 2012 doll.	Growth Rate	Source
DME Israel			
0001	850	.	PROXY(W. Asia(Maddison))
1000	1,011	0.02	PROXY(W. Asia(Maddison))
1500	961	0.01	PROXY(Other W. Asia(Maddison))
1600	961	0.00	INTERPOL(Maddison)
1700	961	0.00	PROXY(Other W. Asia(Maddison))
1820	961	0.00	1820(Palestine(Maddison))
1870	1,175	0.40	1870(Palestine(Maddison))
1880	1,323	1.19	INTERPOL(Maddison)
1890	1,489	1.19	INTERPOL(Maddison)
1900	1,677	1.19	INTERPOL(Maddison)
1913	1,956	1.19	1913(Palestine(Maddison))
1920	2,281	2.22	INTERPOL(Maddison)
1929	2,780	2.22	INTERPOL(Maddison)
1938	3,387	2.22	INTERPOL(Maddison)
1950	4,408	2.22	50(Maddison)
1960	7,304	5.18	60(Maddison)
1970	12,694	5.68	70(Maddison)
1980	17,278	3.13	80(WB)
1990	20,487	1.72	90(WB)
2000	26,166	2.48	00(WB)
2010	30,111	1.41	10(WB)
2012	31,345	2.03	12(WB)
2020	37,224	2.17	FORECAST
2030	45,277	1.98	FORECAST
DME Italy			
0001	1,266	.	0001(Maddison)
1000	704	0.06	1000(Maddison)
1500	1,721	0.18	1500(Maddison)
1600	1,721	0.00	1600(Maddison)
1700	1,721	0.00	1700(Maddison)
1820	1,748	0.01	1820(Maddison)
1870	2,346	0.59	1870(Maddison)
1880	2,474	0.53	1880(Maddison)
1890	2,609	0.53	1890(Maddison)
1900	2,793	0.69	1900(Maddison)
1913	4,012	2.82	1913(Maddison)
1920	4,048	0.13	1920(Maddison)
1929	4,840	2.00	1929(Maddison)
1938	5,189	0.78	1938(Maddison)
1950	5,480	0.46	50(Maddison)
1960	9,804	5.99	60(Maddison)
1970	17,025	5.67	70(Maddison)
1980	24,021	3.50	80(WB)
1990	30,789	2.51	90(WB)
2000	36,034	1.59	00(WB)
2010	35,120	0.26	10(WB)

Year	GDP at PPP Per Capita, 2012 doll.	Growth Rate	Source
2012	34,926	0.28	12(WB)
2020	38,218	1.13	FORECAST
2030	43,889	1.39	FORECAST
		AFR Ivory Coast	
0001	.	.	
1000	.	.	
1500	.	.	
1600	.	.	
1700	.	.	
1820	.	.	
1870	.	.	
1880	.	.	
1890	.	.	
1900	.	.	
1913	.	.	
1920	.	.	
1929	.	.	
1938	.	.	
1950	1,629	.	50(Maddison)
1960	1,906	1.58	60(Maddison)
1970	2,593	3.12	70(Maddison)
1980	2,938	1.26	80(WB)
1990	2,297	2.43	90(WB)
2000	2,099	0.90	00(WB)
2010	2,010	0.44	10(WB)
2012	2,006	0.09	12(WB)
2020	2,037	0.19	FORECAST
2030	2,170	0.63	FORECAST
		LAM Jamaica	
0001	405	.	0001(MIN)
1000	598	0.04	1000(MIN)
1500	785	0.05	1500(MIN)
1600	838	0.06	INTERPOL(Maddison)
1700	1,121	0.29	PROXY(Caribbean cs(Maddison))
1820	1,095	0.02	1820(Maddison)
1870	837	0.54	1870(Maddison)
1880	866	0.34	INTERPOL(Maddison)
1890	897	0.34	INTERPOL(Maddison)
1900	928	0.34	INTERPOL(Maddison)
1913	970	0.34	1913(Maddison)
1920	1,100	1.81	INTERPOL(Maddison)
1929	1,294	1.81	INTERPOL(Maddison)
1938	1,521	1.81	1938(Maddison)
1950	2,077	2.63	50(Maddison)
1960	4,009	6.80	60(Maddison)
1970	5,705	3.59	70(Maddison)

Year	GDP at PPP Per Capita, 2012 doll.	Growth Rate	Source
1980	4,676	1.97	80(Maddison)
1990	5,367	1.39	90(Maddison)
2000	4,901	0.90	00(CIA)WEIGHT(US(WB))
2010	9,221	6.52	10(CIA)WEIGHT(US(WB))
2012	9,000	1.21	12(CIA)
2020	11,803	3.45	FORECAST
2030	14,988	2.42	FORECAST
		DME JAPAN	
0001	434	.	0001(MIN)
1000	665	0.04	1000(Maddison)
1500	782	0.03	1500(Maddison)
1600	814	0.04	1600(Maddison)
1700	892	0.09	1700(Maddison)
1820	1,047	0.13	1820(Maddison)
1870	1,153	0.19	1870(Maddison)
1880	1,350	1.59	1880(Maddison)
1890	1,584	1.61	1890(Maddison)
1900	1,847	1.55	1900(Maddison)
1913	2,170	1.25	1913(Maddison)
1920	2,654	2.91	1920(Maddison)
1929	3,170	2.00	1929(Maddison)
1938	3,832	2.13	1938(Maddison)
1950	3,006	2.00	50(Maddison)
1960	6,216	7.54	60(Maddison)
1970	15,067	9.26	70(Maddison)
1980	20,866	3.31	80(WB)
1990	30,873	4.00	90(WB)
2000	32,775	0.60	00(WB)
2010	35,171	0.71	10(WB)
2012	35,618	0.63	12(WB)
2020	40,492	1.62	FORECAST
2030	47,901	1.69	FORECAST
		DME JERSEY	
0001	.	.	
1000	.	.	
1500	.	.	
1600	.	.	
1700	.	.	
1820	.	.	
1870	.	.	
1880	.	.	
1890	.	.	
1900	.	.	
1913	.	.	
1920	.	.	
1929	.	.	

Year	GDP at PPP Per Capita, 2012 doll.	Growth Rate	Source
1938	.	.	
1950	9,742	.	PROXY(9 European cs(Maddison))
1960	14,116	3.78	INTERPOL(9 European cs(Maddison))
1970	20,454	3.78	INTERPOL(9 European cs(Maddison))
1980	26,092	2.46	INTERPOL(9 European cs(Maddison))
1990	31,515	1.91	99(CIA)WEIGHT(US(Maddison))
2000	34,282	0.85	99(CIA)WEIGHT(US(WB))
2010	64,601	6.54	05(CIA)WEIGHT(US(WB))
2012	66,564	1.51	05(CIA)WEIGHT(US(WB))
2020	91,356	4.04	FORECAST
2030	117,421	2.54	FORECAST
MEA Jordan			
0001	814	.	PROXY(W. Asia(Maddison))
1000	968	0.02	PROXY(W. Asia(Maddison))
1500	920	0.01	PROXY(Other W. Asia(Maddison))
1600	920	0.00	INTERPOL(Maddison)
1700	920	0.00	PROXY(Other W. Asia(Maddison))
1820	920	0.00	1820(Maddison)
1870	1,125	0.40	1870(Maddison)
1880	1,215	0.77	INTERPOL(Maddison)
1890	1,312	0.77	INTERPOL(Maddison)
1900	1,416	0.77	INTERPOL(Maddison)
1913	1,565	0.77	1913(Maddison)
1920	1,723	1.38	INTERPOL(Maddison)
1929	1,950	1.38	INTERPOL(Maddison)
1938	2,207	1.38	INTERPOL(Maddison)
1950	2,602	1.38	50(Maddison)
1960	3,209	2.12	60(Maddison)
1970	2,954	0.82	70(Maddison)
1980	4,784	4.94	80(WB)
1990	4,047	1.66	90(WB)
2000	4,187	0.34	00(WB)
2010	5,994	3.65	10(WB)
2012	6,037	0.36	12(WB)
2020	7,172	2.18	FORECAST
2030	8,726	1.98	FORECAST
USR Kazakhstan			
0001	455	.	0001(MIN)
1000	715	0.05	1000(MIN)
1500	1,001	0.07	PROXY(USSR(Maddison))
1600	1,108	0.10	PROXY(USSR(Maddison))
1700	1,224	0.10	PROXY(USSR(Maddison))
1820	1,381	0.10	PROXY(USSR(Maddison))
1870	1,892	0.63	PROXY(USSR(Maddison))
1880	2,071	0.91	INTERPOL(Maddison)
1890	2,268	0.91	INTERPOL(Maddison)
1900	2,482	0.91	PROXY(USSR(Maddison))
1913	2,986	1.43	PROXY(USSR(Maddison))

Year	GDP at PPP Per Capita, 2012 doll.	Growth Rate	Source
1920	1,157	12.67	PROXY(USSR(Davies))
1929	2,856	10.56	PROXY(USSR(Maddison))
1938	4,430	5.00	PROXY(USSR(Maddison))
1950	5,701	2.12	PROXY(USSR(Maddison))
1960	7,255	2.44	PROXY(USSR(Maddison))
1970	9,396	2.62	PROXY(USSR(Maddison))
1980	9,196	0.21	INTERPOL(Kazakhstan(Maddison))
1990	8,067	1.30	90(WB)
2000	6,160	2.66	00(WB)
2010	12,458	7.30	10(WB)
2012	13,672	4.76	12(WB)
2020	19,052	4.23	FORECAST
2030	24,565	2.57	FORECAST
AFR Kenya			
0001	.	.	
1000	.	.	
1500	.	.	
1600	.	.	
1700	.	.	
1820	.	.	
1870	.	.	
1880	.	.	
1890	.	.	
1900	.	.	
1913	.	.	
1920	.	.	
1929	.	.	
1938	.	.	
1950	1,019	.	50(Maddison)
1960	1,122	0.97	60(Maddison)
1970	1,397	2.21	70(Maddison)
1980	1,554	1.07	80(WB)
1990	1,608	0.34	90(WB)
2000	1,460	0.96	00(WB)
2010	1,678	1.41	10(WB)
2012	1,737	1.73	12(WB)
2020	1,895	1.09	FORECAST
2030	2,170	1.37	FORECAST
SEA Kiribati			
0001	.	.	
1000	.	.	
1500	.	.	
1600	.	.	
1700	.	.	
1820	.	.	

Year	GDP at PPP Per Capita, 2012 doll.	Growth Rate	Source
1870	.	.	
1880	.	.	
1890	.	.	
1900	.	.	
1913	.	.	
1920	.	.	
1929	.	.	
1938	.	.	
1950	915	.	PROXY(14 Pacific is(Maddison))
1960	1,261	3.26	INTERPOL(14 Pacific is(Maddison))
1970	1,739	3.26	INTERPOL(14 Pacific is(Maddison))
1980	2,171	2.24	80(WB)
1990	1,893	1.36	90(WB)
2000	2,672	3.51	00(WB)
2010	2,550	0.47	10(WB)
2012	2,618	1.33	12(WB)
2020	2,902	1.29	FORECAST
2030	3,368	1.50	FORECAST
		CPA Korea, North	
0001	704	.	PROXY(China(Maddison))
1000	704	0.00	PROXY(China(Maddison))
1500	939	0.06	1500(Maddison)
1600	939	0.00	INTERPOL(Maddison)
1700	939	0.00	1700(Maddison)
1820	939	0.00	1820(Maddison)
1870	945	0.01	1870(Maddison)
1880	1,015	0.71	INTERPOL(Maddison)
1890	1,090	0.71	INTERPOL(Maddison)
1900	1,170	0.71	INTERPOL(Maddison)
1913	1,283	0.71	1913(Maddison)
1920	1,579	3.01	1920(Maddison)
1929	1,587	0.05	1929(Maddison)
1938	2,283	4.13	1938(Maddison)
1950	1,205	5.19	50(Maddison)
1960	1,734	3.71	60(Maddison)
1970	3,078	5.91	70(Maddison)
1980	4,488	3.84	80(Maddison)
1990	4,488	0.00	90(Maddison)
2000	2,546	5.51	00(EST)WEIGHT(US(WB))
2010	2,377	0.68	10(EST)WEIGHT(US(WB))
2012	2,402	0.51	12(EST)
2020	2,505	0.53	FORECAST
2030	2,750	0.94	FORECAST
		SEA Korea, South	
0001	704	.	PROXY(China(Maddison))
1000	704	0.00	PROXY(China(Maddison))
1500	939	0.06	1500(Maddison)

Year	GDP at PPP Per Capita, 2012 doll.	Growth Rate	Source
1600	939	0.00	INTERPOL(Maddison)
1700	939	0.00	1700(Maddison)
1820	939	0.00	1820(Maddison)
1870	945	0.01	1870(Maddison)
1880	1,015	0.71	INTERPOL(Maddison)
1890	1,090	0.71	INTERPOL(Maddison)
1900	1,170	0.71	INTERPOL(Maddison)
1913	1,283	0.71	1913(Maddison)
1920	1,579	3.01	1920(Maddison)
1929	1,587	0.05	1929(Maddison)
1938	2,283	4.13	1938(Maddison)
1950	1,205	5.19	50(Maddison)
1960	1,685	3.41	60(Maddison)
1970	2,898	5.57	70(Maddison)
1980	5,919	7.40	80(WB)
1990	12,050	7.37	90(WB)
2000	20,179	5.29	00(WB)
2010	28,721	3.59	10(WB)
2012	30,011	2.22	12(WB)
2020	43,599	4.78	FORECAST
2030	56,586	2.64	FORECAST
EEU Kosovo			
0001	324	.	0001(MIN)
1000	436	0.03	1000(MIN)
1500	528	0.04	1500(MIN)
1600	552	0.04	1600(MIN)
1700	577	0.05	1700(MIN)
1820	611	0.05	1820(MIN)
1870	626	0.05	PROXY(Yugoslavia(Maddison))
1880	743	1.72	PROXY(Yugoslavia(Maddison))
1890	881	1.72	PROXY(Yugoslavia(Maddison))
1900	943	0.68	PROXY(Yugoslavia(Maddison))
1913	1,105	1.23	PROXY(Yugoslavia(Maddison))
1920	1,077	0.36	PROXY(Yugoslavia(Maddison))
1929	1,425	3.16	PROXY(Yugoslavia(Maddison))
1938	1,417	0.07	PROXY(Yugoslavia(Maddison))
1950	1,621	1.13	PROXY(Yugoslavia(Maddison))
1960	2,769	5.50	PROXY(Yugoslavia(Maddison))
1970	4,622	5.26	PROXY(Yugoslavia(Maddison))
1980	8,155	5.84	PROXY(Yugoslavia(Maddison))
1990	7,704	0.57	PROXY(Serbia & Montenegro(Maddison
2000	3,955	6.45	PROXY(Serbia)
2010	6,492	5.08	10(CIA)WEIGHT(US(WB))
2012	7,500	7.49	12(CIA)
2020	10,301	4.05	FORECAST
2030	13,243	2.54	FORECAST
MEA Kuwait			
0001	761	.	PROXY(W. Asia(Maddison))

Year	GDP at PPP Per Capita, 2012 doll.	Growth Rate	Source
1000	906	0.02	PROXY(W. Asia(Maddison))
1500	861	0.01	AVG(Arabia(Maddison))
1600	861	0.00	INTERPOL(Maddison)
1700	861	0.00	AVG(Arabia(Maddison))
1820	861	0.00	AVG(Arabia(Maddison))
1870	900	0.09	AVG(Arabia(Maddison))
1880	909	0.10	INTERPOL(Maddison)
1890	918	0.10	INTERPOL(Maddison)
1900	927	0.10	INTERPOL(Maddison)
1913	939	0.10	AVG(Arabia(Maddison))
1920	1,954	11.04	INTERPOL(Maddison)
1929	5,014	11.04	INTERPOL(Maddison)
1938	12,864	11.04	INTERPOL(Maddison)
1950	45,190	11.04	50(Maddison)
1960	45,197	0.00	60(Maddison)
1970	44,995	0.04	70(Maddison)
1980	47,742	0.59	80(WB)
1990	50,425	0.55	90(Maddison)WEIGHT(80(WB))
2000	46,516	0.80	00(WB)
2010	46,510	0.00	10(WB)
2012	46,385	0.13	12(WB)
2020	46,756	0.10	FORECAST
2030	49,383	0.55	FORECAST

USR Kyrgyzstan

Year	GDP at PPP Per Capita, 2012 doll.	Growth Rate	Source
0001	338	.	0001(MIN)
1000	462	0.03	1000(MIN)
1500	567	0.04	1500(MIN)
1600	594	0.05	1600(MIN)
1700	624	0.05	1700(MIN)
1820	663	0.05	PROXY(USSR(Maddison))
1870	909	0.63	PROXY(USSR(Maddison))
1880	995	0.91	INTERPOL(Maddison)
1890	1,090	0.91	INTERPOL(Maddison)
1900	1,193	0.91	PROXY(USSR(Maddison))
1913	1,435	1.43	PROXY(USSR(Maddison))
1920	556	12.67	PROXY(USSR(Davies))
1929	1,372	10.56	PROXY(USSR(Maddison))
1938	2,129	5.00	PROXY(USSR(Maddison))
1950	2,739	2.12	PROXY(USSR(Maddison))
1960	3,208	1.59	PROXY(USSR(Maddison))
1970	3,822	1.77	PROXY(USSR(Maddison))
1980	3,463	0.98	INTERPOL(Kyrgyzstan(Maddison))
1990	2,868	1.87	90(WB)
2000	1,727	4.95	00(WB)
2010	2,314	2.97	10(WB)
2012	2,360	0.99	12(WB)
2020	2,683	1.62	FORECAST
2030	3,174	1.70	FORECAST

Year	GDP at PPP Per Capita, 2012 doll.	Growth Rate	Source
CPA Laos			
0001	393	.	0001(MIN)
1000	572	0.04	1000(MIN)
1500	741	0.05	PROXY(Other E. Asia(Maddison))
1600	754	0.02	PROXY(Other E. Asia(Maddison))
1700	750	0.01	PROXY(Other E. Asia(Maddison))
1820	760	0.01	PROXY(26 E. Asian cs(Maddison))
1870	731	0.08	PROXY(26 E. Asian cs(Maddison))
1880	791	0.80	INTERPOL(Maddison)
1890	856	0.79	INTERPOL(Maddison)
1900	927	0.79	INTERPOL(Maddison)
1913	1,028	0.79	PROXY(26 E. Asian cs(Maddison))
1920	1,014	0.19	INTERPOL(Maddison)
1929	997	0.19	INTERPOL(Maddison)
1938	981	0.19	INTERPOL(Maddison)
1950	959	0.19	50(Maddison)
1960	981	0.22	60(Maddison)
1970	998	0.17	70(Maddison)
1980	1,079	0.78	80(Maddison)
1990	1,061	0.17	90(WB)
2000	1,525	3.70	00(WB)
2010	2,559	5.31	10(WB)
2012	2,879	6.07	12(WB)
2020	4,032	4.30	FORECAST
2030	5,204	2.58	FORECAST
USR Latvia			
0001	458	.	0001(MIN)
1000	722	0.05	1000(MIN)
1500	1,014	0.07	PROXY(USSR(Maddison))
1600	1,122	0.10	PROXY(USSR(Maddison))
1700	1,240	0.10	PROXY(USSR(Maddison))
1820	1,398	0.10	PROXY(USSR(Maddison))
1870	1,917	0.63	PROXY(USSR(Maddison))
1880	2,098	0.91	INTERPOL(Maddison)
1890	2,297	0.91	INTERPOL(Maddison)
1900	2,514	0.91	PROXY(USSR(Maddison))
1913	3,024	1.43	PROXY(USSR(Maddison))
1920	2,645	1.90	PROXY(Finland(Maddison))
1929	3,893	4.39	PROXY(Finland(Maddison))
1938	5,142	3.14	PROXY(Finland(Maddison))
1950	5,774	0.97	PROXY(USSR(Maddison))
1960	7,729	2.96	PROXY(USSR(Maddison))
1970	10,543	3.15	PROXY(USSR(Maddison))
1980	12,000	1.30	80(WB)
1990	14,907	2.19	90(WB)

Year	GDP at PPP Per Capita, 2012 doll.	Growth Rate	Source
2000	11,255	2.77	00(WB)
2010	18,927	5.34	10(WB)
2012	21,810	7.35	12(WB)
2020	29,937	4.04	FORECAST
2030	38,480	2.54	FORECAST
MEA Lebanon			
0001	911	.	PROXY(W. Asia(Maddison))
1000	1,084	0.02	PROXY(W. Asia(Maddison))
1500	1,030	0.01	PROXY(Other W. Asia(Maddison))
1600	1,030	0.00	INTERPOL(Maddison)
1700	1,030	0.00	PROXY(Other W. Asia(Maddison))
1820	1,030	0.00	1820(Maddison)
1870	1,321	0.50	1870(Maddison)
1880	1,473	1.10	INTERPOL(Maddison)
1890	1,643	1.10	INTERPOL(Maddison)
1900	1,833	1.10	INTERPOL(Maddison)
1913	2,113	1.10	1913(Maddison)
1920	2,361	1.60	INTERPOL(Maddison)
1929	2,723	1.60	INTERPOL(Maddison)
1938	3,142	1.60	INTERPOL(Maddison)
1950	3,801	1.60	50(Maddison)
1960	4,636	2.01	60(Maddison)
1970	6,998	4.20	70(Maddison)
1980	10,475	4.12	80(Maddison)
1990	7,122	3.79	90(WB)
2000	11,387	4.81	00(WB)
2010	14,027	2.11	10(WB)
2012	14,373	1.23	12(WB)
2020	17,785	2.70	FORECAST
2030	22,090	2.19	FORECAST
AFR Lesotho			
0001	298	.	0001(MIN)
1000	391	0.03	1000(MIN)
1500	463	0.03	1500(MIN)
1600	481	0.04	1600(MIN)
1700	500	0.04	1700(MIN)
1820	525	0.04	1820(MIN)
1870	536	0.04	1870(MIN)
1880	539	0.04	1880(MIN)
1890	541	0.04	1890(MIN)
1900	543	0.04	1900(MIN)
1913	547	0.04	1913(MIN)
1920	548	0.04	1920(MIN)
1929	550	0.04	1929(MIN)
1938	553	0.04	1938(MIN)
1950	556	0.04	50(Maddison)
1960	617	1.06	60(Maddison)
1970	700	1.27	70(Maddison)

Year	GDP at PPP Per Capita, 2012 doll.	Growth Rate	Source
1980	991	3.53	80(WB)
1990	1,167	1.65	90(WB)
2000	1,356	1.51	00(WB)
2010	1,834	3.07	10(WB)
2012	1,931	2.62	12(WB)
2020	2,378	2.63	FORECAST
2030	2,946	2.17	FORECAST
AFR LIBERIA			
0001	.	.	
1000	.	.	
1500	.	.	
1600	.	.	
1700	.	.	
1820	.	.	
1870	.	.	
1880	.	.	
1890	.	.	
1900	.	.	
1913	.	.	
1920	.	.	
1929	.	.	
1938	.	.	
1950	1,651	.	50(Maddison)
1960	1,448	1.30	60(Maddison)
1970	1,306	1.03	70(Maddison)
1980	852	4.18	80(WB)
1990	352	8.47	90(WB)
2000	450	2.51	00(WB)
2010	585	2.64	10(WB)
2012	639	4.54	12(WB)
2020	778	2.49	FORECAST
2030	958	2.11	FORECAST
MEA LIBYA			
0001	673	.	AVG(Other N. Africa(Maddison))
1000	673	0.00	AVG(Other N. Africa(Maddison))
1500	673	0.00	AVG(Other N. Africa(Maddison))
1600	673	0.00	AVG(Other N. Africa(Maddison))
1700	673	0.00	AVG(Other N. Africa(Maddison))
1820	673	0.00	AVG(Other N. Africa(Maddison))
1870	877	0.53	INTERPOL(Maddison)
1880	925	0.53	INTERPOL(Maddison)
1890	975	0.53	INTERPOL(Maddison)
1900	1,029	0.53	INTERPOL(Maddison)
1913	1,102	0.53	INTERPOL(Maddison)
1920	1,144	0.53	INTERPOL(Maddison)
1929	1,200	0.53	INTERPOL(Maddison)

Year	GDP at PPP Per Capita, 2012 doll.	Growth Rate	Source
1938	1,258	0.53	INTERPOL(Maddison)
1950	1,341	0.53	50(Maddison)
1960	2,999	8.38	60(Maddison)
1970	16,463	18.57	70(Maddison)
1980	12,955	2.37	80(Maddison)
1990	5,221	8.69	90(Maddison)
2000	14,726	10.93	00(WB)
2010	17,590	1.79	09(WB)WEIGHT(US(WB))
2012	12,100	17.06	12(CIA)
2020	16,678	4.09	FORECAST
2030	21,457	2.55	FORECAST
		DME LIECHTENSTEIN	
0001	.	.	
1000	.	.	
1500	.	.	
1600	.	.	
1700	.	.	
1820	.	.	
1870	.	.	
1880	.	.	
1890	.	.	
1900	.	.	
1913	.	.	
1920	.	.	
1929	.	.	
1938	.	.	
1950	10,343	.	PROXY(9 European cs(Maddison))
1960	14,954	3.76	INTERPOL(9 European cs(Maddison))
1970	21,621	3.76	INTERPOL(9 European cs(Maddison))
1980	27,540	2.45	INTERPOL(9 European cs(Maddison))
1990	33,226	1.89	90(CIA)
2000	35,236	0.59	99(CIA)WEIGHT(US(WB))
2010	95,550	10.49	09(CIA)WEIGHT(US(WB))
2012	98,435	1.50	09(CIA)WEIGHT(US(WB))
2020	154,941	5.83	FORECAST
2030	202,199	2.70	FORECAST
		USR LITHUANIA	
0001	451	.	0001(MIN)
1000	705	0.04	1000(MIN)
1500	980	0.07	PROXY(USSR(Maddison))
1600	1,085	0.10	PROXY(USSR(Maddison))
1700	1,199	0.10	PROXY(USSR(Maddison))
1820	1,352	0.10	PROXY(USSR(Maddison))
1870	1,853	0.63	PROXY(USSR(Maddison))
1880	2,028	0.91	INTERPOL(Maddison)
1890	2,220	0.91	INTERPOL(Maddison)

Year	GDP at PPP Per Capita, 2012 doll.	Growth Rate	Source
1900	2,431	0.91	PROXY(USSR(Maddison))
1913	2,924	1.43	PROXY(USSR(Maddison))
1920	2,557	1.90	PROXY(Finland(Maddison))
1929	3,763	4.39	PROXY(Finland(Maddison))
1938	4,971	3.14	PROXY(Finland(Maddison))
1950	5,582	0.97	PROXY(USSR(Maddison))
1960	8,135	3.84	PROXY(USSR(Maddison))
1970	12,084	4.04	PROXY(USSR(Maddison))
1980	14,302	1.70	INTERPOL(Lithuanua(Maddison))
1990	15,819	1.01	90(WB)
2000	11,636	3.02	00(WB)
2010	21,134	6.15	10(WB)
2012	24,356	7.35	12(WB)
2020	34,231	4.35	FORECAST
2030	44,206	2.59	FORECAST
DME Luxembourg			
0001	.	.	
1000	.	.	
1500	.	.	
1600	.	.	
1700	.	.	
1820	.	.	
1870	.	.	
1880	.	.	
1890	.	.	
1900	.	.	
1913	.	.	
1920	.	.	
1929	.	.	
1938	.	.	
1950	13,116	.	50(Maddison)
1960	19,554	4.07	INTERPOL(Maddison)
1970	29,153	4.07	INTERPOL(Maddison)
1980	31,768	0.86	80(WB)
1990	52,011	5.05	90(WB)
2000	82,301	4.70	00(WB)
2010	92,510	1.18	10(WB)
2012	89,510	1.63	12(WB)
2020	108,966	2.49	FORECAST
2030	134,301	2.11	FORECAST
SEA Macao			
0001	.	.	
1000	.	.	
1500	.	.	
1600	.	.	
1700	.	.	

Year	GDP at PPP Per Capita, 2012 doll.	Growth Rate	Source
1820	.	.	
1870	.	.	
1880	.	.	
1890	.	.	
1900	.	.	
1913	.	.	
1920	.	.	
1929	.	.	
1938	.	.	
1950	1,618	.	PROXY(Maddison)
1960	3,225	7.14	INTERPOL(Maddison)
1970	6,430	7.14	INTERPOL(Maddison)
1980	18,585	11.20	82(WB)
1990	24,201	2.68	90(WB)
2000	27,033	1.11	00(WB)
2010	67,012	9.50	10(WB)
2012	86,341	13.51	12(WB)
2020	159,422	7.97	FORECAST
2030	206,213	2.61	FORECAST
	EEU Macedonia		
0001	326	.	0001(MIN)
1000	440	0.03	1000(MIN)
1500	534	0.04	1500(MIN)
1600	557	0.04	1600(MIN)
1700	583	0.05	1700(MIN)
1820	618	0.05	1820(MIN)
1870	633	0.05	PROXY(Yugoslavia(Maddison))
1880	751	1.72	INTERPOL(Maddison)
1890	891	1.72	PROXY(Yugoslavia(Maddison))
1900	954	0.68	PROXY(Yugoslavia(Maddison))
1913	1,118	1.23	PROXY(Yugoslavia(Maddison))
1920	1,090	0.36	PROXY(Yugoslavia(Maddison))
1929	1,442	3.16	PROXY(Yugoslavia(Maddison))
1938	1,434	0.07	PROXY(Yugoslavia(Maddison))
1950	1,640	1.13	PROXY(Yugoslavia(Maddison))
1960	2,913	5.91	PROXY(Yugoslavia(Maddison))
1970	5,066	5.69	PROXY(Yugoslavia(Maddison))
1980	9,271	6.23	PROXY(Yugoslavia(Maddison))
1990	9,556	0.30	90(WB)
2000	8,977	0.62	00(WB)
2010	11,532	2.54	10(WB)
2012	11,834	1.30	12(WB)
2020	13,910	2.04	FORECAST
2030	16,818	1.92	FORECAST
	AFR Madagascar		
0001	355	.	0001(MIN)
1000	495	0.03	1000(MIN)

Year	GDP at PPP Per Capita, 2012 doll.	Growth Rate	Source
1500	617	0.04	1500(MIN)
1600	649	0.05	1600(Rest of Africa(Maddison))
1700	649	0.00	1700(Rest of Africa(Maddison))
1820	649	0.00	1820(Rest of Africa(Maddison))
1870	893	0.64	INTERPOL(Maddison)
1880	952	0.64	INTERPOL(Maddison)
1890	1,015	0.64	INTERPOL(Maddison)
1900	1,082	0.64	INTERPOL(Maddison)
1913	1,175	0.64	INTERPOL(Maddison)
1920	1,229	0.64	INTERPOL(Maddison)
1929	1,302	0.64	INTERPOL(Maddison)
1938	1,379	0.64	INTERPOL(Maddison)
1950	1,488	0.64	50(Maddison)
1960	1,747	1.62	60(Maddison)
1970	1,875	0.71	70(Maddison)
1980	1,558	1.84	80(WB)
1990	1,220	2.42	90(WB)
2000	1,010	1.86	00(WB)
2010	970	0.41	10(WB)
2012	962	0.38	12(WB)
2020	966	0.04	FORECAST
2030	1,015	0.49	FORECAST
		AFR MALAWI	
0001	283	.	0001(MIN)
1000	366	0.03	1000(MIN)
1500	429	0.03	1500(MIN)
1600	444	0.03	1600(MIN)
1700	460	0.04	1700(MIN)
1820	482	0.04	1820(MIN)
1870	491	0.04	1870(MIN)
1880	493	0.04	1880(MIN)
1890	495	0.04	1890(MIN)
1900	497	0.04	1900(MIN)
1913	500	0.04	1913(MIN)
1920	501	0.04	1920(MIN)
1929	503	0.04	1929(MIN)
1938	505	0.04	1938(MIN)
1950	507	0.04	50(Maddison)
1960	570	1.18	60(Maddison)
1970	602	0.54	70(Maddison)
1980	795	2.83	80(WB)
1990	656	1.91	90(WB)
2000	758	1.46	00(WB)
2010	751	0.10	10(WB)
2012	753	0.17	12(WB)
2020	788	0.57	FORECAST
2030	868	0.97	FORECAST

Year	GDP at PPP Per Capita, 2012 doll.	Growth Rate	Source
		SEA MALAYSIA	
0001	706	.	PROXY(Other E. Asia(Maddison))
1000	706	0.00	PROXY(Other E. Asia(Maddison))
1500	920	0.05	PROXY(Other E. Asia(Maddison))
1600	937	0.02	PROXY(Other E. Asia(Maddison))
1700	932	0.01	PROXY(Other E. Asia(Maddison))
1820	944	0.01	1820(Maddison)
1870	1,037	0.19	1870(Maddison)
1880	1,086	0.46	INTERPOL(Maddison)
1890	1,138	0.46	INTERPOL(Maddison)
1900	1,191	0.46	INTERPOL(Maddison)
1913	1,408	1.29	1913(Maddison)
1920	1,737	3.04	1920(Maddison)
1929	2,632	4.73	1929(Maddison)
1938	2,130	2.33	1938(Maddison)
1950	2,440	1.14	50(Maddison)
1960	2,378	0.26	60(Maddison)
1970	3,216	3.07	70(Maddison)
1980	5,644	5.78	80(WB)
1990	7,681	3.13	90(WB)
2000	12,089	4.64	00(WB)
2010	15,745	2.68	10(WB)
2012	16,919	3.66	12(WB)
2020	22,591	3.68	FORECAST
2030	28,841	2.47	FORECAST
		SAS MALDIVES	
0001	.	.	
1000	.	.	
1500	.	.	
1600	.	.	
1700	.	.	
1820	.	.	
1870	.	.	
1880	.	.	
1890	.	.	
1900	.	.	
1913	.	.	
1920	.	.	
1929	.	.	
1938	.	.	
1950	852	.	50(Maddison)
1960	1,031	1.93	INTERPOL(Maddison)
1970	1,247	1.93	INTERPOL(Maddison)
1980	1,983	4.75	INTERPOL(Maddison)
1990	3,546	5.98	90(Maddison)
2000	5,109	3.72	00(WB)

Year	GDP at PPP Per Capita, 2012 doll.	Growth Rate	Source
2010	8,384	5.08	10(WB)
2012	8,925	3.17	12(WB)
2020	12,982	4.80	FORECAST
2030	16,852	2.64	FORECAST
		AFR Mali	
0001	.	.	
1000	.	.	
1500	.	.	
1600	.	.	
1700	.	.	
1820	.	.	
1870	.	.	
1880	.	.	
1890	.	.	
1900	.	.	
1913	.	.	
1920	.	.	
1929	.	.	
1938	.	.	
1950	715	.	50(Maddison)
1960	772	0.77	60(Maddison)
1970	781	0.12	70(Maddison)
1980	903	1.46	80(WB)
1990	808	1.10	90(WB)
2000	948	1.61	00(WB)
2010	1,251	2.82	10(WB)
2012	1,204	1.90	12(WB)
2020	1,390	1.81	FORECAST
2030	1,661	1.80	FORECAST
		DME Malta	
0001	.	.	
1000	.	.	
1500	.	.	
1600	.	.	
1700	.	.	
1820	.	.	
1870	.	.	
1880	.	.	
1890	.	.	
1900	.	.	
1913	.	.	
1920	.	.	
1929	.	.	
1938	.	.	

Year	GDP at PPP Per Capita, 2012 doll.	Growth Rate	Source
1950	1,394	.	50(Maddison)
1960	3,274	8.91	INTERPOL(Maddison)
1970	7,689	8.91	INTERPOL(Maddison)
1980	11,900	4.47	80(WB)
1990	15,810	2.88	90(WB)
2000	26,528	5.31	00(WB)
2010	28,475	0.71	10(WB)
2012	28,955	0.84	12(WB)
2020	35,847	2.70	FORECAST
2030	44,535	2.19	FORECAST

SEA Marshall Islands

Year	GDP at PPP Per Capita, 2012 doll.	Growth Rate	Source
0001	.	.	
1000	.	.	
1500	.	.	
1600	.	.	
1700	.	.	
1820	.	.	
1870	.	.	
1880	.	.	
1890	.	.	
1900	.	.	
1913	.	.	
1920	.	.	
1929	.	.	
1938	.	.	
1950	1,527	.	PROXY(14 Pacific is(Maddison))
1960	1,753	1.39	INTERPOL(14 Pacific is(Maddison))
1970	2,013	1.39	INTERPOL(14 Pacific is(Maddison))
1980	2,125	0.54	INTERPOL(14 Pacific is(Maddison))
1990	2,164	0.18	92(CIA)WEIGHT(US(Maddison))
2000	2,226	0.29	01(CIA)WEIGHT(US(WB))
2010	8,453	14.27	12(CIA)WEIGHT(US(WB))
2012	8,700	1.45	12(CIA)
2020	15,084	7.12	FORECAST
2030	19,627	2.67	FORECAST

LAM Martinique

Year	GDP at PPP Per Capita, 2012 doll.	Growth Rate	Source
0001	.	.	
1000	.	.	
1500	.	.	
1600	.	.	
1700	.	.	
1820	.	.	
1870	.	.	
1880	.	.	
1890	.	.	

Year	GDP at PPP Per Capita, 2012 doll.	Growth Rate	Source
1900	.	.	
1913	.	.	
1920	.	.	
1929	.	.	
1938	.	.	
1950	2,065	.	50(Maddison)
1960	3,739	6.11	INTERPOL(Maddison)
1970	6,768	6.11	INTERPOL(Maddison)
1980	8,408	2.19	INTERPOL(Maddison)
1990	8,888	0.56	90(Maddison)
2000	12,637	3.58	01(CIA)WEIGHT(US(WB))
2010	32,318	9.85	10(REG)WEIGHT(US(WB))
2012	31,370	1.48	12(REG)
2020	49,822	5.95	FORECAST
2030	65,026	2.70	FORECAST
AFR Mauritania			
0001	.	.	
1000	.	.	
1500	.	.	
1600	.	.	
1700	.	.	
1820	.	.	
1870	.	.	
1880	.	.	
1890	.	.	
1900	.	.	
1913	.	.	
1920	.	.	
1929	.	.	
1938	.	.	
1950	726	.	50(Maddison)
1960	1,076	4.02	60(Maddison)
1970	2,028	6.54	70(Maddison)
1980	2,088	0.29	80(WB)
1990	1,855	1.18	90(WB)
2000	1,950	0.50	00(WB)
2010	2,402	2.11	10(WB)
2012	2,561	3.25	12(WB)
2020	2,965	1.85	FORECAST
2030	3,550	1.82	FORECAST
AFR Mauritius			
0001	.	.	
1000	.	.	
1500	.	.	
1600	.	.	

Year	GDP at PPP Per Capita, 2012 doll.	Growth Rate	Source
1700	.	.	
1820	.	.	
1870	.	.	
1880	.	.	
1890	.	.	
1900	.	.	
1913	.	.	
1920	.	.	
1929	.	.	
1938	.	.	
1950	3,896	.	50(Maddison)
1960	3,861	0.09	60(Maddison)
1970	3,646	0.57	70(Maddison)
1980	4,747	2.67	80(WB)
1990	7,611	4.83	90(WB)
2000	10,606	3.37	00(WB)
2010	14,052	2.85	10(WB)
2012	14,902	2.98	12(WB)
2020	19,315	3.30	FORECAST
2030	24,434	2.38	FORECAST

AFR Mayotte

Year	GDP at PPP Per Capita, 2012 doll.	Growth Rate	Source
0001	.	.	
1000	.	.	
1500	.	.	
1600	.	.	
1700	.	.	
1820	.	.	
1870	.	.	
1880	.	.	
1890	.	.	
1900	.	.	
1913	.	.	
1920	.	.	
1929	.	.	
1938	.	.	
1950	493	.	PROXY(3 Afr. cs(Maddison))
1960	654	2.86	PROXY(3 Afr. cs(Maddison))
1970	672	0.27	PROXY(3 Afr. cs(Maddison))
1980	773	1.41	PROXY(3 Afr. cs(Maddison))
1990	858	1.06	93(CIA)WEIGHT(US(Maddison))
2000	3,679	15.66	98(CIA)WEIGHT(US(WB))
2010	13,238	13.66	09(CIA)WEIGHT(US(WB))
2012	12,530	2.71	12(REG)
2020	27,640	10.39	FORECAST
2030	34,807	2.33	FORECAST

Year	GDP at PPP Per Capita, 2012 doll.	Growth Rate	Source
		LAM Mexico	
0001	370	.	0001(MIN)
1000	525	0.04	1000(MIN)
1500	665	0.05	1500(Maddison)
1600	710	0.07	1600(Maddison)
1700	889	0.22	1700(Maddison)
1820	1,188	0.24	1820(Maddison)
1870	1,055	0.24	1870(Maddison)
1880	1,292	2.05	INTERPOL(Maddison)
1890	1,582	2.05	1890(Maddison)
1900	2,138	3.06	1900(Maddison)
1913	2,710	1.84	1913(Maddison)
1920	2,853	0.73	1920(Maddison)
1929	2,749	0.41	1929(Maddison)
1938	2,807	0.23	1938(Maddison)
1950	3,701	2.33	50(Maddison)
1960	5,120	3.30	60(Maddison)
1970	7,298	3.61	70(Maddison)
1980	11,160	4.34	80(WB)
1990	10,874	0.26	90(WB)
2000	14,627	3.01	00(WB)
2010	15,486	0.57	10(WB)
2012	16,426	2.99	12(WB)
2020	18,973	1.82	FORECAST
2030	22,688	1.80	FORECAST
		SEA Micronesia	
0001	.	.	
1000	.	.	
1500	.	.	
1600	.	.	
1700	.	.	
1820	.	.	
1870	.	.	
1880	.	.	
1890	.	.	
1900	.	.	
1913	.	.	
1920	.	.	
1929	.	.	
1938	.	.	
1950	2,162	.	PROXY(14 Pacific is(Maddison))
1960	2,478	1.38	INTERPOL(14 Pacific is(Maddison))
1970	2,841	1.38	INTERPOL(14 Pacific is(Maddison))
1980	2,974	0.46	INTERPOL(14 Pacific is(Maddison))
1990	2,996	0.07	90(WB)
2000	3,442	1.40	00(WB)

Year	GDP at PPP Per Capita, 2012 doll.	Growth Rate	Source
2010	3,627	0.53	10(WB)
2012	3,726	1.35	12(WB)
2020	3,993	0.87	FORECAST
2030	4,501	1.20	FORECAST
		USR Moldova	
0001	378	.	0001(MIN)
1000	542	0.04	1000(MIN)
1500	691	0.05	PROXY(USSR(Maddison))
1600	765	0.10	PROXY(USSR(Maddison))
1700	845	0.10	PROXY(USSR(Maddison))
1820	953	0.10	PROXY(USSR(Maddison))
1870	1,307	0.63	PROXY(USSR(Maddison))
1880	1,430	0.91	INTERPOL(Maddison)
1890	1,566	0.91	INTERPOL(Maddison)
1900	1,714	0.91	PROXY(USSR(Maddison))
1913	2,062	1.43	PROXY(USSR(Maddison))
1920	1,222	7.20	PROXY(Romania(Maddison))
1929	1,364	1.23	PROXY(Romania(Maddison))
1938	1,471	0.84	PROXY(Romania(Maddison))
1950	3,936	8.55	PROXY(USSR(Maddison))
1960	5,183	2.79	PROXY(USSR(Maddison))
1970	6,924	2.94	PROXY(USSR(Maddison))
1980	7,789	1.18	INTERPOL(Moldova(Maddison))
1990	8,341	0.69	90(Maddison)
2000	2,077	12.98	00(WB)
2010	3,217	4.47	10(WB)
2012	3,368	2.32	12(WB)
2020	4,175	2.72	FORECAST
2030	5,189	2.20	FORECAST
		DME Monaco	
0001	.	.	
1000	.	.	
1500	.	.	
1600	.	.	
1700	.	.	
1820	.	.	
1870	.	.	
1880	.	.	
1890	.	.	
1900	.	.	
1913	.	.	
1920	.	.	
1929	.	.	
1938	.	.	
1950	8,251	.	PROXY(9 European cs(Maddison))
1960	12,161	3.96	INTERPOL(9 European cs(Maddison))

Year	GDP at PPP Per Capita, 2012 doll.	Growth Rate	Source
1970	17,926	3.96	INTERPOL(9 European cs(Maddison))
1980	23,124	2.58	INTERPOL(9 European cs(Maddison))
1990	28,174	1.99	93(CIA)WEIGHT(US(Maddison))
2000	34,031	1.91	00(CIA)WEIGHT(US(WB))
2010	161,841	16.88	10(CIA)WEIGHT(US(WB))
2012	195,372	9.87	11(CIA)WEIGHT(US(WB))
2020	430,572	10.38	FORECAST
2030	542,295	2.33	FORECAST
		CPA Mongolia	
0001	329	.	0001(MIN)
1000	447	0.03	1000(MIN)
1500	544	0.04	1500(MIN)
1600	568	0.04	1600(MIN)
1700	595	0.05	1700(MIN)
1820	631	0.05	1820(MIN)
1870	648	0.05	1870(MIN)
1880	651	0.05	1880(MIN)
1890	654	0.05	1890(MIN)
1900	658	0.05	INTERPOL(Maddison)
1913	729	0.79	PROXY(26 E. Asian cs(Maddison))
1920	720	0.19	INTERPOL(Maddison)
1929	708	0.19	INTERPOL(Maddison)
1938	696	0.19	INTERPOL(Maddison)
1950	681	0.19	50(Maddison)
1960	984	3.75	60(Maddison)
1970	1,423	3.76	70(Maddison)
1980	2,055	3.75	80(Maddison)
1990	2,783	3.08	90(WB)
2000	2,533	0.93	00(WB)
2010	4,197	5.18	10(WB)
2012	5,374	13.15	12(WB)
2020	7,983	5.07	FORECAST
2030	10,385	2.67	FORECAST
		EEU Montenegro	
0001	381	.	0001(MIN)
1000	547	0.04	1000(MIN)
1500	700	0.05	PROXY(E. Europe(Maddison))
1600	773	0.10	PROXY(E. Europe(Maddison))
1700	855	0.10	PROXY(E. Europe(Maddison))
1820	964	0.10	PROXY(E. Europe(Maddison))
1870	1,013	0.10	PROXY(Yugoslavia(Maddison))
1880	1,202	1.72	INTERPOL(Maddison)
1890	1,426	1.72	PROXY(Yugoslavia(Maddison))
1900	1,525	0.68	PROXY(Yugoslavia(Maddison))
1913	1,787	1.23	PROXY(Yugoslavia(Maddison))
1920	1,743	0.36	PROXY(Yugoslavia(Maddison))
1929	2,307	3.16	PROXY(Yugoslavia(Maddison))
1938	2,293	0.07	PROXY(Yugoslavia(Maddison))

Year	GDP at PPP Per Capita, 2012 doll.	Growth Rate	Source
1950	2,623	1.13	PROXY(Yugoslavia(Maddison))
1960	4,566	5.70	PROXY(Yugoslavia(Maddison))
1970	7,761	5.45	PROXY(Yugoslavia(Maddison))
1980	13,971	6.06	PROXY(Yugoslavia(Maddison))
1990	13,173	0.59	PROXY(Serbia(WB))
2000	9,165	3.56	00(WB)
2010	13,929	4.27	10(WB)
2012	14,358	1.53	12(WB)
2020	17,957	2.84	FORECAST
2030	22,410	2.24	FORECAST
LAM Montserrat			
0001	.	.	
1000	.	.	
1500	.	.	
1600	.	.	
1700	.	.	
1820	.	.	
1870	.	.	
1880	.	.	
1890	.	.	
1900	.	.	
1913	.	.	
1920	.	.	
1929	.	.	
1938	.	.	
1950	2,977	.	PROXY(8 Caribbean cs(Maddison))
1960	3,634	2.01	INTERPOL(8 Caribbean cs(Maddison))
1970	4,436	2.01	INTERPOL(8 Caribbean cs(Maddison))
1980	5,014	1.23	INTERPOL(8 Caribbean cs(Maddison))
1990	5,485	0.90	92(CIA)WEIGHT(US(Maddison))
2000	4,245	2.53	99(CIA)WEIGHT(US(WB))
2010	9,254	8.10	06(CIA)WEIGHT(US(WB))
2012	9,471	1.17	06(CIA)WEIGHT(US(WB))
2020	13,220	4.26	FORECAST
2030	17,051	2.58	FORECAST
MEA Morocco			
0001	438	.	0001(MIN)
1000	673	0.04	1000(Maddison)
1500	673	0.00	1500(Maddison)
1600	673	0.00	1600(Maddison)
1700	673	0.00	1700(Maddison)
1820	673	0.00	1820(Maddison)
1870	881	0.54	1870(Maddison)
1880	930	0.54	INTERPOL(Maddison)
1890	981	0.54	INTERPOL(Maddison)
1900	1,036	0.54	INTERPOL(Maddison)

Year	GDP at PPP Per Capita, 2012 doll.	Growth Rate	Source
1913	1,111	0.54	1913(Maddison)
1920	1,273	1.96	INTERPOL(Maddison)
1929	1,515	1.96	INTERPOL(Maddison)
1938	1,804	1.96	INTERPOL(Maddison)
1950	2,277	1.96	50(Maddison)
1960	1,955	1.51	60(Maddison)
1970	2,202	1.20	70(Maddison)
1980	2,846	2.60	80(WB)
1990	3,302	1.50	90(WB)
2000	3,415	0.34	00(WB)
2010	4,889	3.65	10(WB)
2012	5,220	3.33	12(WB)
2020	6,431	2.64	FORECAST
2030	7,973	2.17	FORECAST
AFR Mozambique			
0001	355	.	0001(MIN)
1000	495	0.03	1000(MIN)
1500	617	0.04	1500(MIN)
1600	649	0.05	1600(Rest of Africa(Maddison))
1700	649	0.00	1700(Rest of Africa(Maddison))
1820	649	0.00	1820(Rest of Africa(Maddison))
1870	956	0.78	INTERPOL(Maddison)
1880	1,032	0.78	INTERPOL(Maddison)
1890	1,115	0.78	INTERPOL(Maddison)
1900	1,205	0.78	INTERPOL(Maddison)
1913	1,332	0.78	INTERPOL(Maddison)
1920	1,406	0.78	INTERPOL(Maddison)
1929	1,507	0.78	INTERPOL(Maddison)
1938	1,616	0.78	INTERPOL(Maddison)
1950	1,773	0.78	50(Maddison)
1960	2,093	1.67	60(Maddison)
1970	2,771	2.85	70(Maddison)
1980	496	15.80	80(WB)
1990	451	0.96	90(WB)
2000	569	2.36	00(WB)
2010	919	4.91	10(WB)
2012	1,007	4.70	12(WB)
2020	1,342	3.65	FORECAST
2030	1,712	2.47	FORECAST
AFR Namibia			
0001	355	.	0001(MIN)
1000	495	0.03	1000(MIN)
1500	617	0.04	1500(MIN)
1600	649	0.05	1600(Rest of Africa(Maddison))
1700	649	0.00	1700(Rest of Africa(Maddison))
1820	649	0.00	1820(Rest of Africa(Maddison))
1870	1,225	1.28	INTERPOL(Maddison)
1880	1,390	1.28	INTERPOL(Maddison)

Year	GDP at PPP Per Capita, 2012 doll.	Growth Rate	Source
1890	1,579	1.28	INTERPOL(Maddison)
1900	1,792	1.28	INTERPOL(Maddison)
1913	2,114	1.28	INTERPOL(Maddison)
1920	2,310	1.28	INTERPOL(Maddison)
1929	2,589	1.28	INTERPOL(Maddison)
1938	2,903	1.28	INTERPOL(Maddison)
1950	3,380	1.28	50(Maddison)
1960	3,955	1.58	60(Maddison)
1970	4,845	2.05	70(Maddison)
1980	5,761	1.75	80(WB)
1990	4,680	2.06	90(WB)
2000	5,161	0.98	00(WB)
2010	6,964	3.04	10(WB)
2012	7,442	3.38	12(WB)
2020	8,952	2.34	FORECAST
2030	10,966	2.05	FORECAST
SEA Nauru			
0001	.	.	
1000	.	.	
1500	.	.	
1600	.	.	
1700	.	.	
1820	.	.	
1870	.	.	
1880	.	.	
1890	.	.	
1900	.	.	
1913	.	.	
1920	.	.	
1929	.	.	
1938	.	.	
1950	9,820	.	PROXY(14 Pacific is(Maddison))
1960	11,300	1.41	INTERPOL(14 Pacific is(Maddison))
1970	13,004	1.41	INTERPOL(14 Pacific is(Maddison))
1980	13,740	0.55	INTERPOL(14 Pacific is(Maddison))
1990	13,997	0.19	93(CIA)WEIGHT(US(Maddison))
2000	6,378	7.56	00(CIA)WEIGHT(US(WB))
2010	5,670	1.17	05(CIA)WEIGHT(US(WB))
2012	5,839	1.48	05(CIA)WEIGHT(US(WB))
2020	5,994	0.33	FORECAST
2030	6,466	0.76	FORECAST
SAS Nepal			
0001	333	.	0001(MIN)
1000	454	0.03	1000(MIN)
1500	555	0.04	1500(MIN)
1600	580	0.05	1600(MIN)

Year	GDP at PPP Per Capita, 2012 doll.	Growth Rate	Source
1700	609	0.05	1700(MIN)
1820	646	0.05	1820(MIN)
1870	663	0.05	1870(MIN)
1880	667	0.05	INTERPOL(Maddison)
1890	716	0.71	INTERPOL(Maddison)
1900	769	0.71	INTERPOL(Maddison)
1913	843	0.71	1913(Maddison)
1920	831	0.22	INTERPOL(Maddison)
1929	814	0.23	INTERPOL(Maddison)
1938	797	0.22	INTERPOL(Maddison)
1950	776	0.22	50(Maddison)
1960	854	0.96	60(Maddison)
1970	833	0.25	70(Maddison)
1980	742	1.15	80(WB)
1990	922	2.19	90(WB)
2000	1,106	1.84	00(WB)
2010	1,380	2.24	10(WB)
2012	1,457	2.74	12(WB)
2020	1,728	2.15	FORECAST
2030	2,100	1.97	FORECAST
DME NETHERLANDS			
0001	665	.	0001(Maddison)
1000	665	0.00	1000(Maddison)
1500	1,191	0.12	1500(Maddison)
1600	2,161	0.60	1600(Maddison)
1700	3,333	0.43	1700(Maddison)
1820	2,876	0.12	1820(Maddison)
1870	4,314	0.81	1870(Maddison)
1880	4,767	1.00	1880(Maddison)
1890	5,200	0.87	1890(Maddison)
1900	5,358	0.30	1900(Maddison)
1913	6,336	1.30	1913(Maddison)
1920	6,604	0.59	1920(Maddison)
1929	8,902	3.37	1929(Maddison)
1938	8,215	0.89	1938(Maddison)
1950	9,383	1.11	50(Maddison)
1960	13,281	3.54	60(Maddison)
1970	19,690	4.02	70(Maddison)
1980	24,614	2.26	80(WB)
1990	29,314	1.76	90(WB)
2000	39,860	3.12	00(WB)
2010	43,870	0.96	10(WB)
2012	43,339	0.61	12(WB)
2020	49,602	1.70	FORECAST
2030	58,954	1.74	FORECAST
SEA NEW CALEDONIA			
0001	.	.	
1000	.	.	

Year	GDP at PPP Per Capita, 2012 doll.	Growth Rate	Source
1500	.	.	
1600	.	.	
1700	.	.	
1820	.	.	
1870	.	.	
1880	.	.	
1890	.	.	
1900	.	.	
1913	.	.	
1920	.	.	
1929	.	.	
1938	.	.	
1950	6,368	.	PROXY(14 Pacific is(Maddison))
1960	7,391	1.50	INTERPOL(14 Pacific is(Maddison))
1970	8,578	1.50	INTERPOL(14 Pacific is(Maddison))
1980	9,094	0.59	INTERPOL(14 Pacific is(Maddison))
1990	9,274	0.20	91(CIA)WEIGHT(US(Maddison))
2000	19,203	7.55	00(CIA)WEIGHT(US(WB))
2010	39,070	7.36	08(CIA)WEIGHT(US(WB))
2012	40,302	1.56	08(CIA)WEIGHT(US(WB))
2020	62,321	5.60	FORECAST
2030	81,289	2.69	FORECAST
		DME New Zealand	
0001	328	.	0001(MIN)
1000	444	0.03	1000(MIN)
1500	540	0.04	1500(MIN)
1600	564	0.04	1600(MIN)
1700	591	0.05	1700(MIN)
1820	626	0.05	1820(Maddison)
1870	4,851	4.18	1870(Maddison)
1880	5,863	1.91	1880(Maddison)
1890	5,876	0.02	1890(Maddison)
1900	6,726	1.36	1900(Maddison)
1913	8,062	1.40	1913(Maddison)
1920	8,827	1.30	1920(Maddison)
1929	8,234	0.77	1929(Maddison)
1938	10,112	2.31	1938(Maddison)
1950	13,232	2.27	50(Maddison)
1960	15,209	1.40	60(Maddison)
1970	18,547	2.00	70(Maddison)
1980	20,990	1.25	80(WB)
1990	24,100	1.39	90(WB)
2000	27,741	1.42	00(WB)
2010	31,586	1.31	10(WB)
2012	32,926	2.10	12(WB)
2020	37,289	1.57	FORECAST
2030	43,991	1.67	FORECAST

Year	GDP at PPP Per Capita, 2012 doll.	Growth Rate	Source
		LAM NICARAGUA	
0001	337	.	0001(MIN)
1000	461	0.03	1000(MIN)
1500	565	0.04	1500(MIN)
1600	592	0.05	1600(MIN)
1700	621	0.05	1700(MIN)
1820	660	0.05	PROXY(Other L. Am.(Maddison))
1870	676	0.05	PROXY(Other L. Am.(Maddison))
1880	806	1.77	INTERPOL(Maddison)
1890	960	1.77	INTERPOL(Maddison)
1900	1,144	1.77	INTERPOL(Maddison)
1913	1,437	1.77	PROXY(Other L. Am.(Maddison))
1920	1,978	4.67	1920(Maddison)
1929	2,738	3.68	1929(Maddison)
1938	1,684	5.26	1938(Maddison)
1950	2,529	3.45	50(Maddison)
1960	3,295	2.68	60(Maddison)
1970	4,993	4.24	70(Maddison)
1980	3,983	2.24	80(WB)
1990	2,686	3.86	90(WB)
2000	3,117	1.50	00(WB)
2010	3,704	1.74	10(WB)
2012	4,006	3.99	12(WB)
2020	4,661	1.91	FORECAST
2030	5,600	1.85	FORECAST
		AFR NIGER	
0001	.	.	
1000	.	.	
1500	.	.	
1600	.	.	
1700	.	.	
1820	.	.	
1870	.	.	
1880	.	.	
1890	.	.	
1900	.	.	
1913	.	.	
1920	.	.	
1929	.	.	
1938	.	.	
1950	1,272	.	50(Maddison)
1960	1,473	1.48	60(Maddison)
1970	1,489	0.11	70(Maddison)
1980	1,282	1.49	80(WB)
1990	899	3.49	90(WB)
2000	660	3.04	00(WB)

Year	GDP at PPP Per Capita, 2012 doll.	Growth Rate	Source
2010	725	0.94	10(WB)
2012	769	3.00	12(WB)
2020	826	0.90	FORECAST
2030	933	1.23	FORECAST
AFR Nigeria			
0001	.	.	
1000	.	.	
1500	.	.	
1600	.	.	
1700	.	.	
1820	.	.	
1870	.	.	
1880	.	.	
1890	.	.	
1900	.	.	
1913	.	.	
1920	.	.	
1929	.	.	
1938	.	.	
1950	1,178	.	50(Maddison)
1960	1,299	0.98	60(Maddison)
1970	1,747	3.01	70(Maddison)
1980	1,998	1.35	80(WB)
1990	1,722	1.48	90(WB)
2000	1,713	0.05	00(WB)
2010	2,441	3.60	10(WB)
2012	2,620	3.61	12(WB)
2020	3,167	2.40	FORECAST
2030	3,889	2.08	FORECAST
SEA Niue			
0001	.	.	
1000	.	.	
1500	.	.	
1600	.	.	
1700	.	.	
1820	.	.	
1870	.	.	
1880	.	.	
1890	.	.	
1900	.	.	
1913	.	.	
1920	.	.	
1929	.	.	
1938	.	.	

Year	GDP at PPP Per Capita, 2012 doll.	Growth Rate	Source
1950	1,178	.	PROXY(14 Pacific is(Maddison))
1960	1,426	1.93	INTERPOL(14 Pacific is(Maddison))
1970	1,727	1.93	INTERPOL(14 Pacific is(Maddison))
1980	1,861	0.75	INTERPOL(14 Pacific is(Maddison))
1990	1,909	0.25	93(CIA)WEIGHT(US(Maddison))
2000	4,008	7.70	00(CIA)WEIGHT(US(WB))
2010	7,268	6.13	03(CIA)WEIGHT(US(WB))
2012	7,564	2.01	03(CIA)WEIGHT(US(WB))
2020	11,308	5.16	FORECAST
2030	14,719	2.67	FORECAST
SEA Northern Mariana Islands			
0001	.	.	
1000	.	.	
1500	.	.	
1600	.	.	
1700	.	.	
1820	.	.	
1870	.	.	
1880	.	.	
1890	.	.	
1900	.	.	
1913	.	.	
1920	.	.	
1929	.	.	
1938	.	.	
1950	11,707	.	PROXY(14 Pacific is(Maddison))
1960	12,913	0.99	INTERPOL(14 Pacific is(Maddison))
1970	14,244	0.99	INTERPOL(14 Pacific is(Maddison))
1980	14,802	0.39	INTERPOL(14 Pacific is(Maddison))
1990	14,995	0.13	92(CIA)WEIGHT(US(Maddison))
2000	15,510	0.34	00(CIA)WEIGHT(US(WB))
2010	14,259	0.84	10(CIA)WEIGHT(US(WB))
2012	14,554	1.03	10(CIA)WEIGHT(US(WB))
2020	14,917	0.31	FORECAST
2030	16,063	0.74	FORECAST
DME Norway			
0001	455	.	0001(MIN)
1000	715	0.05	1000(MIN)
1500	1,002	0.07	1500(Maddison)
1600	1,189	0.17	1600(Maddison)
1700	1,408	0.17	1700(Maddison)
1820	1,728	0.17	1820(Maddison)
1870	2,241	0.52	1870(Maddison)
1880	2,485	1.04	1880(Maddison)
1890	2,781	1.13	1890(Maddison)
1900	3,031	0.87	1900(Maddison)

Year	GDP at PPP Per Capita, 2012 doll.	Growth Rate	Source
1913	3,914	1.99	1913(Maddison)
1920	4,350	1.52	1920(Maddison)
1929	5,433	2.50	1929(Maddison)
1938	6,787	2.50	1938(Maddison)
1950	8,549	1.94	50(Maddison)
1960	11,777	3.26	60(Maddison)
1970	17,292	3.92	70(Maddison)
1980	27,928	4.91	80(WB)
1990	35,906	2.54	90(WB)
2000	60,315	5.32	00(WB)
2010	64,911	0.74	10(WB)
2012	66,141	0.94	12(WB)
2020	80,528	2.49	FORECAST
2030	99,258	2.11	FORECAST
MEA Oman			
0001	761	.	PROXY(W. Asia(Maddison))
1000	906	0.02	PROXY(W. Asia(Maddison))
1500	861	0.01	AVG(Arabia(Maddison))
1600	861	0.00	INTERPOL(Maddison)
1700	861	0.00	AVG(Arabia(Maddison))
1820	861	0.00	AVG(Arabia(Maddison))
1870	900	0.09	AVG(Arabia(Maddison))
1880	909	0.10	INTERPOL(Maddison)
1890	918	0.10	INTERPOL(Maddison)
1900	927	0.10	INTERPOL(Maddison)
1913	939	0.10	AVG(Arabia(Maddison))
1920	946	0.10	INTERPOL(Maddison)
1929	954	0.10	INTERPOL(Maddison)
1938	963	0.10	INTERPOL(Maddison)
1950	975	0.10	50(Maddison)
1960	1,697	5.70	60(Maddison)
1970	8,239	17.12	70(Maddison)
1980	10,140	2.10	80(WB)
1990	15,459	4.31	90(WB)
2000	22,284	3.72	00(WB)
2010	28,317	2.42	10(WB)
2012	26,223	3.77	12(WB)
2020	33,847	3.24	FORECAST
2030	42,757	2.36	FORECAST
SAS Pakistan			
0001	704	.	0001(Undivided India(Maddison))
1000	704	0.00	1000(Undivided India(Maddison))
1500	861	0.04	1500(Undivided India(Maddison))
1600	861	0.00	1600(Undivided India(Maddison))
1700	861	0.00	1700(Undivided India(Maddison))
1820	831	0.03	1820(Maddison)
1870	976	0.32	INTERPOL(Maddison)
1880	1,008	0.32	INTERPOL(Maddison)

Year	GDP at PPP Per Capita, 2012 doll.	Growth Rate	Source
1890	1,041	0.32	INTERPOL(Maddison)
1900	1,075	0.32	1900(Maddison)
1913	1,141	0.46	1913(Maddison)
1920	1,145	0.05	INTERPOL(Maddison)
1929	1,150	0.05	1929(Maddison)
1938	1,064	0.86	1938(Maddison)
1950	1,006	0.47	50(Maddison)
1960	941	0.67	60(Maddison)
1970	1,278	3.11	70(Maddison)
1980	1,444	1.23	80(WB)
1990	1,904	2.80	90(WB)
2000	2,125	1.11	00(WB)
2010	2,655	2.25	10(WB)
2012	2,741	1.62	12(WB)
2020	3,224	2.05	FORECAST
2030	3,899	1.92	FORECAST
SEA PALAU			
0001	.	.	
1000	.	.	
1500	.	.	
1600	.	.	
1700	.	.	
1820	.	.	
1870	.	.	
1880	.	.	
1890	.	.	
1900	.	.	
1913	.	.	
1920	.	.	
1929	.	.	
1938	.	.	
1950	11,490	.	PROXY(14 Pacific is(Maddison))
1960	13,196	1.39	INTERPOL(14 Pacific is(Maddison))
1970	15,155	1.39	INTERPOL(14 Pacific is(Maddison))
1980	16,001	0.54	INTERPOL(14 Pacific is(Maddison))
1990	16,296	0.18	91(WB)WEIGHT(US(Maddison))
2000	18,353	1.20	00(WB)
2010	17,046	0.74	10(WB)
2012	18,722	4.80	12(WB)
2020	20,408	1.08	FORECAST
2030	23,360	1.36	FORECAST
LAM PANAMA			
0001	366	.	0001(MIN)
1000	518	0.03	1000(MIN)
1500	652	0.05	1500(MIN)

Year	GDP at PPP Per Capita, 2012 doll.	Growth Rate	Source
1600	688	0.05	1600(MIN)
1700	728	0.06	1700(MIN)
1820	783	0.06	PROXY(Other L. Am.(Maddison))
1870	802	0.05	PROXY(Other L. Am.(Maddison))
1880	956	1.77	INTERPOL(Maddison)
1890	1,139	1.77	INTERPOL(Maddison)
1900	1,357	1.77	INTERPOL(Maddison)
1913	1,703	1.77	PROXY(Other L. Am.(Maddison))
1920	1,896	1.54	INTERPOL(Maddison)
1929	2,175	1.54	INTERPOL(Maddison)
1938	2,496	1.54	INTERPOL(Maddison)
1950	2,998	1.54	50(Maddison)
1960	3,690	2.10	60(Maddison)
1970	5,786	4.60	70(Maddison)
1980	7,611	2.78	80(WB)
1990	6,984	0.85	90(WB)
2000	9,059	2.63	00(WB)
2010	13,807	4.30	10(WB)
2012	16,346	8.80	12(WB)
2020	22,788	4.24	FORECAST
2030	29,384	2.58	FORECAST

SEA Papua New Guinea

Year	GDP at PPP Per Capita, 2012 doll.	Growth Rate	Source
0001	.	.	
1000	.	.	
1500	.	.	
1600	.	.	
1700	.	.	
1820	.	.	
1870	.	.	
1880	.	.	
1890	.	.	
1900	.	.	
1913	.	.	
1920	.	.	
1929	.	.	
1938	.	.	
1950	1,180	.	50(Maddison)
1960	1,641	3.35	INTERPOL(Maddison)
1970	2,281	3.35	INTERPOL(Maddison)
1980	2,244	0.16	80(WB)
1990	1,971	1.29	90(WB)
2000	2,236	1.27	00(WB)
2010	2,536	1.27	10(WB)
2012	2,851	6.03	12(WB)
2020	3,316	1.91	FORECAST
2030	3,984	1.85	FORECAST

Year	GDP at PPP Per Capita, 2012 doll.	Growth Rate	Source
		LAM Paraguay	
0001	334	.	0001(MIN)
1000	455	0.03	1000(MIN)
1500	555	0.04	1500(MIN)
1600	581	0.05	1600(MIN)
1700	610	0.05	1700(MIN)
1820	647	0.05	PROXY(Other L. Am.(Maddison))
1870	663	0.05	PROXY(Other L. Am.(Maddison))
1880	790	1.77	INTERPOL(Maddison)
1890	941	1.77	INTERPOL(Maddison)
1900	1,121	1.77	INTERPOL(Maddison)
1913	1,408	1.77	PROXY(Other L. Am.(Maddison))
1920	1,567	1.54	INTERPOL(Maddison)
1929	1,798	1.54	INTERPOL(Maddison)
1938	2,063	1.54	INTERPOL(Maddison)
1950	2,479	1.54	50(Maddison)
1960	2,438	0.17	60(Maddison)
1970	2,904	1.76	70(Maddison)
1980	4,951	5.48	80(WB)
1990	5,526	1.11	90(WB)
2000	5,266	0.48	00(WB)
2010	6,063	1.42	10(WB)
2012	6,038	0.20	12(WB)
2020	6,629	1.17	FORECAST
2030	7,634	1.42	FORECAST
		LAM Peru	
0001	358	.	0001(MIN)
1000	501	0.03	1000(MIN)
1500	626	0.04	1500(MIN)
1600	659	0.05	1600(MIN)
1700	696	0.05	1700(MIN)
1820	746	0.06	PROXY(Other L. Am.(Maddison))
1870	764	0.05	PROXY(Other L. Am.(Maddison))
1880	907	1.73	INTERPOL(Maddison)
1890	1,077	1.73	INTERPOL(Maddison)
1900	1,278	1.73	1900(Maddison)
1913	1,623	1.85	1913(Maddison)
1920	2,083	3.63	1920(Maddison)
1929	2,533	2.20	1929(Maddison)
1938	2,749	0.91	1938(Maddison)
1950	3,541	2.13	50(Maddison)
1960	4,829	3.15	60(Maddison)
1970	6,210	2.55	70(Maddison)
1980	7,013	1.22	80(WB)
1990	5,165	3.01	90(WB)
2000	6,320	2.04	00(WB)
2010	9,713	4.39	10(WB)
2012	10,765	5.28	12(WB)

Year	GDP at PPP Per Capita, 2012 doll.	Growth Rate	Source
2020	14,176	3.50	FORECAST
2030	18,024	2.43	FORECAST
		SEA PHILIPPINES	
0001	684	.	PROXY(Other E. Asia(Maddison))
1000	684	0.00	PROXY(Other E. Asia(Maddison))
1500	891	0.05	PROXY(Other E. Asia(Maddison))
1600	907	0.02	PROXY(Other E. Asia(Maddison))
1700	903	0.01	PROXY(Other E. Asia(Maddison))
1820	914	0.01	1820(Maddison)
1870	976	0.13	1870(Maddison)
1880	1,012	0.36	INTERPOL(Maddison)
1890	1,048	0.36	INTERPOL(Maddison)
1900	1,086	0.36	INTERPOL(Maddison)
1913	1,648	3.26	1913(Maddison)
1920	2,017	2.93	1920(Maddison)
1929	2,350	1.71	1929(Maddison)
1938	2,382	0.15	1938(Maddison)
1950	1,674	2.89	50(Maddison)
1960	2,201	2.77	60(Maddison)
1970	2,509	1.32	70(Maddison)
1980	3,222	2.53	80(WB)
1990	2,915	1.00	90(WB)
2000	3,070	0.52	00(WB)
2010	4,057	2.83	10(WB)
2012	4,339	3.41	12(WB)
2020	5,153	2.17	FORECAST
2030	6,268	1.98	FORECAST
		EEU POLAND	
0001	460	.	0001(MIN)
1000	726	0.05	1000(MIN)
1500	1,023	0.07	PROXY(E. Europe(Maddison))
1600	1,130	0.10	PROXY(E. Europe(Maddison))
1700	1,249	0.10	PROXY(E. Europe(Maddison))
1820	1,408	0.10	PROXY(E. Europe(Maddison))
1870	1,480	0.10	1870(Maddison)
1880	1,725	1.54	INTERPOL(Maddison)
1890	2,009	1.54	1890(Maddison)
1900	2,404	1.81	1900(Maddison)
1913	2,721	0.96	1913(Maddison)
1920	2,966	1.24	INTERPOL(Maddison)
1929	3,313	1.24	1929(Maddison)
1938	3,414	0.34	1938(Maddison)
1950	3,829	0.96	50(Maddison)
1960	5,314	3.33	60(Maddison)
1970	7,749	3.84	70(Maddison)
1980	10,604	3.19	80(Maddison)
1990	9,783	0.80	90(WB)
2000	14,303	3.87	00(WB)

Year	GDP at PPP Per Capita, 2012 doll.	Growth Rate	Source
2010	21,562	4.19	10(WB)
2012	22,783	2.79	12(WB)
2020	30,323	3.64	FORECAST
2030	38,675	2.46	FORECAST
		DME Portugal	
0001	704	.	0001(Maddison)
1000	665	0.01	1000(Maddison)
1500	948	0.07	1500(Maddison)
1600	1,158	0.20	1600(Maddison)
1700	1,282	0.10	1700(Maddison)
1820	1,444	0.10	1820(Maddison)
1870	1,526	0.11	1870(Maddison)
1880	1,482	0.29	1880(Maddison)
1890	1,765	1.76	1890(Maddison)
1900	2,037	1.44	1900(Maddison)
1913	1,956	0.31	1913(Maddison)
1920	1,923	0.24	1920(Maddison)
1929	2,519	3.05	1929(Maddison)
1938	2,734	0.91	1938(Maddison)
1950	3,264	1.49	50(Maddison)
1960	4,742	3.81	60(Maddison)
1970	9,141	6.78	70(Maddison)
1980	13,803	4.21	80(WB)
1990	18,916	3.20	90(WB)
2000	25,915	3.20	00(WB)
2010	27,075	0.44	10(WB)
2012	25,958	2.08	12(WB)
2020	30,041	1.84	FORECAST
2030	35,971	1.82	FORECAST
		LAM Puerto Rico	
0001	405	.	0001(MIN)
1000	597	0.04	1000(MIN)
1500	784	0.05	1500(MIN)
1600	837	0.06	1600(MIN)
1700	897	0.07	PROXY(Caribbean cs(Maddison))
1820	876	0.02	PROXY(Other L. Am.(Maddison))
1870	897	0.05	PROXY(Other L. Am.(Maddison))
1880	1,069	1.77	INTERPOL(Maddison)
1890	1,274	1.77	INTERPOL(Maddison)
1900	1,518	1.77	INTERPOL(Maddison)
1913	1,906	1.77	PROXY(Other L. Am.(Maddison))
1920	2,121	1.54	INTERPOL(Maddison)
1929	2,434	1.54	INTERPOL(Maddison)
1938	2,793	1.54	INTERPOL(Maddison)
1950	3,355	1.54	50(Maddison)
1960	5,011	4.09	60(Maddison)
1970	8,521	5.45	70(Maddison)
1980	10,595	2.20	80(Maddison)

Year	GDP at PPP Per Capita, 2012 doll.	Growth Rate	Source
1990	13,166	2.20	90(Maddison)
2000	13,393	0.17	00(CIA)WEIGHT(US(WB))
2010	16,985	2.40	10(CIA)WEIGHT(US(WB))
2012	17,443	1.34	10(CIA)WEIGHT(US(WB))
2020	20,398	1.98	FORECAST
2030	24,586	1.88	FORECAST
		MEA Qatar	
0001	761	.	PROXY(W. Asia(Maddison))
1000	906	0.02	PROXY(W. Asia(Maddison))
1500	861	0.01	AVG(Arabia(Maddison))
1600	861	0.00	INTERPOL(Maddison)
1700	861	0.00	AVG(Arabia(Maddison))
1820	861	0.00	AVG(Arabia(Maddison))
1870	900	0.09	AVG(Arabia(Maddison))
1880	909	0.10	INTERPOL(Maddison)
1890	918	0.10	INTERPOL(Maddison)
1900	927	0.10	INTERPOL(Maddison)
1913	939	0.10	AVG(Arabia(Maddison))
1920	1,973	11.19	INTERPOL(Maddison)
1929	5,125	11.19	INTERPOL(Maddison)
1938	13,315	11.19	INTERPOL(Maddison)
1950	47,551	11.19	50(Maddison)
1960	52,978	1.09	60(Maddison)
1970	53,091	0.02	70(Maddison)
1980	45,908	1.44	80(Maddison)
1990	19,510	8.20	90(CIA)
2000	79,512	15.08	00(WB)
2010	88,491	1.08	10(WB)
2012	91,189	1.51	12(WB)
2020	127,682	4.30	FORECAST
2030	164,779	2.58	FORECAST
		AFR Reunion	
0001	.	.	
1000	.	.	
1500	.	.	
1600	.	.	
1700	.	.	
1820	.	.	
1870	.	.	
1880	.	.	
1890	.	.	
1900	.	.	
1913	.	.	
1920	.	.	
1929	.	.	
1938	.	.	

Year	GDP at PPP Per Capita, 2012 doll.	Growth Rate	Source
1950	3,112	.	50(Maddison)
1960	3,494	1.16	60(Maddison)
1970	5,349	4.35	70(Maddison)
1980	5,685	0.61	80(Maddison)
1990	6,924	1.99	90(Maddison)
2000	6,696	0.33	99(CIA)WEIGHT(US(WB))
2010	30,118	16.22	10(REG)WEIGHT(US(WB))
2012	26,467	6.26	12(REG)
2020	49,236	8.07	FORECAST
2030	63,632	2.60	FORECAST
EEU Romania			
0001	665	.	AVG(Danubian provinces(Maddison))
1000	626	0.01	1000(Maddison)
1500	1,006	0.10	PROXY(E. Europe(Maddison))
1600	1,112	0.10	PROXY(E. Europe(Maddison))
1700	1,230	0.10	PROXY(E. Europe(Maddison))
1820	1,386	0.10	PROXY(E. Europe(Maddison))
1870	1,457	0.10	1870(Maddison)
1880	1,685	1.47	INTERPOL(Maddison)
1890	1,950	1.47	1890(Maddison)
1900	2,214	1.28	1900(Maddison)
1913	2,724	1.61	1913(Maddison)
1920	1,614	7.20	PROXY(Bulgaria(Maddison))
1929	1,803	1.23	1929(Maddison)
1938	1,944	0.84	1938(Maddison)
1950	1,850	0.41	50(Maddison)
1960	3,433	6.38	60(Maddison)
1970	6,312	6.28	70(Maddison)
1980	10,772	5.49	80(WB)
1990	11,140	0.34	90(WB)
2000	9,516	1.56	00(WB)
2010	17,360	6.20	10(WB)
2012	18,063	2.00	12(WB)
2020	24,441	3.85	FORECAST
2030	31,309	2.51	FORECAST
USR Russia			
0001	421	.	0001(MIN)
1000	634	0.04	1000(MIN)
1500	849	0.06	PROXY(USSR(Maddison))
1600	939	0.10	PROXY(USSR(Maddison))
1700	1,038	0.10	PROXY(USSR(Maddison))
1820	1,170	0.10	PROXY(USSR(Maddison))
1870	1,604	0.63	PROXY(USSR(Maddison))
1880	1,756	0.91	INTERPOL(Maddison)
1890	1,922	0.91	INTERPOL(Maddison)
1900	2,104	0.91	PROXY(USSR(Maddison))
1913	2,531	1.43	PROXY(USSR(Maddison))
1920	981	12.67	PROXY(USSR(Davies))

Year	GDP at PPP Per Capita, 2012 doll.	Growth Rate	Source
1929	2,421	10.56	PROXY(USSR(Maddison))
1938	3,756	5.00	PROXY(USSR(Maddison))
1950	4,833	2.12	PROXY(USSR(Maddison))
1960	7,514	4.51	PROXY(USSR(Maddison))
1970	11,955	4.75	PROXY(USSR(Maddison))
1980	14,742	2.12	INTERPOL(Russia(Maddison))
1990	16,919	1.39	90(WB)
2000	11,212	4.03	00(WB)
2010	21,579	6.77	10(WB)
2012	23,589	4.55	12(WB)
2020	33,131	4.34	FORECAST
2030	42,781	2.59	FORECAST
AFR Rwanda			
0001	.	.	
1000	.	.	
1500	.	.	
1600	.	.	
1700	.	.	
1820	.	.	
1870	.	.	
1880	.	.	
1890	.	.	
1900	.	.	
1913	.	.	
1920	.	.	
1929	.	.	
1938	.	.	
1950	856	.	50(Maddison)
1960	894	0.44	60(Maddison)
1970	857	0.42	70(Maddison)
1980	984	1.39	80(WB)
1990	866	1.27	90(WB)
2000	755	1.37	00(WB)
2010	1,214	4.87	10(WB)
2012	1,332	4.75	12(WB)
2020	1,696	3.07	FORECAST
2030	2,132	2.31	FORECAST
AFR Saint Helena			
0001	.	.	
1000	.	.	
1500	.	.	
1600	.	.	
1700	.	.	
1820	.	.	
1870	.	.	

Year	GDP at PPP Per Capita, 2012 doll.	Growth Rate	Source
1880	.	.	
1890	.	.	
1900	.	.	
1913	.	.	
1920	.	.	
1929	.	.	
1938	.	.	
1950	1,991	.	PROXY(3 Afr. cs(Maddison))
1960	3,023	4.26	PROXY(3 Afr. cs(Maddison))
1970	3,148	0.41	PROXY(3 Afr. cs(Maddison))
1980	3,871	2.09	PROXY(3 Afr. cs(Maddison))
1990	4,523	1.57	PROXY(3 Afr. cs(Maddison))
2000	9,133	7.28	98(CIA)WEIGHT(US(WB))
2010	7,972	1.35	10(CIA)WEIGHT(US(WB))
2012	8,347	2.32	10(CIA)WEIGHT(US(WB))
2020	10,116	2.43	FORECAST
2030	12,440	2.09	FORECAST
LAM Saint Kitts and Nevis			
0001	.	.	
1000	.	.	
1500	.	.	
1600	.	.	
1700	.	.	
1820	.	.	
1870	.	.	
1880	.	.	
1890	.	.	
1900	.	.	
1913	.	.	
1920	.	.	
1929	.	.	
1938	.	.	
1950	1,948	.	50(Maddison)
1960	3,819	6.96	INTERPOL(Maddison)
1970	7,487	6.96	INTERPOL(Maddison)
1980	6,413	1.54	80(WB)
1990	11,564	6.07	90(Maddison)
2000	15,930	3.25	00(WB)
2010	17,206	0.77	10(WB)
2012	18,384	3.37	12(WB)
2020	22,640	2.64	FORECAST
2030	28,060	2.17	FORECAST
LAM Saint Lucia			
0001	.	.	
1000	.	.	

Year	GDP at PPP Per Capita, 2012 doll.	Growth Rate	Source
1500	.	.	
1600	.	.	
1700	.	.	
1820	.	.	
1870	.	.	
1880	.	.	
1890	.	.	
1900	.	.	
1913	.	.	
1920	.	.	
1929	.	.	
1938	.	.	
1950	1,150	.	50(Maddison)
1960	1,981	5.59	INTERPOL(Maddison)
1970	3,411	5.59	INTERPOL(Maddison)
1980	4,617	3.07	80(WB)
1990	7,944	5.58	90(WB)
2000	10,377	2.71	00(WB)
2010	11,452	0.99	10(WB)
2012	11,427	0.11	12(WB)
2020	13,591	2.19	FORECAST
2030	16,545	1.99	FORECAST

LAM Saint Martin

Year	GDP at PPP Per Capita, 2012 doll.	Growth Rate	Source
0001	.	.	
1000	.	.	
1500	.	.	
1600	.	.	
1700	.	.	
1820	.	.	
1870	.	.	
1880	.	.	
1890	.	.	
1900	.	.	
1913	.	.	
1920	.	.	
1929	.	.	
1938	.	.	
1950	4,921	.	05(CIA)WEIGHT(Curacao)
1960	6,847	3.36	05(CIA)WEIGHT(Curacao)
1970	9,526	3.36	05(CIA)WEIGHT(Curacao)
1980	9,337	0.20	05(CIA)WEIGHT(Curacao)
1990	7,877	1.69	05(CIA)WEIGHT(Curacao)
2000	11,879	4.19	05(CIA)WEIGHT(Curacao)
2010	21,723	6.22	05(CIA)WEIGHT(US(WB))
2012	22,538	1.86	05(CIA)WEIGHT(US(WB))

Year	GDP at PPP Per Capita, 2012 doll.	Growth Rate	Source
2020	31,655	4.34	FORECAST
2030	40,875	2.59	FORECAST
DME Saint Pierre and Miquelon			
0001	.	.	
1000	.	.	
1500	.	.	
1600	.	.	
1700	.	.	
1820	.	.	
1870	.	.	
1880	.	.	
1890	.	.	
1900	.	.	
1913	.	.	
1920	.	.	
1929	.	.	
1938	.	.	
1950	6,924	.	PROXY(8 Caribbean cs(Maddison))
1960	9,056	2.72	INTERPOL(8 Caribbean cs(Maddison))
1970	11,844	2.72	INTERPOL(8 Caribbean cs(Maddison))
1980	13,971	1.67	INTERPOL(8 Caribbean cs(Maddison))
1990	15,766	1.22	92(CIA)WEIGHT(US(Maddison))
2000	30,550	6.84	96(CIA)WEIGHT(US(WB))
2010	37,691	2.12	06(CIA)WEIGHT(US(WB))
2012	38,886	1.57	06(CIA)WEIGHT(US(WB))
2020	50,033	3.20	FORECAST
2030	63,132	2.35	FORECAST
LAM Saint Vincent and the Grenadines			
0001	.	.	
1000	.	.	
1500	.	.	
1600	.	.	
1700	.	.	
1820	.	.	
1870	.	.	
1880	.	.	
1890	.	.	
1900	.	.	
1913	.	.	
1920	.	.	
1929	.	.	
1938	.	.	
1950	1,845	.	50(Maddison)
1960	2,348	2.44	INTERPOL(Maddison)

Year	GDP at PPP Per Capita, 2012 doll.	Growth Rate	Source
1970	2,988	2.44	INTERPOL(Maddison)
1980	3,665	2.06	80(WB)
1990	6,159	5.33	90(WB)
2000	8,206	2.91	00(WB)
2010	10,789	2.77	10(WB)
2012	11,047	1.19	12(WB)
2020	14,018	3.02	FORECAST
2030	17,597	2.30	FORECAST
		SEA Samoa	
0001	.	.	
1000	.	.	
1500	.	.	
1600	.	.	
1700	.	.	
1820	.	.	
1870	.	.	
1880	.	.	
1890	.	.	
1900	.	.	
1913	.	.	
1920	.	.	
1929	.	.	
1938	.	.	
1950	2,065	.	PROXY(14 Pacific is(Maddison))
1960	2,385	1.45	INTERPOL(14 Pacific is(Maddison))
1970	2,754	1.45	INTERPOL(14 Pacific is(Maddison))
1980	2,802	0.17	82(WB)
1990	2,965	0.57	90(WB)
2000	3,531	1.76	00(WB)
2010	4,371	2.16	10(WB)
2012	4,493	1.37	12(WB)
2020	5,170	1.77	FORECAST
2030	6,167	1.78	FORECAST
		SEA Samoa, American	
0001	.	.	
1000	.	.	
1500	.	.	
1600	.	.	
1700	.	.	
1820	.	.	
1870	.	.	
1880	.	.	
1890	.	.	
1900	.	.	
1913	.	.	

Year	GDP at PPP Per Capita, 2012 doll.	Growth Rate	Source
1920	.	.	
1929	.	.	
1938	.	.	
1950	2,760	.	PROXY(14 Pacific is(Maddison))
1960	3,457	2.28	INTERPOL(14 Pacific is(Maddison))
1970	4,330	2.28	INTERPOL(14 Pacific is(Maddison))
1980	4,730	0.89	INTERPOL(14 Pacific is(Maddison))
1990	4,873	0.30	91(CIA)WEIGHT(US(Maddison))
2000	11,226	8.70	00(CIA)WEIGHT(US(WB))
2010	8,217	3.07	07(CIA)WEIGHT(US(WB))
2012	8,612	2.38	07(CIA)WEIGHT(US(WB))
2020	10,559	2.58	FORECAST
2030	13,059	2.15	FORECAST
		DME San Marino	
0001	.	.	
1000	.	.	
1500	.	.	
1600	.	.	
1700	.	.	
1820	.	.	
1870	.	.	
1880	.	.	
1890	.	.	
1900	.	.	
1913	.	.	
1920	.	.	
1929	.	.	
1938	.	.	
1950	7,431	.	PROXY(9 European cs(Maddison))
1960	11,304	4.28	INTERPOL(9 European cs(Maddison))
1970	17,194	4.28	INTERPOL(9 European cs(Maddison))
1980	22,644	2.79	INTERPOL(9 European cs(Maddison))
1990	28,034	2.16	92(CIA)WEIGHT(US(Maddison))
2000	39,942	3.60	00(CIA)WEIGHT(US(WB))
2010	35,192	1.26	10(CIA)WEIGHT(US(WB))
2012	55,000	25.02	12(CIA)
2020	81,475	5.03	FORECAST
2030	105,970	2.66	FORECAST
		AFR Sao Tome and Principe	
0001	.	.	
1000	.	.	
1500	.	.	
1600	.	.	
1700	.	.	
1820	.	.	

Year	GDP at PPP Per Capita, 2012 doll.	Growth Rate	Source
1870	.	.	
1880	.	.	
1890	.	.	
1900	.	.	
1913	.	.	
1920	.	.	
1929	.	.	
1938	.	.	
1950	1,283	.	50(Maddison)
1960	1,330	0.36	60(Maddison)
1970	1,841	3.31	70(Maddison)
1980	2,279	2.16	80(Maddison)
1990	1,800	2.33	90(Maddison)
2000	1,464	2.04	00(WB)
2010	1,783	1.99	10(WB)
2012	1,822	1.08	12(WB)
2020	2,024	1.32	FORECAST
2030	2,354	1.52	FORECAST
MEA Saudi Arabia			
0001	761	.	PROXY(W. Asia(Maddison))
1000	906	0.02	PROXY(W. Asia(Maddison))
1500	861	0.01	AVG(Arabia(Maddison))
1600	861	0.00	INTERPOL(Maddison)
1700	861	0.00	AVG(Arabia(Maddison))
1820	861	0.00	AVG(Arabia(Maddison))
1870	900	0.09	AVG(Arabia(Maddison))
1880	909	0.10	INTERPOL(Maddison)
1890	918	0.10	INTERPOL(Maddison)
1900	927	0.10	INTERPOL(Maddison)
1913	939	0.10	AVG(Arabia(Maddison))
1920	1,204	3.61	INTERPOL(Maddison)
1929	1,657	3.61	INTERPOL(Maddison)
1938	2,280	3.61	INTERPOL(Maddison)
1950	3,491	3.61	50(Maddison)
1960	6,745	6.81	60(Maddison)
1970	16,267	9.20	70(Maddison)
1980	32,956	7.32	80(WB)
1990	18,023	5.86	90(WB)
2000	22,270	2.14	00(WB)
2010	28,188	2.38	10(WB)
2012	31,214	5.23	12(WB)
2020	40,096	3.18	FORECAST
2030	50,565	2.35	FORECAST
AFR Senegal			
0001	.	.	
1000	.	.	
1500	.	.	

Year	GDP at PPP Per Capita, 2012 doll.	Growth Rate	Source
1600	.	.	
1700	.	.	
1820	.	.	
1870	.	.	
1880	.	.	
1890	.	.	
1900	.	.	
1913	.	.	
1920	.	.	
1929	.	.	
1938	.	.	
1950	1,970	.	50(Maddison)
1960	2,070	0.49	60(Maddison)
1970	1,962	0.53	70(Maddison)
1980	1,744	1.17	80(WB)
1990	1,690	0.31	90(WB)
2000	1,745	0.32	00(WB)
2010	1,913	0.93	10(WB)
2012	1,908	0.13	12(WB)
2020	1,988	0.52	FORECAST
2030	2,181	0.93	FORECAST

EEU Serbia

Year	GDP at PPP Per Capita, 2012 doll.	Growth Rate	Source
0001	665	.	AVG(Danubian provinces(Maddison))
1000	626	0.01	1000(Maddison)
1500	712	0.03	PROXY(E. Europe(Maddison))
1600	786	0.10	PROXY(E. Europe(Maddison))
1700	869	0.10	PROXY(E. Europe(Maddison))
1820	980	0.10	PROXY(E. Europe(Maddison))
1870	1,030	0.10	PROXY(Yugoslavia(Maddison))
1880	1,222	1.72	INTERPOL(Maddison)
1890	1,450	1.72	PROXY(Yugoslavia(Maddison))
1900	1,551	0.68	PROXY(Yugoslavia(Maddison))
1913	1,817	1.23	PROXY(Yugoslavia(Maddison))
1920	1,773	0.36	PROXY(Yugoslavia(Maddison))
1929	2,345	3.16	PROXY(Yugoslavia(Maddison))
1938	2,332	0.07	PROXY(Yugoslavia(Maddison))
1950	2,667	1.13	PROXY(Yugoslavia(Maddison))
1960	4,512	5.40	PROXY(Yugoslavia(Maddison))
1970	7,462	5.16	PROXY(Yugoslavia(Maddison))
1980	13,030	5.73	PROXY(Yugoslavia(Maddison))
1990	12,323	0.56	90(WB)
2000	7,423	4.94	00(WB)
2010	11,687	4.64	10(WB)
2012	11,801	0.49	12(WB)
2020	14,752	2.83	FORECAST

Year	GDP at PPP Per Capita, 2012 doll.	Growth Rate	Source
2030	18,406	2.24	FORECAST
		AFR Seychelles	
0001	.	.	
1000	.	.	
1500	.	.	
1600	.	.	
1700	.	.	
1820	.	.	
1870	.	.	
1880	.	.	
1890	.	.	
1900	.	.	
1913	.	.	
1920	.	.	
1929	.	.	
1938	.	.	
1950	2,992	.	50(Maddison)
1960	4,450	4.05	60(Maddison)
1970	5,792	2.67	70(Maddison)
1980	11,627	7.22	80(WB)
1990	15,227	2.73	90(WB)
2000	21,274	3.40	00(WB)
2010	23,514	1.01	10(WB)
2012	26,572	6.30	12(WB)
2020	33,828	3.06	FORECAST
2030	42,517	2.31	FORECAST
		AFR Sierra Leone	
0001	395	.	0001(MIN)
1000	577	0.04	1000(MIN)
1500	750	0.05	1500(MIN)
1600	798	0.06	1600(MIN)
1700	852	0.07	1700(MIN)
1820	928	0.07	1820(MIN)
1870	963	0.08	1870(MIN)
1880	971	0.08	1880(MIN)
1890	978	0.08	1890(MIN)
1900	986	0.08	1900(MIN)
1913	996	0.08	1913(MIN)
1920	1,002	0.08	1920(MIN)
1929	1,009	0.08	1929(MIN)
1938	1,017	0.08	1938(MIN)
1950	1,027	0.08	50(Maddison)
1960	1,216	1.71	60(Maddison)
1970	1,455	1.81	70(Maddison)
1980	1,323	0.95	80(WB)
1990	1,143	1.45	90(WB)

Year	GDP at PPP Per Capita, 2012 doll.	Growth Rate	Source
2000	863	2.77	00(WB)
2010	1,145	2.86	10(WB)
2012	1,337	8.07	12(WB)
2020	1,640	2.58	FORECAST
2030	2,028	2.15	FORECAST
		SEA SINGAPORE	
0001	399	.	0001(MIN)
1000	585	0.04	1000(MIN)
1500	763	0.05	PROXY(Other E. Asia(Maddison))
1600	777	0.02	PROXY(Other E. Asia(Maddison))
1700	773	0.01	PROXY(Other E. Asia(Maddison))
1820	782	0.01	1820(Maddison)
1870	1,067	0.62	1870(Maddison)
1880	1,235	1.47	INTERPOL(Maddison)
1890	1,430	1.47	INTERPOL(Maddison)
1900	1,655	1.47	INTERPOL(Maddison)
1913	2,001	1.47	1913(Maddison)
1920	2,221	1.50	INTERPOL(Maddison)
1929	2,540	1.50	INTERPOL(Maddison)
1938	2,904	1.50	INTERPOL(Maddison)
1950	3,472	1.50	50(Maddison)
1960	3,843	1.02	60(Maddison)
1970	7,863	7.42	70(Maddison)
1980	17,086	8.07	80(WB)
1990	28,558	5.27	90(WB)
2000	43,412	4.28	00(WB)
2010	59,711	3.24	10(WB)
2012	60,800	0.91	12(WB)
2020	83,191	4.00	FORECAST
2030	106,854	2.53	FORECAST
		LAM SINT MAARTEN	
0001	.	.	
1000	.	.	
1500	.	.	
1600	.	.	
1700	.	.	
1820	.	.	
1870	.	.	
1880	.	.	
1890	.	.	
1900	.	.	
1913	.	.	
1920	.	.	
1929	.	.	
1938	.	.	
1950	5,304	.	06(CIA)WEIGHT(Curacao)

Year	GDP at PPP Per Capita, 2012 doll.	Growth Rate	Source
1960	7,402	3.39	06(CIA)WEIGHT(Curacao)
1970	10,332	3.39	06(CIA)WEIGHT(Curacao)
1980	10,126	0.20	06(CIA)WEIGHT(Curacao)
1990	8,528	1.70	06(CIA)WEIGHT(Curacao)
2000	12,911	4.23	06(CIA)WEIGHT(Curacao)
2010	21,746	5.35	10(CIA)WEIGHT(US(WB))
2012	22,570	1.88	10(CIA)WEIGHT(US(WB))
2020	30,748	3.94	FORECAST
2030	39,455	2.52	FORECAST
EEU Slovakia			
0001	428	.	0001(MIN)
1000	651	0.04	1000(MIN)
1500	880	0.06	PROXY(E. Europe(Maddison))
1600	972	0.10	PROXY(E. Europe(Maddison))
1700	1,075	0.10	PROXY(E. Europe(Maddison))
1820	1,212	0.10	PROXY(Czechoslovakia(Maddison))
1870	1,661	0.63	PROXY(Czechoslovakia(Maddison))
1880	1,889	1.29	INTERPOL(Maddison)
1890	2,148	1.29	PROXY(Czechoslovakia(Maddison))
1900	2,467	1.40	PROXY(Czechoslovakia(Maddison))
1913	2,991	1.49	PROXY(Czechoslovakia(Maddison))
1920	2,758	1.15	PROXY(Czechoslovakia(Maddison))
1929	4,341	5.17	PROXY(Czechoslovakia(Maddison))
1938	4,113	0.60	PROXY(37Czechoslovakia(Maddison))
1950	4,996	1.63	PROXY(Czechoslovakia(Maddison))
1960	7,569	4.24	PROXY(Czechoslovakia(Maddison))
1970	9,798	2.61	PROXY(Czechoslovakia(Maddison))
1980	12,335	2.33	PROXY(Czechoslovakia(Maddison))
1990	13,207	0.69	90(WB)
2000	14,693	1.07	00(WB)
2010	24,601	5.29	10(WB)
2012	25,842	2.49	12(WB)
2020	33,926	3.46	FORECAST
2030	43,097	2.42	FORECAST
EEU Slovenia			
0001	487	.	0001(MIN)
1000	796	0.05	1000(MIN)
1500	1,167	0.08	INTERPOL(Maddison)
1600	1,321	0.12	INTERPOL(Maddison)
1700	1,497	0.12	INTERPOL(Maddison)
1820	1,738	0.12	INTERPOL(Maddison)
1870	1,850	0.12	PROXY(Yugoslavia(Maddison))
1880	2,194	1.72	INTERPOL(Maddison)
1890	2,603	1.72	PROXY(Yugoslavia(Maddison))
1900	2,785	0.68	PROXY(Yugoslavia(Maddison))
1913	3,264	1.23	PROXY(Yugoslavia(Maddison))
1920	3,184	0.36	PROXY(Yugoslavia(Maddison))
1929	4,212	3.16	PROXY(Yugoslavia(Maddison))

Year	GDP at PPP Per Capita, 2012 doll.	Growth Rate	Source
1938	4,187	0.07	PROXY(Yugoslavia(Maddison))
1950	4,789	1.13	PROXY(Yugoslavia(Maddison))
1960	7,622	4.76	PROXY(Yugoslavia(Maddison))
1970	11,889	4.55	PROXY(Yugoslavia(Maddison))
1980	19,454	5.05	PROXY(Yugoslavia(Maddison))
1990	18,574	0.46	90(WB)
2000	22,870	2.10	00(WB)
2010	29,139	2.45	10(WB)
2012	28,476	1.14	12(WB)
2020	33,769	2.15	FORECAST
2030	41,042	1.97	FORECAST
SEA Solomon Islands			
0001	.	.	
1000	.	.	
1500	.	.	
1600	.	.	
1700	.	.	
1820	.	.	
1870	.	.	
1880	.	.	
1890	.	.	
1900	.	.	
1913	.	.	
1920	.	.	
1929	.	.	
1938	.	.	
1950	928	.	PROXY(14 Pacific is(Maddison))
1960	1,179	2.43	INTERPOL(14 Pacific is(Maddison))
1970	1,499	2.43	INTERPOL(14 Pacific is(Maddison))
1980	1,740	1.50	80(WB)
1990	2,645	4.28	90(WB)
2000	2,558	0.33	00(WB)
2010	2,835	1.03	10(WB)
2012	3,076	4.16	12(WB)
2020	3,543	1.78	FORECAST
2030	4,229	1.79	FORECAST
AFR Somalia			
0001	355	.	0001(MIN)
1000	495	0.03	1000(MIN)
1500	617	0.04	1500(MIN)
1600	649	0.05	1600(Rest of Africa(Maddison))
1700	649	0.00	1700(Rest of Africa(Maddison))
1820	649	0.00	1820(Rest of Africa(Maddison))
1870	930	0.72	INTERPOL(Maddison)
1880	1,000	0.72	INTERPOL(Maddison)
1890	1,074	0.72	INTERPOL(Maddison)

Year	GDP at PPP Per Capita, 2012 doll.	Growth Rate	Source
1900	1,154	0.72	INTERPOL(Maddison)
1913	1,268	0.72	INTERPOL(Maddison)
1920	1,333	0.72	INTERPOL(Maddison)
1929	1,422	0.72	INTERPOL(Maddison)
1938	1,517	0.72	INTERPOL(Maddison)
1950	1,654	0.72	50(Maddison)
1960	2,165	2.73	60(Maddison)
1970	1,837	1.63	70(Maddison)
1980	1,610	1.31	80(Maddison)
1990	1,712	0.62	90(Maddison)
2000	830	6.98	00(CIA)WEIGHT(US(WB))
2010	614	2.97	10(CIA)WEIGHT(US(WB))
2012	642	2.23	10(CIA)WEIGHT(US(WB))
2020	665	0.43	FORECAST
2030	724	0.85	FORECAST
AFR South Africa			
0001	355	.	0001(MIN)
1000	495	0.03	1000(MIN)
1500	617	0.04	1500(MIN)
1600	649	0.05	1600(Rest of Africa(Maddison))
1700	649	0.00	1700(Rest of Africa(Maddison))
1820	649	0.00	1820(Maddison)
1870	1,343	1.46	1870(Maddison)
1880	1,552	1.46	INTERPOL(Maddison)
1890	1,795	1.46	INTERPOL(Maddison)
1900	2,076	1.46	INTERPOL(Maddison)
1913	2,507	1.46	1913(Maddison)
1920	2,734	1.25	INTERPOL(Maddison)
1929	3,057	1.25	INTERPOL(Maddison)
1938	3,418	1.25	INTERPOL(Maddison)
1950	3,967	1.25	50(Maddison)
1960	5,300	2.94	60(Maddison)
1970	7,890	4.06	70(Maddison)
1980	9,492	1.87	80(WB)
1990	8,601	0.98	90(WB)
2000	8,627	0.03	00(WB)
2010	10,653	2.13	10(WB)
2012	11,021	1.71	12(WB)
2020	12,445	1.53	FORECAST
2030	14,651	1.65	FORECAST
AFR South Sudan			
0001	324	.	0001(MIN)
1000	437	0.03	1000(MIN)
1500	529	0.04	1500(MIN)
1600	553	0.04	1600(MIN)
1700	578	0.05	1700(MIN)
1820	612	0.05	1820(MIN)
1870	627	0.05	1870(MIN)

Year	GDP at PPP Per Capita, 2012 doll.	Growth Rate	Source
1880	631	0.05	1880(MIN)
1890	634	0.05	1890(MIN)
1900	637	0.05	1900(MIN)
1913	641	0.05	1913(MIN)
1920	644	0.05	1920(MIN)
1929	647	0.05	1929(MIN)
1938	650	0.05	1938(MIN)
1950	654	0.05	PROXY(Sudan(Maddison))
1960	785	1.85	PROXY(Sudan(Maddison))
1970	691	1.27	PROXY(Sudan(Maddison))
1980	715	0.34	PROXY(Sudan(WB))
1990	683	0.45	PROXY(Sudan(WB))
2000	787	1.42	PROXY(Sudan(WB))
2010	1,042	2.85	PROXY(Sudan(WB))
2012	1,100	2.76	12(CIA)
2020	1,301	2.12	FORECAST
2030	1,579	1.95	FORECAST
DME Spain			
0001	779	.	0001(Maddison)
1000	704	0.01	1000(Maddison)
1500	1,034	0.08	1500(Maddison)
1600	1,335	0.26	1600(Maddison)
1700	1,335	0.00	1700(Maddison)
1820	1,577	0.14	1820(Maddison)
1870	1,889	0.36	1870(Maddison)
1880	2,576	3.15	1880(Maddison)
1890	2,541	0.13	1890(Maddison)
1900	2,795	0.96	1900(Maddison)
1913	3,217	1.09	1913(Maddison)
1920	3,407	0.82	1920(Maddison)
1929	4,286	2.58	1929(Maddison)
1938	2,801	4.62	1938(Maddison)
1950	3,425	1.69	50(Maddison)
1960	5,046	3.95	60(Maddison)
1970	11,172	8.27	70(Maddison)
1980	17,122	4.36	80(WB)
1990	22,399	2.72	90(WB)
2000	30,900	3.27	00(WB)
2010	32,826	0.61	10(WB)
2012	32,134	1.06	12(WB)
2020	37,466	1.94	FORECAST
2030	45,074	1.87	FORECAST
SAS Sri Lanka			
0001	644	.	PROXY(Other E. Asia(Maddison))
1000	644	0.00	PROXY(Other E. Asia(Maddison))
1500	839	0.05	PROXY(Other E. Asia(Maddison))
1600	855	0.02	PROXY(Other E. Asia(Maddison))
1700	850	0.01	PROXY(Other E. Asia(Maddison))

Year	GDP at PPP Per Capita, 2012 doll.	Growth Rate	Source
1820	861	0.01	1820(Maddison)
1870	1,332	0.88	1870(Maddison)
1880	1,300	0.24	1880(Maddison)
1890	1,635	2.32	1890(Maddison)
1900	2,019	2.13	1900(Maddison)
1913	1,931	0.34	1913(Maddison)
1920	1,709	1.73	1920(Maddison)
1929	2,091	2.27	1929(Maddison)
1938	1,917	0.96	1938(Maddison)
1950	1,961	0.19	50(Maddison)
1960	1,800	0.85	60(Maddison)
1970	1,838	0.21	70(Maddison)
1980	1,977	0.73	80(WB)
1990	2,552	2.58	90(WB)
2000	3,523	3.28	00(WB)
2010	5,290	4.15	10(WB)
2012	6,146	7.79	12(WB)
2020	8,539	4.20	FORECAST
2030	11,004	2.57	FORECAST
		AFR SUDAN	
0001	428	.	0001(MIN)
1000	649	0.04	1000(Sahel & W. Africa(Maddison))
1500	649	0.00	1500(Sahel & W. Africa(Maddison))
1600	649	0.00	1600(Sahel & W. Africa(Maddison))
1700	649	0.00	1700(Sahel & W. Africa(Maddison))
1820	649	0.00	1820(Sahel & W. Africa(Maddison))
1870	844	0.53	INTERPOL(Maddison)
1880	890	0.53	INTERPOL(Maddison)
1890	938	0.53	INTERPOL(Maddison)
1900	988	0.53	INTERPOL(Maddison)
1913	1,058	0.53	INTERPOL(Maddison)
1920	1,098	0.53	INTERPOL(Maddison)
1929	1,151	0.53	INTERPOL(Maddison)
1938	1,206	0.53	INTERPOL(Maddison)
1950	1,285	0.53	50(Maddison)
1960	1,543	1.85	60(Maddison)
1970	1,357	1.27	70(Maddison)
1980	1,405	0.34	80(WB)
1990	1,342	0.45	90(WB)
2000	1,546	1.42	00(WB)
2010	2,048	2.85	10(WB)
2012	2,162	2.76	12(WB)
2020	2,557	2.12	FORECAST
2030	3,104	1.95	FORECAST
		LAM SURINAME	
0001	.	.	
1000	.	.	
1500	.	.	

Year	GDP at PPP Per Capita, 2012 doll.	Growth Rate	Source
1600	.	.	
1700	.	.	
1820	.	.	
1870	.	.	
1880	.	.	
1890	.	.	
1900	.	.	
1913	.	.	
1920	.	.	
1929	.	.	
1938	.	.	
1950	2,293	.	50(Maddison)
1960	3,316	3.76	INTERPOL(Maddison)
1970	4,796	3.76	INTERPOL(Maddison)
1980	7,217	4.17	80(WB)
1990	5,757	2.24	90(WB)
2000	5,589	0.29	00(WB)
2010	8,101	3.78	10(WB)
2012	8,722	3.76	12(WB)
2020	10,822	2.73	FORECAST
2030	13,458	2.20	FORECAST
DME Svalbard			
0001	.	.	
1000	.	.	
1500	.	.	
1600	.	.	
1700	.	.	
1820	.	.	
1870	.	.	
1880	.	.	
1890	.	.	
1900	.	.	
1913	.	.	
1920	.	.	
1929	.	.	
1938	.	.	
1950	12,986	.	PROXY(Norway(Maddison))
1960	17,890	3.26	PROXY(Norway(Maddison))
1970	26,268	3.92	PROXY(Norway(Maddison))
1980	42,424	4.91	PROXY(Norway(WB))
1990	54,541	2.54	PROXY(Norway(WB))
2000	91,620	5.32	PROXY(Norway(WB))
2010	98,601	0.74	PROXY(Norway(WB))
2012	100,469	0.94	(REG)
2020	122,324	2.49	FORECAST

Year	GDP at PPP Per Capita, 2012 doll.	Growth Rate	Source
2030	150,775	2.11	FORECAST
		AFR SWAZILAND	
0001	355	.	0001(MIN)
1000	495	0.03	1000(MIN)
1500	617	0.04	1500(MIN)
1600	649	0.05	1600(Rest of Africa(Maddison))
1700	649	0.00	1700(Rest of Africa(Maddison))
1820	649	0.00	1820(Rest of Africa(Maddison))
1870	803	0.43	INTERPOL(Maddison)
1880	838	0.43	INTERPOL(Maddison)
1890	874	0.43	INTERPOL(Maddison)
1900	912	0.43	INTERPOL(Maddison)
1913	964	0.43	INTERPOL(Maddison)
1920	993	0.43	INTERPOL(Maddison)
1929	1,032	0.43	INTERPOL(Maddison)
1938	1,072	0.43	INTERPOL(Maddison)
1950	1,128	0.43	50(Maddison)
1960	1,460	2.61	60(Maddison)
1970	2,959	7.32	70(Maddison)
1980	3,522	1.76	80(WB)
1990	5,561	4.67	90(WB)
2000	4,868	1.32	00(WB)
2010	5,359	0.96	10(WB)
2012	5,161	1.86	12(WB)
2020	5,752	1.36	FORECAST
2030	6,704	1.54	FORECAST
		DME SWEDEN	
0001	472	.	0001(MIN)
1000	758	0.05	1000(MIN)
1500	1,088	0.07	1500(Maddison)
1600	1,289	0.17	1600(Maddison)
1700	1,529	0.17	1700(Maddison)
1820	1,875	0.17	1820(Maddison)
1870	2,601	0.66	1870(Maddison)
1880	2,889	1.06	1880(Maddison)
1890	3,264	1.23	1890(Maddison)
1900	4,008	2.07	1900(Maddison)
1913	4,845	1.47	1913(Maddison)
1920	4,385	1.42	1920(Maddison)
1929	6,054	3.65	1929(Maddison)
1938	7,394	2.25	1938(Maddison)
1950	10,546	3.00	50(Maddison)
1960	13,999	2.87	60(Maddison)
1970	21,169	4.22	70(Maddison)
1980	25,540	1.89	80(WB)
1990	30,970	1.95	90(WB)
2000	35,596	1.40	00(WB)
2010	41,857	1.63	10(WB)

Year	GDP at PPP Per Capita, 2012 doll.	Growth Rate	Source
2012	42,866	1.20	12(WB)
2020	49,365	1.78	FORECAST
2030	58,919	1.78	FORECAST
		DME SWITZERLAND	
0001	665	.	0001(Maddison)
1000	642	0.00	1000(Maddison)
1500	989	0.09	1500(Maddison)
1600	1,174	0.17	1600(Maddison)
1700	1,393	0.17	1700(Maddison)
1820	1,706	0.17	1820(Maddison)
1870	3,289	1.32	1870(Maddison)
1880	3,834	1.54	1880(Maddison)
1890	4,979	2.65	1890(Maddison)
1900	5,998	1.88	1900(Maddison)
1913	6,676	0.83	1913(Maddison)
1920	6,751	0.16	1920(Maddison)
1929	9,909	4.36	1929(Maddison)
1938	9,999	0.10	1938(Maddison)
1950	14,184	2.96	50(Maddison)
1960	21,453	4.22	60(Maddison)
1970	31,975	4.07	70(Maddison)
1980	37,846	1.70	80(WB)
1990	45,449	1.85	90(WB)
2000	47,870	0.52	00(WB)
2010	52,798	0.98	10(WB)
2012	53,191	0.37	12(WB)
2020	58,243	1.14	FORECAST
2030	66,923	1.40	FORECAST
		MEA SYRIA	
0001	911	.	PROXY(W. Asia(Maddison))
1000	1,084	0.02	PROXY(W. Asia(Maddison))
1500	1,030	0.01	PROXY(Other W. Asia(Maddison))
1600	1,030	0.00	INTERPOL(Maddison)
1700	1,030	0.00	PROXY(Other W. Asia(Maddison))
1820	1,030	0.00	1820(Maddison)
1870	1,321	0.50	1870(Maddison)
1880	1,473	1.10	INTERPOL(Maddison)
1890	1,643	1.10	INTERPOL(Maddison)
1900	1,833	1.10	INTERPOL(Maddison)
1913	2,113	1.10	1913(Maddison)
1920	2,357	1.58	INTERPOL(Maddison)
1929	2,714	1.58	INTERPOL(Maddison)
1938	3,124	1.58	INTERPOL(Maddison)
1950	3,770	1.58	50(Maddison)
1960	3,725	0.12	60(Maddison)
1970	3,520	0.56	70(Maddison)
1980	4,449	2.37	80(WB)
1990	4,136	0.73	90(WB)

Year	GDP at PPP Per Capita, 2012 doll.	Growth Rate	Source
2000	4,387	0.59	00(WB)
2010	5,006	1.33	10(WB)
2012	4,776	2.33	12(CIA)
2020	5,133	0.91	FORECAST
2030	5,802	1.23	FORECAST
SEA Taiwan			
0001	644	.	PROXY(Other E. Asia(Maddison))
1000	644	0.00	PROXY(Other E. Asia(Maddison))
1500	839	0.05	PROXY(Other E. Asia(Maddison))
1600	855	0.02	PROXY(Other E. Asia(Maddison))
1700	850	0.01	PROXY(Other E. Asia(Maddison))
1820	861	0.01	1820(Maddison)
1870	861	0.00	1870(Maddison)
1880	918	0.65	INTERPOL(Maddison)
1890	980	0.65	INTERPOL(Maddison)
1900	1,045	0.65	INTERPOL(Maddison)
1913	1,169	0.86	1913(Maddison)
1920	1,501	3.63	1920(Maddison)
1929	1,793	2.00	1929(Maddison)
1938	2,037	1.43	1938(Maddison)
1950	1,446	2.82	50(Maddison)
1960	2,309	4.79	60(Maddison)
1970	4,540	6.99	70(Maddison)
1980	8,803	6.85	80(Maddison)
1990	14,651	5.23	90(Maddison)
2000	22,597	4.43	00(CIA)WEIGHT(US(WB))
2010	37,688	5.25	10(CIA)WEIGHT(US(WB))
2012	38,900	1.60	12(CIA)
2020	57,667	5.04	FORECAST
2030	75,009	2.66	FORECAST
USR Tajikistan			
0001	344	.	0001(MIN)
1000	474	0.03	1000(MIN)
1500	585	0.04	1500(MIN)
1600	614	0.05	1600(MIN)
1700	645	0.05	PROXY(USSR(Maddison))
1820	728	0.10	PROXY(USSR(Maddison))
1870	997	0.63	PROXY(USSR(Maddison))
1880	1,092	0.91	INTERPOL(Maddison)
1890	1,195	0.91	INTERPOL(Maddison)
1900	1,308	0.91	PROXY(USSR(Maddison))
1913	1,574	1.43	PROXY(USSR(Maddison))
1920	610	12.67	PROXY(USSR(Davies))
1929	1,505	10.56	PROXY(USSR(Maddison))
1938	2,335	5.00	PROXY(USSR(Maddison))
1950	3,005	2.12	PROXY(USSR(Maddison))

Year	GDP at PPP Per Capita, 2012 doll.	Growth Rate	Source
1960	3,856	2.53	PROXY(USSR(Maddison))
1970	5,035	2.70	PROXY(USSR(Maddison))
1980	4,446	1.24	INTERPOL(Tajikistan(Maddison))
1990	3,418	2.60	90(WB)
2000	1,124	10.52	00(WB)
2010	1,995	5.90	10(WB)
2012	2,192	4.83	12(WB)
2020	2,906	3.59	FORECAST
2030	3,703	2.45	FORECAST
AFR Tanzania			
0001	.	.	
1000	.	.	
1500	.	.	
1600	.	.	
1700	.	.	
1820	.	.	
1870	.	.	
1880	.	.	
1890	.	.	
1900	.	.	
1913	.	.	
1920	.	.	
1929	.	.	
1938	.	.	
1950	663	.	50(Maddison)
1960	745	1.16	60(Maddison)
1970	954	2.51	70(Maddison)
1980	1,035	0.81	80(Maddison)
1990	977	0.58	90(WB)
2000	990	0.14	00(WB)
2010	1,471	4.03	10(WB)
2012	1,575	3.48	12(WB)
2020	1,929	2.57	FORECAST
2030	2,385	2.14	FORECAST
SEA Thailand			
0001	756	.	PROXY(Other E. Asia(Maddison))
1000	756	0.00	PROXY(Other E. Asia(Maddison))
1500	986	0.05	PROXY(Other E. Asia(Maddison))
1600	1,004	0.02	PROXY(Other E. Asia(Maddison))
1700	998	0.01	PROXY(Other E. Asia(Maddison))
1820	1,011	0.01	1820(Maddison)
1870	1,114	0.19	1870(Maddison)
1880	1,169	0.48	INTERPOL(Maddison)
1890	1,227	0.48	1890(Maddison)
1900	1,265	0.31	INTERPOL(Maddison)
1913	1,316	0.31	1913(Maddison)

Year	GDP at PPP Per Capita, 2012 doll.	Growth Rate	Source
1920	1,283	0.37	INTERPOL(Maddison)
1929	1,241	0.37	1929(Maddison)
1938	1,293	0.45	1938(Maddison)
1950	1,278	0.09	50(Maddison)
1960	1,493	1.56	60(Maddison)
1970	2,068	3.31	70(Maddison)
1980	2,750	2.89	80(WB)
1990	4,836	5.81	90(WB)
2000	6,419	2.87	00(WB)
2010	9,129	3.58	10(WB)
2012	9,660	2.87	12(WB)
2020	12,973	3.75	FORECAST
2030	16,587	2.49	FORECAST

AFR Togo

Year	GDP at PPP Per Capita, 2012 doll.	Growth Rate	Source
0001	.	.	
1000	.	.	
1500	.	.	
1600	.	.	
1700	.	.	
1820	.	.	
1870	.	.	
1880	.	.	
1890	.	.	
1900	.	.	
1913	.	.	
1920	.	.	
1929	.	.	
1938	.	.	
1950	898	.	50(Maddison)
1960	1,010	1.18	60(Maddison)
1970	1,338	2.86	70(Maddison)
1980	1,290	0.37	80(WB)
1990	1,102	1.56	90(WB)
2000	1,031	0.66	00(WB)
2010	999	0.32	10(WB)
2012	1,034	1.74	12(WB)
2020	1,063	0.35	FORECAST
2030	1,149	0.78	FORECAST

SEA Tokelau

Year	GDP at PPP Per Capita, 2012 doll.	Growth Rate	Source
0001	.	.	
1000	.	.	
1500	.	.	
1600	.	.	
1700	.	.	
1820	.	.	

Year	GDP at PPP Per Capita, 2012 doll.	Growth Rate	Source
1870	.	.	
1880	.	.	
1890	.	.	
1900	.	.	
1913	.	.	
1920	.	.	
1929	.	.	
1938	.	.	
1950	982	.	PROXY(14 Pacific is(Maddison))
1960	1,146	1.55	INTERPOL(14 Pacific is(Maddison))
1970	1,336	1.55	INTERPOL(14 Pacific is(Maddison))
1980	1,420	0.61	INTERPOL(14 Pacific is(Maddison))
1990	1,449	0.20	93(CIA)WEIGHT(US(Maddison))
2000	1,760	1.97	93(CIA)WEIGHT(US(WB))
2010	1,894	0.73	93(CIA)WEIGHT(US(WB))
2012	1,955	1.62	93(CIA)WEIGHT(US(WB))
2020	2,146	1.17	FORECAST
2030	2,470	1.42	FORECAST
SEA TONGA			
0001	.	.	
1000	.	.	
1500	.	.	
1600	.	.	
1700	.	.	
1820	.	.	
1870	.	.	
1880	.	.	
1890	.	.	
1900	.	.	
1913	.	.	
1920	.	.	
1929	.	.	
1938	.	.	
1950	1,948	.	PROXY(14 Pacific is(Maddison))
1960	2,386	2.05	INTERPOL(14 Pacific is(Maddison))
1970	2,922	2.05	INTERPOL(14 Pacific is(Maddison))
1980	2,748	0.61	81(WB)
1990	3,193	1.51	90(WB)
2000	4,363	3.17	00(WB)
2010	4,736	0.82	10(WB)
2012	4,881	1.52	12(WB)
2020	5,552	1.62	FORECAST
2030	6,570	1.70	FORECAST
LAM TRINIDAD AND TOBAGO			
0001	401	.	0001(MIN)

Year	GDP at PPP Per Capita, 2012 doll.	Growth Rate	Source
1000	590	0.04	1000(MIN)
1500	772	0.05	1500(MIN)
1600	823	0.06	INTERPOL(Maddison)
1700	1,081	0.27	INTERPOL(Maddison)
1820	1,501	0.27	PROXY(Other L. Am.(Maddison))
1870	1,538	0.05	PROXY(Other L. Am.(Maddison))
1880	1,832	1.77	INTERPOL(Maddison)
1890	2,183	1.77	INTERPOL(Maddison)
1900	2,601	1.77	INTERPOL(Maddison)
1913	3,266	1.77	PROXY(Other L. Am.(Maddison))
1920	3,635	1.54	INTERPOL(Maddison)
1929	4,171	1.54	INTERPOL(Maddison)
1938	4,786	1.54	INTERPOL(Maddison)
1950	5,749	1.54	50(Maddison)
1960	9,402	5.04	60(Maddison)
1970	11,901	2.38	70(Maddison)
1980	17,165	3.73	80(WB)
1990	12,127	3.41	90(WB)
2000	16,129	2.89	00(WB)
2010	26,766	5.20	10(WB)
2012	26,550	0.40	12(WB)
2020	34,953	3.50	FORECAST
2030	44,439	2.43	FORECAST

MEA Tunisia

Year	GDP at PPP Per Capita, 2012 doll.	Growth Rate	Source
0001	673	.	PROXY(Other N. Africa(Maddison))
1000	673	0.00	PROXY(Other N. Africa(Maddison))
1500	673	0.00	PROXY(Other N. Africa(Maddison))
1600	673	0.00	PROXY(Other N. Africa(Maddison))
1700	673	0.00	PROXY(Other N. Africa(Maddison))
1820	673	0.00	1820(Maddison)
1870	991	0.78	1870(Maddison)
1880	1,070	0.78	INTERPOL(Maddison)
1890	1,156	0.78	INTERPOL(Maddison)
1900	1,249	0.78	INTERPOL(Maddison)
1913	1,382	0.78	1913(Maddison)
1920	1,444	0.63	INTERPOL(Maddison)
1929	1,528	0.63	INTERPOL(Maddison)
1938	1,618	0.63	INTERPOL(Maddison)
1950	1,745	0.63	50(Maddison)
1960	2,089	1.82	60(Maddison)
1970	2,827	3.07	70(Maddison)
1980	4,534	4.84	80(WB)
1990	5,041	1.06	90(WB)
2000	6,898	3.19	00(WB)
2010	9,696	3.46	10(WB)
2012	9,636	0.31	12(WB)
2020	12,124	2.91	FORECAST
2030	15,168	2.27	FORECAST

Year	GDP at PPP Per Capita, 2012 doll.	Growth Rate	Source
		MEA TURKEY	
0001	831	.	PROXY(W. Asia(Maddison))
1000	988	0.02	PROXY(W. Asia(Maddison))
1500	939	0.01	1500(Maddison)
1600	939	0.00	INTERPOL(Maddison)
1700	939	0.00	1700(Maddison)
1820	1,006	0.06	1820(Maddison)
1870	1,291	0.50	1870(Maddison)
1880	1,412	0.90	INTERPOL(Maddison)
1890	1,545	0.90	INTERPOL(Maddison)
1900	1,689	0.90	INTERPOL(Maddison)
1913	1,898	0.90	1913(Maddison)
1920	1,114	7.33	1923(Maddison)
1929	1,898	6.10	1929(Maddison)
1938	2,698	3.98	1938(Maddison)
1950	2,540	0.50	50(Maddison)
1960	3,499	3.25	60(Maddison)
1970	4,760	3.13	70(Maddison)
1980	6,116	2.54	80(WB)
1990	8,720	3.61	90(WB)
2000	12,648	3.79	00(WB)
2010	16,880	2.93	10(WB)
2012	18,551	4.83	12(WB)
2020	24,773	3.68	FORECAST
2030	31,626	2.47	FORECAST
		USR TURKMENISTAN	
0001	366	.	0001(MIN)
1000	517	0.03	1000(MIN)
1500	652	0.05	1500(MIN)
1600	688	0.05	PROXY(USSR(Maddison))
1700	760	0.10	PROXY(USSR(Maddison))
1820	858	0.10	PROXY(USSR(Maddison))
1870	1,175	0.63	PROXY(USSR(Maddison))
1880	1,287	0.91	INTERPOL(Maddison)
1890	1,408	0.91	INTERPOL(Maddison)
1900	1,542	0.91	PROXY(USSR(Maddison))
1913	1,855	1.43	PROXY(USSR(Maddison))
1920	719	12.67	PROXY(USSR(Davies))
1929	1,774	10.56	PROXY(USSR(Maddison))
1938	2,752	5.00	PROXY(USSR(Maddison))
1950	3,541	2.12	PROXY(USSR(Maddison))
1960	5,177	3.87	PROXY(USSR(Maddison))
1970	7,703	4.05	PROXY(USSR(Maddison))
1980	7,830	0.16	INTERPOL(Turkmenistan(Maddison))
1990	6,962	1.17	90(WB)
2000	4,464	4.35	00(WB)
2010	8,379	6.50	10(WB)

Year	GDP at PPP Per Capita, 2012 doll.	Growth Rate	Source
2012	10,411	11.47	12(WB)
2020	15,255	4.89	FORECAST
2030	19,819	2.65	FORECAST
LAM TURKS AND CAICOS ISLANDS			
0001	.	.	
1000	.	.	
1500	.	.	
1600	.	.	
1700	.	.	
1820	.	.	
1870	.	.	
1880	.	.	
1890	.	.	
1900	.	.	
1913	.	.	
1920	.	.	
1929	.	.	
1938	.	.	
1950	4,155	.	PROXY(8 Caribbean cs(Maddison))
1960	5,508	2.86	INTERPOL(8 Caribbean cs(Maddison))
1970	7,301	2.86	INTERPOL(8 Caribbean cs(Maddison))
1980	8,684	1.75	INTERPOL(8 Caribbean cs(Maddison))
1990	9,860	1.28	92(CIA)WEIGHT(US(Maddison))
2000	11,658	1.69	00(CIA)WEIGHT(US(WB))
2010	30,316	10.03	07(CIA)WEIGHT(US(WB))
2012	31,327	1.65	07(CIA)WEIGHT(US(WB))
2020	48,976	5.74	FORECAST
2030	63,904	2.70	FORECAST
SEA TUVALU			
0001	.	.	
1000	.	.	
1500	.	.	
1600	.	.	
1700	.	.	
1820	.	.	
1870	.	.	
1880	.	.	
1890	.	.	
1900	.	.	
1913	.	.	
1920	.	.	
1929	.	.	
1938	.	.	
1950	786	.	PROXY(14 Pacific is(Maddison))

Year	GDP at PPP Per Capita, 2012 doll.	Growth Rate	Source
1960	914	1.52	INTERPOL(14 Pacific is(Maddison))
1970	1,062	1.52	INTERPOL(14 Pacific is(Maddison))
1980	1,127	0.59	INTERPOL(14 Pacific is(Maddison))
1990	1,150	0.20	93(CIA)WEIGHT(US(Maddison))
2000	1,390	1.92	00(CIA)WEIGHT(US(WB))
2010	3,528	9.76	10(CIA)WEIGHT(US(WB))
2012	3,500	0.40	12(CIA)
2020	5,243	5.18	FORECAST
2030	6,825	2.67	FORECAST
AFR Uganda			
0001	.	.	
1000	.	.	
1500	.	.	
1600	.	.	
1700	.	.	
1820	.	.	
1870	.	.	
1880	.	.	
1890	.	.	
1900	.	.	
1913	.	.	
1920	.	.	
1929	.	.	
1938	.	.	
1950	1,075	.	50(Maddison)
1960	1,019	0.53	60(Maddison)
1970	1,136	1.09	70(Maddison)
1980	686	4.92	80(Maddison)
1990	643	0.65	90(WB)
2000	877	3.16	00(WB)
2010	1,289	3.92	10(WB)
2012	1,330	1.55	12(WB)
2020	1,665	2.85	FORECAST
2030	2,078	2.24	FORECAST
USR Ukraine			
0001	361	.	0001(MIN)
1000	507	0.03	1000(MIN)
1500	635	0.05	PROXY(USSR(Maddison))
1600	702	0.10	PROXY(USSR(Maddison))
1700	776	0.10	PROXY(USSR(Maddison))
1820	876	0.10	PROXY(USSR(Maddison))
1870	1,200	0.63	PROXY(USSR(Maddison))
1880	1,314	0.91	INTERPOL(Maddison)
1890	1,438	0.91	INTERPOL(Maddison)
1900	1,574	0.91	PROXY(USSR(Maddison))
1913	1,894	1.43	PROXY(USSR(Maddison))

Year	GDP at PPP Per Capita, 2012 doll.	Growth Rate	Source
1920	734	12.67	PROXY(USSR(Davies))
1929	1,811	10.56	PROXY(USSR(Maddison))
1938	2,809	5.00	PROXY(USSR(Maddison))
1950	3,615	2.12	PROXY(USSR(Maddison))
1960	4,992	3.28	PROXY(USSR(Maddison))
1970	7,010	3.45	PROXY(USSR(Maddison))
1980	8,224	1.61	INTERPOL(Ukraine(Maddison))
1990	9,191	1.12	90(WB)
2000	4,213	7.50	00(WB)
2010	6,881	5.03	10(WB)
2012	7,298	2.99	12(WB)
2020	9,372	3.18	FORECAST
2030	11,817	2.35	FORECAST
MEA United Arab Emirates			
0001	761	.	PROXY(W. Asia(Maddison))
1000	906	0.02	PROXY(W. Asia(Maddison))
1500	861	0.01	AVG(Arabia(Maddison))
1600	861	0.00	INTERPOL(Maddison)
1700	861	0.00	AVG(Arabia(Maddison))
1820	861	0.00	AVG(Arabia(Maddison))
1870	900	0.09	AVG(Arabia(Maddison))
1880	909	0.10	INTERPOL(Maddison)
1890	918	0.10	INTERPOL(Maddison)
1900	927	0.10	INTERPOL(Maddison)
1913	939	0.10	AVG(Arabia(Maddison))
1920	1,743	9.24	INTERPOL(Maddison)
1929	3,863	9.24	INTERPOL(Maddison)
1938	8,558	9.24	INTERPOL(Maddison)
1950	24,721	9.24	50(Maddison)
1960	54,855	8.30	60(Maddison)
1970	90,599	5.15	70(Maddison)
1980	154,935	5.51	80(WB)
1990	86,187	5.70	90(WB)
2000	86,187	0.00	00(WB)
2010	41,673	7.01	10(WB)
2012	41,397	0.33	12(WB)
2020	43,423	0.60	FORECAST
2030	47,937	0.99	FORECAST
DME United Kingdom			
0001	478	.	0001(MIN)
1000	773	0.05	1000(MIN)
1500	1,117	0.07	1500(Maddison)
1600	1,524	0.31	1600(Maddison)
1700	1,956	0.25	1700(Maddison)
1820	2,670	0.26	1820(Maddison)
1870	4,992	1.26	1870(Maddison)
1880	5,441	0.87	1880(Maddison)
1890	6,273	1.43	1890(Maddison)

Year	GDP at PPP Per Capita, 2012 doll.	Growth Rate	Source
1900	7,029	1.14	1900(Maddison)
1913	7,701	0.70	1913(Maddison)
1920	7,117	1.12	1920(Maddison)
1929	8,611	2.14	1929(Maddison)
1938	9,805	1.45	1938(Maddison)
1950	10,858	0.85	50(Maddison)
1960	13,362	2.10	60(Maddison)
1970	16,438	2.09	70(Maddison)
1980	19,522	1.73	80(WB)
1990	24,913	2.47	90(WB)
2000	32,450	2.68	00(WB)
2010	35,725	0.97	10(WB)
2012	35,722	0.00	12(WB)
2020	40,473	1.57	FORECAST
2030	47,763	1.67	FORECAST
DME United States			
0001	389	.	0001(MIN)
1000	564	0.04	1000(MIN)
1500	729	0.05	1500(MIN)
1600	774	0.06	1600(MIN)
1700	825	0.06	1700(Maddison)
1820	1,967	0.73	1820(Maddison)
1870	3,826	1.34	1870(Maddison)
1880	4,507	1.65	1880(Maddison)
1890	5,308	1.65	1890(Maddison)
1900	6,402	1.89	1900(Maddison)
1913	8,295	2.01	1913(Maddison)
1920	8,688	0.66	1920(Maddison)
1929	10,796	2.44	1929(Maddison)
1938	9,586	1.31	1938(Maddison)
1950	14,962	3.78	50(Maddison)
1960	17,869	1.79	60(Maddison)
1970	23,899	2.95	70(Maddison)
1980	29,775	2.22	80(WB)
1990	37,628	2.37	90(WB)
2000	46,759	2.20	00(WB)
2010	50,169	0.71	10(WB)
2012	51,749	1.56	12(WB)
2020	58,746	1.60	FORECAST
2030	69,425	1.68	FORECAST
LAM Uruguay			
0001	364	.	0001(MIN)
1000	513	0.03	1000(MIN)
1500	645	0.05	AVG(Other Sp. Am.(Maddison))
1600	1,077	0.51	INTERPOL(Maddison)
1700	1,800	0.51	INTERPOL(Maddison)
1820	3,332	0.51	PROXY(Other L. Am.(Maddison))
1870	3,413	0.05	1870(Maddison)

Year	GDP at PPP Per Capita, 2012 doll.	Growth Rate	Source
1880	3,258	0.46	1880(Maddison)
1890	3,360	0.31	1890(Maddison)
1900	3,472	0.33	1900(Maddison)
1913	5,180	3.12	1913(Maddison)
1920	4,184	3.00	1920(Maddison)
1929	6,020	4.12	1929(Maddison)
1938	5,752	0.50	1938(Maddison)
1950	7,291	1.99	50(Maddison)
1960	7,385	0.13	60(Maddison)
1970	7,343	0.06	70(Maddison)
1980	8,869	1.91	80(WB)
1990	8,292	0.67	90(WB)
2000	10,888	2.76	00(WB)
2010	14,342	2.79	10(WB)
2012	15,777	4.88	12(WB)
2020	19,647	2.78	FORECAST
2030	24,474	2.22	FORECAST
USR Uzbekistan			
0001	368	.	0001(MIN)
1000	520	0.03	1000(MIN)
1500	657	0.05	PROXY(USSR(Maddison))
1600	727	0.10	PROXY(USSR(Maddison))
1700	803	0.10	PROXY(USSR(Maddison))
1820	909	0.10	PROXY(USSR(Maddison))
1870	1,241	0.63	PROXY(USSR(Maddison))
1880	1,359	0.91	INTERPOL(Maddison)
1890	1,488	0.91	INTERPOL(Maddison)
1900	1,628	0.91	PROXY(USSR(Maddison))
1913	1,959	1.43	PROXY(USSR(Maddison))
1920	759	12.67	PROXY(USSR(Davies))
1929	1,873	10.56	PROXY(USSR(Maddison))
1938	2,906	5.00	PROXY(USSR(Maddison))
1950	3,740	2.12	PROXY(USSR(Maddison))
1960	4,634	2.17	PROXY(USSR(Maddison))
1970	5,816	2.30	PROXY(USSR(Maddison))
1980	5,837	0.04	INTERPOL(Uzbekistan(Maddison))
1990	5,439	0.70	90(Maddison)
2000	2,326	8.14	00(WB)
2010	3,273	3.47	10(WB)
2012	3,533	3.89	12(WB)
2020	4,237	2.30	FORECAST
2030	5,182	2.03	FORECAST
SEA Vanuatu			
0001	.	.	
1000	.	.	
1500	.	.	
1600	.	.	
1700	.	.	

Year	GDP at PPP Per Capita, 2012 doll.	Growth Rate	Source
1820	.	.	
1870	.	.	
1880	.	.	
1890	.	.	
1900	.	.	
1913	.	.	
1920	.	.	
1929	.	.	
1938	.	.	
1950	2,191	.	PROXY(14 Pacific is(Maddison))
1960	2,557	1.56	INTERPOL(14 Pacific is(Maddison))
1970	2,985	1.56	INTERPOL(14 Pacific is(Maddison))
1980	3,183	0.64	80(WB)
1990	3,945	2.17	90(WB)
2000	4,377	1.05	00(WB)
2010	4,571	0.44	10(WB)
2012	4,531	0.45	12(WB)
2020	4,835	0.81	FORECAST
2030	5,428	1.16	FORECAST
LAM Venezuela			
0001	352	.	0001(MIN)
1000	489	0.03	1000(MIN)
1500	608	0.04	1500(MIN)
1600	639	0.05	1600(MIN)
1700	673	0.05	1700(MIN)
1820	720	0.06	1820(Maddison)
1870	890	0.43	1870(Maddison)
1880	1,006	1.23	INTERPOL(Maddison)
1890	1,137	1.23	INTERPOL(Maddison)
1900	1,285	1.23	1900(Maddison)
1913	1,728	2.30	1913(Maddison)
1920	1,836	0.87	1920(Maddison)
1929	5,361	12.65	1929(Maddison)
1938	6,485	2.14	1938(Maddison)
1950	11,677	5.02	50(Maddison)
1960	13,928	1.78	60(Maddison)
1970	14,599	0.47	70(Maddison)
1980	13,485	0.79	80(WB)
1990	11,545	1.54	90(WB)
2000	11,247	0.26	00(WB)
2010	12,572	1.12	10(WB)
2012	13,267	2.72	12(WB)
2020	14,318	0.96	FORECAST
2030	16,245	1.27	FORECAST
CPA Vietnam			
0001	410	.	0001(MIN)
1000	609	0.04	1000(MIN)

Year	GDP at PPP Per Capita, 2012 doll.	Growth Rate	Source
1500	804	0.06	PROXY(Other E. Asia(Maddison))
1600	819	0.02	PROXY(Other E. Asia(Maddison))
1700	815	0.01	PROXY(Other E. Asia(Maddison))
1820	825	0.01	1820(Maddison)
1870	790	0.09	1870(Maddison)
1880	860	0.85	INTERPOL(Maddison)
1890	936	0.85	INTERPOL(Maddison)
1900	1,019	0.85	INTERPOL(Maddison)
1913	1,138	0.85	1913(Maddison)
1920	1,116	0.27	INTERPOL(Maddison)
1929	1,090	0.27	INTERPOL(Maddison)
1938	1,064	0.27	INTERPOL(Maddison)
1950	1,030	0.27	50(Maddison)
1960	1,147	1.09	60(Maddison)
1970	968	1.68	70(Maddison)
1980	916	0.55	80(Maddison)
1990	1,153	2.33	90(WB)
2000	2,041	5.88	00(WB)
2010	3,458	5.41	10(WB)
2012	3,787	4.65	12(WB)
2020	5,551	4.89	FORECAST
2030	7,212	2.65	FORECAST
LAM Virgin Islands, British			
0001	.	.	
1000	.	.	
1500	.	.	
1600	.	.	
1700	.	.	
1820	.	.	
1870	.	.	
1880	.	.	
1890	.	.	
1900	.	.	
1913	.	.	
1920	.	.	
1929	.	.	
1938	.	.	
1950	7,463	.	PROXY(8 Caribbean cs(Maddison))
1960	9,853	2.82	INTERPOL(8 Caribbean cs(Maddison))
1970	13,008	2.82	INTERPOL(8 Caribbean cs(Maddison))
1980	15,432	1.72	INTERPOL(8 Caribbean cs(Maddison))
1990	17,488	1.26	91(CIA)WEIGHT(US(Maddison))
2000	19,835	1.27	00(CIA)WEIGHT(US(WB))
2010	43,827	8.25	10(CIA)WEIGHT(US(WB))
2012	45,266	1.63	10(CIA)WEIGHT(US(WB))
2020	65,853	4.80	FORECAST
2030	85,484	2.64	FORECAST

Year	GDP at PPP Per Capita, 2012 doll.	Growth Rate	Source
		LAM Virgin Islands, U.S.	
0001	.	.	
1000	.	.	
1500	.	.	
1600	.	.	
1700	.	.	
1820	.	.	
1870	.	.	
1880	.	.	
1890	.	.	
1900	.	.	
1913	.	.	
1920	.	.	
1929	.	.	
1938	.	.	
1950	9,204	.	PROXY(8 Caribbean cs(Maddison))
1960	11,892	2.60	INTERPOL(8 Caribbean cs(Maddison))
1970	15,366	2.60	INTERPOL(8 Caribbean cs(Maddison))
1980	17,990	1.59	INTERPOL(8 Caribbean cs(Maddison))
1990	20,191	1.16	87(CIA)WEIGHT(US(Maddison))
2000	19,877	0.16	00(CIA)WEIGHT(US(WB))
2010	43,796	8.22	10(REG)WEIGHT(US(WB))
2012	45,617	2.06	12(REG)
2020	64,953	4.52	FORECAST
2030	84,064	2.61	FORECAST
		SEA Wallis and Futuna	
0001	.	.	
1000	.	.	
1500	.	.	
1600	.	.	
1700	.	.	
1820	.	.	
1870	.	.	
1880	.	.	
1890	.	.	
1900	.	.	
1913	.	.	
1920	.	.	
1929	.	.	
1938	.	.	
1950	1,871	.	PROXY(14 Pacific is(Maddison))
1960	2,136	1.33	INTERPOL(14 Pacific is(Maddison))
1970	2,439	1.33	INTERPOL(14 Pacific is(Maddison))
1980	2,569	0.52	INTERPOL(14 Pacific is(Maddison))

Year	GDP at PPP Per Capita, 2012 doll.	Growth Rate	Source
1990	2,614	0.17	94(CIA)WEIGHT(US(Maddison))
2000	2,738	0.46	00(CIA)WEIGHT(US(WB))
2010	4,562	5.24	04(CIA)WEIGHT(US(WB))
2012	4,690	1.39	04(CIA)WEIGHT(US(WB))
2020	5,890	2.89	FORECAST
2030	7,364	2.26	FORECAST
MEA West Bank			
0001	.	.	
1000	.	.	
1500	.	.	
1600	.	.	
1700	.	.	
1820	.	.	
1870	.	.	
1880	.	.	
1890	.	.	
1900	.	.	
1913	.	.	
1920	.	.	
1929	.	.	
1938	.	.	
1950	1,681	.	PROXY(West Bank & Gaza(Maddison))
1960	1,964	1.57	PROXY(West Bank & Gaza(Maddison))
1970	2,285	1.53	PROXY(West Bank & Gaza(Maddison))
1980	2,619	1.37	PROXY(West Bank & Gaza(Maddison))
1990	3,003	1.38	PROXY(West Bank & Gaza(Maddison))
2000	2,900	0.35	00(WB)
2010	2,265	2.44	10(CIA)WEIGHT(US(WB))
2012	2,210	1.21	11(CIA)WEIGHT(US(WB))
2020	2,266	0.31	FORECAST
2030	2,441	0.75	FORECAST
AFR Western Sahara			
0001	.	.	
1000	.	.	
1500	.	.	
1600	.	.	
1700	.	.	
1820	.	.	
1870	.	.	
1880	.	.	
1890	.	.	
1900	.	.	
1913	.	.	
1920	.	.	

Year	GDP at PPP Per Capita, 2012 doll.	Growth Rate	Source
1929	.	.	
1938	.	.	
1950	360	.	PROXY(3 Afr. cs(Maddison))
1960	550	4.33	PROXY(3 Afr. cs(Maddison))
1970	573	0.41	PROXY(3 Afr. cs(Maddison))
1980	707	2.12	PROXY(3 Afr. cs(Maddison))
1990	828	1.59	PROXY(3 Afr. cs(Maddison))
2000	2,311	10.81	07(CIA)WEIGHT(US(WB))
2010	2,569	1.06	07(CIA)WEIGHT(US(WB))
2012	2,691	2.36	07(CIA)WEIGHT(US(WB))
2020	3,621	3.78	FORECAST
2030	4,632	2.49	FORECAST
MEA Yemen			
0001	761	.	PROXY(W. Asia(Maddison))
1000	906	0.02	PROXY(W. Asia(Maddison))
1500	861	0.01	AVG(Arabia(Maddison))
1600	861	0.00	INTERPOL(Maddison)
1700	861	0.00	AVG(Arabia(Maddison))
1820	861	0.00	AVG(Arabia(Maddison))
1870	900	0.09	AVG(Arabia(Maddison))
1880	909	0.10	INTERPOL(Maddison)
1890	918	0.10	INTERPOL(Maddison)
1900	927	0.10	INTERPOL(Maddison)
1913	939	0.10	AVG(Arabia(Maddison))
1920	1,016	1.14	INTERPOL(Maddison)
1929	1,125	1.13	INTERPOL(Maddison)
1938	1,245	1.14	INTERPOL(Maddison)
1950	1,426	1.14	50(Maddison)
1960	1,320	0.76	60(Maddison)
1970	1,475	1.12	70(Maddison)
1980	2,409	5.02	80(Maddison)
1990	2,091	1.40	90(WB)
2000	2,448	1.59	00(WB)
2010	2,864	1.58	10(WB)
2012	2,448	7.53	12(WB)
2020	2,747	1.45	FORECAST
2030	3,219	1.60	FORECAST
AFR Zambia			
0001	355	.	0001(MIN)
1000	495	0.03	1000(MIN)
1500	617	0.04	1500(MIN)
1600	649	0.05	1600(Rest of Africa(Maddison))
1700	649	0.00	1700(Rest of Africa(Maddison))
1820	649	0.00	1820(Rest of Africa(Maddison))
1870	777	0.36	INTERPOL(Maddison)
1880	805	0.36	INTERPOL(Maddison)
1890	834	0.36	INTERPOL(Maddison)
1900	865	0.36	INTERPOL(Maddison)

Year	GDP at PPP Per Capita, 2012 doll.	Growth Rate	Source
1913	906	0.36	INTERPOL(Maddison)
1920	929	0.36	INTERPOL(Maddison)
1929	959	0.36	INTERPOL(Maddison)
1938	991	0.36	INTERPOL(Maddison)
1950	1,034	0.36	50(Maddison)
1960	1,625	4.62	60(Maddison)
1970	1,899	1.57	70(Maddison)
1980	1,627	1.54	80(WB)
1990	1,312	2.13	90(WB)
2000	1,133	1.46	00(WB)
2010	1,550	3.18	10(WB)
2012	1,683	4.21	12(WB)
2020	2,006	2.22	FORECAST
2030	2,445	2.00	FORECAST
AFR ZIMBABWE			
0001	355	.	0001(MIN)
1000	495	0.03	1000(MIN)
1500	617	0.04	1500(MIN)
1600	649	0.05	1600(Rest of Africa(Maddison))
1700	649	0.00	1700(Rest of Africa(Maddison))
1820	649	0.00	1820(Rest of Africa(Maddison))
1870	794	0.40	INTERPOL(Maddison)
1880	827	0.40	INTERPOL(Maddison)
1890	861	0.40	INTERPOL(Maddison)
1900	897	0.40	INTERPOL(Maddison)
1913	945	0.40	INTERPOL(Maddison)
1920	972	0.40	INTERPOL(Maddison)
1929	1,008	0.40	INTERPOL(Maddison)
1938	1,045	0.40	INTERPOL(Maddison)
1950	1,097	0.40	50(Maddison)
1960	1,353	2.12	60(Maddison)
1970	1,694	2.27	70(Maddison)
1980	1,706	0.07	80(Maddison)
1990	1,764	0.33	90(Maddison)
2000	2,004	1.29	00(CIA)WEIGHT(US(WB))
2010	460	13.68	10(CIA)WEIGHT(US(WB))
2012	600	14.19	12(CIA)
2020	729	2.47	FORECAST
2030	899	2.11	FORECAST

3. GDP at PPP, by Country

Year	GDP at PPP, mil. 2012 doll.	Growth Rate	Source
SAS Afghanistan			
0001	235	.	POP*GPC
1000	641	0.10	POP*GPC
1500	1,497	0.17	POP*GPC
1600	1,767	0.17	POP*GPC
1700	2,044	0.15	POP*GPC
1820	2,622	0.21	POP*GPC
1870	3,236	0.42	POP*GPC
1880	3,764	1.52	POP*GPC
1890	4,377	1.52	POP*GPC
1900	5,091	1.52	POP*GPC
1913	6,195	1.52	POP*GPC
1920	6,537	0.77	POP*GPC
1929	7,004	0.77	POP*GPC
1938	7,504	0.77	POP*GPC
1950	8,227	0.77	POP*GPC
1960	12,770	4.50	POP*GPC
1970	14,955	1.59	POP*GPC
1980	17,488	1.58	POP*GPC
1990	11,974	3.72	POP*GPC
2000	20,667	5.61	POP*GPC
2010	31,200	4.20	POP*GPC
2012	42,077	16.13	POP*GPC
2020	64,675	5.52	POP*GPC
2030	101,456	4.61	POP*GPC

Year	GDP at PPP, mil. 2012 doll.	Growth Rate	Source
	EEU Albania		
0001	68	.	POP*GPC
1000	93	0.03	POP*GPC
1500	114	0.04	POP*GPC
1600	119	0.05	POP*GPC
1700	187	0.46	POP*GPC
1820	290	0.37	POP*GPC
1870	421	0.75	POP*GPC
1880	535	2.42	POP*GPC
1890	679	2.42	POP*GPC
1900	858	2.36	POP*GPC
1913	1,140	2.21	POP*GPC
1920	1,253	1.37	POP*GPC
1929	1,416	1.36	POP*GPC
1938	1,558	1.07	POP*GPC
1950	1,903	1.68	POP*GPC
1960	3,831	7.25	POP*GPC
1970	7,326	6.70	POP*GPC
1980	11,083	4.23	POP*GPC
1990	12,209	0.97	POP*GPC
2000	15,225	2.23	POP*GPC
2010	26,141	5.55	POP*GPC
2012	26,492	0.67	POP*GPC
2020	36,118	3.95	POP*GPC
2030	46,958	2.66	POP*GPC
	MEA Algeria		
0001	1,346	.	POP*GPC
1000	1,346	0.00	POP*GPC
1500	1,009	0.06	POP*GPC
1600	1,514	0.41	POP*GPC
1700	1,178	0.25	POP*GPC
1820	1,809	0.36	POP*GPC
1870	4,225	1.71	POP*GPC
1880	5,184	2.07	POP*GPC
1890	6,333	2.02	POP*GPC
1900	7,736	2.02	POP*GPC
1913	10,004	2.00	POP*GPC
1920	11,433	1.93	POP*GPC
1929	13,738	2.06	POP*GPC
1938	15,732	1.52	POP*GPC
1950	18,697	1.45	POP*GPC
1960	39,157	7.67	POP*GPC
1970	59,188	4.22	POP*GPC
1980	125,399	7.80	POP*GPC
1990	164,380	2.74	POP*GPC
2000	196,144	1.78	POP*GPC
2010	297,593	4.26	POP*GPC
2012	316,012	3.05	POP*GPC
2020	399,700	2.98	POP*GPC

Year	GDP at PPP, mil. 2012 doll.	Growth Rate	Source
2030	513,771	2.54	POP*GPC
DME Andorra			
0001	.	.	POP*GPC
1000	.	.	POP*GPC
1500	.	.	POP*GPC
1600	.	.	POP*GPC
1700	.	.	POP*GPC
1820	.	.	POP*GPC
1870	.	.	POP*GPC
1880	.	.	POP*GPC
1890	.	.	POP*GPC
1900	.	.	POP*GPC
1913	.	.	POP*GPC
1920	.	.	POP*GPC
1929	.	.	POP*GPC
1938	.	.	POP*GPC
1950	39	.	POP*GPC
1960	76	6.89	POP*GPC
1970	277	13.82	POP*GPC
1980	604	8.10	POP*GPC
1990	1,142	6.57	POP*GPC
2000	1,593	3.38	POP*GPC
2010	3,322	7.63	POP*GPC
2012	2,915	6.33	POP*GPC
2020	3,609	2.71	POP*GPC
2030	4,422	2.05	POP*GPC
AFR Angola			
0001	.	.	POP*GPC
1000	.	.	POP*GPC
1500	.	.	POP*GPC
1600	.	.	POP*GPC
1700	.	.	POP*GPC
1820	.	.	POP*GPC
1870	.	.	POP*GPC
1880	.	.	POP*GPC
1890	.	.	POP*GPC
1900	.	.	POP*GPC
1913	.	.	POP*GPC
1920	.	.	POP*GPC
1929	.	.	POP*GPC
1938	.	.	POP*GPC
1950	6,779	.	POP*GPC
1960	12,316	6.15	POP*GPC
1970	26,440	7.94	POP*GPC
1980	23,252	1.28	POP*GPC
1990	36,788	4.69	POP*GPC
2000	35,087	0.47	POP*GPC
2010	98,198	10.84	POP*GPC
2012	108,373	5.05	POP*GPC

Year	GDP at PPP, mil. 2012 doll.	Growth Rate	Source
2020	189,214	7.21	POP*GPC
2030	316,676	5.28	POP*GPC
LAM Anguilla			
0001	.	.	POP*GPC
1000	.	.	POP*GPC
1500	.	.	POP*GPC
1600	.	.	POP*GPC
1700	.	.	POP*GPC
1820	.	.	POP*GPC
1870	.	.	POP*GPC
1880	.	.	POP*GPC
1890	.	.	POP*GPC
1900	.	.	POP*GPC
1913	.	.	POP*GPC
1920	.	.	POP*GPC
1929	.	.	POP*GPC
1938	.	.	POP*GPC
1950	15	.	POP*GPC
1960	25	5.02	POP*GPC
1970	41	5.02	POP*GPC
1980	57	3.34	POP*GPC
1990	74	2.62	POP*GPC
2000	131	5.90	POP*GPC
2010	192	3.88	POP*GPC
2012	206	3.78	POP*GPC
2020	276	3.69	POP*GPC
2030	403	3.86	POP*GPC
LAM Antigua and Barbuda			
0001	.	.	POP*GPC
1000	.	.	POP*GPC
1500	.	.	POP*GPC
1600	.	.	POP*GPC
1700	.	.	POP*GPC
1820	.	.	POP*GPC
1870	.	.	POP*GPC
1880	.	.	POP*GPC
1890	.	.	POP*GPC
1900	.	.	POP*GPC
1913	.	.	POP*GPC
1920	.	.	POP*GPC
1929	.	.	POP*GPC
1938	.	.	POP*GPC
1950	128	.	POP*GPC
1960	211	5.12	POP*GPC
1970	350	5.16	POP*GPC
1980	504	3.72	POP*GPC
1990	987	6.95	POP*GPC
2000	1,438	3.83	POP*GPC
2010	1,710	1.75	POP*GPC

Year	GDP at PPP, mil. 2012 doll.	Growth Rate	Source
2012	1,714	0.10	POP*GPC
2020	2,168	2.98	POP*GPC
2030	2,843	2.75	POP*GPC
	LAM Argentina		
0001	74	.	POP*GPC
1000	212	0.11	POP*GPC
1500	387	0.12	POP*GPC
1600	331	0.16	POP*GPC
1700	536	0.48	POP*GPC
1820	1,070	0.58	POP*GPC
1870	3,685	2.50	POP*GPC
1880	6,472	5.80	POP*GPC
1890	11,369	5.80	POP*GPC
1900	20,240	5.94	POP*GPC
1913	45,472	6.42	POP*GPC
1920	48,157	0.82	POP*GPC
1929	79,216	5.69	POP*GPC
1938	87,450	1.10	POP*GPC
1950	133,837	3.61	POP*GPC
1960	172,520	2.57	POP*GPC
1970	252,581	3.89	POP*GPC
1980	319,241	2.37	POP*GPC
1990	271,910	1.59	POP*GPC
2000	422,190	4.50	POP*GPC
2010	671,145	4.74	POP*GPC
2012	744,067	5.29	POP*GPC
2020	1,026,210	4.10	POP*GPC
2030	1,382,594	3.03	POP*GPC
	USR Armenia		
0001	16	.	POP*GPC
1000	39	0.09	POP*GPC
1500	130	0.24	POP*GPC
1600	172	0.28	POP*GPC
1700	222	0.25	POP*GPC
1820	348	0.37	POP*GPC
1870	901	1.92	POP*GPC
1880	1,101	2.03	POP*GPC
1890	1,347	2.03	POP*GPC
1900	1,659	2.10	POP*GPC
1913	2,503	3.22	POP*GPC
1920	960	12.79	POP*GPC
1929	2,637	11.88	POP*GPC
1938	4,482	6.07	POP*GPC
1950	6,092	2.59	POP*GPC
1960	9,635	4.69	POP*GPC
1970	15,015	4.54	POP*GPC
1980	19,080	2.42	POP*GPC
1990	21,819	1.35	POP*GPC
2000	13,731	4.53	POP*GPC

Year	GDP at PPP, mil. 2012 doll.	Growth Rate	Source
2010	18,024	2.76	POP*GPC
2012	18,734	1.95	POP*GPC
2020	22,110	2.09	POP*GPC
2030	26,371	1.78	POP*GPC
	LAM Aruba		
0001	.	.	POP*GPC
1000	.	.	POP*GPC
1500	.	.	POP*GPC
1600	.	.	POP*GPC
1700	.	.	POP*GPC
1820	.	.	POP*GPC
1870	.	.	POP*GPC
1880	.	.	POP*GPC
1890	.	.	POP*GPC
1900	.	.	POP*GPC
1913	.	.	POP*GPC
1920	.	.	POP*GPC
1929	.	.	POP*GPC
1938	.	.	POP*GPC
1950	592	.	POP*GPC
1960	887	4.12	POP*GPC
1970	1,271	3.67	POP*GPC
1980	1,497	1.65	POP*GPC
1990	1,793	1.82	POP*GPC
2000	3,325	6.37	POP*GPC
2010	2,322	3.53	POP*GPC
2012	2,548	4.74	POP*GPC
2020	2,900	1.63	POP*GPC
2030	3,409	1.63	POP*GPC
	DME Australia		
0001	92	.	POP*GPC
1000	170	0.06	POP*GPC
1500	302	0.12	POP*GPC
1600	319	0.06	POP*GPC
1700	338	0.06	POP*GPC
1820	271	0.19	POP*GPC
1870	9,091	7.28	POP*GPC
1880	14,732	4.95	POP*GPC
1890	21,675	3.94	POP*GPC
1900	23,492	0.81	POP*GPC
1913	38,905	3.96	POP*GPC
1920	39,960	0.38	POP*GPC
1929	52,676	3.12	POP*GPC
1938	63,591	2.11	POP*GPC
1950	95,329	3.43	POP*GPC
1960	143,919	4.21	POP*GPC
1970	244,854	5.46	POP*GPC
1980	343,367	3.44	POP*GPC
1990	493,419	3.69	POP*GPC

Year	GDP at PPP, mil. 2012 doll.	Growth Rate	Source
2000	667,424	3.07	POP*GPC
2010	900,256	3.04	POP*GPC
2012	980,527	4.36	POP*GPC
2020	1,286,515	3.45	POP*GPC
2030	1,708,915	2.88	POP*GPC
DME Austria			
0001	333	.	POP*GPC
1000	466	0.03	POP*GPC
1500	2,213	0.31	POP*GPC
1600	3,274	0.39	POP*GPC
1700	3,885	0.17	POP*GPC
1820	6,421	0.42	POP*GPC
1870	13,177	1.45	POP*GPC
1880	16,075	2.01	POP*GPC
1890	20,621	2.52	POP*GPC
1900	26,938	2.71	POP*GPC
1913	36,692	2.41	POP*GPC
1920	24,364	5.68	POP*GPC
1929	38,574	5.24	POP*GPC
1938	37,609	0.28	POP*GPC
1950	40,218	0.56	POP*GPC
1960	75,661	6.52	POP*GPC
1970	125,553	5.20	POP*GPC
1980	187,356	4.08	POP*GPC
1990	235,443	2.31	POP*GPC
2000	314,605	2.94	POP*GPC
2010	357,777	1.29	POP*GPC
2012	373,132	2.12	POP*GPC
2020	450,975	2.40	POP*GPC
2030	560,929	2.21	POP*GPC
USR Azerbaijan			
0001	34	.	POP*GPC
1000	79	0.08	POP*GPC
1500	245	0.23	POP*GPC
1600	315	0.25	POP*GPC
1700	399	0.24	POP*GPC
1820	624	0.37	POP*GPC
1870	1,615	1.92	POP*GPC
1880	1,975	2.03	POP*GPC
1890	2,416	2.03	POP*GPC
1900	2,975	2.10	POP*GPC
1913	4,490	3.22	POP*GPC
1920	1,722	12.79	POP*GPC
1929	4,729	11.88	POP*GPC
1938	8,039	6.07	POP*GPC
1950	9,386	1.30	POP*GPC
1960	16,349	5.71	POP*GPC
1970	28,519	5.72	POP*GPC
1980	34,944	2.05	POP*GPC

Year	GDP at PPP, mil. 2012 doll.	Growth Rate	Source
1990	39,019	1.11	POP*GPC
2000	22,899	5.19	POP*GPC
2010	92,049	14.93	POP*GPC
2012	94,172	1.15	POP*GPC
2020	171,037	7.74	POP*GPC
2030	235,631	3.26	POP*GPC
	LAM Bahamas		
0001	.	.	POP*GPC
1000	.	.	POP*GPC
1500	.	.	POP*GPC
1600	.	.	POP*GPC
1700	.	.	POP*GPC
1820	.	.	POP*GPC
1870	.	.	POP*GPC
1880	.	.	POP*GPC
1890	.	.	POP*GPC
1900	.	.	POP*GPC
1913	.	.	POP*GPC
1920	.	.	POP*GPC
1929	.	.	POP*GPC
1938	.	.	POP*GPC
1950	1,183	.	POP*GPC
1960	2,258	6.68	POP*GPC
1970	4,785	7.80	POP*GPC
1980	6,538	3.17	POP*GPC
1990	8,804	3.02	POP*GPC
2000	10,619	1.89	POP*GPC
2010	10,919	0.28	POP*GPC
2012	11,282	1.65	POP*GPC
2020	12,732	1.52	POP*GPC
2030	14,943	1.61	POP*GPC
	MEA Bahrain		
0001	45	.	POP*GPC
1000	55	0.02	POP*GPC
1500	47	0.03	POP*GPC
1600	47	0.00	POP*GPC
1700	47	0.00	POP*GPC
1820	54	0.12	POP*GPC
1870	56	0.09	POP*GPC
1880	60	0.66	POP*GPC
1890	64	0.66	POP*GPC
1900	68	0.66	POP*GPC
1913	75	0.66	POP*GPC
1920	101	4.37	POP*GPC
1929	148	4.37	POP*GPC
1938	217	4.37	POP*GPC
1950	362	4.37	POP*GPC
1960	1,024	10.95	POP*GPC
1970	2,962	11.21	POP*GPC

Year	GDP at PPP, mil. 2012 doll.	Growth Rate	Source
1980	8,237	10.77	POP*GPC
1990	10,250	2.21	POP*GPC
2000	20,545	7.20	POP*GPC
2010	35,443	5.60	POP*GPC
2012	35,219	0.32	POP*GPC
2020	45,793	3.34	POP*GPC
2030	60,000	2.74	POP*GPC
	SAS Bangladesh		
0001	5,054	.	POP*GPC
1000	5,054	0.00	POP*GPC
1500	9,060	0.12	POP*GPC
1600	11,119	0.21	POP*GPC
1700	13,589	0.20	POP*GPC
1820	16,619	0.17	POP*GPC
1870	21,730	0.54	POP*GPC
1880	22,701	0.44	POP*GPC
1890	25,361	1.11	POP*GPC
1900	26,515	0.45	POP*GPC
1913	30,690	1.13	POP*GPC
1920	31,096	0.19	POP*GPC
1929	33,347	0.78	POP*GPC
1938	35,745	0.77	POP*GPC
1950	38,572	0.64	POP*GPC
1960	44,367	1.41	POP*GPC
1970	60,459	3.14	POP*GPC
1980	65,608	0.82	POP*GPC
1990	92,124	3.45	POP*GPC
2000	139,899	4.27	POP*GPC
2010	248,146	5.90	POP*GPC
2012	282,537	6.70	POP*GPC
2020	413,181	4.87	POP*GPC
2030	573,128	3.33	POP*GPC
	LAM Barbados		
0001	.	.	POP*GPC
1000	.	.	POP*GPC
1500	.	.	POP*GPC
1600	.	.	POP*GPC
1700	.	.	POP*GPC
1820	.	.	POP*GPC
1870	.	.	POP*GPC
1880	.	.	POP*GPC
1890	.	.	POP*GPC
1900	.	.	POP*GPC
1913	.	.	POP*GPC
1920	.	.	POP*GPC
1929	.	.	POP*GPC
1938	.	.	POP*GPC
1950	701	.	POP*GPC
1960	1,505	7.94	POP*GPC

Year	GDP at PPP, mil. 2012 doll.	Growth Rate	Source
1970	3,027	7.24	POP*GPC
1980	4,721	4.55	POP*GPC
1990	5,331	1.22	POP*GPC
2000	6,840	2.52	POP*GPC
2010	7,329	0.69	POP*GPC
2012	7,346	0.12	POP*GPC
2020	8,335	1.59	POP*GPC
2030	9,794	1.63	POP*GPC
	USR Belarus		
0001	43	.	POP*GPC
1000	122	0.10	POP*GPC
1500	466	0.27	POP*GPC
1600	645	0.32	POP*GPC
1700	950	0.39	POP*GPC
1820	2,366	0.76	POP*GPC
1870	5,268	1.61	POP*GPC
1880	6,442	2.03	POP*GPC
1890	7,878	2.03	POP*GPC
1900	9,702	2.10	POP*GPC
1913	14,641	3.22	POP*GPC
1920	5,615	12.79	POP*GPC
1929	15,422	11.88	POP*GPC
1938	26,215	6.07	POP*GPC
1950	29,738	1.06	POP*GPC
1960	39,233	2.81	POP*GPC
1970	54,984	3.43	POP*GPC
1980	65,289	1.73	POP*GPC
1990	74,589	1.34	POP*GPC
2000	66,070	1.21	POP*GPC
2010	135,571	7.45	POP*GPC
2012	144,993	3.42	POP*GPC
2020	201,719	4.21	POP*GPC
2030	249,912	2.17	POP*GPC
	DME Belgium		
0001	211	.	POP*GPC
1000	266	0.02	POP*GPC
1500	1,917	0.40	POP*GPC
1600	2,444	0.24	POP*GPC
1700	3,580	0.38	POP*GPC
1820	7,088	0.57	POP*GPC
1870	21,467	2.24	POP*GPC
1880	26,576	2.16	POP*GPC
1890	32,701	2.10	POP*GPC
1900	39,229	1.84	POP*GPC
1913	50,624	1.98	POP*GPC
1920	46,822	1.11	POP*GPC
1929	63,523	3.45	POP*GPC
1938	63,319	0.04	POP*GPC
1950	73,839	1.29	POP*GPC

Year	GDP at PPP, mil. 2012 doll.	Growth Rate	Source
1960	103,067	3.39	POP*GPC
1970	173,998	5.38	POP*GPC
1980	250,714	3.72	POP*GPC
1990	308,880	2.11	POP*GPC
2000	385,381	2.24	POP*GPC
2010	445,249	1.45	POP*GPC
2012	451,494	0.70	POP*GPC
2020	530,792	2.04	POP*GPC
2030	655,550	2.13	POP*GPC
	LAM Belize		
0001	.	.	POP*GPC
1000	.	.	POP*GPC
1500	.	.	POP*GPC
1600	.	.	POP*GPC
1700	.	.	POP*GPC
1820	.	.	POP*GPC
1870	.	.	POP*GPC
1880	.	.	POP*GPC
1890	.	.	POP*GPC
1900	.	.	POP*GPC
1913	.	.	POP*GPC
1920	.	.	POP*GPC
1929	.	.	POP*GPC
1938	.	.	POP*GPC
1950	172	.	POP*GPC
1960	264	4.36	POP*GPC
1970	407	4.44	POP*GPC
1980	587	3.72	POP*GPC
1990	941	4.84	POP*GPC
2000	1,623	5.60	POP*GPC
2010	2,430	4.12	POP*GPC
2012	2,628	3.99	POP*GPC
2020	3,576	3.93	POP*GPC
2030	5,018	3.45	POP*GPC
	AFR Benin		
0001	.	.	POP*GPC
1000	.	.	POP*GPC
1500	.	.	POP*GPC
1600	.	.	POP*GPC
1700	.	.	POP*GPC
1820	.	.	POP*GPC
1870	.	.	POP*GPC
1880	.	.	POP*GPC
1890	.	.	POP*GPC
1900	.	.	POP*GPC
1913	.	.	POP*GPC
1920	.	.	POP*GPC
1929	.	.	POP*GPC
1938	.	.	POP*GPC

Year	GDP at PPP, mil. 2012 doll.	Growth Rate	Source
1950	2,838	.	POP*GPC
1960	4,492	4.70	POP*GPC
1970	5,068	1.22	POP*GPC
1980	5,893	1.52	POP*GPC
1990	7,642	2.63	POP*GPC
2000	11,095	3.80	POP*GPC
2010	14,172	2.48	POP*GPC
2012	14,556	1.35	POP*GPC
2020	18,171	2.81	POP*GPC
2030	24,503	3.03	POP*GPC
	DME Bermuda		
0001	.	.	POP*GPC
1000	.	.	POP*GPC
1500	.	.	POP*GPC
1600	.	.	POP*GPC
1700	.	.	POP*GPC
1820	.	.	POP*GPC
1870	.	.	POP*GPC
1880	.	.	POP*GPC
1890	.	.	POP*GPC
1900	.	.	POP*GPC
1913	.	.	POP*GPC
1920	.	.	POP*GPC
1929	.	.	POP*GPC
1938	.	.	POP*GPC
1950	102	.	POP*GPC
1960	198	6.89	POP*GPC
1970	412	7.60	POP*GPC
1980	547	2.87	POP*GPC
1990	648	1.72	POP*GPC
2000	2,149	12.74	POP*GPC
2010	5,493	9.84	POP*GPC
2012	5,773	2.51	POP*GPC
2020	11,003	8.40	POP*GPC
2030	14,428	2.75	POP*GPC
	SAS Bhutan		
0001	.	.	POP*GPC
1000	.	.	POP*GPC
1500	.	.	POP*GPC
1600	.	.	POP*GPC
1700	.	.	POP*GPC
1820	.	.	POP*GPC
1870	.	.	POP*GPC
1880	.	.	POP*GPC
1890	.	.	POP*GPC
1900	.	.	POP*GPC
1913	.	.	POP*GPC
1920	.	.	POP*GPC
1929	.	.	POP*GPC

Year	GDP at PPP, mil. 2012 doll.	Growth Rate	Source
1938	.	.	POP*GPC
1950	132	.	POP*GPC
1960	178	3.00	POP*GPC
1970	276	4.49	POP*GPC
1980	462	5.31	POP*GPC
1990	1,261	10.56	POP*GPC
2000	1,810	3.68	POP*GPC
2010	4,169	8.70	POP*GPC
2012	4,942	8.88	POP*GPC
2020	8,648	7.24	POP*GPC
2030	12,239	3.53	POP*GPC
LAM Bolivia			
0001	154	.	POP*GPC
1000	441	0.11	POP*GPC
1500	807	0.12	POP*GPC
1600	511	0.46	POP*GPC
1700	615	0.19	POP*GPC
1820	863	0.28	POP*GPC
1870	1,201	0.66	POP*GPC
1880	1,492	2.20	POP*GPC
1890	1,854	2.20	POP*GPC
1900	2,304	2.20	POP*GPC
1913	3,209	2.58	POP*GPC
1920	4,056	3.40	POP*GPC
1929	5,163	2.72	POP*GPC
1938	6,572	2.72	POP*GPC
1950	8,150	1.81	POP*GPC
1960	8,324	0.21	POP*GPC
1970	14,454	5.67	POP*GPC
1980	21,910	4.25	POP*GPC
1990	21,467	0.20	POP*GPC
2000	32,489	4.23	POP*GPC
2010	47,859	3.95	POP*GPC
2012	53,557	5.79	POP*GPC
2020	72,394	3.84	POP*GPC
2030	101,854	3.47	POP*GPC
EEU Bosnia			
0001	85	.	POP*GPC
1000	136	0.05	POP*GPC
1500	217	0.09	POP*GPC
1600	278	0.25	POP*GPC
1700	293	0.05	POP*GPC
1820	592	0.59	POP*GPC
1870	963	0.98	POP*GPC
1880	1,050	0.86	POP*GPC
1890	1,350	2.54	POP*GPC
1900	1,665	2.12	POP*GPC
1913	2,373	2.76	POP*GPC
1920	2,116	1.63	POP*GPC

Year	GDP at PPP, mil. 2012 doll.	Growth Rate	Source
1929	3,199	4.70	POP*GPC
1938	3,603	1.33	POP*GPC
1950	4,176	1.24	POP*GPC
1960	8,401	7.24	POP*GPC
1970	15,496	6.31	POP*GPC
1980	29,560	6.67	POP*GPC
1990	30,786	0.41	POP*GPC
2000	22,282	3.18	POP*GPC
2010	35,722	4.83	POP*GPC
2012	36,095	0.52	POP*GPC
2020	43,929	2.49	POP*GPC
2030	52,199	1.74	POP*GPC
AFR Botswana			
0001	10	.	POP*GPC
1000	18	0.06	POP*GPC
1500	42	0.17	POP*GPC
1600	44	0.04	POP*GPC
1700	45	0.04	POP*GPC
1820	52	0.12	POP*GPC
1870	92	1.14	POP*GPC
1880	103	1.14	POP*GPC
1890	115	1.14	POP*GPC
1900	129	1.14	POP*GPC
1913	149	1.14	POP*GPC
1920	162	1.14	POP*GPC
1929	179	1.14	POP*GPC
1938	198	1.14	POP*GPC
1950	235	1.42	POP*GPC
1960	383	5.03	POP*GPC
1970	947	9.46	POP*GPC
1980	4,271	16.25	POP*GPC
1990	12,061	10.94	POP*GPC
2000	20,008	5.19	POP*GPC
2010	29,366	3.91	POP*GPC
2012	33,132	6.22	POP*GPC
2020	51,661	5.71	POP*GPC
2030	75,674	3.89	POP*GPC
LAM Brazil			
0001	123	.	POP*GPC
1000	350	0.10	POP*GPC
1500	636	0.12	POP*GPC
1600	536	0.17	POP*GPC
1700	898	0.52	POP*GPC
1820	4,556	1.36	POP*GPC
1870	10,931	1.77	POP*GPC
1880	13,879	2.42	POP*GPC
1890	17,642	2.43	POP*GPC
1900	19,080	0.79	POP*GPC
1913	30,027	3.55	POP*GPC

Year	GDP at PPP, mil. 2012 doll.	Growth Rate	Source
1920	41,296	4.66	POP*GPC
1929	58,526	3.95	POP*GPC
1938	78,831	3.36	POP*GPC
1950	141,221	4.98	POP*GPC
1960	270,161	6.70	POP*GPC
1970	474,229	5.79	POP*GPC
1980	1,013,479	7.89	POP*GPC
1990	1,188,141	1.60	POP*GPC
2000	1,526,600	2.54	POP*GPC
2010	2,192,294	3.69	POP*GPC
2012	2,274,691	1.86	POP*GPC
2020	2,837,518	2.80	POP*GPC
2030	3,624,210	2.48	POP*GPC
SEA Brunei			
0001	.	.	POP*GPC
1000	.	.	POP*GPC
1500	.	.	POP*GPC
1600	.	.	POP*GPC
1700	.	.	POP*GPC
1820	.	.	POP*GPC
1870	.	.	POP*GPC
1880	.	.	POP*GPC
1890	.	.	POP*GPC
1900	.	.	POP*GPC
1913	.	.	POP*GPC
1920	.	.	POP*GPC
1929	.	.	POP*GPC
1938	.	.	POP*GPC
1950	351	.	POP*GPC
1960	1,155	12.66	POP*GPC
1970	3,310	11.11	POP*GPC
1980	10,387	12.11	POP*GPC
1990	7,137	3.68	POP*GPC
2000	17,985	9.68	POP*GPC
2010	19,910	1.02	POP*GPC
2012	21,005	2.71	POP*GPC
2020	28,936	4.09	POP*GPC
2030	40,123	3.32	POP*GPC
EEU Bulgaria			
0001	333	.	POP*GPC
1000	501	0.04	POP*GPC
1500	726	0.07	POP*GPC
1600	1,254	0.55	POP*GPC
1700	1,387	0.10	POP*GPC
1820	2,735	0.57	POP*GPC
1870	3,399	0.44	POP*GPC
1880	4,553	2.96	POP*GPC
1890	6,097	2.96	POP*GPC
1900	7,655	2.30	POP*GPC

Year	GDP at PPP, mil. 2012 doll.	Growth Rate	Source
1913	11,330	3.06	POP*GPC
1920	7,215	6.24	POP*GPC
1929	10,987	4.78	POP*GPC
1938	16,383	4.54	POP*GPC
1950	18,733	1.12	POP*GPC
1960	35,322	6.55	POP*GPC
1970	61,609	5.72	POP*GPC
1980	80,511	2.71	POP*GPC
1990	102,003	2.39	POP*GPC
2000	75,118	3.01	POP*GPC
2010	114,273	4.28	POP*GPC
2012	117,270	1.30	POP*GPC
2020	145,395	2.72	POP*GPC
2030	172,655	1.73	POP*GPC
AFR Burkina Faso			
0001	.	.	POP*GPC
1000	.	.	POP*GPC
1500	.	.	POP*GPC
1600	.	.	POP*GPC
1700	.	.	POP*GPC
1820	.	.	POP*GPC
1870	.	.	POP*GPC
1880	.	.	POP*GPC
1890	.	.	POP*GPC
1900	.	.	POP*GPC
1913	.	.	POP*GPC
1920	.	.	POP*GPC
1929	.	.	POP*GPC
1938	.	.	POP*GPC
1950	3,246	.	POP*GPC
1960	4,216	2.65	POP*GPC
1970	5,265	2.25	POP*GPC
1980	5,694	0.79	POP*GPC
1990	8,023	3.49	POP*GPC
2000	12,901	4.86	POP*GPC
2010	22,722	5.82	POP*GPC
2012	25,904	6.77	POP*GPC
2020	39,799	5.51	POP*GPC
2030	64,344	4.92	POP*GPC
CPA Burma			
0001	249	.	POP*GPC
1000	678	0.10	POP*GPC
1500	1,579	0.17	POP*GPC
1600	1,864	0.17	POP*GPC
1700	2,156	0.15	POP*GPC
1820	2,765	0.21	POP*GPC
1870	3,348	0.38	POP*GPC
1880	4,776	3.62	POP*GPC
1890	6,813	3.62	POP*GPC

Year	GDP at PPP, mil. 2012 doll.	Growth Rate	Source
1900	9,939	3.85	POP*GPC
1913	13,212	2.21	POP*GPC
1920	15,003	1.83	POP*GPC
1929	19,459	2.93	POP*GPC
1938	18,696	0.44	POP*GPC
1950	12,076	3.58	POP*GPC
1960	19,469	4.89	POP*GPC
1970	26,244	3.03	POP*GPC
1980	39,954	4.29	POP*GPC
1990	47,273	1.70	POP*GPC
2000	81,091	5.54	POP*GPC
2010	81,673	0.07	POP*GPC
2012	87,322	3.40	POP*GPC
2020	106,221	2.48	POP*GPC
2030	135,005	2.43	POP*GPC
AFR Burundi			
0001	9	.	POP*GPC
1000	116	0.26	POP*GPC
1500	275	0.17	POP*GPC
1600	333	0.19	POP*GPC
1700	396	0.17	POP*GPC
1820	541	0.26	POP*GPC
1870	764	0.69	POP*GPC
1880	819	0.70	POP*GPC
1890	878	0.70	POP*GPC
1900	941	0.70	POP*GPC
1913	1,030	0.70	POP*GPC
1920	1,081	0.70	POP*GPC
1929	1,151	0.70	POP*GPC
1938	1,225	0.70	POP*GPC
1950	1,331	0.70	POP*GPC
1960	1,610	1.92	POP*GPC
1970	1,872	1.52	POP*GPC
1980	2,157	1.43	POP*GPC
1990	2,877	2.92	POP*GPC
2000	3,522	2.04	POP*GPC
2010	4,631	2.77	POP*GPC
2012	4,813	1.95	POP*GPC
2020	5,621	1.96	POP*GPC
2030	6,802	1.92	POP*GPC
CPA Cambodia			
0001	133	.	POP*GPC
1000	344	0.10	POP*GPC
1500	766	0.16	POP*GPC
1600	904	0.17	POP*GPC
1700	1,046	0.15	POP*GPC
1820	1,342	0.21	POP*GPC
1870	1,465	0.18	POP*GPC

Year	GDP at PPP, mil. 2012 doll.	Growth Rate	Source
1880	1,667	1.30	POP*GPC
1890	1,922	1.43	POP*GPC
1900	2,215	1.43	POP*GPC
1913	2,666	1.43	POP*GPC
1920	2,825	0.83	POP*GPC
1929	3,044	0.83	POP*GPC
1938	3,280	0.83	POP*GPC
1950	3,624	0.83	POP*GPC
1960	6,124	5.39	POP*GPC
1970	7,535	2.09	POP*GPC
1980	8,623	1.36	POP*GPC
1990	12,458	3.75	POP*GPC
2000	16,859	3.07	POP*GPC
2010	32,552	6.80	POP*GPC
2012	36,689	6.16	POP*GPC
2020	54,044	4.96	POP*GPC
2030	76,963	3.60	POP*GPC
	AFR CAMEROON		
0001	.	.	POP*GPC
1000	.	.	POP*GPC
1500	.	.	POP*GPC
1600	.	.	POP*GPC
1700	.	.	POP*GPC
1820	.	.	POP*GPC
1870	.	.	POP*GPC
1880	.	.	POP*GPC
1890	.	.	POP*GPC
1900	.	.	POP*GPC
1913	.	.	POP*GPC
1920	.	.	POP*GPC
1929	.	.	POP*GPC
1938	.	.	POP*GPC
1950	5,132	.	POP*GPC
1960	7,513	3.88	POP*GPC
1970	11,942	4.74	POP*GPC
1980	20,608	5.61	POP*GPC
1990	28,315	3.23	POP*GPC
2000	32,505	1.39	POP*GPC
2010	43,862	3.04	POP*GPC
2012	47,747	4.33	POP*GPC
2020	60,556	3.02	POP*GPC
2030	81,736	3.04	POP*GPC
	DME CANADA		
0001	28	.	POP*GPC
1000	78	0.10	POP*GPC
1500	152	0.13	POP*GPC
1600	160	0.05	POP*GPC
1700	135	0.17	POP*GPC

Year	GDP at PPP, mil. 2012 doll.	Growth Rate	Source
1820	1,154	1.81	POP*GPC
1870	10,029	4.42	POP*GPC
1880	12,458	2.19	POP*GPC
1890	18,301	3.92	POP*GPC
1900	24,858	3.11	POP*GPC
1913	54,641	6.25	POP*GPC
1920	53,156	0.39	POP*GPC
1929	81,677	4.89	POP*GPC
1938	81,467	0.03	POP*GPC
1950	159,856	5.78	POP*GPC
1960	247,856	4.48	POP*GPC
1970	418,504	5.38	POP*GPC
1980	641,347	4.36	POP*GPC
1990	847,230	2.82	POP*GPC
2000	1,138,465	3.00	POP*GPC
2010	1,341,418	1.65	POP*GPC
2012	1,416,659	2.77	POP*GPC
2020	1,690,602	2.23	POP*GPC
2030	2,131,855	2.35	POP*GPC
AFR Cape Verde			
0001	.	.	POP*GPC
1000	.	.	POP*GPC
1500	.	.	POP*GPC
1600	.	.	POP*GPC
1700	.	.	POP*GPC
1820	.	.	POP*GPC
1870	.	.	POP*GPC
1880	.	.	POP*GPC
1890	.	.	POP*GPC
1900	.	.	POP*GPC
1913	.	.	POP*GPC
1920	.	.	POP*GPC
1929	.	.	POP*GPC
1938	.	.	POP*GPC
1950	103	.	POP*GPC
1960	148	3.69	POP*GPC
1970	205	3.35	POP*GPC
1980	268	2.69	POP*GPC
1990	440	5.09	POP*GPC
2000	1,202	10.57	POP*GPC
2010	2,260	6.52	POP*GPC
2012	2,445	4.01	POP*GPC
2020	3,979	6.28	POP*GPC
2030	5,604	3.48	POP*GPC
LAM Cayman Islands			
0001	.	.	POP*GPC
1000	.	.	POP*GPC
1500	.	.	POP*GPC
1600	.	.	POP*GPC

Year	GDP at PPP, mil. 2012 doll.	Growth Rate	Source
1700	.	.	POP*GPC
1820	.	.	POP*GPC
1870	.	.	POP*GPC
1880	.	.	POP*GPC
1890	.	.	POP*GPC
1900	.	.	POP*GPC
1913	.	.	POP*GPC
1920	.	.	POP*GPC
1929	.	.	POP*GPC
1938	.	.	POP*GPC
1950	94	.	POP*GPC
1960	166	5.80	POP*GPC
1970	273	5.12	POP*GPC
1980	550	7.26	POP*GPC
1990	953	5.65	POP*GPC
2000	1,607	5.36	POP*GPC
2010	2,725	5.42	POP*GPC
2012	2,814	1.62	POP*GPC
2020	3,402	2.40	POP*GPC
2030	4,257	2.27	POP*GPC

AFR Central African Republic

Year	GDP at PPP, mil. 2012 doll.	Growth Rate	Source
0001	.	.	POP*GPC
1000	.	.	POP*GPC
1500	.	.	POP*GPC
1600	.	.	POP*GPC
1700	.	.	POP*GPC
1820	.	.	POP*GPC
1870	.	.	POP*GPC
1880	.	.	POP*GPC
1890	.	.	POP*GPC
1900	.	.	POP*GPC
1913	.	.	POP*GPC
1920	.	.	POP*GPC
1929	.	.	POP*GPC
1938	.	.	POP*GPC
1950	1,587	.	POP*GPC
1960	1,994	2.31	POP*GPC
1970	2,270	1.31	POP*GPC
1980	2,338	0.29	POP*GPC
1990	2,653	1.27	POP*GPC
2000	3,072	1.48	POP*GPC
2010	4,817	4.60	POP*GPC
2012	5,445	6.32	POP*GPC
2020	7,443	3.99	POP*GPC
2030	10,877	3.87	POP*GPC

Year	GDP at PPP, mil. 2012 doll.	Growth Rate	Source
AFR Chad			
0001	.	.	POP*GPC
1000	.	.	POP*GPC
1500	.	.	POP*GPC
1600	.	.	POP*GPC
1700	.	.	POP*GPC
1820	.	.	POP*GPC
1870	.	.	POP*GPC
1880	.	.	POP*GPC
1890	.	.	POP*GPC
1900	.	.	POP*GPC
1913	.	.	POP*GPC
1920	.	.	POP*GPC
1929	.	.	POP*GPC
1938	.	.	POP*GPC
1950	1,943	.	POP*GPC
1960	3,111	4.82	POP*GPC
1970	4,027	2.62	POP*GPC
1980	3,765	0.67	POP*GPC
1990	6,366	5.39	POP*GPC
2000	8,340	2.74	POP*GPC
2010	24,316	11.29	POP*GPC
2012	26,338	4.07	POP*GPC
2020	44,294	6.71	POP*GPC
2030	72,578	5.06	POP*GPC
LAM Chile			
0001	106	.	POP*GPC
1000	303	0.11	POP*GPC
1500	552	0.12	POP*GPC
1600	394	0.34	POP*GPC
1700	528	0.29	POP*GPC
1820	837	0.39	POP*GPC
1870	3,926	3.14	POP*GPC
1880	5,472	3.38	POP*GPC
1890	7,627	3.38	POP*GPC
1900	10,216	2.96	POP*GPC
1913	16,043	3.53	POP*GPC
1920	16,390	0.31	POP*GPC
1929	25,773	5.16	POP*GPC
1938	27,191	0.60	POP*GPC
1950	36,420	2.47	POP*GPC
1960	47,239	2.64	POP*GPC
1970	66,850	3.53	POP*GPC
1980	76,823	1.40	POP*GPC
1990	114,080	4.03	POP*GPC
2000	218,952	6.74	POP*GPC
2010	314,923	3.70	POP*GPC
2012	356,552	6.40	POP*GPC
2020	510,950	4.60	POP*GPC

Year	GDP at PPP, mil. 2012 doll.	Growth Rate	Source
2030	689,931	3.05	POP*GPC
	CPA China		
0001	41,969	.	POP*GPC
1000	41,547	0.00	POP*GPC
1500	96,708	0.17	POP*GPC
1600	150,225	0.44	POP*GPC
1700	129,569	0.15	POP*GPC
1820	357,724	0.85	POP*GPC
1870	296,914	0.37	POP*GPC
1880	308,076	0.37	POP*GPC
1890	321,107	0.42	POP*GPC
1900	341,137	0.61	POP*GPC
1913	377,600	0.78	POP*GPC
1920	410,924	1.22	POP*GPC
1929	428,529	0.47	POP*GPC
1938	451,450	0.58	POP*GPC
1950	386,474	1.29	POP*GPC
1960	552,968	3.65	POP*GPC
1970	647,609	1.59	POP*GPC
1980	856,698	2.84	POP*GPC
1990	1,988,657	8.79	POP*GPC
2000	4,154,457	7.65	POP*GPC
2010	10,528,805	9.75	POP*GPC
2012	12,270,138	7.95	POP*GPC
2020	22,998,958	8.17	POP*GPC
2030	29,893,111	2.66	POP*GPC
	LAM Colombia		
0001	159	.	POP*GPC
1000	446	0.10	POP*GPC
1500	799	0.12	POP*GPC
1600	503	0.46	POP*GPC
1700	602	0.18	POP*GPC
1820	1,072	0.48	POP*GPC
1870	2,178	1.43	POP*GPC
1880	3,068	3.49	POP*GPC
1890	4,322	3.49	POP*GPC
1900	6,087	3.48	POP*GPC
1913	10,048	3.93	POP*GPC
1920	12,202	2.81	POP*GPC
1929	18,419	4.68	POP*GPC
1938	25,097	3.50	POP*GPC
1950	42,343	4.46	POP*GPC
1960	60,816	3.69	POP*GPC
1970	98,670	4.96	POP*GPC
1980	164,505	5.24	POP*GPC
1990	234,999	3.63	POP*GPC
2000	294,334	2.28	POP*GPC
2010	426,821	3.79	POP*GPC
2012	471,983	5.16	POP*GPC

Year	GDP at PPP, mil. 2012 doll.	Growth Rate	Source
2020	614,409	3.35	POP*GPC
2030	810,866	2.81	POP*GPC
AFR Comoros			
0001	.	.	POP*GPC
1000	.	.	POP*GPC
1500	.	.	POP*GPC
1600	.	.	POP*GPC
1700	.	.	POP*GPC
1820	.	.	POP*GPC
1870	.	.	POP*GPC
1880	.	.	POP*GPC
1890	.	.	POP*GPC
1900	.	.	POP*GPC
1913	.	.	POP*GPC
1920	.	.	POP*GPC
1929	.	.	POP*GPC
1938	.	.	POP*GPC
1950	130	.	POP*GPC
1960	252	6.85	POP*GPC
1970	529	7.71	POP*GPC
1980	458	1.44	POP*GPC
1990	620	3.08	POP*GPC
2000	704	1.29	POP*GPC
2010	852	1.92	POP*GPC
2012	891	2.26	POP*GPC
2020	1,045	2.01	POP*GPC
2030	1,277	2.02	POP*GPC
AFR Congo, Democratic Republic of the			
0001	.	.	POP*GPC
1000	.	.	POP*GPC
1500	.	.	POP*GPC
1600	.	.	POP*GPC
1700	.	.	POP*GPC
1820	.	.	POP*GPC
1870	.	.	POP*GPC
1880	.	.	POP*GPC
1890	.	.	POP*GPC
1900	.	.	POP*GPC
1913	.	.	POP*GPC
1920	.	.	POP*GPC
1929	.	.	POP*GPC
1938	.	.	POP*GPC
1950	12,103	.	POP*GPC
1960	17,701	3.87	POP*GPC
1970	23,617	2.93	POP*GPC
1980	24,317	0.29	POP*GPC
1990	27,049	1.07	POP*GPC
2000	15,612	5.35	POP*GPC
2010	25,292	4.94	POP*GPC

Year	GDP at PPP, mil. 2012 doll.	Growth Rate	Source
2012	28,888	6.87	POP*GPC
2020	40,006	4.15	POP*GPC
2030	58,795	3.93	POP*GPC

AFR Congo, Republic of the

Year	GDP at PPP, mil. 2012 doll.	Growth Rate	Source
0001	.	.	POP*GPC
1000	.	.	POP*GPC
1500	.	.	POP*GPC
1600	.	.	POP*GPC
1700	.	.	POP*GPC
1820	.	.	POP*GPC
1870	.	.	POP*GPC
1880	.	.	POP*GPC
1890	.	.	POP*GPC
1900	.	.	POP*GPC
1913	.	.	POP*GPC
1920	.	.	POP*GPC
1929	.	.	POP*GPC
1938	.	.	POP*GPC
1950	1,630	.	POP*GPC
1960	2,419	4.03	POP*GPC
1970	3,816	4.66	POP*GPC
1980	6,670	5.74	POP*GPC
1990	10,508	4.65	POP*GPC
2000	11,417	0.83	POP*GPC
2010	17,326	4.26	POP*GPC
2012	18,411	3.08	POP*GPC
2020	24,207	3.48	POP*GPC
2030	34,713	3.67	POP*GPC

SEA Cook Islands

Year	GDP at PPP, mil. 2012 doll.	Growth Rate	Source
0001	.	.	POP*GPC
1000	.	.	POP*GPC
1500	.	.	POP*GPC
1600	.	.	POP*GPC
1700	.	.	POP*GPC
1820	.	.	POP*GPC
1870	.	.	POP*GPC
1880	.	.	POP*GPC
1890	.	.	POP*GPC
1900	.	.	POP*GPC
1913	.	.	POP*GPC
1920	.	.	POP*GPC
1929	.	.	POP*GPC
1938	.	.	POP*GPC
1950	20	.	POP*GPC
1960	30	4.48	POP*GPC
1970	47	4.48	POP*GPC
1980	64	3.11	POP*GPC
1990	82	2.53	POP*GPC
2000	130	4.74	POP*GPC

Year	GDP at PPP, mil. 2012 doll.	Growth Rate	Source
2010	118	0.97	POP*GPC
2012	115	1.44	POP*GPC
2020	99	1.83	POP*GPC
2030	74	2.87	POP*GPC
	LAM Costa Rica		
0001	9	.	POP*GPC
1000	26	0.11	POP*GPC
1500	47	0.12	POP*GPC
1600	30	0.46	POP*GPC
1700	36	0.19	POP*GPC
1820	51	0.28	POP*GPC
1870	113	1.61	POP*GPC
1880	174	4.43	POP*GPC
1890	268	4.43	POP*GPC
1900	413	4.43	POP*GPC
1913	649	3.55	POP*GPC
1920	1,067	7.36	POP*GPC
1929	1,213	1.43	POP*GPC
1938	1,732	4.04	POP*GPC
1950	2,648	3.60	POP*GPC
1960	5,348	7.28	POP*GPC
1970	10,161	6.63	POP*GPC
1980	17,056	5.32	POP*GPC
1990	22,014	2.58	POP*GPC
2000	35,381	4.86	POP*GPC
2010	50,841	3.69	POP*GPC
2012	55,435	4.42	POP*GPC
2020	74,953	3.84	POP*GPC
2030	100,078	2.93	POP*GPC
	EEU Croatia		
0001	146	.	POP*GPC
1000	255	0.06	POP*GPC
1500	436	0.11	POP*GPC
1600	589	0.30	POP*GPC
1700	652	0.10	POP*GPC
1820	1,393	0.63	POP*GPC
1870	2,316	1.02	POP*GPC
1880	2,978	2.54	POP*GPC
1890	3,828	2.54	POP*GPC
1900	4,723	2.12	POP*GPC
1913	6,732	2.76	POP*GPC
1920	6,002	1.63	POP*GPC
1929	9,073	4.70	POP*GPC
1938	10,221	1.33	POP*GPC
1950	11,846	1.24	POP*GPC
1960	21,233	6.01	POP*GPC
1970	36,838	5.66	POP*GPC
1980	67,568	6.25	POP*GPC
1990	65,672	0.28	POP*GPC

Year	GDP at PPP, mil. 2012 doll.	Growth Rate	Source
2000	68,895	0.48	POP*GPC
2010	89,482	2.65	POP*GPC
2012	89,417	0.04	POP*GPC
2020	104,308	1.94	POP*GPC
2030	123,267	1.68	POP*GPC
LAM Cuba			
0001	14	.	POP*GPC
1000	41	0.11	POP*GPC
1500	78	0.13	POP*GPC
1600	33	0.85	POP*GPC
1700	88	0.99	POP*GPC
1820	506	1.46	POP*GPC
1870	1,140	1.64	POP*GPC
1880	1,461	2.52	POP*GPC
1890	1,873	2.52	POP*GPC
1900	2,402	2.52	POP*GPC
1913	4,422	4.81	POP*GPC
1920	6,067	4.62	POP*GPC
1929	9,597	5.23	POP*GPC
1938	9,410	0.22	POP*GPC
1950	18,954	6.01	POP*GPC
1960	22,713	1.83	POP*GPC
1970	26,117	1.41	POP*GPC
1980	38,270	3.89	POP*GPC
1990	46,006	1.86	POP*GPC
2000	32,631	3.38	POP*GPC
2010	118,381	13.75	POP*GPC
2012	121,973	1.51	POP*GPC
2020	208,186	6.91	POP*GPC
2030	268,436	2.57	POP*GPC
LAM Curacao			
0001	.	.	POP*GPC
1000	.	.	POP*GPC
1500	.	.	POP*GPC
1600	.	.	POP*GPC
1700	.	.	POP*GPC
1820	.	.	POP*GPC
1870	.	.	POP*GPC
1880	.	.	POP*GPC
1890	.	.	POP*GPC
1900	.	.	POP*GPC
1913	.	.	POP*GPC
1920	.	.	POP*GPC
1929	.	.	POP*GPC
1938	.	.	POP*GPC
1950	526	.	POP*GPC
1960	893	5.44	POP*GPC
1970	1,461	5.04	POP*GPC
1980	1,461	0.00	POP*GPC

Year	GDP at PPP, mil. 2012 doll.	Growth Rate	Source
1990	1,204	1.91	POP*GPC
2000	1,689	3.44	POP*GPC
2010	3,004	5.92	POP*GPC
2012	3,174	2.79	POP*GPC
2020	4,420	4.23	POP*GPC
2030	5,751	2.67	POP*GPC
MEA Cyprus			
0001	172	.	POP*GPC
1000	141	0.02	POP*GPC
1500	43	0.23	POP*GPC
1600	73	0.52	POP*GPC
1700	80	0.09	POP*GPC
1820	149	0.52	POP*GPC
1870	323	1.56	POP*GPC
1880	414	2.51	POP*GPC
1890	530	2.51	POP*GPC
1900	673	2.42	POP*GPC
1913	867	1.97	POP*GPC
1920	1,073	3.08	POP*GPC
1929	1,476	3.61	POP*GPC
1938	1,899	2.84	POP*GPC
1950	1,455	2.19	POP*GPC
1960	2,917	7.20	POP*GPC
1970	5,401	6.35	POP*GPC
1980	9,692	6.02	POP*GPC
1990	18,189	6.50	POP*GPC
2000	26,979	4.02	POP*GPC
2010	36,756	3.14	POP*GPC
2012	35,793	1.32	POP*GPC
2020	46,631	3.36	POP*GPC
2030	61,660	2.83	POP*GPC
EEU Czech Republic			
0001	329	.	POP*GPC
1000	647	0.07	POP*GPC
1500	2,179	0.24	POP*GPC
1600	3,611	0.51	POP*GPC
1700	3,993	0.10	POP*GPC
1820	7,657	0.54	POP*GPC
1870	13,923	1.20	POP*GPC
1880	16,666	1.81	POP*GPC
1890	19,949	1.81	POP*GPC
1900	24,728	2.17	POP*GPC
1913	32,700	2.17	POP*GPC
1920	29,552	1.44	POP*GPC
1929	49,749	5.96	POP*GPC
1938	49,573	0.04	POP*GPC
1950	51,090	0.25	POP*GPC
1960	86,179	5.37	POP*GPC
1970	121,797	3.52	POP*GPC

Year	GDP at PPP, mil. 2012 doll.	Growth Rate	Source
1980	171,682	3.49	POP*GPC
1990	199,321	1.50	POP*GPC
2000	205,023	0.28	POP*GPC
2010	285,592	3.37	POP*GPC
2012	287,954	0.41	POP*GPC
2020	348,641	2.42	POP*GPC
2030	424,243	1.98	POP*GPC
	DME Denmark		
0001	87	.	POP*GPC
1000	285	0.12	POP*GPC
1500	693	0.18	POP*GPC
1600	890	0.25	POP*GPC
1700	1,138	0.25	POP*GPC
1820	2,303	0.59	POP*GPC
1870	5,918	1.91	POP*GPC
1880	7,102	1.84	POP*GPC
1890	9,057	2.46	POP*GPC
1900	12,091	2.93	POP*GPC
1913	18,261	3.22	POP*GPC
1920	20,252	1.49	POP*GPC
1929	27,939	3.64	POP*GPC
1938	34,056	2.22	POP*GPC
1950	46,403	2.61	POP*GPC
1960	65,059	3.44	POP*GPC
1970	105,380	4.94	POP*GPC
1980	133,715	2.41	POP*GPC
1990	168,569	2.34	POP*GPC
2000	222,946	2.84	POP*GPC
2010	237,363	0.63	POP*GPC
2012	239,819	0.52	POP*GPC
2020	272,063	1.59	POP*GPC
2030	325,413	1.81	POP*GPC
	AFR Djibouti		
0001	.	.	POP*GPC
1000	.	.	POP*GPC
1500	.	.	POP*GPC
1600	.	.	POP*GPC
1700	.	.	POP*GPC
1820	.	.	POP*GPC
1870	.	.	POP*GPC
1880	.	.	POP*GPC
1890	.	.	POP*GPC
1900	.	.	POP*GPC
1913	.	.	POP*GPC
1920	.	.	POP*GPC
1929	.	.	POP*GPC
1938	.	.	POP*GPC
1950	141	.	POP*GPC
1960	253	6.02	POP*GPC

Year	GDP at PPP, mil. 2012 doll.	Growth Rate	Source
1970	604	9.10	POP*GPC
1980	1,086	6.04	POP*GPC
1990	1,672	4.41	POP*GPC
2000	1,479	1.22	POP*GPC
2010	2,222	4.15	POP*GPC
2012	2,296	1.64	POP*GPC
2020	3,025	3.51	POP*GPC
2030	4,214	3.37	POP*GPC
LAM Dominica			
0001	.	.	POP*GPC
1000	.	.	POP*GPC
1500	.	.	POP*GPC
1600	.	.	POP*GPC
1700	.	.	POP*GPC
1820	.	.	POP*GPC
1870	.	.	POP*GPC
1880	.	.	POP*GPC
1890	.	.	POP*GPC
1900	.	.	POP*GPC
1913	.	.	POP*GPC
1920	.	.	POP*GPC
1929	.	.	POP*GPC
1938	.	.	POP*GPC
1950	128	.	POP*GPC
1960	198	4.44	POP*GPC
1970	303	4.35	POP*GPC
1980	336	1.03	POP*GPC
1990	571	5.45	POP*GPC
2000	667	1.57	POP*GPC
2010	907	3.12	POP*GPC
2012	888	1.06	POP*GPC
2020	1,132	3.08	POP*GPC
2030	1,460	2.57	POP*GPC
LAM Dominican Republic			
0001	2	.	POP*GPC
1000	5	0.10	POP*GPC
1500	9	0.12	POP*GPC
1600	4	0.86	POP*GPC
1700	10	0.97	POP*GPC
1820	62	1.54	POP*GPC
1870	174	2.08	POP*GPC
1880	225	2.61	POP*GPC
1890	291	2.61	POP*GPC
1900	465	4.80	POP*GPC
1913	685	3.02	POP*GPC
1920	893	3.87	POP*GPC
1929	1,414	5.24	POP*GPC
1938	2,135	4.68	POP*GPC
1950	3,782	4.88	POP*GPC

Year	GDP at PPP, mil. 2012 doll.	Growth Rate	Source
1960	6,931	6.25	POP*GPC
1970	11,717	5.39	POP*GPC
1980	23,788	7.34	POP*GPC
1990	29,892	2.31	POP*GPC
2000	54,169	6.13	POP*GPC
2010	89,085	5.10	POP*GPC
2012	96,639	4.15	POP*GPC
2020	141,503	4.88	POP*GPC
2030	195,967	3.31	POP*GPC
SEA East Timor			
0001	.	.	POP*GPC
1000	.	.	POP*GPC
1500	.	.	POP*GPC
1600	.	.	POP*GPC
1700	.	.	POP*GPC
1820	.	.	POP*GPC
1870	.	.	POP*GPC
1880	.	.	POP*GPC
1890	.	.	POP*GPC
1900	.	.	POP*GPC
1913	.	.	POP*GPC
1920	.	.	POP*GPC
1929	.	.	POP*GPC
1938	.	.	POP*GPC
1950	285	.	POP*GPC
1960	389	3.16	POP*GPC
1970	534	3.20	POP*GPC
1980	528	0.10	POP*GPC
1990	722	3.17	POP*GPC
2000	911	2.35	POP*GPC
2010	1,694	6.40	POP*GPC
2012	1,898	5.86	POP*GPC
2020	2,773	4.85	POP*GPC
2030	4,153	4.12	POP*GPC
LAM Ecuador			
0001	69	.	POP*GPC
1000	197	0.10	POP*GPC
1500	358	0.12	POP*GPC
1600	226	0.46	POP*GPC
1700	272	0.18	POP*GPC
1820	381	0.28	POP*GPC
1870	790	1.47	POP*GPC
1880	1,048	2.87	POP*GPC
1890	1,391	2.87	POP*GPC
1900	1,847	2.87	POP*GPC
1913	2,798	3.25	POP*GPC
1920	3,300	2.39	POP*GPC
1929	4,078	2.38	POP*GPC
1938	5,715	3.82	POP*GPC

Year	GDP at PPP, mil. 2012 doll.	Growth Rate	Source
1950	9,874	4.66	POP*GPC
1960	16,484	5.26	POP*GPC
1970	28,572	5.65	POP*GPC
1980	57,192	7.19	POP*GPC
1990	74,470	2.68	POP*GPC
2000	87,403	1.61	POP*GPC
2010	126,255	3.75	POP*GPC
2012	146,068	7.56	POP*GPC
2020	186,734	3.12	POP*GPC
2030	247,376	2.85	POP*GPC
MEA Egypt			
0001	3,130	.	POP*GPC
1000	3,912	0.02	POP*GPC
1500	2,973	0.05	POP*GPC
1600	3,717	0.22	POP*GPC
1700	3,345	0.11	POP*GPC
1820	3,266	0.02	POP*GPC
1870	6,494	1.38	POP*GPC
1880	8,174	2.33	POP*GPC
1890	10,137	2.18	POP*GPC
1900	12,836	2.39	POP*GPC
1913	17,200	2.28	POP*GPC
1920	18,398	0.97	POP*GPC
1929	19,948	0.90	POP*GPC
1938	22,696	1.44	POP*GPC
1950	29,137	2.10	POP*GPC
1960	42,508	3.85	POP*GPC
1970	66,991	4.65	POP*GPC
1980	135,081	7.26	POP*GPC
1990	229,371	5.44	POP*GPC
2000	312,978	3.16	POP*GPC
2010	517,428	5.16	POP*GPC
2012	548,000	2.91	POP*GPC
2020	768,205	4.31	POP*GPC
2030	1,068,945	3.36	POP*GPC
LAM El Salvador			
0001	33	.	POP*GPC
1000	94	0.10	POP*GPC
1500	169	0.12	POP*GPC
1600	106	0.46	POP*GPC
1700	127	0.18	POP*GPC
1820	178	0.28	POP*GPC
1870	363	1.44	POP*GPC
1880	423	1.55	POP*GPC
1890	585	3.28	POP*GPC
1900	808	3.28	POP*GPC
1913	1,334	3.94	POP*GPC
1920	1,706	3.57	POP*GPC
1929	2,297	3.36	POP*GPC

Year	GDP at PPP, mil. 2012 doll.	Growth Rate	Source
1938	2,431	0.63	POP*GPC
1950	4,546	5.35	POP*GPC
1960	7,656	5.35	POP*GPC
1970	14,271	6.43	POP*GPC
1980	20,794	3.84	POP*GPC
1990	19,289	0.75	POP*GPC
2000	34,047	5.85	POP*GPC
2010	41,052	1.89	POP*GPC
2012	42,575	1.84	POP*GPC
2020	51,703	2.46	POP*GPC
2030	64,194	2.19	POP*GPC
AFR Equatorial Guinea			
0001	.	.	POP*GPC
1000	.	.	POP*GPC
1500	.	.	POP*GPC
1600	.	.	POP*GPC
1700	.	.	POP*GPC
1820	.	.	POP*GPC
1870	.	.	POP*GPC
1880	.	.	POP*GPC
1890	.	.	POP*GPC
1900	.	.	POP*GPC
1913	.	.	POP*GPC
1920	.	.	POP*GPC
1929	.	.	POP*GPC
1938	.	.	POP*GPC
1950	178	.	POP*GPC
1960	289	4.94	POP*GPC
1970	575	7.12	POP*GPC
1980	484	1.71	POP*GPC
1990	851	5.81	POP*GPC
2000	5,125	19.67	POP*GPC
2010	20,470	14.85	POP*GPC
2012	22,012	3.70	POP*GPC
2020	55,965	12.37	POP*GPC
2030	86,684	4.47	POP*GPC
AFR Eritrea			
0001	8	.	POP*GPC
1000	21	0.09	POP*GPC
1500	48	0.17	POP*GPC
1600	56	0.15	POP*GPC
1700	64	0.14	POP*GPC
1820	84	0.23	POP*GPC
1870	179	1.52	POP*GPC
1880	209	1.52	POP*GPC
1890	243	1.52	POP*GPC
1900	282	1.52	POP*GPC
1913	344	1.52	POP*GPC
1920	382	1.52	POP*GPC

Year	GDP at PPP, mil. 2012 doll.	Growth Rate	Source
1929	438	1.52	POP*GPC
1938	501	1.52	POP*GPC
1950	601	1.52	POP*GPC
1960	687	1.34	POP*GPC
1970	1,196	5.70	POP*GPC
1980	1,735	3.79	POP*GPC
1990	2,010	1.48	POP*GPC
2000	2,500	2.20	POP*GPC
2010	2,689	0.73	POP*GPC
2012	3,108	7.49	POP*GPC
2020	4,109	3.55	POP*GPC
2030	5,705	3.34	POP*GPC
USR Estonia			
0001	6	.	POP*GPC
1000	21	0.12	POP*GPC
1500	89	0.29	POP*GPC
1600	124	0.34	POP*GPC
1700	185	0.40	POP*GPC
1820	467	0.78	POP*GPC
1870	1,039	1.61	POP*GPC
1880	1,271	2.03	POP*GPC
1890	1,554	2.03	POP*GPC
1900	1,914	2.10	POP*GPC
1913	2,889	3.22	POP*GPC
1920	2,501	2.04	POP*GPC
1929	4,095	5.63	POP*GPC
1938	5,928	4.19	POP*GPC
1950	7,127	1.55	POP*GPC
1960	10,933	4.37	POP*GPC
1970	17,266	4.68	POP*GPC
1980	22,125	2.51	POP*GPC
1990	26,157	1.69	POP*GPC
2000	20,167	2.57	POP*GPC
2010	27,889	3.29	POP*GPC
2012	31,572	6.40	POP*GPC
2020	39,987	3.00	POP*GPC
2030	49,122	2.08	POP*GPC
AFR Ethiopia			
0001	118	.	POP*GPC
1000	296	0.09	POP*GPC
1500	678	0.17	POP*GPC
1600	786	0.15	POP*GPC
1700	900	0.14	POP*GPC
1820	1,179	0.23	POP*GPC
1870	2,510	1.52	POP*GPC
1880	2,919	1.52	POP*GPC
1890	3,396	1.52	POP*GPC
1900	3,950	1.52	POP*GPC
1913	4,808	1.52	POP*GPC

Year	GDP at PPP, mil. 2012 doll.	Growth Rate	Source
1920	5,345	1.52	POP*GPC
1929	6,124	1.52	POP*GPC
1938	7,017	1.52	POP*GPC
1950	8,413	1.52	POP*GPC
1960	10,573	2.31	POP*GPC
1970	18,260	5.62	POP*GPC
1980	24,234	2.87	POP*GPC
1990	29,871	2.11	POP*GPC
2000	36,567	2.04	POP*GPC
2010	79,709	8.10	POP*GPC
2012	93,303	8.19	POP*GPC
2020	144,031	5.58	POP*GPC
2030	214,535	4.06	POP*GPC
DME Falkland Islands			
0001	.	.	POP*GPC
1000	.	.	POP*GPC
1500	.	.	POP*GPC
1600	.	.	POP*GPC
1700	.	.	POP*GPC
1820	.	.	POP*GPC
1870	.	.	POP*GPC
1880	.	.	POP*GPC
1890	.	.	POP*GPC
1900	.	.	POP*GPC
1913	.	.	POP*GPC
1920	.	.	POP*GPC
1929	.	.	POP*GPC
1938	.	.	POP*GPC
1950	25	.	POP*GPC
1960	33	2.73	POP*GPC
1970	43	2.73	POP*GPC
1980	50	1.67	POP*GPC
1990	57	1.22	POP*GPC
2000	86	4.20	POP*GPC
2010	178	7.57	POP*GPC
2012	189	2.93	POP*GPC
2020	279	5.03	POP*GPC
2030	407	3.82	POP*GPC
DME Faroe Islands			
0001	.	.	POP*GPC
1000	.	.	POP*GPC
1500	.	.	POP*GPC
1600	.	.	POP*GPC
1700	.	.	POP*GPC
1820	.	.	POP*GPC
1870	.	.	POP*GPC
1880	.	.	POP*GPC
1890	.	.	POP*GPC
1900	.	.	POP*GPC

Year	GDP at PPP, mil. 2012 doll.	Growth Rate	Source
1913	.	.	POP*GPC
1920	.	.	POP*GPC
1929	.	.	POP*GPC
1938	.	.	POP*GPC
1950	203	.	POP*GPC
1960	326	4.87	POP*GPC
1970	549	5.35	POP*GPC
1980	778	3.56	POP*GPC
1990	1,056	3.10	POP*GPC
2000	1,180	1.11	POP*GPC
2010	1,526	2.61	POP*GPC
2012	1,555	0.94	POP*GPC
2020	1,889	2.46	POP*GPC
2030	2,377	2.33	POP*GPC
	SEA Fiji		
0001	.	.	POP*GPC
1000	.	.	POP*GPC
1500	.	.	POP*GPC
1600	.	.	POP*GPC
1700	.	.	POP*GPC
1820	.	.	POP*GPC
1870	.	.	POP*GPC
1880	.	.	POP*GPC
1890	.	.	POP*GPC
1900	.	.	POP*GPC
1913	.	.	POP*GPC
1920	.	.	POP*GPC
1929	.	.	POP*GPC
1938	.	.	POP*GPC
1950	1,332	.	POP*GPC
1960	1,807	3.10	POP*GPC
1970	2,389	2.83	POP*GPC
1980	2,806	1.62	POP*GPC
1990	3,217	1.37	POP*GPC
2000	3,754	1.56	POP*GPC
2010	4,078	0.83	POP*GPC
2012	4,175	1.18	POP*GPC
2020	4,479	0.88	POP*GPC
2030	5,166	1.44	POP*GPC
	DME Finland		
0001	8	.	POP*GPC
1000	22	0.11	POP*GPC
1500	213	0.45	POP*GPC
1600	337	0.46	POP*GPC
1700	399	0.17	POP*GPC
1820	1,429	1.07	POP*GPC
1870	3,129	1.58	POP*GPC
1880	3,700	1.69	POP*GPC
1890	5,109	3.28	POP*GPC

Year	GDP at PPP, mil. 2012 doll.	Growth Rate	Source
1900	6,906	3.06	POP*GPC
1913	9,999	2.89	POP*GPC
1920	9,050	1.41	POP*GPC
1929	14,558	5.42	POP*GPC
1938	20,533	3.90	POP*GPC
1950	26,681	2.21	POP*GPC
1960	44,353	5.21	POP*GPC
1970	72,947	5.10	POP*GPC
1980	105,188	3.73	POP*GPC
1990	143,139	3.13	POP*GPC
2000	174,385	1.99	POP*GPC
2010	208,179	1.79	POP*GPC
2012	212,192	0.96	POP*GPC
2020	254,752	2.31	POP*GPC
2030	316,718	2.20	POP*GPC
DME France			
0001	3,701	.	POP*GPC
1000	4,323	0.02	POP*GPC
1500	17,065	0.27	POP*GPC
1600	24,347	0.36	POP*GPC
1700	30,575	0.23	POP*GPC
1820	55,503	0.50	POP*GPC
1870	112,846	1.43	POP*GPC
1880	129,531	1.39	POP*GPC
1890	148,775	1.39	POP*GPC
1900	182,711	2.08	POP*GPC
1913	226,118	1.65	POP*GPC
1920	196,941	1.95	POP*GPC
1929	303,883	4.94	POP*GPC
1938	293,242	0.40	POP*GPC
1950	344,251	1.35	POP*GPC
1960	543,800	4.68	POP*GPC
1970	945,753	5.69	POP*GPC
1980	1,302,394	3.25	POP*GPC
1990	1,657,535	2.44	POP*GPC
2000	2,047,810	2.14	POP*GPC
2010	2,289,757	1.12	POP*GPC
2012	2,337,236	1.03	POP*GPC
2020	2,675,765	1.71	POP*GPC
2030	3,183,418	1.75	POP*GPC
SEA French Polynesia			
0001	.	.	POP*GPC
1000	.	.	POP*GPC
1500	.	.	POP*GPC
1600	.	.	POP*GPC
1700	.	.	POP*GPC
1820	.	.	POP*GPC
1870	.	.	POP*GPC
1880	.	.	POP*GPC

Year	GDP at PPP, mil. 2012 doll.	Growth Rate	Source
1890	.	.	POP*GPC
1900	.	.	POP*GPC
1913	.	.	POP*GPC
1920	.	.	POP*GPC
1929	.	.	POP*GPC
1938	.	.	POP*GPC
1950	426	.	POP*GPC
1960	643	4.20	POP*GPC
1970	1,070	5.22	POP*GPC
1980	1,555	3.81	POP*GPC
1990	2,053	2.82	POP*GPC
2000	3,591	5.75	POP*GPC
2010	6,342	5.85	POP*GPC
2012	6,732	3.03	POP*GPC
2020	9,503	4.40	POP*GPC
2030	12,878	3.09	POP*GPC
AFR Gabon			
0001	.	.	POP*GPC
1000	.	.	POP*GPC
1500	.	.	POP*GPC
1600	.	.	POP*GPC
1700	.	.	POP*GPC
1820	.	.	POP*GPC
1870	.	.	POP*GPC
1880	.	.	POP*GPC
1890	.	.	POP*GPC
1900	.	.	POP*GPC
1913	.	.	POP*GPC
1920	.	.	POP*GPC
1929	.	.	POP*GPC
1938	.	.	POP*GPC
1950	2,023	.	POP*GPC
1960	3,840	6.62	POP*GPC
1970	7,081	6.31	POP*GPC
1980	12,766	6.07	POP*GPC
1990	15,967	2.26	POP*GPC
2000	18,844	1.67	POP*GPC
2010	22,046	1.58	POP*GPC
2012	24,652	5.74	POP*GPC
2020	30,956	2.89	POP*GPC
2030	41,490	2.97	POP*GPC
AFR Gambia			
0001	.	.	POP*GPC
1000	.	.	POP*GPC
1500	.	.	POP*GPC
1600	.	.	POP*GPC
1700	.	.	POP*GPC
1820	.	.	POP*GPC
1870	.	.	POP*GPC

Year	GDP at PPP, mil. 2012 doll.	Growth Rate	Source
1880	.	.	POP*GPC
1890	.	.	POP*GPC
1900	.	.	POP*GPC
1913	.	.	POP*GPC
1920	.	.	POP*GPC
1929	.	.	POP*GPC
1938	.	.	POP*GPC
1950	279	.	POP*GPC
1960	425	4.30	POP*GPC
1970	762	6.01	POP*GPC
1980	1,296	5.45	POP*GPC
1990	1,780	3.23	POP*GPC
2000	2,564	3.71	POP*GPC
2010	3,527	3.24	POP*GPC
2012	3,501	0.38	POP*GPC
2020	4,329	2.69	POP*GPC
2030	5,601	2.61	POP*GPC
MEA Gaza Strip			
0001	.	.	POP*GPC
1000	.	.	POP*GPC
1500	.	.	POP*GPC
1600	.	.	POP*GPC
1700	.	.	POP*GPC
1820	.	.	POP*GPC
1870	.	.	POP*GPC
1880	.	.	POP*GPC
1890	.	.	POP*GPC
1900	.	.	POP*GPC
1913	.	.	POP*GPC
1920	.	.	POP*GPC
1929	.	.	POP*GPC
1938	.	.	POP*GPC
1950	275	.	POP*GPC
1960	380	3.30	POP*GPC
1970	464	2.03	POP*GPC
1980	671	3.76	POP*GPC
1990	1,034	4.42	POP*GPC
2000	1,713	5.17	POP*GPC
2010	2,034	1.74	POP*GPC
2012	2,146	2.71	POP*GPC
2020	2,714	2.98	POP*GPC
2030	3,495	2.56	POP*GPC
USR Georgia			
0001	43	.	POP*GPC
1000	106	0.09	POP*GPC
1500	346	0.24	POP*GPC
1600	459	0.28	POP*GPC
1700	592	0.25	POP*GPC
1820	926	0.37	POP*GPC

Year	GDP at PPP, mil. 2012 doll.	Growth Rate	Source
1870	2,398	1.92	POP*GPC
1880	2,932	2.03	POP*GPC
1890	3,586	2.03	POP*GPC
1900	4,416	2.10	POP*GPC
1913	6,664	3.22	POP*GPC
1920	3,909	7.34	POP*GPC
1929	7,020	6.72	POP*GPC
1938	11,933	6.07	POP*GPC
1950	15,439	2.17	POP*GPC
1960	23,328	4.21	POP*GPC
1970	34,592	4.02	POP*GPC
1980	39,791	1.41	POP*GPC
1990	37,072	0.71	POP*GPC
2000	10,440	11.90	POP*GPC
2010	22,399	7.93	POP*GPC
2012	26,242	8.24	POP*GPC
2020	37,124	4.43	POP*GPC
2030	44,471	1.82	POP*GPC
DME Germany			
0001	1,915	.	POP*GPC
1000	2,246	0.02	POP*GPC
1500	12,919	0.35	POP*GPC
1600	19,805	0.43	POP*GPC
1700	21,360	0.08	POP*GPC
1820	41,973	0.56	POP*GPC
1870	112,897	2.00	POP*GPC
1880	135,529	1.84	POP*GPC
1890	180,880	2.93	POP*GPC
1900	254,050	3.46	POP*GPC
1913	371,388	2.96	POP*GPC
1920	266,430	4.63	POP*GPC
1929	410,393	4.92	POP*GPC
1938	535,770	3.01	POP*GPC
1950	415,265	2.10	POP*GPC
1960	927,989	8.37	POP*GPC
1970	1,456,958	4.61	POP*GPC
1980	1,989,435	3.16	POP*GPC
1990	2,520,685	2.40	POP*GPC
2000	2,990,962	1.73	POP*GPC
2010	3,297,337	0.98	POP*GPC
2012	3,460,217	2.44	POP*GPC
2020	3,988,877	1.79	POP*GPC
2030	4,659,470	1.57	POP*GPC
AFR Ghana			
0001	66	.	POP*GPC
1000	211	0.12	POP*GPC
1500	405	0.13	POP*GPC
1600	540	0.29	POP*GPC
1700	728	0.30	POP*GPC

Year	GDP at PPP, mil. 2012 doll.	Growth Rate	Source
1820	892	0.17	POP*GPC
1870	1,084	0.39	POP*GPC
1880	1,160	0.68	POP*GPC
1890	1,241	0.68	POP*GPC
1900	1,474	1.73	POP*GPC
1913	2,497	4.14	POP*GPC
1920	3,202	3.62	POP*GPC
1929	4,409	3.62	POP*GPC
1938	6,071	3.62	POP*GPC
1950	9,300	3.62	POP*GPC
1960	13,022	3.42	POP*GPC
1970	15,487	1.75	POP*GPC
1980	15,369	0.08	POP*GPC
1990	20,158	2.75	POP*GPC
2000	27,063	2.99	POP*GPC
2010	44,209	5.03	POP*GPC
2012	52,732	9.22	POP*GPC
2020	74,973	4.50	POP*GPC
2030	112,347	4.13	POP*GPC
	DME Gibraltar		
0001	.	.	POP*GPC
1000	.	.	POP*GPC
1500	.	.	POP*GPC
1600	.	.	POP*GPC
1700	.	.	POP*GPC
1820	.	.	POP*GPC
1870	.	.	POP*GPC
1880	.	.	POP*GPC
1890	.	.	POP*GPC
1900	.	.	POP*GPC
1913	.	.	POP*GPC
1920	.	.	POP*GPC
1929	.	.	POP*GPC
1938	.	.	POP*GPC
1950	70	.	POP*GPC
1960	117	5.35	POP*GPC
1970	205	5.75	POP*GPC
1980	324	4.68	POP*GPC
1990	427	2.80	POP*GPC
2000	978	8.64	POP*GPC
2010	1,352	3.30	POP*GPC
2012	1,413	2.23	POP*GPC
2020	2,035	4.66	POP*GPC
2030	2,608	2.51	POP*GPC
	DME Greece		
0001	1,721	.	POP*GPC
1000	689	0.09	POP*GPC
1500	678	0.00	POP*GPC
1600	1,134	0.52	POP*GPC

Year	GDP at PPP, mil. 2012 doll.	Growth Rate	Source
1700	1,244	0.09	POP*GPC
1820	2,319	0.52	POP*GPC
1870	5,036	1.56	POP*GPC
1880	6,451	2.51	POP*GPC
1890	8,262	2.51	POP*GPC
1900	10,490	2.42	POP*GPC
1913	13,515	1.97	POP*GPC
1920	16,714	3.08	POP*GPC
1929	22,997	3.61	POP*GPC
1938	29,579	2.84	POP*GPC
1950	22,673	2.19	POP*GPC
1960	45,298	7.17	POP*GPC
1970	105,570	8.83	POP*GPC
1980	182,963	5.65	POP*GPC
1990	196,213	0.70	POP*GPC
2000	272,321	3.33	POP*GPC
2010	319,417	1.61	POP*GPC
2012	282,695	5.92	POP*GPC
2020	338,890	2.29	POP*GPC
2030	412,218	1.98	POP*GPC
DME Greenland			
0001	.	.	POP*GPC
1000	.	.	POP*GPC
1500	.	.	POP*GPC
1600	.	.	POP*GPC
1700	.	.	POP*GPC
1820	.	.	POP*GPC
1870	.	.	POP*GPC
1880	.	.	POP*GPC
1890	.	.	POP*GPC
1900	.	.	POP*GPC
1913	.	.	POP*GPC
1920	.	.	POP*GPC
1929	.	.	POP*GPC
1938	.	.	POP*GPC
1950	157	.	POP*GPC
1960	328	7.68	POP*GPC
1970	669	7.37	POP*GPC
1980	932	3.38	POP*GPC
1990	1,267	3.11	POP*GPC
2000	1,444	1.32	POP*GPC
2010	2,111	3.87	POP*GPC
2012	2,155	1.03	POP*GPC
2020	2,685	2.79	POP*GPC
2030	3,349	2.23	POP*GPC
LAM Grenada			
0001	.	.	POP*GPC
1000	.	.	POP*GPC
1500	.	.	POP*GPC

Year	GDP at PPP, mil. 2012 doll.	Growth Rate	Source
1600	.	.	POP*GPC
1700	.	.	POP*GPC
1820	.	.	POP*GPC
1870	.	.	POP*GPC
1880	.	.	POP*GPC
1890	.	.	POP*GPC
1900	.	.	POP*GPC
1913	.	.	POP*GPC
1920	.	.	POP*GPC
1929	.	.	POP*GPC
1938	.	.	POP*GPC
1950	111	.	POP*GPC
1960	195	5.80	POP*GPC
1970	306	4.59	POP*GPC
1980	371	1.93	POP*GPC
1990	622	5.32	POP*GPC
2000	953	4.35	POP*GPC
2010	1,116	1.59	POP*GPC
2012	1,126	0.42	POP*GPC
2020	1,426	3.00	POP*GPC
2030	1,759	2.12	POP*GPC
	LAM Guadeloupe		
0001	.	.	POP*GPC
1000	.	.	POP*GPC
1500	.	.	POP*GPC
1600	.	.	POP*GPC
1700	.	.	POP*GPC
1820	.	.	POP*GPC
1870	.	.	POP*GPC
1880	.	.	POP*GPC
1890	.	.	POP*GPC
1900	.	.	POP*GPC
1913	.	.	POP*GPC
1920	.	.	POP*GPC
1929	.	.	POP*GPC
1938	.	.	POP*GPC
1950	562	.	POP*GPC
1960	1,159	7.51	POP*GPC
1970	2,179	6.52	POP*GPC
1980	2,705	2.19	POP*GPC
1990	3,082	1.31	POP*GPC
2000	4,834	4.60	POP*GPC
2010	12,579	10.04	POP*GPC
2012	12,160	1.68	POP*GPC
2020	19,532	6.10	POP*GPC
2030	26,101	2.94	POP*GPC
	SEA Guam		
0001	.	.	POP*GPC
1000	.	.	POP*GPC

Year	GDP at PPP, mil. 2012 doll.	Growth Rate	Source
1500	.	.	POP*GPC
1600	.	.	POP*GPC
1700	.	.	POP*GPC
1820	.	.	POP*GPC
1870	.	.	POP*GPC
1880	.	.	POP*GPC
1890	.	.	POP*GPC
1900	.	.	POP*GPC
1913	.	.	POP*GPC
1920	.	.	POP*GPC
1929	.	.	POP*GPC
1938	.	.	POP*GPC
1950	892	.	POP*GPC
1960	1,162	2.68	POP*GPC
1970	1,721	4.00	POP*GPC
1980	2,301	2.95	POP*GPC
1990	2,941	2.48	POP*GPC
2000	4,152	3.51	POP*GPC
2010	4,728	1.31	POP*GPC
2012	4,924	2.05	POP*GPC
2020	5,770	2.00	POP*GPC
2030	7,347	2.45	POP*GPC
LAM Guatemala			
0001	86	.	POP*GPC
1000	252	0.11	POP*GPC
1500	467	0.12	POP*GPC
1600	297	0.45	POP*GPC
1700	359	0.19	POP*GPC
1820	507	0.29	POP*GPC
1870	943	1.25	POP*GPC
1880	1,195	2.40	POP*GPC
1890	1,514	2.40	POP*GPC
1900	1,919	2.40	POP*GPC
1913	2,755	2.82	POP*GPC
1920	3,179	2.07	POP*GPC
1929	4,718	4.49	POP*GPC
1938	7,343	5.04	POP*GPC
1950	9,687	2.34	POP*GPC
1960	13,915	3.69	POP*GPC
1970	21,744	4.56	POP*GPC
1980	33,099	4.29	POP*GPC
1990	36,630	1.02	POP*GPC
2000	51,479	3.46	POP*GPC
2010	70,922	3.26	POP*GPC
2012	75,987	3.51	POP*GPC
2020	99,053	3.37	POP*GPC
2030	138,273	3.39	POP*GPC

Year	GDP at PPP, mil. 2012 doll.	Growth Rate	Source
DME Guernsey			
0001	.	.	POP*GPC
1000	.	.	POP*GPC
1500	.	.	POP*GPC
1600	.	.	POP*GPC
1700	.	.	POP*GPC
1820	.	.	POP*GPC
1870	.	.	POP*GPC
1880	.	.	POP*GPC
1890	.	.	POP*GPC
1900	.	.	POP*GPC
1913	.	.	POP*GPC
1920	.	.	POP*GPC
1929	.	.	POP*GPC
1938	.	.	POP*GPC
1950	332	.	POP*GPC
1960	494	4.05	POP*GPC
1970	814	5.13	POP*GPC
1980	1,082	2.89	POP*GPC
1990	1,507	3.37	POP*GPC
2000	1,701	1.22	POP*GPC
2010	3,285	6.80	POP*GPC
2012	3,420	2.04	POP*GPC
2020	4,910	4.63	POP*GPC
2030	6,579	2.97	POP*GPC
LAM Guiana, French			
0001	.	.	POP*GPC
1000	.	.	POP*GPC
1500	.	.	POP*GPC
1600	.	.	POP*GPC
1700	.	.	POP*GPC
1820	.	.	POP*GPC
1870	.	.	POP*GPC
1880	.	.	POP*GPC
1890	.	.	POP*GPC
1900	.	.	POP*GPC
1913	.	.	POP*GPC
1920	.	.	POP*GPC
1929	.	.	POP*GPC
1938	.	.	POP*GPC
1950	216	.	POP*GPC
1960	242	1.13	POP*GPC
1970	349	3.75	POP*GPC
1980	474	3.11	POP*GPC
1990	812	5.52	POP*GPC
2000	1,370	5.37	POP*GPC
2010	5,990	15.90	POP*GPC
2012	5,566	3.60	POP*GPC

Year	GDP at PPP, mil. 2012 doll.	Growth Rate	Source
2020	11,153	9.08	POP*GPC
2030	18,025	4.92	POP*GPC
AFR Guinea			
0001	37	.	POP*GPC
1000	110	0.11	POP*GPC
1500	200	0.12	POP*GPC
1600	264	0.27	POP*GPC
1700	351	0.29	POP*GPC
1820	422	0.16	POP*GPC
1870	639	0.83	POP*GPC
1880	695	0.83	POP*GPC
1890	755	0.83	POP*GPC
1900	820	0.83	POP*GPC
1913	913	0.83	POP*GPC
1920	968	0.83	POP*GPC
1929	1,043	0.83	POP*GPC
1938	1,124	0.83	POP*GPC
1950	1,242	0.83	POP*GPC
1960	2,266	6.20	POP*GPC
1970	3,274	3.75	POP*GPC
1980	4,310	2.79	POP*GPC
1990	5,604	2.66	POP*GPC
2000	8,215	3.90	POP*GPC
2010	10,231	2.22	POP*GPC
2012	11,030	3.83	POP*GPC
2020	14,120	3.14	POP*GPC
2030	19,532	3.30	POP*GPC
AFR GuineaBissau			
0001	8	.	POP*GPC
1000	23	0.11	POP*GPC
1500	42	0.12	POP*GPC
1600	55	0.27	POP*GPC
1700	73	0.28	POP*GPC
1820	88	0.15	POP*GPC
1870	134	0.83	POP*GPC
1880	145	0.83	POP*GPC
1890	158	0.83	POP*GPC
1900	171	0.83	POP*GPC
1913	191	0.83	POP*GPC
1920	202	0.83	POP*GPC
1929	218	0.83	POP*GPC
1938	235	0.83	POP*GPC
1950	259	0.83	POP*GPC
1960	451	5.70	POP*GPC
1970	775	5.55	POP*GPC
1980	961	2.18	POP*GPC
1990	1,492	4.50	POP*GPC
2000	1,423	0.47	POP*GPC
2010	1,841	2.61	POP*GPC

Year	GDP at PPP, mil. 2012 doll.	Growth Rate	Source
2012	1,811	0.82	POP*GPC
2020	2,242	2.70	POP*GPC
2030	3,015	3.01	POP*GPC
	LAM GUYANA		
0001	.	.	POP*GPC
1000	.	.	POP*GPC
1500	.	.	POP*GPC
1600	.	.	POP*GPC
1700	.	.	POP*GPC
1820	.	.	POP*GPC
1870	.	.	POP*GPC
1880	.	.	POP*GPC
1890	.	.	POP*GPC
1900	.	.	POP*GPC
1913	.	.	POP*GPC
1920	.	.	POP*GPC
1929	.	.	POP*GPC
1938	.	.	POP*GPC
1950	723	.	POP*GPC
1960	1,067	3.97	POP*GPC
1970	1,532	3.68	POP*GPC
1980	1,970	2.55	POP*GPC
1990	1,425	3.19	POP*GPC
2000	2,081	3.86	POP*GPC
2010	2,324	1.11	POP*GPC
2012	2,533	4.40	POP*GPC
2020	3,034	2.28	POP*GPC
2030	3,769	2.19	POP*GPC
	LAM HAITI		
0001	15	.	POP*GPC
1000	41	0.10	POP*GPC
1500	74	0.12	POP*GPC
1600	31	0.86	POP*GPC
1700	82	0.97	POP*GPC
1820	514	1.54	POP*GPC
1870	841	0.99	POP*GPC
1880	936	1.08	POP*GPC
1890	1,042	1.08	POP*GPC
1900	1,161	1.08	POP*GPC
1913	1,767	3.29	POP*GPC
1920	2,209	3.24	POP*GPC
1929	2,852	2.88	POP*GPC
1938	3,672	2.85	POP*GPC
1950	5,297	3.10	POP*GPC
1960	6,102	1.42	POP*GPC
1970	6,485	0.61	POP*GPC
1980	11,122	5.54	POP*GPC
1990	11,079	0.04	POP*GPC
2000	10,963	0.11	POP*GPC

Year	GDP at PPP, mil. 2012 doll.	Growth Rate	Source
2010	11,067	0.09	POP*GPC
2012	11,853	3.49	POP*GPC
2020	13,534	1.67	POP*GPC
2030	16,446	1.97	POP*GPC
LAM Honduras			
0001	17	.	POP*GPC
1000	47	0.10	POP*GPC
1500	83	0.11	POP*GPC
1600	52	0.47	POP*GPC
1700	62	0.18	POP*GPC
1820	86	0.27	POP*GPC
1870	263	2.27	POP*GPC
1880	284	0.77	POP*GPC
1890	363	2.49	POP*GPC
1900	465	2.49	POP*GPC
1913	770	3.96	POP*GPC
1920	1,435	9.30	POP*GPC
1929	2,182	4.76	POP*GPC
1938	1,902	1.51	POP*GPC
1950	2,940	3.70	POP*GPC
1960	4,416	4.15	POP*GPC
1970	6,874	4.53	POP*GPC
1980	11,329	5.12	POP*GPC
1990	14,357	2.40	POP*GPC
2000	20,299	3.52	POP*GPC
2010	30,604	4.19	POP*GPC
2012	33,027	3.88	POP*GPC
2020	43,793	3.59	POP*GPC
2030	60,373	3.26	POP*GPC
SEA Hong Kong			
0001	2	.	POP*GPC
1000	2	0.00	POP*GPC
1500	5	0.17	POP*GPC
1600	8	0.44	POP*GPC
1700	7	0.15	POP*GPC
1820	19	0.85	POP*GPC
1870	131	3.97	POP*GPC
1880	201	4.32	POP*GPC
1890	306	4.32	POP*GPC
1900	507	5.16	POP*GPC
1913	975	5.16	POP*GPC
1920	1,439	5.73	POP*GPC
1929	1,993	3.69	POP*GPC
1938	4,294	8.90	POP*GPC
1950	7,764	5.06	POP*GPC
1960	15,051	6.84	POP*GPC
1970	35,087	8.83	POP*GPC
1980	82,376	8.91	POP*GPC
1990	160,419	6.89	POP*GPC

Year	GDP at PPP, mil. 2012 doll.	Growth Rate	Source
2000	230,708	3.70	POP*GPC
2010	343,873	4.07	POP*GPC
2012	363,566	2.82	POP*GPC
2020	524,760	4.69	POP*GPC
2030	728,901	3.34	POP*GPC
	EEU Hungary		
0001	200	.	POP*GPC
1000	313	0.05	POP*GPC
1500	1,394	0.30	POP*GPC
1600	1,564	0.12	POP*GPC
1700	2,106	0.30	POP*GPC
1820	6,687	0.97	POP*GPC
1870	10,111	0.83	POP*GPC
1880	12,423	2.08	POP*GPC
1890	15,264	2.08	POP*GPC
1900	18,759	2.08	POP*GPC
1913	25,739	2.46	POP*GPC
1920	21,261	2.69	POP*GPC
1929	33,255	5.10	POP*GPC
1938	38,086	1.52	POP*GPC
1950	36,239	0.41	POP*GPC
1960	64,710	5.97	POP*GPC
1970	104,199	4.88	POP*GPC
1980	152,053	3.85	POP*GPC
1990	172,871	1.29	POP*GPC
2000	180,941	0.46	POP*GPC
2010	224,792	2.19	POP*GPC
2012	223,558	0.27	POP*GPC
2020	254,599	1.64	POP*GPC
2030	295,430	1.50	POP*GPC
	DME Iceland		
0001	.	.	POP*GPC
1000	17	.	POP*GPC
1500	38	0.16	POP*GPC
1600	49	0.25	POP*GPC
1700	63	0.25	POP*GPC
1820	73	0.13	POP*GPC
1870	168	1.66	POP*GPC
1880	189	1.22	POP*GPC
1890	214	1.22	POP*GPC
1900	283	2.82	POP*GPC
1913	409	2.88	POP*GPC
1920	451	1.40	POP*GPC
1929	646	4.08	POP*GPC
1938	817	2.64	POP*GPC
1950	1,192	3.21	POP*GPC
1960	2,281	6.70	POP*GPC
1970	4,111	6.06	POP*GPC
1980	6,068	3.97	POP*GPC

Year	GDP at PPP, mil. 2012 doll.	Growth Rate	Source
1990	7,936	2.72	POP*GPC
2000	9,727	2.06	POP*GPC
2010	12,049	2.16	POP*GPC
2012	12,563	2.11	POP*GPC
2020	15,188	2.40	POP*GPC
2030	19,348	2.45	POP*GPC
	SAS India		
0001	44,310	.	POP*GPC
1000	44,310	0.00	POP*GPC
1500	79,430	0.12	POP*GPC
1600	97,482	0.21	POP*GPC
1700	119,145	0.20	POP*GPC
1820	145,703	0.17	POP*GPC
1870	185,280	0.48	POP*GPC
1880	196,107	0.57	POP*GPC
1890	221,983	1.25	POP*GPC
1900	231,570	0.42	POP*GPC
1913	261,351	0.93	POP*GPC
1920	249,329	0.67	POP*GPC
1929	287,067	1.58	POP*GPC
1938	299,731	0.48	POP*GPC
1950	358,281	1.50	POP*GPC
1960	477,013	2.90	POP*GPC
1970	615,692	2.58	POP*GPC
1980	762,819	2.17	POP*GPC
1990	1,302,715	5.50	POP*GPC
2000	2,140,903	5.09	POP*GPC
2010	4,259,456	7.12	POP*GPC
2012	4,779,027	5.92	POP*GPC
2020	7,491,408	5.78	POP*GPC
2030	10,644,522	3.58	POP*GPC
	SEA Indonesia		
0001	2,200	.	POP*GPC
1000	4,073	0.06	POP*GPC
1500	9,460	0.17	POP*GPC
1600	10,606	0.11	POP*GPC
1700	11,890	0.11	POP*GPC
1820	17,168	0.31	POP*GPC
1870	29,599	1.10	POP*GPC
1880	34,057	1.41	POP*GPC
1890	38,812	1.32	POP*GPC
1900	49,700	2.50	POP*GPC
1913	70,638	2.74	POP*GPC
1920	79,445	1.69	POP*GPC
1929	109,601	3.64	POP*GPC
1938	125,272	1.50	POP*GPC
1950	104,550	1.50	POP*GPC
1960	128,261	2.07	POP*GPC
1970	169,739	2.84	POP*GPC

Year	GDP at PPP, mil. 2012 doll.	Growth Rate	Source
1980	290,032	5.50	POP*GPC
1990	517,496	5.96	POP*GPC
2000	655,987	2.40	POP*GPC
2010	1,060,535	4.92	POP*GPC
2012	1,193,641	6.09	POP*GPC
2020	1,658,554	4.20	POP*GPC
2030	2,235,884	3.03	POP*GPC
MEA Iran			
0001	3,621	.	POP*GPC
1000	4,442	0.02	POP*GPC
1500	3,756	0.03	POP*GPC
1600	4,199	0.11	POP*GPC
1700	4,695	0.11	POP*GPC
1820	6,036	0.21	POP*GPC
1870	9,468	0.90	POP*GPC
1880	10,879	1.40	POP*GPC
1890	12,500	1.40	POP*GPC
1900	14,362	1.40	POP*GPC
1913	17,204	1.40	POP*GPC
1920	20,681	2.66	POP*GPC
1929	26,204	2.66	POP*GPC
1938	33,202	2.66	POP*GPC
1950	45,522	2.66	POP*GPC
1960	79,354	5.71	POP*GPC
1970	217,673	10.62	POP*GPC
1980	294,598	3.07	POP*GPC
1990	352,833	1.82	POP*GPC
2000	549,022	4.52	POP*GPC
2010	921,800	5.32	POP*GPC
2012	930,499	0.47	POP*GPC
2020	1,248,740	3.75	POP*GPC
2030	1,622,745	2.65	POP*GPC
MEA Iraq			
0001	862	.	POP*GPC
1000	1,058	0.02	POP*GPC
1500	894	0.03	POP*GPC
1600	896	0.00	POP*GPC
1700	896	0.00	POP*GPC
1820	1,006	0.10	POP*GPC
1870	1,778	1.15	POP*GPC
1880	2,158	1.96	POP*GPC
1890	2,619	1.96	POP*GPC
1900	3,179	1.96	POP*GPC
1913	4,089	1.96	POP*GPC
1920	4,964	2.81	POP*GPC
1929	6,370	2.81	POP*GPC
1938	8,174	2.81	POP*GPC
1950	11,398	2.81	POP*GPC
1960	33,715	11.45	POP*GPC

Year	GDP at PPP, mil. 2012 doll.	Growth Rate	Source
1970	59,456	5.84	POP*GPC
1980	158,496	10.30	POP*GPC
1990	115,057	3.15	POP*GPC
2000	144,261	2.29	POP*GPC
2010	204,452	3.55	POP*GPC
2012	250,620	10.72	POP*GPC
2020	370,525	5.01	POP*GPC
2030	577,582	4.54	POP*GPC
DME Ireland			
0001	48	.	POP*GPC
1000	179	0.13	POP*GPC
1500	469	0.19	POP*GPC
1600	685	0.38	POP*GPC
1700	1,533	0.81	POP*GPC
1820	6,934	1.27	POP*GPC
1870	10,710	0.87	POP*GPC
1880	11,372	0.60	POP*GPC
1890	11,403	0.03	POP*GPC
1900	11,945	0.47	POP*GPC
1913	13,240	0.79	POP*GPC
1920	12,419	0.91	POP*GPC
1929	12,979	0.49	POP*GPC
1938	14,027	0.87	POP*GPC
1950	16,043	1.13	POP*GPC
1960	19,629	2.04	POP*GPC
1970	30,770	4.60	POP*GPC
1980	50,728	5.13	POP*GPC
1990	73,250	3.74	POP*GPC
2000	153,733	7.70	POP*GPC
2010	195,380	2.43	POP*GPC
2012	200,536	1.31	POP*GPC
2020	271,610	3.86	POP*GPC
2030	364,906	3.00	POP*GPC
DME Isle of Man			
0001	.	.	POP*GPC
1000	.	.	POP*GPC
1500	.	.	POP*GPC
1600	.	.	POP*GPC
1700	.	.	POP*GPC
1820	.	.	POP*GPC
1870	.	.	POP*GPC
1880	.	.	POP*GPC
1890	.	.	POP*GPC
1900	.	.	POP*GPC
1913	.	.	POP*GPC
1920	.	.	POP*GPC
1929	.	.	POP*GPC
1938	.	.	POP*GPC
1950	265	.	POP*GPC

Year	GDP at PPP, mil. 2012 doll.	Growth Rate	Source
1960	349	2.79	POP*GPC
1970	581	5.24	POP*GPC
1980	919	4.69	POP*GPC
1990	1,221	2.89	POP*GPC
2000	1,894	4.48	POP*GPC
2010	4,706	9.53	POP*GPC
2012	4,965	2.71	POP*GPC
2020	8,172	6.43	POP*GPC
2030	11,012	3.03	POP*GPC
DME Israel			
0001	153	.	POP*GPC
1000	188	0.02	POP*GPC
1500	159	0.03	POP*GPC
1600	155	0.03	POP*GPC
1700	151	0.03	POP*GPC
1820	176	0.13	POP*GPC
1870	279	0.92	POP*GPC
1880	352	2.33	POP*GPC
1890	444	2.35	POP*GPC
1900	560	2.35	POP*GPC
1913	757	2.35	POP*GPC
1920	1,108	5.59	POP*GPC
1929	1,808	5.59	POP*GPC
1938	2,949	5.59	POP*GPC
1950	5,545	5.40	POP*GPC
1960	15,266	10.66	POP*GPC
1970	36,177	9.01	POP*GPC
1980	64,725	5.99	POP*GPC
1990	92,192	3.60	POP*GPC
2000	159,558	5.64	POP*GPC
2010	219,990	3.26	POP*GPC
2012	236,877	3.77	POP*GPC
2020	317,109	3.71	POP*GPC
2030	436,924	3.26	POP*GPC
DME Italy			
0001	10,128	.	POP*GPC
1000	3,521	0.11	POP*GPC
1500	18,074	0.33	POP*GPC
1600	22,549	0.22	POP*GPC
1700	22,894	0.02	POP*GPC
1820	35,266	0.36	POP*GPC
1870	65,417	1.24	POP*GPC
1880	73,068	1.11	POP*GPC
1890	82,698	1.25	POP*GPC
1900	94,054	1.30	POP*GPC
1913	149,449	3.63	POP*GPC
1920	151,397	0.19	POP*GPC
1929	195,873	2.90	POP*GPC
1938	225,303	1.57	POP*GPC

Year	GDP at PPP, mil. 2012 doll.	Growth Rate	Source
1950	258,134	1.14	POP*GPC
1960	485,496	6.52	POP*GPC
1970	907,847	6.46	POP*GPC
1980	1,350,480	4.05	POP*GPC
1990	1,749,789	2.62	POP*GPC
2000	2,077,191	1.73	POP*GPC
2010	2,076,136	0.01	POP*GPC
2012	2,082,113	0.14	POP*GPC
2020	2,329,409	1.41	POP*GPC
2030	2,722,809	1.57	POP*GPC
AFR Ivory Coast			
0001	.	.	POP*GPC
1000	.	.	POP*GPC
1500	.	.	POP*GPC
1600	.	.	POP*GPC
1700	.	.	POP*GPC
1820	.	.	POP*GPC
1870	.	.	POP*GPC
1880	.	.	POP*GPC
1890	.	.	POP*GPC
1900	.	.	POP*GPC
1913	.	.	POP*GPC
1920	.	.	POP*GPC
1929	.	.	POP*GPC
1938	.	.	POP*GPC
1950	4,081	.	POP*GPC
1960	6,817	5.27	POP*GPC
1970	14,465	7.81	POP*GPC
1980	25,244	5.73	POP*GPC
1990	28,692	1.29	POP*GPC
2000	35,444	2.14	POP*GPC
2010	42,320	1.79	POP*GPC
2012	44,022	1.99	POP*GPC
2020	51,944	2.09	POP*GPC
2030	64,487	2.19	POP*GPC
LAM Jamaica			
0001	9	.	POP*GPC
1000	28	0.11	POP*GPC
1500	54	0.13	POP*GPC
1600	23	0.85	POP*GPC
1700	77	1.22	POP*GPC
1820	439	1.46	POP*GPC
1870	418	0.10	POP*GPC
1880	489	1.58	POP*GPC
1890	571	1.58	POP*GPC
1900	668	1.58	POP*GPC
1913	812	1.51	POP*GPC
1920	941	2.12	POP*GPC
1929	1,274	3.43	POP*GPC

Year	GDP at PPP, mil. 2012 doll.	Growth Rate	Source
1938	1,769	3.71	POP*GPC
1950	2,913	4.25	POP*GPC
1960	6,531	8.41	POP*GPC
1970	10,663	5.02	POP*GPC
1980	9,969	0.67	POP*GPC
1990	12,693	2.45	POP*GPC
2000	12,655	0.03	POP*GPC
2010	24,815	6.97	POP*GPC
2012	24,393	0.85	POP*GPC
2020	32,752	3.75	POP*GPC
2030	41,801	2.47	POP*GPC
	DME Japan		
0001	1,303	.	POP*GPC
1000	4,988	0.13	POP*GPC
1500	12,049	0.18	POP*GPC
1600	15,054	0.22	POP*GPC
1700	24,083	0.47	POP*GPC
1820	32,453	0.25	POP*GPC
1870	39,716	0.40	POP*GPC
1880	49,706	2.27	POP*GPC
1890	63,467	2.47	POP*GPC
1900	81,437	2.52	POP*GPC
1913	112,151	2.49	POP*GPC
1920	148,140	4.06	POP*GPC
1929	200,508	3.42	POP*GPC
1938	275,463	3.59	POP*GPC
1950	251,383	0.76	POP*GPC
1960	575,024	8.63	POP*GPC
1970	1,562,630	10.51	POP*GPC
1980	2,418,685	4.47	POP*GPC
1990	3,774,309	4.55	POP*GPC
2000	4,157,896	0.97	POP*GPC
2010	4,504,409	0.80	POP*GPC
2012	4,542,373	0.42	POP*GPC
2020	5,090,130	1.43	POP*GPC
2030	5,800,240	1.31	POP*GPC
	DME Jersey		
0001	.	.	POP*GPC
1000	.	.	POP*GPC
1500	.	.	POP*GPC
1600	.	.	POP*GPC
1700	.	.	POP*GPC
1820	.	.	POP*GPC
1870	.	.	POP*GPC
1880	.	.	POP*GPC
1890	.	.	POP*GPC
1900	.	.	POP*GPC
1913	.	.	POP*GPC
1920	.	.	POP*GPC

Year	GDP at PPP, mil. 2012 doll.	Growth Rate	Source
1929	.	.	POP*GPC
1938	.	.	POP*GPC
1950	555	.	POP*GPC
1960	889	4.82	POP*GPC
1970	1,411	4.73	POP*GPC
1980	1,983	3.46	POP*GPC
1990	2,647	2.93	POP*GPC
2000	2,983	1.20	POP*GPC
2010	6,266	7.71	POP*GPC
2012	6,563	2.34	POP*GPC
2020	9,592	4.86	POP*GPC
2030	12,916	3.02	POP*GPC
MEA Jordan			
0001	174	.	POP*GPC
1000	213	0.02	POP*GPC
1500	180	0.03	POP*GPC
1600	175	0.03	POP*GPC
1700	171	0.03	POP*GPC
1820	200	0.13	POP*GPC
1870	299	0.81	POP*GPC
1880	344	1.40	POP*GPC
1890	395	1.40	POP*GPC
1900	454	1.40	POP*GPC
1913	545	1.40	POP*GPC
1920	635	2.22	POP*GPC
1929	774	2.22	POP*GPC
1938	943	2.22	POP*GPC
1950	1,228	2.22	POP*GPC
1960	2,872	8.86	POP*GPC
1970	4,924	5.54	POP*GPC
1980	10,999	8.37	POP*GPC
1990	13,825	2.31	POP*GPC
2000	20,090	3.81	POP*GPC
2010	36,243	6.08	POP*GPC
2012	38,142	2.59	POP*GPC
2020	52,335	4.03	POP*GPC
2030	72,736	3.35	POP*GPC
USR Kazakhstan			
0001	211	.	POP*GPC
1000	553	0.10	POP*GPC
1500	1,083	0.13	POP*GPC
1600	1,370	0.23	POP*GPC
1700	1,703	0.22	POP*GPC
1820	2,873	0.44	POP*GPC
1870	5,315	1.24	POP*GPC
1880	6,500	2.03	POP*GPC
1890	7,949	2.03	POP*GPC
1900	9,790	2.10	POP*GPC
1913	14,774	3.22	POP*GPC

Year	GDP at PPP, mil. 2012 doll.	Growth Rate	Source
1920	5,667	12.79	POP*GPC
1929	15,562	11.88	POP*GPC
1938	26,453	6.07	POP*GPC
1950	38,157	3.10	POP*GPC
1960	72,417	6.62	POP*GPC
1970	123,142	5.45	POP*GPC
1980	137,944	1.14	POP*GPC
1990	135,327	0.19	POP*GPC
2000	91,681	3.82	POP*GPC
2010	203,210	8.28	POP*GPC
2012	229,811	6.34	POP*GPC
2020	350,455	5.42	POP*GPC
2030	482,303	3.24	POP*GPC
	AFR Kenya		
0001	.	.	POP*GPC
1000	.	.	POP*GPC
1500	.	.	POP*GPC
1600	.	.	POP*GPC
1700	.	.	POP*GPC
1820	.	.	POP*GPC
1870	.	.	POP*GPC
1880	.	.	POP*GPC
1890	.	.	POP*GPC
1900	.	.	POP*GPC
1913	.	.	POP*GPC
1920	.	.	POP*GPC
1929	.	.	POP*GPC
1938	.	.	POP*GPC
1950	6,236	.	POP*GPC
1960	9,156	3.92	POP*GPC
1970	15,714	5.55	POP*GPC
1980	25,386	4.91	POP*GPC
1990	37,553	3.99	POP*GPC
2000	44,671	1.75	POP*GPC
2010	68,547	4.37	POP*GPC
2012	74,593	4.32	POP*GPC
2020	94,468	3.00	POP*GPC
2030	122,726	2.65	POP*GPC
	SEA Kiribati		
0001	.	.	POP*GPC
1000	.	.	POP*GPC
1500	.	.	POP*GPC
1600	.	.	POP*GPC
1700	.	.	POP*GPC
1820	.	.	POP*GPC
1870	.	.	POP*GPC
1880	.	.	POP*GPC
1890	.	.	POP*GPC
1900	.	.	POP*GPC

Year	GDP at PPP, mil. 2012 doll.	Growth Rate	Source
1913	.	.	POP*GPC
1920	.	.	POP*GPC
1929	.	.	POP*GPC
1938	.	.	POP*GPC
1950	30	.	POP*GPC
1960	52	5.53	POP*GPC
1970	85	5.12	POP*GPC
1980	126	3.98	POP*GPC
1990	134	0.65	POP*GPC
2000	227	5.39	POP*GPC
2010	260	1.36	POP*GPC
2012	279	3.60	POP*GPC
2020	351	2.91	POP*GPC
2030	465	2.84	POP*GPC
CPA Korea, North			
0001	540	.	POP*GPC
1000	1,000	0.06	POP*GPC
1500	2,375	0.17	POP*GPC
1600	2,933	0.21	POP*GPC
1700	3,622	0.21	POP*GPC
1820	4,080	0.10	POP*GPC
1870	4,264	0.09	POP*GPC
1880	4,666	0.91	POP*GPC
1890	5,117	0.93	POP*GPC
1900	5,588	0.88	POP*GPC
1913	6,284	0.91	POP*GPC
1920	8,806	4.94	POP*GPC
1929	10,460	1.93	POP*GPC
1938	17,789	6.08	POP*GPC
1950	11,732	3.41	POP*GPC
1960	18,977	4.93	POP*GPC
1970	43,858	8.74	POP*GPC
1980	77,369	5.84	POP*GPC
1990	90,402	1.57	POP*GPC
2000	58,015	4.34	POP*GPC
2010	57,828	0.03	POP*GPC
2012	59,051	1.05	POP*GPC
2020	64,238	1.06	POP*GPC
2030	73,380	1.34	POP*GPC
SEA Korea, South			
0001	1,168	.	POP*GPC
1000	2,162	0.06	POP*GPC
1500	5,136	0.17	POP*GPC
1600	6,342	0.21	POP*GPC
1700	7,832	0.21	POP*GPC
1820	8,821	0.10	POP*GPC
1870	9,218	0.09	POP*GPC
1880	9,946	0.76	POP*GPC
1890	10,730	0.76	POP*GPC

Year	GDP at PPP, mil. 2012 doll.	Growth Rate	Source
1900	11,577	0.76	POP*GPC
1913	13,588	1.24	POP*GPC
1920	18,638	4.62	POP*GPC
1929	21,764	1.74	POP*GPC
1938	35,117	5.46	POP*GPC
1950	25,118	2.75	POP*GPC
1960	42,260	5.34	POP*GPC
1970	91,111	7.99	POP*GPC
1980	221,736	9.30	POP*GPC
1990	517,905	8.85	POP*GPC
2000	929,410	6.02	POP*GPC
2010	1,419,117	4.32	POP*GPC
2012	1,497,670	2.73	POP*GPC
2020	2,242,518	5.18	POP*GPC
2030	2,951,535	2.79	POP*GPC
EEU Kosovo			
0001	25	.	POP*GPC
1000	36	0.04	POP*GPC
1500	56	0.09	POP*GPC
1600	71	0.24	POP*GPC
1700	74	0.05	POP*GPC
1820	149	0.58	POP*GPC
1870	242	0.97	POP*GPC
1880	311	2.54	POP*GPC
1890	400	2.54	POP*GPC
1900	494	2.12	POP*GPC
1913	704	2.76	POP*GPC
1920	627	1.63	POP*GPC
1929	948	4.70	POP*GPC
1938	1,068	1.33	POP*GPC
1950	1,238	1.24	POP*GPC
1960	2,622	7.79	POP*GPC
1970	5,634	7.95	POP*GPC
1980	12,403	8.21	POP*GPC
1990	14,345	1.46	POP*GPC
2000	6,723	7.30	POP*GPC
2010	11,782	5.77	POP*GPC
2012	13,777	8.13	POP*GPC
2020	19,912	4.71	POP*GPC
2030	27,359	3.23	POP*GPC
MEA Kuwait			
0001	59	.	POP*GPC
1000	73	0.02	POP*GPC
1500	61	0.03	POP*GPC
1600	61	0.00	POP*GPC
1700	61	0.00	POP*GPC
1820	71	0.12	POP*GPC
1870	74	0.09	POP*GPC
1880	79	0.66	POP*GPC

Year	GDP at PPP, mil. 2012 doll.	Growth Rate	Source
1890	85	0.66	POP*GPC
1900	90	0.66	POP*GPC
1913	98	0.66	POP*GPC
1920	217	12.02	POP*GPC
1929	604	12.02	POP*GPC
1938	1,678	12.02	POP*GPC
1950	6,552	12.02	POP*GPC
1960	13,197	7.25	POP*GPC
1970	33,656	9.81	POP*GPC
1980	65,406	6.87	POP*GPC
1990	107,456	5.09	POP*GPC
2000	104,010	0.33	POP*GPC
2010	165,854	4.78	POP*GPC
2012	176,570	3.18	POP*GPC
2020	210,916	2.25	POP*GPC
2030	263,310	2.24	POP*GPC
USR Kyrgyzstan			
0001	39	.	POP*GPC
1000	89	0.08	POP*GPC
1500	153	0.11	POP*GPC
1600	183	0.18	POP*GPC
1700	216	0.17	POP*GPC
1820	343	0.39	POP*GPC
1870	635	1.24	POP*GPC
1880	776	2.03	POP*GPC
1890	949	2.03	POP*GPC
1900	1,169	2.10	POP*GPC
1913	1,764	3.22	POP*GPC
1920	677	12.79	POP*GPC
1929	1,858	11.88	POP*GPC
1938	3,159	6.07	POP*GPC
1950	4,766	3.49	POP*GPC
1960	6,970	3.87	POP*GPC
1970	11,329	4.98	POP*GPC
1980	12,561	1.04	POP*GPC
1990	12,604	0.03	POP*GPC
2000	8,431	3.94	POP*GPC
2010	12,604	4.10	POP*GPC
2012	13,137	2.09	POP*GPC
2020	16,436	2.84	POP*GPC
2030	21,563	2.75	POP*GPC
CPA Laos			
0001	33	.	POP*GPC
1000	88	0.10	POP*GPC
1500	204	0.17	POP*GPC
1600	241	0.17	POP*GPC
1700	278	0.15	POP*GPC
1820	357	0.21	POP*GPC
1870	552	0.87	POP*GPC

Year	GDP at PPP, mil. 2012 doll.	Growth Rate	Source
1880	688	2.23	POP*GPC
1890	858	2.23	POP*GPC
1900	1,070	2.23	POP*GPC
1913	1,425	2.23	POP*GPC
1920	1,432	0.07	POP*GPC
1929	1,441	0.07	POP*GPC
1938	1,450	0.07	POP*GPC
1950	1,462	0.07	POP*GPC
1960	2,089	3.64	POP*GPC
1970	2,685	2.54	POP*GPC
1980	3,490	2.66	POP*GPC
1990	4,446	2.45	POP*GPC
2000	7,999	6.05	POP*GPC
2010	16,007	7.18	POP*GPC
2012	18,762	8.26	POP*GPC
2020	29,322	5.74	POP*GPC
2030	41,651	3.57	POP*GPC
USR Latvia			
0001	11	.	POP*GPC
1000	35	0.11	POP*GPC
1500	146	0.29	POP*GPC
1600	202	0.32	POP*GPC
1700	298	0.39	POP*GPC
1820	742	0.76	POP*GPC
1870	1,652	1.61	POP*GPC
1880	2,020	2.03	POP*GPC
1890	2,470	2.03	POP*GPC
1900	3,042	2.10	POP*GPC
1913	4,591	3.22	POP*GPC
1920	3,974	2.04	POP*GPC
1929	6,507	5.63	POP*GPC
1938	9,419	4.19	POP*GPC
1950	11,254	1.49	POP*GPC
1960	16,478	3.89	POP*GPC
1970	24,946	4.23	POP*GPC
1980	30,155	1.91	POP*GPC
1990	39,713	2.79	POP*GPC
2000	26,674	3.90	POP*GPC
2010	39,709	4.06	POP*GPC
2012	44,630	6.02	POP*GPC
2020	58,976	3.55	POP*GPC
2030	72,457	2.08	POP*GPC
MEA Lebanon			
0001	297	.	POP*GPC
1000	365	0.02	POP*GPC
1500	308	0.03	POP*GPC
1600	300	0.03	POP*GPC
1700	293	0.03	POP*GPC
1820	342	0.13	POP*GPC

Year	GDP at PPP, mil. 2012 doll.	Growth Rate	Source
1870	629	1.23	POP*GPC
1880	754	1.83	POP*GPC
1890	903	1.83	POP*GPC
1900	1,083	1.83	POP*GPC
1913	1,371	1.83	POP*GPC
1920	1,782	3.82	POP*GPC
1929	2,497	3.82	POP*GPC
1938	3,499	3.82	POP*GPC
1950	5,485	3.82	POP*GPC
1960	8,280	4.20	POP*GPC
1970	16,676	7.25	POP*GPC
1980	30,368	6.18	POP*GPC
1990	24,499	2.12	POP*GPC
2000	43,170	5.83	POP*GPC
2010	57,860	2.97	POP*GPC
2012	59,355	1.28	POP*GPC
2020	75,460	3.05	POP*GPC
2030	95,760	2.41	POP*GPC
AFR Lesotho			
0001	1	.	POP*GPC
1000	6	0.14	POP*GPC
1500	14	0.17	POP*GPC
1600	17	0.19	POP*GPC
1700	25	0.40	POP*GPC
1820	41	0.41	POP*GPC
1870	99	1.79	POP*GPC
1880	118	1.79	POP*GPC
1890	141	1.79	POP*GPC
1900	168	1.79	POP*GPC
1913	212	1.79	POP*GPC
1920	239	1.79	POP*GPC
1929	281	1.79	POP*GPC
1938	330	1.79	POP*GPC
1950	408	1.79	POP*GPC
1960	530	2.66	POP*GPC
1970	747	3.49	POP*GPC
1980	1,347	6.07	POP*GPC
1990	1,987	3.97	POP*GPC
2000	2,598	2.72	POP*GPC
2010	3,521	3.09	POP*GPC
2012	3,728	2.91	POP*GPC
2020	4,681	2.89	POP*GPC
2030	5,751	2.08	POP*GPC
AFR Liberia			
0001	.	.	POP*GPC
1000	.	.	POP*GPC
1500	.	.	POP*GPC
1600	.	.	POP*GPC
1700	.	.	POP*GPC

Year	GDP at PPP, mil. 2012 doll.	Growth Rate	Source
1820	.	.	POP*GPC
1870	.	.	POP*GPC
1880	.	.	POP*GPC
1890	.	.	POP*GPC
1900	.	.	POP*GPC
1913	.	.	POP*GPC
1920	.	.	POP*GPC
1929	.	.	POP*GPC
1938	.	.	POP*GPC
1950	1,360	.	POP*GPC
1960	1,616	1.74	POP*GPC
1970	1,881	1.53	POP*GPC
1980	1,638	1.37	POP*GPC
1990	748	7.54	POP*GPC
2000	1,282	5.54	POP*GPC
2010	2,235	5.71	POP*GPC
2012	2,581	7.46	POP*GPC
2020	3,845	5.11	POP*GPC
2030	5,993	4.54	POP*GPC
MEA Libya			
0001	269	.	POP*GPC
1000	336	0.02	POP*GPC
1500	336	0.00	POP*GPC
1600	336	0.00	POP*GPC
1700	336	0.00	POP*GPC
1820	362	0.06	POP*GPC
1870	579	0.94	POP*GPC
1880	636	0.94	POP*GPC
1890	699	0.94	POP*GPC
1900	768	0.94	POP*GPC
1913	868	0.94	POP*GPC
1920	927	0.94	POP*GPC
1929	1,009	0.94	POP*GPC
1938	1,098	0.94	POP*GPC
1950	1,380	1.92	POP*GPC
1960	4,045	11.35	POP*GPC
1970	32,827	23.29	POP*GPC
1980	39,682	1.91	POP*GPC
1990	22,628	5.46	POP*GPC
2000	73,997	12.58	POP*GPC
2010	107,475	3.80	POP*GPC
2012	73,057	17.55	POP*GPC
2020	115,798	5.93	POP*GPC
2030	166,786	3.72	POP*GPC
DME Liechtenstein			
0001	.	.	POP*GPC
1000	.	.	POP*GPC
1500	.	.	POP*GPC
1600	.	.	POP*GPC

Year	GDP at PPP, mil. 2012 doll.	Growth Rate	Source
1700	.	.	POP*GPC
1820	.	.	POP*GPC
1870	.	.	POP*GPC
1880	.	.	POP*GPC
1890	.	.	POP*GPC
1900	.	.	POP*GPC
1913	.	.	POP*GPC
1920	.	.	POP*GPC
1929	.	.	POP*GPC
1938	.	.	POP*GPC
1950	145	.	POP*GPC
1960	239	5.15	POP*GPC
1970	454	6.62	POP*GPC
1980	689	4.25	POP*GPC
1990	964	3.42	POP*GPC
2000	1,163	1.90	POP*GPC
2010	3,440	11.46	POP*GPC
2012	3,609	2.43	POP*GPC
2020	6,043	6.65	POP*GPC
2030	8,492	3.46	POP*GPC
USR Lithuania			
0001	17	.	POP*GPC
1000	53	0.11	POP*GPC
1500	219	0.29	POP*GPC
1600	303	0.32	POP*GPC
1700	447	0.39	POP*GPC
1820	1,112	0.76	POP*GPC
1870	2,476	1.61	POP*GPC
1880	3,028	2.03	POP*GPC
1890	3,703	2.03	POP*GPC
1900	4,561	2.10	POP*GPC
1913	6,883	3.22	POP*GPC
1920	5,958	2.04	POP*GPC
1929	9,756	5.63	POP*GPC
1938	14,122	4.19	POP*GPC
1950	14,251	0.08	POP*GPC
1960	22,494	4.67	POP*GPC
1970	37,921	5.36	POP*GPC
1980	49,142	2.63	POP*GPC
1990	58,500	1.76	POP*GPC
2000	40,727	3.56	POP*GPC
2010	65,515	4.87	POP*GPC
2012	73,278	5.76	POP*GPC
2020	98,550	3.77	POP*GPC
2030	122,407	2.19	POP*GPC
DME Luxembourg			
0001	.	.	POP*GPC
1000	.	.	POP*GPC
1500	.	.	POP*GPC

Year	GDP at PPP, mil. 2012 doll.	Growth Rate	Source
1600	.	.	POP*GPC
1700	.	.	POP*GPC
1820	.	.	POP*GPC
1870	.	.	POP*GPC
1880	.	.	POP*GPC
1890	.	.	POP*GPC
1900	.	.	POP*GPC
1913	.	.	POP*GPC
1920	.	.	POP*GPC
1929	.	.	POP*GPC
1938	.	.	POP*GPC
1950	3,882	.	POP*GPC
1960	6,140	4.69	POP*GPC
1970	9,883	4.87	POP*GPC
1980	11,563	1.58	POP*GPC
1990	19,816	5.53	POP*GPC
2000	35,801	6.09	POP*GPC
2010	46,902	2.74	POP*GPC
2012	47,680	0.83	POP*GPC
2020	64,726	3.89	POP*GPC
2030	88,236	3.15	POP*GPC
SEA Macao			
0001	.	.	POP*GPC
1000	.	.	POP*GPC
1500	.	.	POP*GPC
1600	.	.	POP*GPC
1700	.	.	POP*GPC
1820	.	.	POP*GPC
1870	.	.	POP*GPC
1880	.	.	POP*GPC
1890	.	.	POP*GPC
1900	.	.	POP*GPC
1913	.	.	POP*GPC
1920	.	.	POP*GPC
1929	.	.	POP*GPC
1938	.	.	POP*GPC
1950	332	.	POP*GPC
1960	558	5.34	POP*GPC
1970	1,633	11.34	POP*GPC
1980	4,684	11.11	POP*GPC
1990	9,003	6.75	POP*GPC
2000	11,651	2.61	POP*GPC
2010	36,254	12.02	POP*GPC
2012	49,658	17.04	POP*GPC
2020	108,407	10.25	POP*GPC
2030	153,628	3.55	POP*GPC
EEU Macedonia			
0001	37	.	POP*GPC
1000	58	0.05	POP*GPC

Year	GDP at PPP, mil. 2012 doll.	Growth Rate	Source
1500	91	0.09	POP*GPC
1600	116	0.24	POP*GPC
1700	121	0.05	POP*GPC
1820	243	0.58	POP*GPC
1870	394	0.97	POP*GPC
1880	507	2.54	POP*GPC
1890	652	2.54	POP*GPC
1900	804	2.12	POP*GPC
1913	1,146	2.76	POP*GPC
1920	1,022	1.63	POP*GPC
1929	1,545	4.70	POP*GPC
1938	1,740	1.33	POP*GPC
1950	2,017	1.24	POP*GPC
1960	4,055	7.23	POP*GPC
1970	7,944	6.95	POP*GPC
1980	16,641	7.68	POP*GPC
1990	18,242	0.92	POP*GPC
2000	18,034	0.11	POP*GPC
2010	23,699	2.77	POP*GPC
2012	24,391	1.45	POP*GPC
2020	28,766	2.08	POP*GPC
2030	34,274	1.77	POP*GPC
AFR Madagascar			
0001	0	.	POP*GPC
1000	99	0.57	POP*GPC
1500	432	0.30	POP*GPC
1600	520	0.18	POP*GPC
1700	649	0.22	POP*GPC
1820	1,093	0.43	POP*GPC
1870	2,144	1.36	POP*GPC
1880	2,453	1.36	POP*GPC
1890	2,807	1.36	POP*GPC
1900	3,212	1.36	POP*GPC
1913	3,827	1.36	POP*GPC
1920	4,206	1.36	POP*GPC
1929	4,748	1.36	POP*GPC
1938	5,360	1.36	POP*GPC
1950	6,301	1.36	POP*GPC
1960	8,916	3.53	POP*GPC
1970	12,282	3.26	POP*GPC
1980	13,411	0.88	POP*GPC
1990	13,759	0.26	POP*GPC
2000	15,876	1.44	POP*GPC
2010	20,218	2.45	POP*GPC
2012	21,174	2.34	POP*GPC
2020	26,038	2.62	POP*GPC
2030	33,911	2.68	POP*GPC

Year	GDP at PPP, mil. 2012 doll.	Growth Rate	Source
AFR Malawi			
0001	7	.	POP*GPC
1000	63	0.22	POP*GPC
1500	147	0.17	POP*GPC
1600	167	0.13	POP*GPC
1700	189	0.12	POP*GPC
1820	222	0.13	POP*GPC
1870	454	1.44	POP*GPC
1880	524	1.44	POP*GPC
1890	605	1.44	POP*GPC
1900	698	1.44	POP*GPC
1913	841	1.44	POP*GPC
1920	929	1.44	POP*GPC
1929	1,057	1.44	POP*GPC
1938	1,203	1.44	POP*GPC
1950	1,428	1.44	POP*GPC
1960	2,010	3.48	POP*GPC
1970	2,727	3.10	POP*GPC
1980	4,963	6.17	POP*GPC
1990	6,151	2.17	POP*GPC
2000	8,513	3.30	POP*GPC
2010	11,188	2.77	POP*GPC
2012	11,970	3.44	POP*GPC
2020	16,302	3.94	POP*GPC
2030	24,463	4.14	POP*GPC
SEA Malaysia			
0001	36	.	POP*GPC
1000	67	0.06	POP*GPC
1500	155	0.17	POP*GPC
1600	183	0.17	POP*GPC
1700	211	0.15	POP*GPC
1820	271	0.21	POP*GPC
1870	830	2.27	POP*GPC
1880	1,223	3.96	POP*GPC
1890	1,803	3.96	POP*GPC
1900	2,659	3.96	POP*GPC
1913	4,343	3.85	POP*GPC
1920	6,158	5.11	POP*GPC
1929	11,360	7.04	POP*GPC
1938	11,090	0.27	POP*GPC
1950	14,906	2.50	POP*GPC
1960	20,038	3.00	POP*GPC
1970	35,092	5.76	POP*GPC
1980	75,973	8.03	POP*GPC
1990	137,348	6.10	POP*GPC
2000	268,357	6.93	POP*GPC
2010	445,969	5.21	POP*GPC
2012	503,159	6.22	POP*GPC

Year	GDP at PPP, mil. 2012 doll.	Growth Rate	Source
2020	743,185	5.00	POP*GPC
2030	1,071,890	3.73	POP*GPC
SAS Maldives			
0001	.	.	POP*GPC
1000	.	.	POP*GPC
1500	.	.	POP*GPC
1600	.	.	POP*GPC
1700	.	.	POP*GPC
1820	.	.	POP*GPC
1870	.	.	POP*GPC
1880	.	.	POP*GPC
1890	.	.	POP*GPC
1900	.	.	POP*GPC
1913	.	.	POP*GPC
1920	.	.	POP*GPC
1929	.	.	POP*GPC
1938	.	.	POP*GPC
1950	67	.	POP*GPC
1960	102	4.25	POP*GPC
1970	151	3.99	POP*GPC
1980	313	7.58	POP*GPC
1990	766	9.35	POP*GPC
2000	1,390	6.14	POP*GPC
2010	2,683	6.80	POP*GPC
2012	2,950	4.86	POP*GPC
2020	4,726	6.07	POP*GPC
2030	6,589	3.38	POP*GPC
AFR Mali			
0001	.	.	POP*GPC
1000	.	.	POP*GPC
1500	.	.	POP*GPC
1600	.	.	POP*GPC
1700	.	.	POP*GPC
1820	.	.	POP*GPC
1870	.	.	POP*GPC
1880	.	.	POP*GPC
1890	.	.	POP*GPC
1900	.	.	POP*GPC
1913	.	.	POP*GPC
1920	.	.	POP*GPC
1929	.	.	POP*GPC
1938	.	.	POP*GPC
1950	2,637	.	POP*GPC
1960	3,469	2.78	POP*GPC
1970	4,331	2.24	POP*GPC
1980	6,158	3.58	POP*GPC
1990	6,728	0.89	POP*GPC
2000	10,226	4.28	POP*GPC
2010	18,246	5.96	POP*GPC

Year	GDP at PPP, mil. 2012 doll.	Growth Rate	Source
2012	18,657	1.12	POP*GPC
2020	27,273	4.86	POP*GPC
2030	42,559	4.55	POP*GPC
	DME MALTA		
0001	.	.	POP*GPC
1000	.	.	POP*GPC
1500	.	.	POP*GPC
1600	.	.	POP*GPC
1700	.	.	POP*GPC
1820	.	.	POP*GPC
1870	.	.	POP*GPC
1880	.	.	POP*GPC
1890	.	.	POP*GPC
1900	.	.	POP*GPC
1913	.	.	POP*GPC
1920	.	.	POP*GPC
1929	.	.	POP*GPC
1938	.	.	POP*GPC
1950	435	.	POP*GPC
1960	1,025	8.95	POP*GPC
1970	2,337	8.59	POP*GPC
1980	3,891	5.23	POP*GPC
1990	5,818	4.10	POP*GPC
2000	10,346	5.92	POP*GPC
2010	11,760	1.29	POP*GPC
2012	12,016	1.08	POP*GPC
2020	15,271	3.04	POP*GPC
2030	19,106	2.27	POP*GPC
	SEA MARSHALL ISLANDS		
0001	.	.	POP*GPC
1000	.	.	POP*GPC
1500	.	.	POP*GPC
1600	.	.	POP*GPC
1700	.	.	POP*GPC
1820	.	.	POP*GPC
1870	.	.	POP*GPC
1880	.	.	POP*GPC
1890	.	.	POP*GPC
1900	.	.	POP*GPC
1913	.	.	POP*GPC
1920	.	.	POP*GPC
1929	.	.	POP*GPC
1938	.	.	POP*GPC
1950	17	.	POP*GPC
1960	26	4.58	POP*GPC
1970	44	5.35	POP*GPC
1980	66	4.05	POP*GPC
1990	95	3.75	POP*GPC
2000	114	1.78	POP*GPC

Year	GDP at PPP, mil. 2012 doll.	Growth Rate	Source
2010	448	14.71	POP*GPC
2012	465	1.83	POP*GPC
2020	890	8.47	POP*GPC
2030	1,256	3.51	POP*GPC
LAM Martinique			
0001	.	.	POP*GPC
1000	.	.	POP*GPC
1500	.	.	POP*GPC
1600	.	.	POP*GPC
1700	.	.	POP*GPC
1820	.	.	POP*GPC
1870	.	.	POP*GPC
1880	.	.	POP*GPC
1890	.	.	POP*GPC
1900	.	.	POP*GPC
1913	.	.	POP*GPC
1920	.	.	POP*GPC
1929	.	.	POP*GPC
1938	.	.	POP*GPC
1950	459	.	POP*GPC
1960	1,054	8.68	POP*GPC
1970	2,200	7.63	POP*GPC
1980	2,741	2.22	POP*GPC
1990	3,200	1.56	POP*GPC
2000	4,840	4.23	POP*GPC
2010	12,701	10.13	POP*GPC
2012	12,203	1.98	POP*GPC
2020	19,530	6.06	POP*GPC
2030	25,490	2.70	POP*GPC
AFR Mauritania			
0001	.	.	POP*GPC
1000	.	.	POP*GPC
1500	.	.	POP*GPC
1600	.	.	POP*GPC
1700	.	.	POP*GPC
1820	.	.	POP*GPC
1870	.	.	POP*GPC
1880	.	.	POP*GPC
1890	.	.	POP*GPC
1900	.	.	POP*GPC
1913	.	.	POP*GPC
1920	.	.	POP*GPC
1929	.	.	POP*GPC
1938	.	.	POP*GPC
1950	502	.	POP*GPC
1960	1,202	9.12	POP*GPC
1970	2,614	8.08	POP*GPC
1980	3,226	2.12	POP*GPC
1990	3,571	1.02	POP*GPC

Year	GDP at PPP, mil. 2012 doll.	Growth Rate	Source
2000	4,876	3.17	POP*GPC
2010	7,699	4.67	POP*GPC
2012	8,601	5.70	POP*GPC
2020	11,873	4.11	POP*GPC
2030	17,223	3.79	POP*GPC
	AFR Mauritius		
0001	.	.	POP*GPC
1000	.	.	POP*GPC
1500	.	.	POP*GPC
1600	.	.	POP*GPC
1700	.	.	POP*GPC
1820	.	.	POP*GPC
1870	.	.	POP*GPC
1880	.	.	POP*GPC
1890	.	.	POP*GPC
1900	.	.	POP*GPC
1913	.	.	POP*GPC
1920	.	.	POP*GPC
1929	.	.	POP*GPC
1938	.	.	POP*GPC
1950	1,866	.	POP*GPC
1960	2,556	3.19	POP*GPC
1970	3,023	1.69	POP*GPC
1980	4,585	4.26	POP*GPC
1990	8,060	5.80	POP*GPC
2000	12,504	4.49	POP*GPC
2010	17,312	3.31	POP*GPC
2012	18,518	3.43	POP*GPC
2020	24,916	3.78	POP*GPC
2030	32,278	2.62	POP*GPC
	AFR Mayotte		
0001	.	.	POP*GPC
1000	.	.	POP*GPC
1500	.	.	POP*GPC
1600	.	.	POP*GPC
1700	.	.	POP*GPC
1820	.	.	POP*GPC
1870	.	.	POP*GPC
1880	.	.	POP*GPC
1890	.	.	POP*GPC
1900	.	.	POP*GPC
1913	.	.	POP*GPC
1920	.	.	POP*GPC
1929	.	.	POP*GPC
1938	.	.	POP*GPC
1950	8	.	POP*GPC
1960	16	6.91	POP*GPC
1970	24	3.71	POP*GPC
1980	40	5.50	POP*GPC

Year	GDP at PPP, mil. 2012 doll.	Growth Rate	Source
1990	76	6.64	POP*GPC
2000	541	21.61	POP*GPC
2010	2,701	17.45	POP*GPC
2012	2,712	0.22	POP*GPC
2020	7,325	13.22	POP*GPC
2030	11,277	4.41	POP*GPC
LAM Mexico			
0001	815	.	POP*GPC
1000	2,365	0.11	POP*GPC
1500	4,988	0.15	POP*GPC
1600	1,776	1.03	POP*GPC
1700	4,000	0.82	POP*GPC
1820	7,824	0.56	POP*GPC
1870	9,723	0.44	POP*GPC
1880	13,433	3.28	POP*GPC
1890	18,556	3.28	POP*GPC
1900	29,086	4.60	POP*GPC
1913	40,573	2.59	POP*GPC
1920	42,505	0.67	POP*GPC
1929	46,397	0.98	POP*GPC
1938	55,319	1.97	POP*GPC
1950	102,666	5.29	POP*GPC
1960	196,704	6.72	POP*GPC
1970	378,538	6.77	POP*GPC
1980	767,564	7.32	POP*GPC
1990	916,759	1.79	POP*GPC
2000	1,439,873	4.62	POP*GPC
2010	1,741,186	1.92	POP*GPC
2012	1,915,028	4.87	POP*GPC
2020	2,386,590	2.79	POP*GPC
2030	3,068,634	2.55	POP*GPC
SEA Micronesia			
0001	.	.	POP*GPC
1000	.	.	POP*GPC
1500	.	.	POP*GPC
1600	.	.	POP*GPC
1700	.	.	POP*GPC
1820	.	.	POP*GPC
1870	.	.	POP*GPC
1880	.	.	POP*GPC
1890	.	.	POP*GPC
1900	.	.	POP*GPC
1913	.	.	POP*GPC
1920	.	.	POP*GPC
1929	.	.	POP*GPC
1938	.	.	POP*GPC
1950	69	.	POP*GPC
1960	112	4.89	POP*GPC
1970	173	4.51	POP*GPC

Year	GDP at PPP, mil. 2012 doll.	Growth Rate	Source
1980	217	2.28	POP*GPC
1990	288	2.85	POP*GPC
2000	368	2.51	POP*GPC
2010	374	0.14	POP*GPC
2012	381	1.02	POP*GPC
2020	399	0.58	POP*GPC
2030	464	1.50	POP*GPC
	USR Moldova		
0001	12	.	POP*GPC
1000	34	0.11	POP*GPC
1500	130	0.27	POP*GPC
1600	180	0.32	POP*GPC
1700	266	0.39	POP*GPC
1820	662	0.76	POP*GPC
1870	1,473	1.61	POP*GPC
1880	1,802	2.03	POP*GPC
1890	2,203	2.03	POP*GPC
1900	2,714	2.10	POP*GPC
1913	4,095	3.22	POP*GPC
1920	2,402	7.34	POP*GPC
1929	2,984	2.44	POP*GPC
1938	3,526	1.87	POP*GPC
1950	9,215	8.34	POP*GPC
1960	15,568	5.38	POP*GPC
1970	24,892	4.80	POP*GPC
1980	31,232	2.30	POP*GPC
1990	36,399	1.54	POP*GPC
2000	8,773	13.26	POP*GPC
2010	12,659	3.74	POP*GPC
2012	13,198	2.11	POP*GPC
2020	15,500	2.03	POP*GPC
2030	18,058	1.54	POP*GPC
	DME Monaco		
0001	.	.	POP*GPC
1000	.	.	POP*GPC
1500	.	.	POP*GPC
1600	.	.	POP*GPC
1700	.	.	POP*GPC
1820	.	.	POP*GPC
1870	.	.	POP*GPC
1880	.	.	POP*GPC
1890	.	.	POP*GPC
1900	.	.	POP*GPC
1913	.	.	POP*GPC
1920	.	.	POP*GPC
1929	.	.	POP*GPC
1938	.	.	POP*GPC
1950	149	.	POP*GPC
1960	255	5.57	POP*GPC

Year	GDP at PPP, mil. 2012 doll.	Growth Rate	Source
1970	430	5.35	POP*GPC
1980	624	3.79	POP*GPC
1990	845	3.08	POP*GPC
2000	1,191	3.49	POP*GPC
2010	5,826	17.20	POP*GPC
2012	7,176	10.98	POP*GPC
2020	16,362	10.85	POP*GPC
2030	21,150	2.60	POP*GPC
CPA Mongolia			
0001	36	.	POP*GPC
1000	91	0.09	POP*GPC
1500	197	0.15	POP*GPC
1600	239	0.19	POP*GPC
1700	291	0.20	POP*GPC
1820	391	0.25	POP*GPC
1870	433	0.20	POP*GPC
1880	443	0.24	POP*GPC
1890	454	0.24	POP*GPC
1900	465	0.24	POP*GPC
1913	529	0.99	POP*GPC
1920	525	0.11	POP*GPC
1929	520	0.11	POP*GPC
1938	515	0.11	POP*GPC
1950	508	0.10	POP*GPC
1960	916	6.06	POP*GPC
1970	1,775	6.84	POP*GPC
1980	3,418	6.77	POP*GPC
1990	5,805	5.44	POP*GPC
2000	6,042	0.40	POP*GPC
2010	11,068	6.24	POP*GPC
2012	14,462	14.31	POP*GPC
2020	24,124	6.60	POP*GPC
2030	34,719	3.71	POP*GPC
EEU Montenegro			
0001	14	.	POP*GPC
1000	23	0.05	POP*GPC
1500	38	0.10	POP*GPC
1600	52	0.30	POP*GPC
1700	57	0.10	POP*GPC
1820	122	0.63	POP*GPC
1870	204	1.02	POP*GPC
1880	262	2.54	POP*GPC
1890	336	2.54	POP*GPC
1900	415	2.12	POP*GPC
1913	592	2.76	POP*GPC
1920	528	1.63	POP*GPC
1929	797	4.70	POP*GPC
1938	898	1.33	POP*GPC
1950	1,041	1.24	POP*GPC

Year	GDP at PPP, mil. 2012 doll.	Growth Rate	Source
1960	2,132	7.43	POP*GPC
1970	4,028	6.57	POP*GPC
1980	8,048	7.17	POP*GPC
1990	8,022	0.03	POP*GPC
2000	5,802	3.19	POP*GPC
2010	8,636	4.06	POP*GPC
2012	8,902	1.53	POP*GPC
2020	11,205	2.92	POP*GPC
2030	13,939	2.21	POP*GPC
	LAM Montserrat		
0001	.	.	POP*GPC
1000	.	.	POP*GPC
1500	.	.	POP*GPC
1600	.	.	POP*GPC
1700	.	.	POP*GPC
1820	.	.	POP*GPC
1870	.	.	POP*GPC
1880	.	.	POP*GPC
1890	.	.	POP*GPC
1900	.	.	POP*GPC
1913	.	.	POP*GPC
1920	.	.	POP*GPC
1929	.	.	POP*GPC
1938	.	.	POP*GPC
1950	17	.	POP*GPC
1960	27	4.35	POP*GPC
1970	41	4.35	POP*GPC
1980	54	2.93	POP*GPC
1990	68	2.33	POP*GPC
2000	27	8.80	POP*GPC
2010	47	5.70	POP*GPC
2012	49	1.62	POP*GPC
2020	59	2.40	POP*GPC
2030	64	0.75	POP*GPC
	MEA Morocco		
0001	438	.	POP*GPC
1000	1,346	0.11	POP*GPC
1500	1,009	0.06	POP*GPC
1600	1,514	0.41	POP*GPC
1700	1,178	0.25	POP*GPC
1820	1,809	0.36	POP*GPC
1870	3,327	1.23	POP*GPC
1880	3,767	1.25	POP*GPC
1890	4,266	1.25	POP*GPC
1900	4,831	1.25	POP*GPC
1913	5,679	1.25	POP*GPC
1920	7,232	3.51	POP*GPC
1929	9,869	3.51	POP*GPC
1938	13,467	3.51	POP*GPC

Year	GDP at PPP, mil. 2012 doll.	Growth Rate	Source
1950	20,385	3.51	POP*GPC
1960	24,285	1.77	POP*GPC
1970	35,029	3.73	POP*GPC
1980	55,465	4.70	POP*GPC
1990	79,255	3.63	POP*GPC
2000	96,005	1.94	POP*GPC
2010	154,624	4.88	POP*GPC
2012	168,627	4.43	POP*GPC
2020	224,815	3.66	POP*GPC
2030	302,061	3.00	POP*GPC
	AFR Mozambique		
0001	18	.	POP*GPC
1000	149	0.21	POP*GPC
1500	617	0.29	POP*GPC
1600	812	0.27	POP*GPC
1700	974	0.18	POP*GPC
1820	1,361	0.28	POP*GPC
1870	3,049	1.63	POP*GPC
1880	3,583	1.63	POP*GPC
1890	4,210	1.63	POP*GPC
1900	4,947	1.63	POP*GPC
1913	6,101	1.63	POP*GPC
1920	6,830	1.63	POP*GPC
1929	7,897	1.63	POP*GPC
1938	9,131	1.63	POP*GPC
1950	11,081	1.63	POP*GPC
1960	15,641	3.51	POP*GPC
1970	25,786	5.13	POP*GPC
1980	6,008	13.56	POP*GPC
1990	5,857	0.25	POP*GPC
2000	10,243	5.75	POP*GPC
2010	20,599	7.24	POP*GPC
2012	23,694	7.25	POP*GPC
2020	38,378	6.21	POP*GPC
2030	62,689	5.03	POP*GPC
	AFR Namibia		
0001	14	.	POP*GPC
1000	27	0.06	POP*GPC
1500	66	0.18	POP*GPC
1600	70	0.05	POP*GPC
1700	70	0.00	POP*GPC
1820	77	0.08	POP*GPC
1870	249	2.38	POP*GPC
1880	315	2.38	POP*GPC
1890	399	2.38	POP*GPC
1900	505	2.38	POP*GPC
1913	685	2.38	POP*GPC
1920	808	2.39	POP*GPC
1929	999	2.38	POP*GPC

Year	GDP at PPP, mil. 2012 doll.	Growth Rate	Source
1938	1,235	2.38	POP*GPC
1950	1,568	2.01	POP*GPC
1960	2,385	4.28	POP*GPC
1970	3,779	4.71	POP*GPC
1980	5,836	4.44	POP*GPC
1990	6,622	1.27	POP*GPC
2000	9,785	3.98	POP*GPC
2010	14,423	3.96	POP*GPC
2012	15,852	4.84	POP*GPC
2020	21,620	3.96	POP*GPC
2030	30,157	3.38	POP*GPC
	SEA Nauru		
0001	.	.	POP*GPC
1000	.	.	POP*GPC
1500	.	.	POP*GPC
1600	.	.	POP*GPC
1700	.	.	POP*GPC
1820	.	.	POP*GPC
1870	.	.	POP*GPC
1880	.	.	POP*GPC
1890	.	.	POP*GPC
1900	.	.	POP*GPC
1913	.	.	POP*GPC
1920	.	.	POP*GPC
1929	.	.	POP*GPC
1938	.	.	POP*GPC
1950	29	.	POP*GPC
1960	45	4.37	POP*GPC
1970	91	7.25	POP*GPC
1980	110	1.90	POP*GPC
1990	126	1.37	POP*GPC
2000	64	6.58	POP*GPC
2010	57	1.17	POP*GPC
2012	58	1.13	POP*GPC
2020	60	0.41	POP*GPC
2030	71	1.73	POP*GPC
	SAS Nepal		
0001	230	.	POP*GPC
1000	579	0.09	POP*GPC
1500	1,260	0.16	POP*GPC
1600	1,529	0.19	POP*GPC
1700	1,865	0.20	POP*GPC
1820	2,509	0.25	POP*GPC
1870	3,117	0.44	POP*GPC
1880	3,294	0.55	POP*GPC
1890	3,718	1.22	POP*GPC
1900	4,063	0.89	POP*GPC
1913	4,756	1.22	POP*GPC
1920	5,079	0.94	POP*GPC

Year	GDP at PPP, mil. 2012 doll.	Growth Rate	Source
1929	5,519	0.93	POP*GPC
1938	6,000	0.93	POP*GPC
1950	6,708	0.93	POP*GPC
1960	8,572	2.48	POP*GPC
1970	9,934	1.49	POP*GPC
1980	10,885	0.92	POP*GPC
1990	17,436	4.82	POP*GPC
2000	27,446	4.64	POP*GPC
2010	36,088	2.78	POP*GPC
2012	39,134	4.13	POP*GPC
2020	52,451	3.73	POP*GPC
2030	72,411	3.28	POP*GPC
DME Netherlands			
0001	133	.	POP*GPC
1000	200	0.04	POP*GPC
1500	1,131	0.35	POP*GPC
1600	3,242	1.06	POP*GPC
1700	6,333	0.67	POP*GPC
1820	6,710	0.05	POP*GPC
1870	15,575	1.70	POP*GPC
1880	19,271	2.15	POP*GPC
1890	23,582	2.04	POP*GPC
1900	27,551	1.57	POP*GPC
1913	39,056	2.72	POP*GPC
1920	45,222	2.12	POP*GPC
1929	69,279	4.85	POP*GPC
1938	71,351	0.33	POP*GPC
1950	94,673	2.38	POP*GPC
1960	152,650	4.89	POP*GPC
1970	256,370	5.32	POP*GPC
1980	348,288	3.11	POP*GPC
1990	438,310	2.33	POP*GPC
2000	634,816	3.77	POP*GPC
2010	728,499	1.39	POP*GPC
2012	725,339	0.22	POP*GPC
2020	851,465	2.02	POP*GPC
2030	1,038,766	2.01	POP*GPC
SEA New Caledonia			
0001	.	.	POP*GPC
1000	.	.	POP*GPC
1500	.	.	POP*GPC
1600	.	.	POP*GPC
1700	.	.	POP*GPC
1820	.	.	POP*GPC
1870	.	.	POP*GPC
1880	.	.	POP*GPC
1890	.	.	POP*GPC
1900	.	.	POP*GPC
1913	.	.	POP*GPC

Year	GDP at PPP, mil. 2012 doll.	Growth Rate	Source
1920	.	.	POP*GPC
1929	.	.	POP*GPC
1938	.	.	POP*GPC
1950	414	.	POP*GPC
1960	584	3.50	POP*GPC
1970	961	5.11	POP*GPC
1980	1,264	2.78	POP*GPC
1990	1,567	2.17	POP*GPC
2000	4,052	9.96	POP*GPC
2010	9,728	9.15	POP*GPC
2012	10,329	3.04	POP*GPC
2020	17,575	6.87	POP*GPC
2030	25,281	3.70	POP*GPC
DME New Zealand			
0001	18	.	POP*GPC
1000	32	0.06	POP*GPC
1500	54	0.11	POP*GPC
1600	56	0.04	POP*GPC
1700	59	0.05	POP*GPC
1820	63	0.05	POP*GPC
1870	1,412	6.43	POP*GPC
1880	3,049	8.00	POP*GPC
1890	3,908	2.51	POP*GPC
1900	5,428	3.34	POP*GPC
1913	9,046	4.01	POP*GPC
1920	10,955	2.77	POP*GPC
1929	12,113	1.12	POP*GPC
1938	16,220	3.30	POP*GPC
1950	25,261	3.76	POP*GPC
1960	36,151	3.65	POP*GPC
1970	52,302	3.76	POP*GPC
1980	65,994	2.35	POP*GPC
1990	83,192	2.34	POP*GPC
2000	107,081	2.56	POP*GPC
2010	137,968	2.57	POP*GPC
2012	145,855	2.82	POP*GPC
2020	176,898	2.44	POP*GPC
2030	226,336	2.50	POP*GPC
LAM Nicaragua			
0001	24	.	POP*GPC
1000	66	0.10	POP*GPC
1500	118	0.11	POP*GPC
1600	74	0.46	POP*GPC
1700	89	0.18	POP*GPC
1820	123	0.27	POP*GPC
1870	228	1.24	POP*GPC
1880	305	2.96	POP*GPC
1890	409	2.96	POP*GPC
1900	547	2.96	POP*GPC

Year	GDP at PPP, mil. 2012 doll.	Growth Rate	Source
1913	830	3.27	POP*GPC
1920	1,266	6.21	POP*GPC
1929	1,862	4.38	POP*GPC
1938	1,313	3.81	POP*GPC
1950	3,275	7.91	POP*GPC
1960	5,843	5.96	POP*GPC
1970	11,974	7.44	POP*GPC
1980	12,913	0.76	POP*GPC
1990	11,068	1.53	POP*GPC
2000	15,816	3.63	POP*GPC
2010	21,440	3.09	POP*GPC
2012	23,860	5.49	POP*GPC
2020	30,774	3.23	POP*GPC
2030	40,541	2.79	POP*GPC
AFR Niger			
0001	.	.	POP*GPC
1000	.	.	POP*GPC
1500	.	.	POP*GPC
1600	.	.	POP*GPC
1700	.	.	POP*GPC
1820	.	.	POP*GPC
1870	.	.	POP*GPC
1880	.	.	POP*GPC
1890	.	.	POP*GPC
1900	.	.	POP*GPC
1913	.	.	POP*GPC
1920	.	.	POP*GPC
1929	.	.	POP*GPC
1938	.	.	POP*GPC
1950	2,809	.	POP*GPC
1960	4,787	5.48	POP*GPC
1970	6,513	3.13	POP*GPC
1980	7,524	1.45	POP*GPC
1990	6,998	0.72	POP*GPC
2000	7,210	0.30	POP*GPC
2010	11,247	4.55	POP*GPC
2012	12,802	6.69	POP*GPC
2020	18,236	4.52	POP*GPC
2030	28,788	4.67	POP*GPC
AFR Nigeria			
0001	.	.	POP*GPC
1000	.	.	POP*GPC
1500	.	.	POP*GPC
1600	.	.	POP*GPC
1700	.	.	POP*GPC
1820	.	.	POP*GPC
1870	.	.	POP*GPC
1880	.	.	POP*GPC
1890	.	.	POP*GPC

Year	GDP at PPP, mil. 2012 doll.	Growth Rate	Source
1900	.	.	POP*GPC
1913	.	.	POP*GPC
1920	.	.	POP*GPC
1929	.	.	POP*GPC
1938	.	.	POP*GPC
1950	37,467	.	POP*GPC
1960	59,656	4.76	POP*GPC
1970	100,215	5.32	POP*GPC
1980	150,957	4.18	POP*GPC
1990	167,964	1.07	POP*GPC
2000	212,809	2.39	POP*GPC
2010	394,400	6.36	POP*GPC
2012	445,639	6.30	POP*GPC
2020	657,707	4.99	POP*GPC
2030	1,025,177	4.54	POP*GPC
SEA Niue			
0001	.	.	POP*GPC
1000	.	.	POP*GPC
1500	.	.	POP*GPC
1600	.	.	POP*GPC
1700	.	.	POP*GPC
1820	.	.	POP*GPC
1870	.	.	POP*GPC
1880	.	.	POP*GPC
1890	.	.	POP*GPC
1900	.	.	POP*GPC
1913	.	.	POP*GPC
1920	.	.	POP*GPC
1929	.	.	POP*GPC
1938	.	.	POP*GPC
1950	1	.	POP*GPC
1960	1	4.73	POP*GPC
1970	2	4.73	POP*GPC
1980	3	3.21	POP*GPC
1990	4	2.56	POP*GPC
2000	8	8.19	POP*GPC
2010	10	1.51	POP*GPC
2012	10	1.24	POP*GPC
2020	10	0.78	POP*GPC
2030	9	1.59	POP*GPC
SEA Northern Mariana Islands			
0001	.	.	POP*GPC
1000	.	.	POP*GPC
1500	.	.	POP*GPC
1600	.	.	POP*GPC
1700	.	.	POP*GPC
1820	.	.	POP*GPC
1870	.	.	POP*GPC
1880	.	.	POP*GPC

Year	GDP at PPP, mil. 2012 doll.	Growth Rate	Source
1890	.	.	POP*GPC
1900	.	.	POP*GPC
1913	.	.	POP*GPC
1920	.	.	POP*GPC
1929	.	.	POP*GPC
1938	.	.	POP*GPC
1950	70	.	POP*GPC
1960	116	5.16	POP*GPC
1970	171	3.93	POP*GPC
1980	252	3.94	POP*GPC
1990	660	10.12	POP*GPC
2000	1,070	4.96	POP*GPC
2010	770	3.24	POP*GPC
2012	744	1.73	POP*GPC
2020	835	1.46	POP*GPC
2030	1,028	2.10	POP*GPC
	DME Norway		
0001	46	.	POP*GPC
1000	143	0.11	POP*GPC
1500	300	0.15	POP*GPC
1600	476	0.46	POP*GPC
1700	704	0.39	POP*GPC
1820	1,676	0.73	POP*GPC
1870	3,888	1.70	POP*GPC
1880	4,769	2.06	POP*GPC
1890	5,553	1.53	POP*GPC
1900	6,759	1.99	POP*GPC
1913	9,577	2.72	POP*GPC
1920	11,419	2.55	POP*GPC
1929	15,186	3.22	POP*GPC
1938	19,926	3.06	POP*GPC
1950	27,912	2.85	POP*GPC
1960	42,198	4.22	POP*GPC
1970	67,042	4.74	POP*GPC
1980	114,115	5.46	POP*GPC
1990	152,276	2.93	POP*GPC
2000	270,873	5.93	POP*GPC
2010	318,971	1.65	POP*GPC
2012	332,469	2.09	POP*GPC
2020	446,607	3.76	POP*GPC
2030	602,990	3.05	POP*GPC
	MEA Oman		
0001	228	.	POP*GPC
1000	280	0.02	POP*GPC
1500	237	0.03	POP*GPC
1600	237	0.00	POP*GPC
1700	237	0.00	POP*GPC
1820	274	0.12	POP*GPC
1870	330	0.38	POP*GPC

Year	GDP at PPP, mil. 2012 doll.	Growth Rate	Source
1880	349	0.54	POP*GPC
1890	368	0.54	POP*GPC
1900	389	0.54	POP*GPC
1913	417	0.54	POP*GPC
1920	422	0.17	POP*GPC
1929	429	0.17	POP*GPC
1938	435	0.17	POP*GPC
1950	445	0.17	POP*GPC
1960	1,020	8.66	POP*GPC
1970	6,451	20.26	POP*GPC
1980	12,016	6.42	POP*GPC
1990	27,734	8.72	POP*GPC
2000	50,452	6.17	POP*GPC
2010	77,675	4.41	POP*GPC
2012	75,503	1.41	POP*GPC
2020	110,410	4.87	POP*GPC
2030	152,729	3.30	POP*GPC
SAS Pakistan			
0001	3,450	.	POP*GPC
1000	3,450	0.00	POP*GPC
1500	6,184	0.12	POP*GPC
1600	7,589	0.21	POP*GPC
1700	9,275	0.20	POP*GPC
1820	11,343	0.17	POP*GPC
1870	15,705	0.65	POP*GPC
1880	16,624	0.57	POP*GPC
1890	18,818	1.25	POP*GPC
1900	19,936	0.58	POP*GPC
1913	22,825	1.05	POP*GPC
1920	23,444	0.38	POP*GPC
1929	26,238	1.26	POP*GPC
1938	28,431	0.90	POP*GPC
1950	39,692	2.82	POP*GPC
1960	48,655	2.06	POP*GPC
1970	86,281	5.90	POP*GPC
1980	123,074	3.62	POP*GPC
1990	226,204	6.28	POP*GPC
2000	323,938	3.66	POP*GPC
2010	489,504	4.21	POP*GPC
2012	521,541	3.22	POP*GPC
2020	689,042	3.54	POP*GPC
2030	947,018	3.23	POP*GPC
SEA Palau			
0001	.	.	POP*GPC
1000	.	.	POP*GPC
1500	.	.	POP*GPC
1600	.	.	POP*GPC
1700	.	.	POP*GPC
1820	.	.	POP*GPC

Year	GDP at PPP, mil. 2012 doll.	Growth Rate	Source
1870	.	.	POP*GPC
1880	.	.	POP*GPC
1890	.	.	POP*GPC
1900	.	.	POP*GPC
1913	.	.	POP*GPC
1920	.	.	POP*GPC
1929	.	.	POP*GPC
1938	.	.	POP*GPC
1950	80	.	POP*GPC
1960	119	3.97	POP*GPC
1970	182	4.35	POP*GPC
1980	208	1.35	POP*GPC
1990	244	1.63	POP*GPC
2000	349	3.62	POP*GPC
2010	349	0.02	POP*GPC
2012	389	5.48	POP*GPC
2020	449	1.82	POP*GPC
2030	537	1.81	POP*GPC
LAM Panama			
0001	13	.	POP*GPC
1000	38	0.11	POP*GPC
1500	69	0.12	POP*GPC
1600	44	0.46	POP*GPC
1700	53	0.19	POP*GPC
1820	74	0.28	POP*GPC
1870	141	1.30	POP*GPC
1880	192	3.14	POP*GPC
1890	262	3.14	POP*GPC
1900	357	3.14	POP*GPC
1913	593	3.98	POP*GPC
1920	923	6.53	POP*GPC
1929	1,101	1.97	POP*GPC
1938	1,597	4.23	POP*GPC
1950	2,677	4.40	POP*GPC
1960	4,192	4.59	POP*GPC
1970	8,818	7.72	POP*GPC
1980	15,084	5.52	POP*GPC
1990	17,280	1.37	POP*GPC
2000	27,547	4.77	POP*GPC
2010	50,562	6.26	POP*GPC
2012	61,900	10.65	POP*GPC
2020	97,509	5.84	POP*GPC
2030	142,073	3.84	POP*GPC
SEA Papua New Guinea			
0001	.	.	POP*GPC
1000	.	.	POP*GPC
1500	.	.	POP*GPC
1600	.	.	POP*GPC
1700	.	.	POP*GPC

Year	GDP at PPP, mil. 2012 doll.	Growth Rate	Source
1820	.	.	POP*GPC
1870	.	.	POP*GPC
1880	.	.	POP*GPC
1890	.	.	POP*GPC
1900	.	.	POP*GPC
1913	.	.	POP*GPC
1920	.	.	POP*GPC
1929	.	.	POP*GPC
1938	.	.	POP*GPC
1950	1,753	.	POP*GPC
1960	2,819	4.87	POP*GPC
1970	5,051	6.01	POP*GPC
1980	6,386	2.37	POP*GPC
1990	7,260	1.29	POP*GPC
2000	11,607	4.80	POP*GPC
2010	17,397	4.13	POP*GPC
2012	20,340	8.13	POP*GPC
2020	28,466	4.29	POP*GPC
2030	41,147	3.75	POP*GPC
LAM Paraguay			
0001	18	.	POP*GPC
1000	50	0.10	POP*GPC
1500	89	0.11	POP*GPC
1600	56	0.46	POP*GPC
1700	67	0.18	POP*GPC
1820	93	0.27	POP*GPC
1870	255	2.04	POP*GPC
1880	317	2.23	POP*GPC
1890	396	2.23	POP*GPC
1900	493	2.23	POP*GPC
1913	837	4.14	POP*GPC
1920	1,096	3.93	POP*GPC
1929	1,547	3.91	POP*GPC
1938	2,189	3.94	POP*GPC
1950	3,651	4.35	POP*GPC
1960	4,656	2.46	POP*GPC
1970	7,192	4.44	POP*GPC
1980	15,704	8.12	POP*GPC
1990	23,209	3.98	POP*GPC
2000	28,533	2.09	POP*GPC
2010	38,655	3.08	POP*GPC
2012	39,486	1.07	POP*GPC
2020	47,676	2.38	POP*GPC
2030	60,874	2.47	POP*GPC
LAM Peru			
0001	180	.	POP*GPC
1000	511	0.10	POP*GPC
1500	926	0.12	POP*GPC
1600	585	0.46	POP*GPC

Year	GDP at PPP, mil. 2012 doll.	Growth Rate	Source
1700	702	0.18	POP*GPC
1820	982	0.28	POP*GPC
1870	1,991	1.42	POP*GPC
1880	2,678	3.01	POP*GPC
1890	3,603	3.01	POP*GPC
1900	4,847	3.01	POP*GPC
1913	7,041	2.91	POP*GPC
1920	9,720	4.71	POP*GPC
1929	13,412	3.64	POP*GPC
1938	16,752	2.50	POP*GPC
1950	27,027	4.07	POP*GPC
1960	47,955	5.90	POP*GPC
1970	81,933	5.50	POP*GPC
1980	121,284	4.00	POP*GPC
1990	111,392	0.85	POP*GPC
2000	163,044	3.88	POP*GPC
2010	281,179	5.60	POP*GPC
2012	318,070	6.36	POP*GPC
2020	452,412	4.50	POP*GPC
2030	620,812	3.21	POP*GPC
SEA Philippines			
0001	104	.	POP*GPC
1000	192	0.06	POP*GPC
1500	446	0.17	POP*GPC
1600	717	0.48	POP*GPC
1700	1,128	0.45	POP*GPC
1820	1,989	0.47	POP*GPC
1870	4,944	1.84	POP*GPC
1880	5,793	1.60	POP*GPC
1890	6,788	1.60	POP*GPC
1900	7,955	1.60	POP*GPC
1913	15,463	5.25	POP*GPC
1920	21,633	4.91	POP*GPC
1929	30,297	3.81	POP*GPC
1938	37,950	2.53	POP*GPC
1950	33,481	1.04	POP*GPC
1960	59,566	5.93	POP*GPC
1970	91,760	4.42	POP*GPC
1980	155,014	5.38	POP*GPC
1990	177,633	1.37	POP*GPC
2000	235,628	2.87	POP*GPC
2010	375,824	4.78	POP*GPC
2012	408,666	4.28	POP*GPC
2020	547,072	3.71	POP*GPC
2030	765,970	3.42	POP*GPC
EEU Poland			
0001	207	.	POP*GPC
1000	871	0.14	POP*GPC
1500	4,091	0.31	POP*GPC

Year	GDP at PPP, mil. 2012 doll.	Growth Rate	Source
1600	5,649	0.32	POP*GPC
1700	7,497	0.28	POP*GPC
1820	14,682	0.56	POP*GPC
1870	24,966	1.07	POP*GPC
1880	33,859	3.09	POP*GPC
1890	45,920	3.09	POP*GPC
1900	59,489	2.62	POP*GPC
1913	72,685	1.55	POP*GPC
1920	71,084	0.32	POP*GPC
1929	92,281	2.94	POP*GPC
1938	106,061	1.56	POP*GPC
1950	95,056	0.91	POP*GPC
1960	157,091	5.15	POP*GPC
1970	252,060	4.84	POP*GPC
1980	377,262	4.12	POP*GPC
1990	372,061	0.14	POP*GPC
2000	546,802	3.93	POP*GPC
2010	829,200	4.25	POP*GPC
2012	877,433	2.87	POP*GPC
2020	1,173,573	3.70	POP*GPC
2030	1,464,484	2.24	POP*GPC
	DME Portugal		
0001	282	.	POP*GPC
1000	399	0.03	POP*GPC
1500	948	0.17	POP*GPC
1600	1,274	0.30	POP*GPC
1700	2,563	0.70	POP*GPC
1820	4,762	0.52	POP*GPC
1870	6,602	0.66	POP*GPC
1880	6,832	0.34	POP*GPC
1890	8,875	2.65	POP*GPC
1900	11,010	2.18	POP*GPC
1913	11,682	0.46	POP*GPC
1920	11,595	0.11	POP*GPC
1929	16,883	4.26	POP*GPC
1938	20,471	2.16	POP*GPC
1950	27,560	2.51	POP*GPC
1960	42,856	4.51	POP*GPC
1970	82,671	6.79	POP*GPC
1980	134,961	5.02	POP*GPC
1990	187,700	3.35	POP*GPC
2000	265,244	3.52	POP*GPC
2010	285,564	0.74	POP*GPC
2012	274,872	1.89	POP*GPC
2020	320,600	1.94	POP*GPC
2030	385,752	1.87	POP*GPC
	LAM Puerto Rico		
0001	6	.	POP*GPC
1000	17	0.11	POP*GPC

Year	GDP at PPP, mil. 2012 doll.	Growth Rate	Source
1500	33	0.13	POP*GPC
1600	14	0.85	POP*GPC
1700	38	0.99	POP*GPC
1820	217	1.46	POP*GPC
1870	579	1.98	POP*GPC
1880	787	3.12	POP*GPC
1890	1,070	3.12	POP*GPC
1900	1,456	3.12	POP*GPC
1913	2,251	3.41	POP*GPC
1920	2,783	3.08	POP*GPC
1929	3,714	3.26	POP*GPC
1938	5,055	3.48	POP*GPC
1950	7,441	3.27	POP*GPC
1960	11,816	4.73	POP*GPC
1970	23,194	6.98	POP*GPC
1980	34,010	3.90	POP*GPC
1990	46,567	3.19	POP*GPC
2000	51,040	0.92	POP*GPC
2010	63,218	2.16	POP*GPC
2012	64,363	0.90	POP*GPC
2020	71,965	1.41	POP*GPC
2030	79,168	0.96	POP*GPC
MEA Qatar			
0001	10	.	POP*GPC
1000	13	0.02	POP*GPC
1500	11	0.03	POP*GPC
1600	11	0.00	POP*GPC
1700	11	0.00	POP*GPC
1820	12	0.12	POP*GPC
1870	13	0.09	POP*GPC
1880	14	0.66	POP*GPC
1890	15	0.66	POP*GPC
1900	16	0.66	POP*GPC
1913	17	0.66	POP*GPC
1920	38	12.18	POP*GPC
1929	106	12.18	POP*GPC
1938	299	12.18	POP*GPC
1950	1,189	12.18	POP*GPC
1960	2,384	7.21	POP*GPC
1970	5,893	9.47	POP*GPC
1980	10,513	5.96	POP*GPC
1990	9,111	1.42	POP*GPC
2000	46,992	17.83	POP*GPC
2010	148,133	12.17	POP*GPC
2012	171,360	7.55	POP*GPC
2020	282,816	6.46	POP*GPC
2030	393,493	3.36	POP*GPC

Year	GDP at PPP, mil. 2012 doll.	Growth Rate	Source
	AFR Reunion		
0001	.	.	POP*GPC
1000	.	.	POP*GPC
1500	.	.	POP*GPC
1600	.	.	POP*GPC
1700	.	.	POP*GPC
1820	.	.	POP*GPC
1870	.	.	POP*GPC
1880	.	.	POP*GPC
1890	.	.	POP*GPC
1900	.	.	POP*GPC
1913	.	.	POP*GPC
1920	.	.	POP*GPC
1929	.	.	POP*GPC
1938	.	.	POP*GPC
1950	759	.	POP*GPC
1960	1,181	4.51	POP*GPC
1970	2,391	7.31	POP*GPC
1980	2,882	1.89	POP*GPC
1990	4,161	3.74	POP*GPC
2000	4,842	1.53	POP*GPC
2010	24,847	17.77	POP*GPC
2012	22,292	5.28	POP*GPC
2020	44,805	9.12	POP*GPC
2030	62,232	3.34	POP*GPC
	EEU Romania		
0001	532	.	POP*GPC
1000	501	0.01	POP*GPC
1500	2,013	0.28	POP*GPC
1600	2,224	0.10	POP*GPC
1700	3,074	0.32	POP*GPC
1820	8,854	0.89	POP*GPC
1870	13,373	0.83	POP*GPC
1880	16,446	2.09	POP*GPC
1890	20,225	2.09	POP*GPC
1900	24,357	1.88	POP*GPC
1913	34,129	2.63	POP*GPC
1920	19,922	7.40	POP*GPC
1929	25,151	2.62	POP*GPC
1938	30,321	2.10	POP*GPC
1950	30,170	0.04	POP*GPC
1960	63,192	7.67	POP*GPC
1970	127,835	7.30	POP*GPC
1980	239,140	6.46	POP*GPC
1990	258,532	0.78	POP*GPC
2000	213,482	1.90	POP*GPC
2010	352,884	5.15	POP*GPC
2012	359,633	0.95	POP*GPC
2020	476,640	3.58	POP*GPC

Year	GDP at PPP, mil. 2012 doll.	Growth Rate	Source
2030	581,977	2.02	POP*GPC
USR Russia			
0001	593	.	POP*GPC
1000	1,743	0.11	POP*GPC
1500	6,946	0.28	POP*GPC
1600	9,574	0.32	POP*GPC
1700	14,130	0.39	POP*GPC
1820	35,801	0.78	POP*GPC
1870	80,699	1.64	POP*GPC
1880	98,688	2.03	POP*GPC
1890	120,687	2.03	POP*GPC
1900	148,630	2.10	POP*GPC
1913	224,301	3.22	POP*GPC
1920	86,028	12.79	POP*GPC
1929	236,264	11.88	POP*GPC
1938	401,613	6.07	POP*GPC
1950	492,682	1.72	POP*GPC
1960	901,020	6.22	POP*GPC
1970	1,558,873	5.63	POP*GPC
1980	2,044,021	2.75	POP*GPC
1990	2,508,098	2.07	POP*GPC
2000	1,644,432	4.13	POP*GPC
2010	3,084,444	6.49	POP*GPC
2012	3,377,570	4.64	POP*GPC
2020	4,696,674	4.21	POP*GPC
2030	5,867,069	2.25	POP*GPC
AFR Rwanda			
0001	.	.	POP*GPC
1000	.	.	POP*GPC
1500	.	.	POP*GPC
1600	.	.	POP*GPC
1700	.	.	POP*GPC
1820	.	.	POP*GPC
1870	.	.	POP*GPC
1880	.	.	POP*GPC
1890	.	.	POP*GPC
1900	.	.	POP*GPC
1913	.	.	POP*GPC
1920	.	.	POP*GPC
1929	.	.	POP*GPC
1938	.	.	POP*GPC
1950	1,851	.	POP*GPC
1960	2,478	2.96	POP*GPC
1970	3,214	2.64	POP*GPC
1980	5,096	4.72	POP*GPC
1990	6,158	1.91	POP*GPC
2000	6,110	0.08	POP*GPC
2010	12,108	7.08	POP*GPC
2012	13,991	7.50	POP*GPC

Year	GDP at PPP, mil. 2012 doll.	Growth Rate	Source
2020	22,114	5.89	POP*GPC
2030	34,798	4.64	POP*GPC
	AFR Saint Helena		
0001	.	.	POP*GPC
1000	.	.	POP*GPC
1500	.	.	POP*GPC
1600	.	.	POP*GPC
1700	.	.	POP*GPC
1820	.	.	POP*GPC
1870	.	.	POP*GPC
1880	.	.	POP*GPC
1890	.	.	POP*GPC
1900	.	.	POP*GPC
1913	.	.	POP*GPC
1920	.	.	POP*GPC
1929	.	.	POP*GPC
1938	.	.	POP*GPC
1950	13	.	POP*GPC
1960	20	4.26	POP*GPC
1970	21	0.41	POP*GPC
1980	26	2.09	POP*GPC
1990	30	1.57	POP*GPC
2000	66	8.14	POP*GPC
2010	61	0.74	POP*GPC
2012	65	2.71	POP*GPC
2020	82	3.02	POP*GPC
2030	107	2.68	POP*GPC
	LAM Saint Kitts and Nevis		
0001	.	.	POP*GPC
1000	.	.	POP*GPC
1500	.	.	POP*GPC
1600	.	.	POP*GPC
1700	.	.	POP*GPC
1820	.	.	POP*GPC
1870	.	.	POP*GPC
1880	.	.	POP*GPC
1890	.	.	POP*GPC
1900	.	.	POP*GPC
1913	.	.	POP*GPC
1920	.	.	POP*GPC
1929	.	.	POP*GPC
1938	.	.	POP*GPC
1950	95	.	POP*GPC
1960	195	7.39	POP*GPC
1970	344	5.87	POP*GPC
1980	282	1.97	POP*GPC
1990	486	5.58	POP*GPC
2000	733	4.20	POP*GPC
2010	860	1.62	POP*GPC

Year	GDP at PPP, mil. 2012 doll.	Growth Rate	Source
2012	933	4.12	POP*GPC
2020	1,223	3.44	POP*GPC
2030	1,599	2.72	POP*GPC
LAM Saint Lucia			
0001	.	.	POP*GPC
1000	.	.	POP*GPC
1500	.	.	POP*GPC
1600	.	.	POP*GPC
1700	.	.	POP*GPC
1820	.	.	POP*GPC
1870	.	.	POP*GPC
1880	.	.	POP*GPC
1890	.	.	POP*GPC
1900	.	.	POP*GPC
1913	.	.	POP*GPC
1920	.	.	POP*GPC
1929	.	.	POP*GPC
1938	.	.	POP*GPC
1950	95	.	POP*GPC
1960	178	6.45	POP*GPC
1970	355	7.12	POP*GPC
1980	545	4.38	POP*GPC
1990	1,096	7.24	POP*GPC
2000	1,629	4.04	POP*GPC
2010	1,901	1.55	POP*GPC
2012	1,935	0.89	POP*GPC
2020	2,528	3.40	POP*GPC
2030	3,243	2.52	POP*GPC
LAM Saint Martin			
0001	.	.	POP*GPC
1000	.	.	POP*GPC
1500	.	.	POP*GPC
1600	.	.	POP*GPC
1700	.	.	POP*GPC
1820	.	.	POP*GPC
1870	.	.	POP*GPC
1880	.	.	POP*GPC
1890	.	.	POP*GPC
1900	.	.	POP*GPC
1913	.	.	POP*GPC
1920	.	.	POP*GPC
1929	.	.	POP*GPC
1938	.	.	POP*GPC
1950	17	.	POP*GPC
1960	29	5.38	POP*GPC
1970	52	5.89	POP*GPC
1980	71	3.15	POP*GPC
1990	237	12.83	POP*GPC
2000	337	3.61	POP*GPC

Year	GDP at PPP, mil. 2012 doll.	Growth Rate	Source
2010	657	6.90	POP*GPC
2012	698	3.07	POP*GPC
2020	1,038	5.10	POP*GPC
2030	1,442	3.33	POP*GPC
	DME Saint Pierre and Miquelon		
0001	.	.	POP*GPC
1000	.	.	POP*GPC
1500	.	.	POP*GPC
1600	.	.	POP*GPC
1700	.	.	POP*GPC
1820	.	.	POP*GPC
1870	.	.	POP*GPC
1880	.	.	POP*GPC
1890	.	.	POP*GPC
1900	.	.	POP*GPC
1913	.	.	POP*GPC
1920	.	.	POP*GPC
1929	.	.	POP*GPC
1938	.	.	POP*GPC
1950	21	.	POP*GPC
1960	34	5.08	POP*GPC
1970	55	5.07	POP*GPC
1980	77	3.37	POP*GPC
1990	100	2.64	POP*GPC
2000	211	7.76	POP*GPC
2010	227	0.73	POP*GPC
2012	227	0.05	POP*GPC
2020	261	1.77	POP*GPC
2030	286	0.93	POP*GPC
	LAM Saint Vincent and the Grenadines		
0001	.	.	POP*GPC
1000	.	.	POP*GPC
1500	.	.	POP*GPC
1600	.	.	POP*GPC
1700	.	.	POP*GPC
1820	.	.	POP*GPC
1870	.	.	POP*GPC
1880	.	.	POP*GPC
1890	.	.	POP*GPC
1900	.	.	POP*GPC
1913	.	.	POP*GPC
1920	.	.	POP*GPC
1929	.	.	POP*GPC
1938	.	.	POP*GPC
1950	124	.	POP*GPC
1960	190	4.40	POP*GPC
1970	263	3.29	POP*GPC
1980	359	3.17	POP*GPC
1990	659	6.26	POP*GPC

Year	GDP at PPP, mil. 2012 doll.	Growth Rate	Source
2000	903	3.20	POP*GPC
2010	1,090	1.90	POP*GPC
2012	1,138	2.18	POP*GPC
2020	1,472	3.27	POP*GPC
2030	1,865	2.40	POP*GPC
SEA Samoa			
0001	.	.	POP*GPC
1000	.	.	POP*GPC
1500	.	.	POP*GPC
1600	.	.	POP*GPC
1700	.	.	POP*GPC
1820	.	.	POP*GPC
1870	.	.	POP*GPC
1880	.	.	POP*GPC
1890	.	.	POP*GPC
1900	.	.	POP*GPC
1913	.	.	POP*GPC
1920	.	.	POP*GPC
1929	.	.	POP*GPC
1938	.	.	POP*GPC
1950	169	.	POP*GPC
1960	262	4.48	POP*GPC
1970	391	4.08	POP*GPC
1980	434	1.05	POP*GPC
1990	477	0.95	POP*GPC
2000	618	2.62	POP*GPC
2010	813	2.78	POP*GPC
2012	848	2.10	POP*GPC
2020	1,003	2.13	POP*GPC
2030	1,258	2.29	POP*GPC
SEA Samoa, American			
0001	.	.	POP*GPC
1000	.	.	POP*GPC
1500	.	.	POP*GPC
1600	.	.	POP*GPC
1700	.	.	POP*GPC
1820	.	.	POP*GPC
1870	.	.	POP*GPC
1880	.	.	POP*GPC
1890	.	.	POP*GPC
1900	.	.	POP*GPC
1913	.	.	POP*GPC
1920	.	.	POP*GPC
1929	.	.	POP*GPC
1938	.	.	POP*GPC
1950	52	.	POP*GPC
1960	69	2.80	POP*GPC
1970	117	5.39	POP*GPC
1980	151	2.62	POP*GPC

Year	GDP at PPP, mil. 2012 doll.	Growth Rate	Source
1990	229	4.23	POP*GPC
2000	640	10.82	POP*GPC
2010	452	3.42	POP*GPC
2012	472	2.19	POP*GPC
2020	570	2.39	POP*GPC
2030	679	1.76	POP*GPC
	DME San Marino		
0001	.	.	POP*GPC
1000	.	.	POP*GPC
1500	.	.	POP*GPC
1600	.	.	POP*GPC
1700	.	.	POP*GPC
1820	.	.	POP*GPC
1870	.	.	POP*GPC
1880	.	.	POP*GPC
1890	.	.	POP*GPC
1900	.	.	POP*GPC
1913	.	.	POP*GPC
1920	.	.	POP*GPC
1929	.	.	POP*GPC
1938	.	.	POP*GPC
1950	97	.	POP*GPC
1960	170	5.79	POP*GPC
1970	327	6.78	POP*GPC
1980	476	3.83	POP*GPC
1990	673	3.53	POP*GPC
2000	1,078	4.83	POP*GPC
2010	1,126	0.43	POP*GPC
2012	1,782	25.79	POP*GPC
2020	2,689	5.28	POP*GPC
2030	3,603	2.97	POP*GPC
	AFR Sao Tome and Principe		
0001	.	.	POP*GPC
1000	.	.	POP*GPC
1500	.	.	POP*GPC
1600	.	.	POP*GPC
1700	.	.	POP*GPC
1820	.	.	POP*GPC
1870	.	.	POP*GPC
1880	.	.	POP*GPC
1890	.	.	POP*GPC
1900	.	.	POP*GPC
1913	.	.	POP*GPC
1920	.	.	POP*GPC
1929	.	.	POP*GPC
1938	.	.	POP*GPC
1950	77	.	POP*GPC
1960	85	1.01	POP*GPC
1970	136	4.82	POP*GPC

Year	GDP at PPP, mil. 2012 doll.	Growth Rate	Source
1980	217	4.74	POP*GPC
1990	209	0.36	POP*GPC
2000	206	0.11	POP*GPC
2010	317	4.40	POP*GPC
2012	344	4.02	POP*GPC
2020	447	3.36	POP*GPC
2030	612	3.18	POP*GPC
MEA Saudi Arabia			
0001	1,501	.	POP*GPC
1000	1,841	0.02	POP*GPC
1500	1,557	0.03	POP*GPC
1600	1,557	0.00	POP*GPC
1700	1,557	0.00	POP*GPC
1820	1,800	0.12	POP*GPC
1870	2,104	0.31	POP*GPC
1880	2,192	0.41	POP*GPC
1890	2,285	0.41	POP*GPC
1900	2,381	0.41	POP*GPC
1913	2,513	0.41	POP*GPC
1920	3,332	4.12	POP*GPC
1929	4,791	4.12	POP*GPC
1938	6,887	4.12	POP*GPC
1950	11,175	4.12	POP*GPC
1960	31,824	11.03	POP*GPC
1970	99,375	12.06	POP*GPC
1980	330,284	12.76	POP*GPC
1990	289,472	1.31	POP*GPC
2000	474,609	5.07	POP*GPC
2010	769,166	4.95	POP*GPC
2012	907,968	8.65	POP*GPC
2020	1,310,712	4.70	POP*GPC
2030	1,874,985	3.65	POP*GPC
AFR Senegal			
0001	.	.	POP*GPC
1000	.	.	POP*GPC
1500	.	.	POP*GPC
1600	.	.	POP*GPC
1700	.	.	POP*GPC
1820	.	.	POP*GPC
1870	.	.	POP*GPC
1880	.	.	POP*GPC
1890	.	.	POP*GPC
1900	.	.	POP*GPC
1913	.	.	POP*GPC
1920	.	.	POP*GPC
1929	.	.	POP*GPC
1938	.	.	POP*GPC
1950	5,010	.	POP*GPC
1960	6,768	3.05	POP*GPC

Year	GDP at PPP, mil. 2012 doll.	Growth Rate	Source
1970	8,473	2.27	POP*GPC
1980	9,784	1.45	POP*GPC
1990	12,417	2.41	POP*GPC
2000	16,519	2.90	POP*GPC
2010	23,572	3.62	POP*GPC
2012	24,736	2.44	POP*GPC
2020	31,289	2.98	POP*GPC
2030	42,490	3.11	POP*GPC
	EEU Serbia		
0001	359	.	POP*GPC
1000	394	0.01	POP*GPC
1500	577	0.08	POP*GPC
1600	778	0.30	POP*GPC
1700	861	0.10	POP*GPC
1820	1,840	0.63	POP*GPC
1870	3,061	1.02	POP*GPC
1880	3,935	2.54	POP*GPC
1890	5,058	2.54	POP*GPC
1900	6,241	2.12	POP*GPC
1913	8,895	2.76	POP*GPC
1920	7,930	1.63	POP*GPC
1929	11,988	4.70	POP*GPC
1938	13,505	1.33	POP*GPC
1950	15,652	1.24	POP*GPC
1960	30,045	6.74	POP*GPC
1970	54,082	6.05	POP*GPC
1980	98,875	6.22	POP*GPC
1990	95,946	0.30	POP*GPC
2000	55,795	5.28	POP*GPC
2010	84,461	4.23	POP*GPC
2012	84,531	0.04	POP*GPC
2020	101,849	2.36	POP*GPC
2030	120,908	1.73	POP*GPC
	AFR Seychelles		
0001	.	.	POP*GPC
1000	.	.	POP*GPC
1500	.	.	POP*GPC
1600	.	.	POP*GPC
1700	.	.	POP*GPC
1820	.	.	POP*GPC
1870	.	.	POP*GPC
1880	.	.	POP*GPC
1890	.	.	POP*GPC
1900	.	.	POP*GPC
1913	.	.	POP*GPC
1920	.	.	POP*GPC
1929	.	.	POP*GPC
1938	.	.	POP*GPC
1950	102	.	POP*GPC

Year	GDP at PPP, mil. 2012 doll.	Growth Rate	Source
1960	182	6.02	POP*GPC
1970	301	5.14	POP*GPC
1980	733	9.29	POP*GPC
1990	1,081	3.97	POP*GPC
2000	1,702	4.64	POP*GPC
2010	2,140	2.32	POP*GPC
2012	2,345	4.68	POP*GPC
2020	3,247	4.15	POP*GPC
2030	4,167	2.52	POP*GPC
	AFR Sierra Leone		
0001	40	.	POP*GPC
1000	135	0.12	POP*GPC
1500	275	0.14	POP*GPC
1600	373	0.30	POP*GPC
1700	512	0.32	POP*GPC
1820	644	0.19	POP*GPC
1870	993	0.87	POP*GPC
1880	1,084	0.87	POP*GPC
1890	1,182	0.87	POP*GPC
1900	1,290	0.87	POP*GPC
1913	1,445	0.88	POP*GPC
1920	1,536	0.88	POP*GPC
1929	1,661	0.88	POP*GPC
1938	1,797	0.88	POP*GPC
1950	1,996	0.88	POP*GPC
1960	2,659	2.91	POP*GPC
1970	3,772	3.56	POP*GPC
1980	4,182	1.04	POP*GPC
1990	4,553	0.85	POP*GPC
2000	3,576	2.39	POP*GPC
2010	6,717	6.51	POP*GPC
2012	8,187	10.40	POP*GPC
2020	11,769	4.64	POP*GPC
2030	17,304	3.93	POP*GPC
	SEA Singapore		
0001	0	.	POP*GPC
1000	1	0.10	POP*GPC
1500	2	0.17	POP*GPC
1600	3	0.17	POP*GPC
1700	3	0.15	POP*GPC
1820	4	0.21	POP*GPC
1870	90	6.46	POP*GPC
1880	142	4.70	POP*GPC
1890	224	4.70	POP*GPC
1900	356	4.71	POP*GPC
1913	646	4.70	POP*GPC
1920	869	4.31	POP*GPC
1929	1,460	5.94	POP*GPC
1938	2,062	3.91	POP*GPC

Year	GDP at PPP, mil. 2012 doll.	Growth Rate	Source
1950	3,549	4.63	POP*GPC
1960	6,280	5.87	POP*GPC
1970	16,308	10.01	POP*GPC
1980	41,263	9.73	POP*GPC
1990	86,159	7.64	POP*GPC
2000	174,865	7.33	POP*GPC
2010	303,153	5.66	POP*GPC
2012	323,386	3.28	POP*GPC
2020	515,034	5.99	POP*GPC
2030	769,453	4.10	POP*GPC
LAM Sint Maarten			
0001	.	.	POP*GPC
1000	.	.	POP*GPC
1500	.	.	POP*GPC
1600	.	.	POP*GPC
1700	.	.	POP*GPC
1820	.	.	POP*GPC
1870	.	.	POP*GPC
1880	.	.	POP*GPC
1890	.	.	POP*GPC
1900	.	.	POP*GPC
1913	.	.	POP*GPC
1920	.	.	POP*GPC
1929	.	.	POP*GPC
1938	.	.	POP*GPC
1950	12	.	POP*GPC
1960	20	5.42	POP*GPC
1970	67	12.83	POP*GPC
1980	126	6.50	POP*GPC
1990	250	7.11	POP*GPC
2000	394	4.67	POP*GPC
2010	826	7.68	POP*GPC
2012	870	2.59	POP*GPC
2020	1,254	4.68	POP*GPC
2030	1,679	2.96	POP*GPC
EEU Slovakia			
0001	120	.	POP*GPC
1000	227	0.06	POP*GPC
1500	738	0.24	POP*GPC
1600	1,223	0.51	POP*GPC
1700	1,352	0.10	POP*GPC
1820	2,593	0.54	POP*GPC
1870	4,715	1.20	POP*GPC
1880	5,644	1.81	POP*GPC
1890	6,755	1.81	POP*GPC
1900	8,374	2.17	POP*GPC
1913	11,073	2.17	POP*GPC
1920	10,007	1.44	POP*GPC
1929	16,846	5.96	POP*GPC

Year	GDP at PPP, mil. 2012 doll.	Growth Rate	Source
1938	16,787	0.04	POP*GPC
1950	17,301	0.25	POP*GPC
1960	31,373	6.13	POP*GPC
1970	44,365	3.53	POP*GPC
1980	61,380	3.30	POP*GPC
1990	69,416	1.24	POP*GPC
2000	79,359	1.35	POP*GPC
2010	132,330	5.25	POP*GPC
2012	139,742	2.76	POP*GPC
2020	187,036	3.71	POP*GPC
2030	237,724	2.43	POP*GPC
EEU Slovenia			
0001	66	.	POP*GPC
1000	125	0.06	POP*GPC
1500	236	0.13	POP*GPC
1600	327	0.33	POP*GPC
1700	370	0.12	POP*GPC
1820	816	0.66	POP*GPC
1870	1,374	1.05	POP*GPC
1880	1,766	2.54	POP*GPC
1890	2,271	2.54	POP*GPC
1900	2,801	2.12	POP*GPC
1913	3,993	2.76	POP*GPC
1920	3,560	1.63	POP*GPC
1929	5,381	4.70	POP*GPC
1938	6,062	1.33	POP*GPC
1950	7,026	1.24	POP*GPC
1960	12,042	5.54	POP*GPC
1970	19,854	5.13	POP*GPC
1980	35,639	6.02	POP*GPC
1990	35,791	0.04	POP*GPC
2000	45,397	2.41	POP*GPC
2010	59,705	2.78	POP*GPC
2012	58,555	0.97	POP*GPC
2020	71,252	2.48	POP*GPC
2030	87,090	2.03	POP*GPC
SEA Solomon Islands			
0001	.	.	POP*GPC
1000	.	.	POP*GPC
1500	.	.	POP*GPC
1600	.	.	POP*GPC
1700	.	.	POP*GPC
1820	.	.	POP*GPC
1870	.	.	POP*GPC
1880	.	.	POP*GPC
1890	.	.	POP*GPC
1900	.	.	POP*GPC
1913	.	.	POP*GPC
1920	.	.	POP*GPC

Year	GDP at PPP, mil. 2012 doll.	Growth Rate	Source
1929	.	.	POP*GPC
1938	.	.	POP*GPC
1950	84	.	POP*GPC
1960	139	5.24	POP*GPC
1970	240	5.59	POP*GPC
1980	398	5.21	POP*GPC
1990	820	7.48	POP*GPC
2000	1,062	2.62	POP*GPC
2010	1,503	3.53	POP*GPC
2012	1,779	8.80	POP*GPC
2020	2,427	3.96	POP*GPC
2030	3,578	3.96	POP*GPC
AFR Somalia			
0001	71	.	POP*GPC
1000	198	0.10	POP*GPC
1500	494	0.18	POP*GPC
1600	520	0.05	POP*GPC
1700	617	0.17	POP*GPC
1820	649	0.04	POP*GPC
1870	1,274	1.36	POP*GPC
1880	1,458	1.36	POP*GPC
1890	1,668	1.36	POP*GPC
1900	1,909	1.36	POP*GPC
1913	2,274	1.36	POP*GPC
1920	2,499	1.36	POP*GPC
1929	2,822	1.36	POP*GPC
1938	3,186	1.36	POP*GPC
1950	3,745	1.36	POP*GPC
1960	6,399	5.50	POP*GPC
1970	6,737	0.52	POP*GPC
1980	9,327	3.31	POP*GPC
1990	11,458	2.08	POP*GPC
2000	6,230	5.91	POP*GPC
2010	6,001	0.37	POP*GPC
2012	6,477	3.89	POP*GPC
2020	7,814	2.37	POP*GPC
2030	10,883	3.37	POP*GPC
AFR South Africa			
0001	33	.	POP*GPC
1000	138	0.14	POP*GPC
1500	345	0.18	POP*GPC
1600	423	0.20	POP*GPC
1700	605	0.36	POP*GPC
1820	938	0.37	POP*GPC
1870	3,420	2.62	POP*GPC
1880	4,854	3.57	POP*GPC
1890	6,891	3.57	POP*GPC
1900	9,782	3.57	POP*GPC
1913	15,425	3.57	POP*GPC

Year	GDP at PPP, mil. 2012 doll.	Growth Rate	Source
1920	19,570	3.46	POP*GPC
1929	26,577	3.46	POP*GPC
1938	36,092	3.46	POP*GPC
1950	53,934	3.40	POP*GPC
1960	92,200	5.51	POP*GPC
1970	177,539	6.77	POP*GPC
1980	275,992	4.51	POP*GPC
1990	316,041	1.36	POP*GPC
2000	387,108	2.05	POP*GPC
2010	541,446	3.41	POP*GPC
2012	576,522	3.19	POP*GPC
2020	681,082	2.11	POP*GPC
2030	834,392	2.05	POP*GPC
AFR South Sudan			
0001	112	.	POP*GPC
1000	227	0.07	POP*GPC
1500	366	0.10	POP*GPC
1600	401	0.09	POP*GPC
1700	440	0.09	POP*GPC
1820	546	0.18	POP*GPC
1870	664	0.39	POP*GPC
1880	690	0.39	POP*GPC
1890	718	0.39	POP*GPC
1900	747	0.39	POP*GPC
1913	786	0.39	POP*GPC
1920	808	0.40	POP*GPC
1929	837	0.40	POP*GPC
1938	868	0.40	POP*GPC
1950	1,038	1.51	POP*GPC
1960	1,437	3.30	POP*GPC
1970	1,646	1.37	POP*GPC
1980	2,407	3.87	POP*GPC
1990	3,056	2.42	POP*GPC
2000	4,952	4.94	POP*GPC
2010	9,984	7.26	POP*GPC
2012	11,620	7.88	POP*GPC
2020	18,942	6.30	POP*GPC
2030	29,500	4.53	POP*GPC
DME Spain			
0001	2,922	.	POP*GPC
1000	2,817	0.00	POP*GPC
1500	7,034	0.18	POP*GPC
1600	10,999	0.45	POP*GPC
1700	11,706	0.06	POP*GPC
1820	19,249	0.42	POP*GPC
1870	30,600	0.93	POP*GPC
1880	43,424	3.56	POP*GPC
1890	45,126	0.39	POP*GPC
1900	51,889	1.41	POP*GPC

Year	GDP at PPP, mil. 2012 doll.	Growth Rate	Source
1913	65,193	1.77	POP*GPC
1920	72,330	1.50	POP*GPC
1929	99,481	3.60	POP*GPC
1938	70,808	3.71	POP*GPC
1950	95,460	2.52	POP*GPC
1960	154,621	4.94	POP*GPC
1970	378,467	9.36	POP*GPC
1980	641,853	5.42	POP*GPC
1990	881,441	3.22	POP*GPC
2000	1,254,201	3.59	POP*GPC
2010	1,508,964	1.87	POP*GPC
2012	1,518,003	0.30	POP*GPC
2020	1,849,995	2.50	POP*GPC
2030	2,318,480	2.28	POP*GPC
SAS Sri Lanka			
0001	195	.	POP*GPC
1000	361	0.06	POP*GPC
1500	839	0.17	POP*GPC
1600	936	0.11	POP*GPC
1700	1,020	0.09	POP*GPC
1820	1,044	0.02	POP*GPC
1870	3,710	2.57	POP*GPC
1880	3,928	0.57	POP*GPC
1890	5,467	3.36	POP*GPC
1900	7,897	3.75	POP*GPC
1913	9,290	1.26	POP*GPC
1920	8,971	0.50	POP*GPC
1929	11,852	3.14	POP*GPC
1938	11,588	0.25	POP*GPC
1950	14,390	1.82	POP*GPC
1960	18,032	2.28	POP*GPC
1970	23,080	2.50	POP*GPC
1980	29,827	2.60	POP*GPC
1990	44,250	4.02	POP*GPC
2000	66,046	4.09	POP*GPC
2010	105,962	4.84	POP*GPC
2012	124,873	8.56	POP*GPC
2020	185,287	5.06	POP*GPC
2030	251,596	3.11	POP*GPC
AFR Sudan			
0001	708	.	POP*GPC
1000	1,611	0.08	POP*GPC
1500	2,149	0.06	POP*GPC
1600	2,256	0.05	POP*GPC
1700	2,363	0.05	POP*GPC
1820	2,769	0.13	POP*GPC
1870	4,274	0.87	POP*GPC
1880	4,661	0.87	POP*GPC
1890	5,083	0.87	POP*GPC

Year	GDP at PPP, mil. 2012 doll.	Growth Rate	Source
1900	5,544	0.87	POP*GPC
1913	6,206	0.87	POP*GPC
1920	6,595	0.87	POP*GPC
1929	7,130	0.87	POP*GPC
1938	7,709	0.87	POP*GPC
1950	9,766	1.99	POP*GPC
1960	13,511	3.30	POP*GPC
1970	15,479	1.37	POP*GPC
1980	22,636	3.87	POP*GPC
1990	28,742	2.42	POP*GPC
2000	41,848	3.83	POP*GPC
2010	67,565	4.91	POP*GPC
2012	73,988	4.64	POP*GPC
2020	100,154	3.86	POP*GPC
2030	143,820	3.68	POP*GPC
LAM Suriname			
0001	.	.	POP*GPC
1000	.	.	POP*GPC
1500	.	.	POP*GPC
1600	.	.	POP*GPC
1700	.	.	POP*GPC
1820	.	.	POP*GPC
1870	.	.	POP*GPC
1880	.	.	POP*GPC
1890	.	.	POP*GPC
1900	.	.	POP*GPC
1913	.	.	POP*GPC
1920	.	.	POP*GPC
1929	.	.	POP*GPC
1938	.	.	POP*GPC
1950	493	.	POP*GPC
1960	962	6.91	POP*GPC
1970	1,784	6.37	POP*GPC
1980	2,641	4.00	POP*GPC
1990	2,343	1.19	POP*GPC
2000	2,610	1.09	POP*GPC
2010	4,302	5.12	POP*GPC
2012	4,770	5.30	POP*GPC
2020	6,320	3.58	POP*GPC
2030	8,317	2.78	POP*GPC
DME Svalbard			
0001	.	.	POP*GPC
1000	.	.	POP*GPC
1500	.	.	POP*GPC
1600	.	.	POP*GPC
1700	.	.	POP*GPC
1820	.	.	POP*GPC
1870	.	.	POP*GPC
1880	.	.	POP*GPC

Year	GDP at PPP, mil. 2012 doll.	Growth Rate	Source
1890	.	.	POP*GPC
1900	.	.	POP*GPC
1913	.	.	POP*GPC
1920	.	.	POP*GPC
1929	.	.	POP*GPC
1938	.	.	POP*GPC
1950	39	.	POP*GPC
1960	60	4.22	POP*GPC
1970	95	4.74	POP*GPC
1980	161	5.46	POP*GPC
1990	215	2.93	POP*GPC
2000	221	0.29	POP*GPC
2010	204	0.82	POP*GPC
2012	198	1.45	POP*GPC
2020	267	3.83	POP*GPC
2030	361	3.05	POP*GPC
	AFR Swaziland		
0001	1	.	POP*GPC
1000	3	0.14	POP*GPC
1500	7	0.18	POP*GPC
1600	8	0.20	POP*GPC
1700	12	0.36	POP*GPC
1820	19	0.37	POP*GPC
1870	55	2.18	POP*GPC
1880	68	2.18	POP*GPC
1890	85	2.18	POP*GPC
1900	105	2.18	POP*GPC
1913	139	2.18	POP*GPC
1920	161	2.18	POP*GPC
1929	196	2.18	POP*GPC
1938	238	2.18	POP*GPC
1950	308	2.18	POP*GPC
1960	510	5.16	POP*GPC
1970	1,320	9.99	POP*GPC
1980	2,124	4.87	POP*GPC
1990	4,799	8.49	POP*GPC
2000	5,180	0.77	POP*GPC
2010	6,355	2.07	POP*GPC
2012	6,295	0.47	POP*GPC
2020	7,713	2.57	POP*GPC
2030	9,801	2.43	POP*GPC
	DME Sweden		
0001	94	.	POP*GPC
1000	303	0.12	POP*GPC
1500	598	0.14	POP*GPC
1600	980	0.49	POP*GPC
1700	1,926	0.68	POP*GPC
1820	4,846	0.77	POP*GPC
1870	10,843	1.62	POP*GPC

Year	GDP at PPP, mil. 2012 doll.	Growth Rate	Source
1880	13,207	1.99	POP*GPC
1890	15,603	1.68	POP*GPC
1900	20,507	2.77	POP*GPC
1913	27,232	2.21	POP*GPC
1920	25,765	0.79	POP*GPC
1929	37,011	4.11	POP*GPC
1938	46,567	2.58	POP*GPC
1950	73,966	3.93	POP*GPC
1960	104,962	3.56	POP*GPC
1970	170,244	4.96	POP*GPC
1980	212,236	2.23	POP*GPC
1990	265,069	2.25	POP*GPC
2000	315,805	1.77	POP*GPC
2010	392,532	2.20	POP*GPC
2012	408,088	1.96	POP*GPC
2020	500,415	2.58	POP*GPC
2030	624,185	2.23	POP*GPC
DME Switzerland			
0001	200	.	POP*GPC
1000	192	0.00	POP*GPC
1500	643	0.24	POP*GPC
1600	1,174	0.60	POP*GPC
1700	1,671	0.35	POP*GPC
1820	3,387	0.59	POP*GPC
1870	8,733	1.91	POP*GPC
1880	10,884	2.23	POP*GPC
1890	14,694	3.05	POP*GPC
1900	19,794	3.02	POP*GPC
1913	25,795	2.06	POP*GPC
1920	26,173	0.21	POP*GPC
1929	39,852	4.78	POP*GPC
1938	41,917	0.56	POP*GPC
1950	66,579	3.93	POP*GPC
1960	114,299	5.55	POP*GPC
1970	197,637	5.63	POP*GPC
1980	239,152	1.92	POP*GPC
1990	305,054	2.46	POP*GPC
2000	343,900	1.21	POP*GPC
2010	413,301	1.86	POP*GPC
2012	425,375	1.45	POP*GPC
2020	493,434	1.87	POP*GPC
2030	589,656	1.80	POP*GPC
MEA Syria			
0001	1,197	.	POP*GPC
1000	1,468	0.02	POP*GPC
1500	1,241	0.03	POP*GPC
1600	1,210	0.03	POP*GPC
1700	1,179	0.03	POP*GPC
1820	1,377	0.13	POP*GPC

Year	GDP at PPP, mil. 2012 doll.	Growth Rate	Source
1870	2,089	0.84	POP*GPC
1880	2,459	1.64	POP*GPC
1890	2,895	1.64	POP*GPC
1900	3,408	1.64	POP*GPC
1913	4,212	1.64	POP*GPC
1920	5,227	3.13	POP*GPC
1929	6,897	3.13	POP*GPC
1938	9,102	3.13	POP*GPC
1950	13,175	3.13	POP*GPC
1960	17,011	2.59	POP*GPC
1970	22,416	2.80	POP*GPC
1980	39,625	5.86	POP*GPC
1990	50,970	2.55	POP*GPC
2000	70,148	3.25	POP*GPC
2010	102,187	3.83	POP*GPC
2012	100,817	0.67	POP*GPC
2020	123,598	2.58	POP*GPC
2030	161,643	2.72	POP*GPC
SEA Taiwan			
0001	39	.	POP*GPC
1000	72	0.06	POP*GPC
1500	168	0.17	POP*GPC
1600	382	0.83	POP*GPC
1700	850	0.80	POP*GPC
1820	1,721	0.59	POP*GPC
1870	2,018	0.32	POP*GPC
1880	2,223	0.97	POP*GPC
1890	2,449	0.97	POP*GPC
1900	2,994	2.03	POP*GPC
1913	4,055	2.36	POP*GPC
1920	5,607	4.74	POP*GPC
1929	8,057	4.11	POP*GPC
1938	11,569	4.10	POP*GPC
1950	11,016	0.41	POP*GPC
1960	24,635	8.38	POP*GPC
1970	66,201	10.39	POP*GPC
1980	155,296	8.90	POP*GPC
1990	297,110	6.70	POP*GPC
2000	501,320	5.37	POP*GPC
2010	872,025	5.69	POP*GPC
2012	905,842	1.92	POP*GPC
2020	1,360,589	5.22	POP*GPC
2030	1,765,120	2.64	POP*GPC
USR Tajikistan			
0001	40	.	POP*GPC
1000	91	0.08	POP*GPC
1500	157	0.11	POP*GPC
1600	188	0.18	POP*GPC
1700	223	0.17	POP*GPC

Year	GDP at PPP, mil. 2012 doll.	Growth Rate	Source
1820	376	0.44	POP*GPC
1870	695	1.24	POP*GPC
1880	850	2.03	POP*GPC
1890	1,039	2.03	POP*GPC
1900	1,280	2.10	POP*GPC
1913	1,931	3.22	POP*GPC
1920	741	12.79	POP*GPC
1929	2,034	11.88	POP*GPC
1938	3,458	6.07	POP*GPC
1950	4,603	2.41	POP*GPC
1960	8,028	5.72	POP*GPC
1970	14,814	6.32	POP*GPC
1980	17,576	1.72	POP*GPC
1990	18,127	0.31	POP*GPC
2000	6,950	9.14	POP*GPC
2010	15,021	8.01	POP*GPC
2012	17,172	6.92	POP*GPC
2020	25,461	5.05	POP*GPC
2030	36,739	3.73	POP*GPC
AFR Tanzania			
0001	.	.	POP*GPC
1000	.	.	POP*GPC
1500	.	.	POP*GPC
1600	.	.	POP*GPC
1700	.	.	POP*GPC
1820	.	.	POP*GPC
1870	.	.	POP*GPC
1880	.	.	POP*GPC
1890	.	.	POP*GPC
1900	.	.	POP*GPC
1913	.	.	POP*GPC
1920	.	.	POP*GPC
1929	.	.	POP*GPC
1938	.	.	POP*GPC
1950	5,265	.	POP*GPC
1960	7,503	3.61	POP*GPC
1970	12,984	5.64	POP*GPC
1980	19,340	4.06	POP*GPC
1990	24,892	2.56	POP*GPC
2000	33,709	3.08	POP*GPC
2010	62,418	6.35	POP*GPC
2012	70,464	6.25	POP*GPC
2020	107,539	5.43	POP*GPC
2030	172,733	4.85	POP*GPC
SEA Thailand			
0001	459	.	POP*GPC
1000	849	0.06	POP*GPC
1500	1,972	0.17	POP*GPC
1600	2,245	0.13	POP*GPC

Year	GDP at PPP, mil. 2012 doll.	Growth Rate	Source
1700	2,496	0.11	POP*GPC
1820	4,716	0.53	POP*GPC
1870	6,434	0.62	POP*GPC
1880	7,256	1.21	POP*GPC
1890	8,183	1.21	POP*GPC
1900	9,259	1.24	POP*GPC
1913	11,435	1.64	POP*GPC
1920	12,572	1.36	POP*GPC
1929	14,963	1.95	POP*GPC
1938	19,363	2.91	POP*GPC
1950	26,346	2.60	POP*GPC
1960	41,076	4.54	POP*GPC
1970	76,697	6.44	POP*GPC
1980	129,343	5.37	POP*GPC
1990	266,925	7.51	POP*GPC
2000	391,712	3.91	POP*GPC
2010	597,092	4.31	POP*GPC
2012	640,643	3.58	POP*GPC
2020	891,914	4.22	POP*GPC
2030	1,168,769	2.74	POP*GPC
AFR Togo			
0001	.	.	POP*GPC
1000	.	.	POP*GPC
1500	.	.	POP*GPC
1600	.	.	POP*GPC
1700	.	.	POP*GPC
1820	.	.	POP*GPC
1870	.	.	POP*GPC
1880	.	.	POP*GPC
1890	.	.	POP*GPC
1900	.	.	POP*GPC
1913	.	.	POP*GPC
1920	.	.	POP*GPC
1929	.	.	POP*GPC
1938	.	.	POP*GPC
1950	1,194	.	POP*GPC
1960	1,594	2.93	POP*GPC
1970	2,807	5.82	POP*GPC
1980	3,441	2.06	POP*GPC
1990	4,041	1.62	POP*GPC
2000	4,774	1.68	POP*GPC
2010	6,120	2.51	POP*GPC
2012	6,700	4.63	POP*GPC
2020	8,069	2.35	POP*GPC
2030	10,315	2.49	POP*GPC
SEA Tokelau			
0001	.	.	POP*GPC
1000	.	.	POP*GPC
1500	.	.	POP*GPC

Year	GDP at PPP, mil. 2012 doll.	Growth Rate	Source
1600	.	.	POP*GPC
1700	.	.	POP*GPC
1820	.	.	POP*GPC
1870	.	.	POP*GPC
1880	.	.	POP*GPC
1890	.	.	POP*GPC
1900	.	.	POP*GPC
1913	.	.	POP*GPC
1920	.	.	POP*GPC
1929	.	.	POP*GPC
1938	.	.	POP*GPC
1950	1	.	POP*GPC
1960	1	4.35	POP*GPC
1970	1	4.33	POP*GPC
1980	2	3.06	POP*GPC
1990	2	2.51	POP*GPC
2000	3	0.41	POP*GPC
2010	3	0.32	POP*GPC
2012	3	0.45	POP*GPC
2020	3	0.63	POP*GPC
2030	3	0.88	POP*GPC
SEA Tonga			
0001	.	.	POP*GPC
1000	.	.	POP*GPC
1500	.	.	POP*GPC
1600	.	.	POP*GPC
1700	.	.	POP*GPC
1820	.	.	POP*GPC
1870	.	.	POP*GPC
1880	.	.	POP*GPC
1890	.	.	POP*GPC
1900	.	.	POP*GPC
1913	.	.	POP*GPC
1920	.	.	POP*GPC
1929	.	.	POP*GPC
1938	.	.	POP*GPC
1950	97	.	POP*GPC
1960	155	4.76	POP*GPC
1970	234	4.19	POP*GPC
1980	253	0.78	POP*GPC
1990	307	1.95	POP*GPC
2000	432	3.49	POP*GPC
2010	488	1.22	POP*GPC
2012	503	1.52	POP*GPC
2020	588	1.99	POP*GPC
2030	729	2.17	POP*GPC
LAM Trinidad and Tobago			
0001	1	.	POP*GPC
1000	4	0.11	POP*GPC

Year	GDP at PPP, mil. 2012 doll.	Growth Rate	Source
1500	8	0.13	POP*GPC
1600	3	0.85	POP*GPC
1700	11	1.20	POP*GPC
1820	90	1.76	POP*GPC
1870	191	1.51	POP*GPC
1880	294	4.42	POP*GPC
1890	453	4.42	POP*GPC
1900	697	4.42	POP*GPC
1913	1,150	3.92	POP*GPC
1920	1,414	3.00	POP*GPC
1929	1,660	1.80	POP*GPC
1938	2,192	3.14	POP*GPC
1950	3,840	4.78	POP*GPC
1960	7,785	7.32	POP*GPC
1970	11,199	3.70	POP*GPC
1980	18,573	5.19	POP*GPC
1990	14,977	2.13	POP*GPC
2000	20,371	3.12	POP*GPC
2010	35,277	5.64	POP*GPC
2012	35,451	0.25	POP*GPC
2020	47,605	3.75	POP*GPC
2030	59,681	2.29	POP*GPC
MEA Tunisia			
0001	538	.	POP*GPC
1000	673	0.02	POP*GPC
1500	538	0.04	POP*GPC
1600	673	0.22	POP*GPC
1700	538	0.22	POP*GPC
1820	589	0.07	POP*GPC
1870	1,165	1.37	POP*GPC
1880	1,402	1.87	POP*GPC
1890	1,687	1.87	POP*GPC
1900	2,031	1.87	POP*GPC
1913	2,584	1.87	POP*GPC
1920	3,043	2.37	POP*GPC
1929	3,756	2.37	POP*GPC
1938	4,635	2.37	POP*GPC
1950	6,136	2.37	POP*GPC
1960	8,818	3.69	POP*GPC
1970	14,492	5.09	POP*GPC
1980	29,276	7.28	POP*GPC
1990	41,408	3.53	POP*GPC
2000	65,900	4.76	POP*GPC
2010	102,268	4.49	POP*GPC
2012	103,768	0.73	POP*GPC
2020	139,948	3.81	POP*GPC
2030	184,111	2.78	POP*GPC

Year	GDP at PPP, mil. 2012 doll.	Growth Rate	Source
MEA Turkey			
0001	5,704	.	POP*GPC
1000	6,995	0.02	POP*GPC
1500	5,915	0.03	POP*GPC
1600	6,830	0.14	POP*GPC
1700	7,887	0.14	POP*GPC
1820	10,136	0.21	POP*GPC
1870	15,225	0.82	POP*GPC
1880	17,611	1.47	POP*GPC
1890	20,371	1.47	POP*GPC
1900	23,563	1.47	POP*GPC
1913	28,472	1.47	POP*GPC
1920	15,461	8.35	POP*GPC
1929	27,912	6.78	POP*GPC
1938	45,906	5.68	POP*GPC
1950	54,564	1.45	POP*GPC
1960	96,233	5.84	POP*GPC
1970	167,698	5.71	POP*GPC
1980	271,797	4.95	POP*GPC
1990	480,628	5.87	POP*GPC
2000	812,662	5.39	POP*GPC
2010	1,234,522	4.27	POP*GPC
2012	1,394,855	6.30	POP*GPC
2020	2,024,053	4.76	POP*GPC
2030	2,773,176	3.20	POP*GPC
USR Turkmenistan			
0001	36	.	POP*GPC
1000	85	0.09	POP*GPC
1500	149	0.11	POP*GPC
1600	180	0.19	POP*GPC
1700	224	0.22	POP*GPC
1820	378	0.44	POP*GPC
1870	699	1.24	POP*GPC
1880	855	2.03	POP*GPC
1890	1,046	2.03	POP*GPC
1900	1,288	2.10	POP*GPC
1913	1,943	3.22	POP*GPC
1920	745	12.79	POP*GPC
1929	2,047	11.88	POP*GPC
1938	3,480	6.07	POP*GPC
1950	4,263	1.71	POP*GPC
1960	8,205	6.77	POP*GPC
1970	16,800	7.43	POP*GPC
1980	22,511	2.97	POP*GPC
1990	25,466	1.24	POP*GPC
2000	19,576	2.60	POP*GPC
2010	41,402	7.78	POP*GPC
2012	52,630	12.75	POP*GPC
2020	84,346	6.07	POP*GPC

Year	GDP at PPP, mil. 2012 doll.	Growth Rate	Source
2030	119,450	3.54	POP*GPC
LAM Turks and Caicos Islands			
0001	.	.	POP*GPC
1000	.	.	POP*GPC
1500	.	.	POP*GPC
1600	.	.	POP*GPC
1700	.	.	POP*GPC
1820	.	.	POP*GPC
1870	.	.	POP*GPC
1880	.	.	POP*GPC
1890	.	.	POP*GPC
1900	.	.	POP*GPC
1913	.	.	POP*GPC
1920	.	.	POP*GPC
1929	.	.	POP*GPC
1938	.	.	POP*GPC
1950	19	.	POP*GPC
1960	32	5.22	POP*GPC
1970	41	2.69	POP*GPC
1980	65	4.74	POP*GPC
1990	114	5.71	POP*GPC
2000	220	6.81	POP*GPC
2010	940	15.62	POP*GPC
2012	1,016	3.98	POP*GPC
2020	2,278	10.62	POP*GPC
2030	4,666	7.43	POP*GPC
SEA Tuvalu			
0001	.	.	POP*GPC
1000	.	.	POP*GPC
1500	.	.	POP*GPC
1600	.	.	POP*GPC
1700	.	.	POP*GPC
1820	.	.	POP*GPC
1870	.	.	POP*GPC
1880	.	.	POP*GPC
1890	.	.	POP*GPC
1900	.	.	POP*GPC
1913	.	.	POP*GPC
1920	.	.	POP*GPC
1929	.	.	POP*GPC
1938	.	.	POP*GPC
1950	4	.	POP*GPC
1960	5	1.52	POP*GPC
1970	6	3.39	POP*GPC
1980	9	3.53	POP*GPC
1990	10	1.39	POP*GPC
2000	13	1.92	POP*GPC
2010	39	11.98	POP*GPC
2012	39	0.50	POP*GPC

Year	GDP at PPP, mil. 2012 doll.	Growth Rate	Source
2020	63	6.09	POP*GPC
2030	82	2.67	POP*GPC
AFR Uganda			
0001	.	.	POP*GPC
1000	.	.	POP*GPC
1500	.	.	POP*GPC
1600	.	.	POP*GPC
1700	.	.	POP*GPC
1820	.	.	POP*GPC
1870	.	.	POP*GPC
1880	.	.	POP*GPC
1890	.	.	POP*GPC
1900	.	.	POP*GPC
1913	.	.	POP*GPC
1920	.	.	POP*GPC
1929	.	.	POP*GPC
1938	.	.	POP*GPC
1950	5,545	.	POP*GPC
1960	7,400	2.93	POP*GPC
1970	11,036	4.08	POP*GPC
1980	8,247	2.87	POP*GPC
1990	10,639	2.58	POP*GPC
2000	20,107	6.57	POP*GPC
2010	40,620	7.29	POP*GPC
2012	44,727	4.93	POP*GPC
2020	72,446	6.21	POP*GPC
2030	121,563	5.31	POP*GPC
USR Ukraine			
0001	190	.	POP*GPC
1000	534	0.10	POP*GPC
1500	2,007	0.27	POP*GPC
1600	2,775	0.32	POP*GPC
1700	4,088	0.39	POP*GPC
1820	10,181	0.76	POP*GPC
1870	22,666	1.61	POP*GPC
1880	27,719	2.03	POP*GPC
1890	33,897	2.03	POP*GPC
1900	41,746	2.10	POP*GPC
1913	62,999	3.22	POP*GPC
1920	24,163	12.79	POP*GPC
1929	66,359	11.88	POP*GPC
1938	112,801	6.07	POP*GPC
1950	133,427	1.41	POP*GPC
1960	213,554	4.82	POP*GPC
1970	331,677	4.50	POP*GPC
1980	411,465	2.18	POP*GPC
1990	476,954	1.49	POP*GPC
2000	207,183	8.00	POP*GPC
2010	315,542	4.30	POP*GPC

Year	GDP at PPP, mil. 2012 doll.	Growth Rate	Source
2012	333,049	2.74	POP*GPC
2020	410,886	2.66	POP*GPC
2030	487,621	1.73	POP*GPC
	MEA United Arab Emirates		
0001	29	.	POP*GPC
1000	36	0.02	POP*GPC
1500	30	0.03	POP*GPC
1600	30	0.00	POP*GPC
1700	30	0.00	POP*GPC
1820	35	0.12	POP*GPC
1870	37	0.09	POP*GPC
1880	39	0.66	POP*GPC
1890	42	0.66	POP*GPC
1900	45	0.66	POP*GPC
1913	49	0.66	POP*GPC
1920	96	10.21	POP*GPC
1929	231	10.21	POP*GPC
1938	554	10.21	POP*GPC
1950	1,780	10.21	POP*GPC
1960	4,937	10.74	POP*GPC
1970	21,019	15.59	POP*GPC
1980	157,414	22.30	POP*GPC
1990	155,911	0.10	POP*GPC
2000	261,404	5.30	POP*GPC
2010	313,049	1.82	POP*GPC
2012	329,898	2.66	POP*GPC
2020	398,359	2.39	POP*GPC
2030	502,806	2.36	POP*GPC
	DME United Kingdom		
0001	357	.	POP*GPC
1000	1,443	0.14	POP*GPC
1500	4,113	0.21	POP*GPC
1600	8,781	0.76	POP*GPC
1700	15,643	0.58	POP*GPC
1820	52,943	1.02	POP*GPC
1870	146,356	2.05	POP*GPC
1880	175,898	1.86	POP*GPC
1890	219,576	2.24	POP*GPC
1900	270,118	2.09	POP*GPC
1913	328,228	1.51	POP*GPC
1920	311,138	0.76	POP*GPC
1929	393,298	2.64	POP*GPC
1938	465,694	1.90	POP*GPC
1950	546,073	1.34	POP*GPC
1960	699,807	2.51	POP*GPC
1970	914,492	2.71	POP*GPC
1980	1,099,683	1.86	POP*GPC
1990	1,425,969	2.63	POP*GPC
2000	1,910,854	2.97	POP*GPC

Year	GDP at PPP, mil. 2012 doll.	Growth Rate	Source
2010	2,245,040	1.62	POP*GPC
2012	2,277,784	0.73	POP*GPC
2020	2,804,032	2.63	POP*GPC
2030	3,515,909	2.29	POP*GPC
DME United States			
0001	265	.	POP*GPC
1000	734	0.10	POP*GPC
1500	1,457	0.14	POP*GPC
1600	1,161	0.23	POP*GPC
1700	825	0.34	POP*GPC
1820	19,633	2.68	POP*GPC
1870	153,964	4.21	POP*GPC
1880	227,402	3.98	POP*GPC
1890	336,005	3.98	POP*GPC
1900	489,039	3.82	POP*GPC
1913	809,667	3.95	POP*GPC
1920	928,585	1.98	POP*GPC
1929	1,319,742	3.98	POP*GPC
1938	1,250,776	0.59	POP*GPC
1950	2,278,203	5.12	POP*GPC
1960	3,228,373	3.55	POP*GPC
1970	4,896,307	4.25	POP*GPC
1980	6,780,639	3.31	POP*GPC
1990	9,399,767	3.32	POP*GPC
2000	13,204,165	3.46	POP*GPC
2010	15,539,778	1.64	POP*GPC
2012	16,261,009	2.29	POP*GPC
2020	19,813,222	2.50	POP*GPC
2030	25,420,199	2.52	POP*GPC
LAM Uruguay			
0001	8	.	POP*GPC
1000	22	0.11	POP*GPC
1500	40	0.12	POP*GPC
1600	40	0.00	POP*GPC
1700	76	0.64	POP*GPC
1820	183	0.74	POP*GPC
1870	1,171	3.78	POP*GPC
1880	1,512	2.59	POP*GPC
1890	2,305	4.31	POP*GPC
1900	3,177	3.26	POP*GPC
1913	6,096	5.14	POP*GPC
1920	5,737	0.86	POP*GPC
1929	10,144	6.54	POP*GPC
1938	11,229	1.14	POP*GPC
1950	16,324	3.17	POP*GPC
1960	18,742	1.39	POP*GPC
1970	20,627	0.96	POP*GPC
1980	25,853	2.28	POP*GPC
1990	25,780	0.03	POP*GPC

Year	GDP at PPP, mil. 2012 doll.	Growth Rate	Source
2000	35,061	3.12	POP*GPC
2010	47,028	2.98	POP*GPC
2012	51,931	5.08	POP*GPC
2020	66,055	3.05	POP*GPC
2030	84,214	2.46	POP*GPC
USR Uzbekistan			
0001	182	.	POP*GPC
1000	428	0.09	POP*GPC
1500	757	0.11	POP*GPC
1600	957	0.23	POP*GPC
1700	1,190	0.22	POP*GPC
1820	2,015	0.44	POP*GPC
1870	3,716	1.23	POP*GPC
1880	4,544	2.03	POP*GPC
1890	5,557	2.03	POP*GPC
1900	6,843	2.10	POP*GPC
1913	10,327	3.22	POP*GPC
1920	3,961	12.79	POP*GPC
1929	10,878	11.88	POP*GPC
1938	18,491	6.07	POP*GPC
1950	23,535	2.03	POP*GPC
1960	39,533	5.32	POP*GPC
1970	69,437	5.79	POP*GPC
1980	93,356	3.00	POP*GPC
1990	111,661	1.81	POP*GPC
2000	56,969	6.51	POP*GPC
2010	91,655	4.87	POP*GPC
2012	103,571	6.30	POP*GPC
2020	137,721	3.63	POP*GPC
2030	182,649	2.86	POP*GPC
SEA Vanuatu			
0001	.	.	POP*GPC
1000	.	.	POP*GPC
1500	.	.	POP*GPC
1600	.	.	POP*GPC
1700	.	.	POP*GPC
1820	.	.	POP*GPC
1870	.	.	POP*GPC
1880	.	.	POP*GPC
1890	.	.	POP*GPC
1900	.	.	POP*GPC
1913	.	.	POP*GPC
1920	.	.	POP*GPC
1929	.	.	POP*GPC
1938	.	.	POP*GPC
1950	105	.	POP*GPC
1960	164	4.52	POP*GPC
1970	257	4.60	POP*GPC
1980	372	3.79	POP*GPC

Year	GDP at PPP, mil. 2012 doll.	Growth Rate	Source
1990	588	4.67	POP*GPC
2000	827	3.48	POP*GPC
2010	1,102	2.91	POP*GPC
2012	1,163	2.76	POP*GPC
2020	1,494	3.18	POP*GPC
2030	2,008	3.00	POP*GPC
	LAM Venezuela		
0001	96	.	POP*GPC
1000	272	0.10	POP*GPC
1500	490	0.12	POP*GPC
1600	309	0.46	POP*GPC
1700	370	0.18	POP*GPC
1820	517	0.28	POP*GPC
1870	1,472	2.12	POP*GPC
1880	1,964	2.93	POP*GPC
1890	2,529	2.56	POP*GPC
1900	3,266	2.59	POP*GPC
1913	4,965	3.27	POP*GPC
1920	5,492	1.45	POP*GPC
1929	17,472	13.72	POP*GPC
1938	23,494	3.35	POP*GPC
1950	59,482	8.05	POP*GPC
1960	105,324	5.88	POP*GPC
1970	155,934	4.00	POP*GPC
1980	202,756	2.66	POP*GPC
1990	227,272	1.15	POP*GPC
2000	273,434	1.87	POP*GPC
2010	356,663	2.69	POP*GPC
2012	391,824	4.81	POP*GPC
2020	466,937	2.22	POP*GPC
2030	588,590	2.34	POP*GPC
	CPA Vietnam		
0001	476	.	POP*GPC
1000	1,310	0.10	POP*GPC
1500	3,085	0.17	POP*GPC
1600	3,642	0.17	POP*GPC
1700	4,212	0.15	POP*GPC
1820	5,402	0.21	POP*GPC
1870	8,320	0.87	POP*GPC
1880	10,431	2.29	POP*GPC
1890	13,078	2.29	POP*GPC
1900	16,397	2.29	POP*GPC
1913	22,001	2.29	POP*GPC
1920	23,055	0.67	POP*GPC
1929	24,486	0.67	POP*GPC
1938	26,006	0.67	POP*GPC
1950	28,179	0.67	POP*GPC
1960	36,318	2.57	POP*GPC
1970	41,215	1.27	POP*GPC

Year	GDP at PPP, mil. 2012 doll.	Growth Rate	Source
1980	49,193	1.79	POP*GPC
1990	77,560	4.66	POP*GPC
2000	158,452	7.41	POP*GPC
2010	300,655	6.61	POP*GPC
2012	336,277	5.76	POP*GPC
2020	534,618	5.97	POP*GPC
2030	744,696	3.37	POP*GPC
LAM Virgin Islands, British			
0001	.	.	POP*GPC
1000	.	.	POP*GPC
1500	.	.	POP*GPC
1600	.	.	POP*GPC
1700	.	.	POP*GPC
1820	.	.	POP*GPC
1870	.	.	POP*GPC
1880	.	.	POP*GPC
1890	.	.	POP*GPC
1900	.	.	POP*GPC
1913	.	.	POP*GPC
1920	.	.	POP*GPC
1929	.	.	POP*GPC
1938	.	.	POP*GPC
1950	43	.	POP*GPC
1960	71	5.17	POP*GPC
1970	117	5.17	POP*GPC
1980	164	3.43	POP*GPC
1990	214	2.69	POP*GPC
2000	389	6.14	POP*GPC
2010	1,093	10.88	POP*GPC
2012	1,410	13.58	POP*GPC
2020	2,792	8.91	POP*GPC
2030	5,328	6.68	POP*GPC
LAM Virgin Islands, U.S.			
0001	.	.	POP*GPC
1000	.	.	POP*GPC
1500	.	.	POP*GPC
1600	.	.	POP*GPC
1700	.	.	POP*GPC
1820	.	.	POP*GPC
1870	.	.	POP*GPC
1880	.	.	POP*GPC
1890	.	.	POP*GPC
1900	.	.	POP*GPC
1913	.	.	POP*GPC
1920	.	.	POP*GPC
1929	.	.	POP*GPC
1938	.	.	POP*GPC
1950	249	.	POP*GPC
1960	392	4.68	POP*GPC

Year	GDP at PPP, mil. 2012 doll.	Growth Rate	Source
1970	968	9.45	POP*GPC
1980	1,745	6.07	POP*GPC
1990	2,059	1.67	POP*GPC
2000	2,167	0.51	POP*GPC
2010	4,642	7.92	POP*GPC
2012	4,805	1.74	POP*GPC
2020	6,495	3.84	POP*GPC
2030	7,650	1.65	POP*GPC
	SEA Wallis and Futuna		
0001	.	.	POP*GPC
1000	.	.	POP*GPC
1500	.	.	POP*GPC
1600	.	.	POP*GPC
1700	.	.	POP*GPC
1820	.	.	POP*GPC
1870	.	.	POP*GPC
1880	.	.	POP*GPC
1890	.	.	POP*GPC
1900	.	.	POP*GPC
1913	.	.	POP*GPC
1920	.	.	POP*GPC
1929	.	.	POP*GPC
1938	.	.	POP*GPC
1950	10	.	POP*GPC
1960	15	4.12	POP*GPC
1970	23	4.12	POP*GPC
1980	31	2.97	POP*GPC
1990	39	2.48	POP*GPC
2000	42	0.71	POP*GPC
2010	70	5.28	POP*GPC
2012	72	1.75	POP*GPC
2020	92	2.98	POP*GPC
2030	116	2.35	POP*GPC
	MEA West Bank		
0001	.	.	POP*GPC
1000	.	.	POP*GPC
1500	.	.	POP*GPC
1600	.	.	POP*GPC
1700	.	.	POP*GPC
1820	.	.	POP*GPC
1870	.	.	POP*GPC
1880	.	.	POP*GPC
1890	.	.	POP*GPC
1900	.	.	POP*GPC
1913	.	.	POP*GPC
1920	.	.	POP*GPC
1929	.	.	POP*GPC
1938	.	.	POP*GPC
1950	1,297	.	POP*GPC

Year	GDP at PPP, mil. 2012 doll.	Growth Rate	Source
1960	1,581	2.00	POP*GPC
1970	1,390	1.28	POP*GPC
1980	1,920	3.29	POP*GPC
1990	3,036	4.69	POP*GPC
2000	6,307	7.58	POP*GPC
2010	6,409	0.16	POP*GPC
2012	6,617	1.60	POP*GPC
2020	7,971	2.36	POP*GPC
2030	10,073	2.37	POP*GPC
AFR Western Sahara			
0001	.	.	POP*GPC
1000	.	.	POP*GPC
1500	.	.	POP*GPC
1600	.	.	POP*GPC
1700	.	.	POP*GPC
1820	.	.	POP*GPC
1870	.	.	POP*GPC
1880	.	.	POP*GPC
1890	.	.	POP*GPC
1900	.	.	POP*GPC
1913	.	.	POP*GPC
1920	.	.	POP*GPC
1929	.	.	POP*GPC
1938	.	.	POP*GPC
1950	5	.	POP*GPC
1960	15	11.82	POP*GPC
1970	51	12.72	POP*GPC
1980	88	5.56	POP*GPC
1990	180	7.44	POP*GPC
2000	776	15.77	POP*GPC
2010	1,264	4.99	POP*GPC
2012	1,407	5.52	POP*GPC
2020	2,361	6.68	POP*GPC
2030	3,803	4.88	POP*GPC
MEA Yemen			
0001	1,862	.	POP*GPC
1000	2,283	0.02	POP*GPC
1500	1,931	0.03	POP*GPC
1600	1,931	0.00	POP*GPC
1700	1,931	0.00	POP*GPC
1820	2,232	0.12	POP*GPC
1870	2,555	0.27	POP*GPC
1880	2,669	0.44	POP*GPC
1890	2,789	0.44	POP*GPC
1900	2,913	0.44	POP*GPC
1913	3,083	0.44	POP*GPC
1920	3,582	2.16	POP*GPC
1929	4,343	2.16	POP*GPC
1938	5,267	2.16	POP*GPC

Year	GDP at PPP, mil. 2012 doll.	Growth Rate	Source
1950	6,810	2.16	POP*GPC
1960	7,753	1.31	POP*GPC
1970	10,472	3.05	POP*GPC
1980	22,001	7.71	POP*GPC
1990	25,967	1.67	POP*GPC
2000	43,378	5.27	POP*GPC
2010	68,553	4.68	POP*GPC
2012	62,499	4.52	POP*GPC
2020	88,547	4.45	POP*GPC
2030	133,070	4.16	POP*GPC
AFR Zambia			
0001	8	.	POP*GPC
1000	77	0.22	POP*GPC
1500	192	0.18	POP*GPC
1600	222	0.15	POP*GPC
1700	242	0.09	POP*GPC
1820	271	0.10	POP*GPC
1870	651	1.77	POP*GPC
1880	775	1.77	POP*GPC
1890	924	1.77	POP*GPC
1900	1,100	1.77	POP*GPC
1913	1,382	1.77	POP*GPC
1920	1,562	1.77	POP*GPC
1929	1,828	1.77	POP*GPC
1938	2,140	1.77	POP*GPC
1950	2,641	1.77	POP*GPC
1960	5,288	7.19	POP*GPC
1970	8,069	4.32	POP*GPC
1980	9,181	1.30	POP*GPC
1990	10,311	1.17	POP*GPC
2000	11,307	0.93	POP*GPC
2010	20,119	5.93	POP*GPC
2012	23,552	8.20	POP*GPC
2020	35,712	5.34	POP*GPC
2030	57,788	4.93	POP*GPC
AFR Zimbabwe			
0001	9	.	POP*GPC
1000	86	0.22	POP*GPC
1500	214	0.18	POP*GPC
1600	248	0.15	POP*GPC
1700	270	0.09	POP*GPC
1820	303	0.10	POP*GPC
1870	744	1.81	POP*GPC
1880	890	1.81	POP*GPC
1890	1,065	1.81	POP*GPC
1900	1,275	1.81	POP*GPC
1913	1,610	1.81	POP*GPC
1920	1,826	1.81	POP*GPC
1929	2,146	1.81	POP*GPC

Year	GDP at PPP, mil. 2012 doll.	Growth Rate	Source
1938	2,523	1.81	POP*GPC
1950	3,130	1.81	POP*GPC
1960	5,426	5.66	POP*GPC
1970	9,341	5.58	POP*GPC
1980	12,233	2.73	POP*GPC
1990	17,910	3.89	POP*GPC
2000	23,684	2.83	POP*GPC
2010	5,833	13.08	POP*GPC
2012	7,773	15.44	POP*GPC
2020	11,142	4.60	POP*GPC
2030	15,564	3.40	POP*GPC

Appendix: Methodology and Definitions

Definition of Gross Domestic Product at Purchasing Power Parities

Typically, GDP is translated into U.S. dollars. The market foreign currency exchange rate, however, does not necessarily reflect differences in the actual purchasing power of different countries. The use of purchasing power parities (PPPs) is intended to eliminate this distortion. Purchasing power parities indicate how many currency units are needed in one country to buy the amount of goods and services that can be purchased for a currency unit in another country.

Definition of Population

The population of a country includes all residents regardless of legal status or citizenship — except for refugees not permanently settled in the country of asylum, who are generally considered part of the population of their country of origin. The values shown are midyear estimates.[1]

My principal source for Population for the latest years is the Encyclopedia Britannica. This population data is changed from year to year; I assume that the data from the latest edition of the *Encyclopedia Britannica Book of the Year* is the most correct. However, their population data is one year ahead of the year of their current yearbook. For example, the 2012 yearbook provides population data for 1960, 1970, 1980, 1990, 2000, 2010, 2013, 2020 (forecast), and 2030 (forecast). I could have taken the population data for 2012 from the previous year's *Britannica Book of the Year*, but the whole population time series from 1960 through 2030 is somewhat shifted in the previous year edition of the *Britannica Book of the Year* compared with their latest edition. I also use the Britannica population data for all these years in the annual companion to this handbook, *Quality of Life, Balance of Powers, and Nuclear Weapons*. So, in order for *Two Thousand Years* to by in sync with *Quality of Life, Balance of Powers, and Nuclear Weapons*, and to use general population time series from the latest edition of the *Britannica Book of the Year*, I use in this handbook population data for the current year (2012) calculated from the current edition of the *Britannica Book of the Year* according to the formula:

1 Economics: The World Bank.

POP2012 = POP2010 * (POP2013 / POP2010)2/3

where

POP2010 is population in 2010 according to the current edition of the Britannica Book of the Year;

POP2012 is calculated population in 2012;

POP2013 is population in 2013 according to the current edition of the Britannica Book of the Year.

Definition of the GDP Historical Data Since AD 1

I used information about GDP Per Capita in purchasing power parities for 1950 and the latest (current) year as the basis points. I also appropriated Angus Maddison's[2] hypothesis that GDP Per Capita in purchasing power parities cannot be less than 400 USD in 1990 prices, and utilized a logarithmic interpolation technique to slightly adjust Maddison's statistical curves for years other than basis years.

It is customary in historical comparisons of the countries of the world to use Gross Domestic Product (GDP) in purchasing power parities. If GDP in market exchange rates is used, then the historical picture becomes distorted in favor of the countries that have strong currencies in the last year of observations. In effect, many less developed countries would appear too weak in the past, having GDP per capita less than the minimum level of 400 dollars in 1990 prices.

The data is given for countries within their current (latest year) boundaries.

I interpolated per capita GDP at purchasing power parities. The reason I interpolated per capita as opposed to gross data is that per capita growth rates are more invariant than the gross growth rates (the latter to some degree depend on the growth rates of the population, which vary by time and country).

For years prior to 1950, the principal source of per capita GDP at purchasing power parities (GDP at PPP) is Angus Maddison.

For years after 1950, there are two main sources of per capita GDP at PPP: Angus Maddison for 1950 through 2000 and World Bank for 1980 through the current year. There is a small discrepancy between these two main sources. In order to harmonize these two sources, a four-step iteration was used:

The Angus Maddison data is in 1990 prices. There is also data from the World Bank for 1990 in current (that is 1990) prices. I assumed that the World Bank data, where available, is more correct. The Angus Maddison data was adjusted accordingly:

```
If G1990-WB exists then
Do;
     G1960-Maddison = G1960-Maddison * (G1990-WB / G1990-Maddison)1/4;
     G1970-Maddison = G1970-Maddison * (G1990-WB / G1990-Maddison)2/4;
     G1980-Maddison = G1980-Maddison * (G1990-WB / G1990-Maddison)3/4;
     G2000-Maddison = G2000-Maddison * (G1990-WB / G1990-Maddison));
     G1990-Maddison = G1990-WB;
End;
where
```

G1990-WB	per capita GDP at PPP in 1990 (in 1990 prices [WB])
G1960-Maddison	per capita GDP at PPP in 1960 (in 1990 prices [Maddison])
G1970-Maddison	per capita GDP at PPP in 1970 (in 1990 prices [Maddison])
G1980-Maddison	per capita GDP at PPP in 1980 (in 1990 prices [Maddison])
G1990-Maddison	per capita GDP at PPP in 1990 (in 1990 prices [Maddison])
G2000-Maddison	per capita GDP at PPP in 2000 (in 1990 prices [Maddison])

2 Economics: Maddison (1995), (2001), (2003), (2007).

Generally, the historical data available from the World Bank is in 2005 prices. Where this data existed for years prior to 2000, I assumed it to be more correct than Angus Maddison's data and made the following adjustment to results of the first step:

```
If G1980-WB exists then
Do;
        G1990-Maddison = G1980-Maddison * (G1990-WB / G1980-WB);
        G2000-Maddison = G1980-Maddison * (G2000-WB / G1980-WB);
End;
Else
If G1990-WB exists then
        G2000-Maddison = G1990-Maddison * (G2000-WB / G1990-WB);
```

where

G1980-WB	per capita GDP at PPP in 1980 (in 2005 prices [World Bank])
G1990-WB	per capita GDP at PPP in 1990 (in 2005 prices [World Bank])
G2000-WB	per capita GDP at PPP in 2000 (in 2005 prices [World Bank])
G1980-Maddison	per capita GDP at PPP in 1980 (in 2005 prices [Maddison])
G1990-Maddison	per capita GDP at PPP in 1990 (in 2005 prices [Maddison])
G2000-Maddison	per capita GDP at PPP in 2000 (in 1990 prices [Maddison])

For the year 2000 (the year of the change between 1990 and 2005 series) I computed per capita GDP at PPP in 1990 prices as a geometric average of the number according to Maddison and the number in 2005 prices weighted as per the U.S. ratio according to the following formula:

G2000-Maddison = (G2000-Maddison * (G2000-WB * (G-US-2000-Maddison / G-US-2000-WB))1/2;

where

G2000-Maddison	per capita GDP at PPP in 2000 (in 1990 prices [Maddison])
G2000-WB	per capita GDP at PPP in 2000 (in 2005 prices [World Bank])
G-US-2000-Maddison	U.S. per capita GDP at PPP(in 1990 prices [Maddison])
G-US-2000-WB	U.S. per capita GDP at PPP (in 2005 prices [World Bank])

After the first three adjustments, there are still general problems which I would call a "cross-country statistical parallax." These problems manifest themselves in the fact that, for any country, if we take per capita GDP at PPP for 1950 (in whatever year's constant prices), and multiply it by the index of per capita GDP at PPP for the current year (in the same year's constant prices), the result will, generally speaking, be somewhat (and sometimes substantially) different from the direct estimate of per capita GDP at PPP for the current year (in the same year's constant prices). For example, it can be noted that data for per capita GDP at PPP in constant prices for Switzerland would overestimate the GDP deflator of that country in comparison with the United States. So, if we take the ratio of the per capita GDP at PPP of Switzerland to that of the United States in 1950, and multiply it by the index per capita GDP at PPP of Switzeralnd for 1990 (or any other current year), the result would be consistently lower than the ratio of the per capita GDP at PPP of Swizerland to that of the United

States when measured directly in 1990 (or any other current year). Conversely, for some countries we would underestimate the inflation in comparison with the United States. Usually, however, for a given country, there is consistently either underestimation or overestimation of inflation in comparison with the United States. I have assumed that the degree of such overestimation or underestimation of inflation for a given country would be constant for the entire period after 1950.

To adjust for the cross-country statistical parallax I have been using logarithmic interpolation.

The reason I use logarithmic interpolation, as opposed to exponential interpolation, is that exponential interpolation may often result in negative growth rates of per capita GDP, which seems unlikely. Logarithmic interpolation does not change the nature of the growth over an observed period: positive growth rates remain positive, negative ones remain negative. Moreover, periods of faster growth remain periods of faster growth and periods of slower growth remain periods of slower growth. The economic rationale for such an interpolation is that its most common use is when there is unaccounted inflation in the statistics of real growth. As a rule, such inflation is higher when economic growth is faster. So it makes sense to assume that the unaccounted deflator should be proportionally higher with higher growth rates. To achieve an interpolation with such qualities, I had to assume that over the period of 1950 to the current year there existed a constant degree to which the reported national growth rates should be raised in order to achieve the observed growth rates between 1950 and the current year. I weighted the growth rates of every country relative to the growth rates of the United States. Such a hypothesis produces a more credible growth curve than the one which would have been acquired if exponential interpolation were used.

The corresponding formulas for the interpolation of per capita GDP are:

$$Gyear_{corrected} = Gyear_{current} * (Gyear_{current} / Gcurrent_{current}) ** (\log((Gcurrent_{current} * G - UScurrent_{1990}) / (G19501990 * G - UScurrentcurrent)) / \log(Gcurrent1990 / G19501990))$$

where

$$Gyear_{current} = Gyear_{1990} * (Gcurrent_{current} / Gcurrent_{1990})$$

$$G1950_{current} = (G19501990 / G - US19501990) * G - US1950_{current}$$

$$G - US1950_{current} = G - US19501990 * (G - UScurrent_{current} / G - UScurrent_{1990})$$

$$Gcurrent_{1990} = G2000_{1990} * (Gcurrent_{2005} / G2000_{2005})$$

$$G - UScurrent_{1990} = G - US2000_{1990} * (G - UScurrent_{2005} / G\text{-}US2000_{2005})$$

The notations are identified below:

GPCPPP	per capita GDP at purchasing power parities
$Gyear_{corrected}$	GPCPPP for a particular year after the interpolation
$Gyear_{current}$	GPCPPP for a particular year in current-year prices
$Gyear_{1990}$	GPCPPP for a particular year in 1990 prices
$G1950_{1990}$	GPCPPP for the year 1950 in 1990 prices
$G\text{-}US1950_{1990}$	GPCPPP of the U.S. for the year 1950 in 1990 prices
$Gcurrent_{current}$	GPCPPP for the current year in current-year prices

$G\text{-}UScurrent_{current}$	GPCPPP of the U.S. for the current year in current-year prices
$G1950_{current}$	GPCPPP for the year 1950 in current-year prices
$G\text{-}US1950_{current}$	GPCPPP of the U.S. for the year 1950 in current-year prices
$Gcurrent_{1990}$	GPCPPP for the current year in 1990 prices
$G\text{-}UScurrent_{1990}$	GPCPPP of the U.S. for the current year in 1990 prices
$G2000_{1990}$	GPCPPP for the year 2000 in 1990 prices
$G\text{-}US2000_{1990}$	GPCPPP of the U.S. for the year 2000 in 1990 prices
$Gcurrent_{2005}$	GPCPPP for the current year in 2005 prices
$G\text{-}UScurrent_{2005}$	GPCPPP of the U.S. for the current year in 2005 prices
$G2000_{2005}$	GPCPPP for the year 2000 in 2005 prices
$G\text{-}US2000_{2005}$	GPCPPP of the U.S. for the year 2000 in 2005 prices

For the years prior to 1950, I used the formula:

$$Gyear_{current} = Gyear1990 * (G1950_{current} / G19501990)$$

Exceptions

My general rule was to take all available data from Angus Maddison and the World Bank (the emphasis here is on "all": I did not skip any applicable data from Angus Maddison and the World Bank for any year where it existed). When the data was unavailable from these sources, I took the CIA data. This rule, with application of the above described four-step algorithm, worked very well for about 230 countries for years after 1950.

Benin, Burundi, Iraq, Moldova, Mozambique, Qatar, and Uzbekistan were exceptions. For the latter countries I had to consider their special historical circumstances and make some modifications to the general rule of selecting all the available sources (for these countries, that amounted to ignoring some available but unreliable data or data leading to illogical results). Here is a summary of ignored data:

CODE	YEAR	USED DATA	SOURCE	IGNORED DATA	SOURCE OF IGNORED DATA
			Benin		
1	1950	1,084	50(Maddison)		
1	1960	978	60(Maddison)		
1	1970	1,027	70(Maddison)		
1	1980	1,133	80(Maddison)		
2	1980	1,076.29	80(WB)		
1	1990	1,147	90(Maddison)		
A	1990	.		799.34	90(WB)
2	1990	1,100.03	90(WB)		
1	2000	1,323	00(Maddison)		
2	2000	1,232.18	00(WB)		
2	2010	1,321.27	10(WB)		
2	2012	1,364.20	12(WB)		
3	2012	1,557.16	12(WB)		

CODE	YEAR	USED DATA	SOURCE	IGNORED DATA	SOURCE OF IGNORED DATA
			Burundi		
1	1950	360	50(Maddison)		
1	1960	444	60(Maddison)		
1	1970	542	70(Maddison)		
1	1980	627	80(Maddison)		
2	1980	604.81	80(WB)		
1	1990	484.61	90(WB) WEIGHT(US(WB))	734	90(Maddison)
A	1990	500.35	90(WB)		
2	1990	688.56	90(WB)		
1	2000	325.48	00(WB) WEIGHT(US(WB))	575	00(Maddison)
2	2000	474.00	00(WB)		
2	2010	475.38	10(WB)		
2	2012	482.95	12(WB)		
3	2012	551.27	12(WB)		
			Iraq		
1	1950	1,364	50(Maddison)		
1	1960	2,735	60(Maddison)		
1	1970	3,473	70(Maddison)		
1	1980	6,377	80(Maddison)		
2	1980	.			
1	1990	3,840.41	90(Maddison) WEIGHT(00(WB))	2,458	90(Maddison)
A	1990	.			
2	1990	.			
1	2000	3,175.51	00(WB) WEIGHT(US Maddison))	1,221	00(Maddison)
2	2000	5,392.28	00(WB)		
2	2010	5,724.27	10(WB)		
2	2012	6,531.51	12(WB)		
3	2012	7,434.83	12(WB)		
			Moldova		
1	1950	2,515.58	PROXY(USSR(Maddison))		
1	1960	3,493.13	PROXY(USSR(Maddison))		
1	1970	4,936.44	PROXY(USSR(Maddison))		
1	1980	5,681.00	INTERPOL(Moldova(Maddison))		
2	1980	.			
1	1990	6,165	90(Maddison)		
A	1990	.			
2	1990	.			

CODE	YEAR	USED DATA	SOURCE	IGNORED DATA	SOURCE OF IGNORED DATA
1	2000	1,137.97	00(WB) WEIGHT(US(WB))	2,128	00(Maddison)
2	2000	1,657.25	00(WB)		
2	2010	2,793.39	10(WB)		
2	2012	2,950.88	12(WB)		
3	2012	3,368.28	12(WB)		
			Mozambique		
1	1950	1,133	50(Maddison)		
1	1960	1,327	60(Maddison)		
1	1970	1,743	70(Maddison)		
1	1980	309.73	80(WB) WEIGHT(US(WB))	1,220	80(Maddison)
2	1980	434.92	80(WB)		
1	1990	278.03	90(WB) WEIGHT(US(WB))	1,115	90(Maddison)
A	1990	287.06	90(WB)		
2	1990	395.04	90(WB)		
1	2000	342.39	00(WB) WEIGHT(US(WB))	1,432	00(Maddison)
2	2000	498.63	00(WB)		
2	2010	805.05	10(WB)		
2	2012	882.42	12(WB)		
3	2012	1,007.23	12(WB)		
			Qatar		
1	1950	30,387	50(Maddison)		
1	1960	33,104	60(Maddison)		
1	1970	33,160	70(Maddison)		
1	1980	29,552	80(Maddison)		
2	1980	.			
1	1990	15,000	90(CIA)	6,804	90(Maddison)
A	1990	.			
2	1990	.			
1	2000	44,309.99	00(WB) WEIGHT(US(WB))	8,042	00(Maddison)
2	2000	64,529.85	00(WB)		
2	2010	70,239.31	10(WB)		
2	2012	71,931.40	12(WB)		
3	2012	91,189.11	12(WB)		
			Uzbekistan		
1	1950	2,389.92	PROXY(USSR(Maddison))		
1	1960	3,318.63	PROXY(USSR(Maddison))		
1	1970	4,698.86	PROXY(USSR(Maddison))		
1	1980	4,725.39	INTERPOL(Uzbekistan(Maddison))		

CODE	YEAR	USED DATA	SOURCE	IGNORED DATA	SOURCE OF IGNORED DATA
2	1980	.			
1	1990	4,241	90(Maddison)		
A	1990	.			
2	1990	.			
1	2000	1,120.83	00(WB) WEIGHT(US(WB))	3,408	00(Maddison)
2	2000	1,632.30	00(WB)		
2	2010	2,753.56	10(WB)		
2	2012	3,095.28	12(WB)		
3	2012	3,533.11	12(WB)		

where

CODE = 1 for per capita GDP at PPP in 1990 prices;

CODE= 2 for per capita GDP at PPP in 2005 prices;

CODE = A for alternative data of per capita GDP at PPP in 1990 in 1990 prices according to the World Bank;

CODE = 3 for per capita GDP at PPP in 2012 in 2012 prices.

Special care was taken for calculation of GDP of the former U.S.S.R. for the year of 1920. In order to calculate an index of GDP 1913-1920, I used partial data for two sectors of the economy: agriculture and industry. The production of grain in these years constituted (Davies(1994), p. 320):

Production of grain	
1913	79.7 million tons
1920	44.5 million tons

Gross industrial production constituted (ibid., p. 321):

Gross industrial production	
1913	8,431
1920	1,718

Agriculture accounted for 50.7 percent of national income in 1913. Assuming that non-agricultural sectors of the economy shrank by 1920 in the same proportion as the industrial production, I obtained the following putative index of GDP:

GDP Index	
1913	100
1920	38.354

Special care was also taken for calculating the GDP of North Korea for the years after 1990. The available CIA estimates are inexact and tend to underestimate North Korean GDP at PPP. Our calculations are as follows:

Year	GDP Growth Rate	Source of GDP Growth Rate	GDP Index	WB US GDP Deflator	GDP, Bil. Current USD	GDP, Bil. 1990 USD	Population, Thousands	GDP Per Capita, 1990 Prices	GDP Per Capita, Current Prices
2012	1.3	CIA	65.293	114.145	59.054	37.365	24,589	1519.58	2401.64
2011	0.8	CIA	64.455						
2010	-05.	CIA	63.943	110.023	55.743	36.592	24,326	1504.23	2309.50
2009	-0.9	CIA	64.264						
2008	3.7	CIA	64.848						
2007	-2.3	CIA	62.534						
2006	-1.1	CIA	64.006						
2005	1.0	CIA	64.718	100.000	51.280	37.036			
2004	1.0	CIA	64.077						
2003	1.0	CIA	63.443						
2002	1.0	CIA	62.815						
2001	-3.0	CIA	62.193						
2000	-3.0	CIA	64.117	88.714	45.069	36.692	22,785	1610.36	1978.01
1999	1.0	CIA	66.100						
1998	-5.0	CIA	65.446						
1997	-3.7	CIA	68.890						
1996	-5.0	CIA	71.537						
1995	-17.0	Maddison	75.302						
1994	0.0	CIA	90.725						
1993	0.3	CIA	90.725						
1992	-7.7	Maddison	90.454						
1991	-2.0	CIA	98.000						
1990			100.000					2841	

Angus Maddison postulated that GDP per capita in purchasing power parities cannot be less than $400 in 1990 prices. However, if you look at some African countries in recent decades, you will see that many countries appear to have had less than that level of GDP per capita in PPP for prolonged periods of time. So I decided to use a modification of Angus Maddison's postulate, by supposing that at a per capita GDP of around 400 (1990 US dollars), the growth rate of GDP per capita becomes very slow. I postulated that at the level of 400 (1990 dollars), the annual growth rate would be 0.05%. Moreover, I postulated that at a level around or below 400 (1990 dollars), the annual growth rate would be proportional to the ratio of the current year level of GDP per capita to 400 (1990 dollars).

The formula for calculating the previous benchmark year GDP per capita is:

```
Previous_GDP = Current_GDP;
DO I = 1 TO Number_of_years_in_period;
Previous_GDP = Previous_GDP
/ (1 + Base_growth_rate * (Previous_GDP / Base_GDP_level));
END;
```

where

Current_GDP	Current year GDP per capita in PPP (1990 prices)
Previous_GDP	Previous year GDP per capita in PPP (1990 prices)
I	Iteration counter
Number_of_years_in_period	Total number of years in period
Base_growth_rate	Assumed to be 0.05%
Base_GDP_level	GDP per capita in PPP equal to 400 (1990 dollars)

References

Central Intelligence Agency, *The World Factbook*, annual

Davies, R. W., Mark Harrison, S. G. Wheatcroft, Eds. (1994) *The Economic Transformation of the Soviet Union, 1913-1945*, Cambridge University Press, Cambridge

Encyclopedia Britannica, Book of the Year, annual

Maddison, Angus (1995) *Monitoring the World Economy, 1820-1992*, OECD, Paris

________ (2001) *The World Economy: A Millennial Perspective*, OECD, Paris

________ (2003) *The World Economy: Historical Statistics*, OECD, Paris

________ *(2007) Contours of the World Economy, 1–2030AD*, Oxford University Press, New York

Mitchell, B.R. *(2003)(1) International Historical Statistics: Africa, Asia and Oceania, 1750-2000*, Palgrave Macmillan, London

________ (2003)(2) *International Historical Statistics: Europe, 1750-2000*, Palgrave Macmillan, London

________ (2003)(3) *International Historical Statistics: The Americas, 1750-2000*, Palgrave Macmillan, London

The World Bank World Development Indicators Online

Wikipedia

Made in the USA
Coppell, TX
16 March 2026

73966192R00236